Behavior Modification
in
Educational Settings

Behavior Modification

in

Educational Settings

Edited by

ROGER D. KLEIN, Ph.D.
Learning Research and Development Center
University of Pittsburgh
Pittsburgh, Pennsylvania

WALTER G. HAPKIEWICZ, Ph.D.
Department of Educational Psychology
Michigan State University
East Lansing, Michigan

AUBREY H. RODEN, Ph.D.
Department of Educational Psychology
State University of New York at Buffalo
Buffalo, New York

CHARLES C THOMAS • PUBLISHER
Springfield • Illinois • U.S.A.

Published and Distributed Throughout the World by
CHARLES C THOMAS • PUBLISHER
BANNERSTONE HOUSE
301–327 East Lawrence Avenue, Springfield, Illinois, U.S.A.

© *1973, by* CHARLES C THOMAS • PUBLISHER
ISBN 0-398-02538-X
Library of Congress Card Catalog Number: 72-75923

With THOMAS BOOKS *careful attention is given to all details of
manufacturing and design. It is the Publisher's desire to present books
that are satisfactory as to their physical qualities and artistic possibilities
and appropriate for their particular use.* THOMAS BOOKS *will be true
to those laws of quality that assure a good name and good will.*

Printed in the United States of America
CC-11

To Our Wives, Colleagues and Students

Preface

Teachers have traditionally directed considerable attention toward the development of academic, social and emotional behaviors in children. More recently, psychologists have also become concerned with these educational goals and have attempted to provide teachers with the best possible methods for achieving them. Nevertheless, when teachers or prospective teachers have enrolled in courses such as educational psychology, many have been thoroughly disappointed by the lack of relevance that these courses have had for actual classroom practice. All too frequently, the "teacher-student" is presented with watered-down versions of various learning theories which fail to bridge the gap between laboratory research and teaching procedures. Typically, the psychologists' jargon has been merely translated into educational jargon. The really critical and difficult tasks have still been left to the individual teacher.

Teachers are frequently confronted with children who do not consistently attend to either their work or to the teacher. Other students rarely complete assignments or show high error rates on homework as well as on tests. Many of these same children often display social responses which might be classified under the general heading of disruptive classroom behaviors. Included in this category are such actions as a high rate of talking and calling out, verbal and physical aggression, noncompliance with instructions and out-of-seat behavior. Disruptive behaviors, however, are only one of several types of inappropriate social behaviors that are observed in the classroom. Other common examples include failure to interact with peers, avoidance of certain activities or games and inability to cooperate with classmates.

The emotional behaviors of children also present difficulties in the classroom. Because of the highly competitive nature of our present educational and social systems, great emphasis is placed upon the performance of students on tests. It is, therefore, not

vii

unusual to observe a large number of children who exhibit symptoms of anxiety when confronted with regular examinations. Maladaptive emotional behavior is not limited to testing situations alone, and numerous students develop a strong dislike for specific subject matter, and at times for the entire school setting. For some children, dislike for school becomes so intense that the resultant fear has been termed "school phobia."

Most teachers, whether in regular public school classrooms or in special education units, find that during the course of a school year they are faced with several children who exhibit some kind of academic, social, or emotional behavior problem. The difficulty might be considered relatively mild, such as the poor attention span of a normal elementary school child, or quite severe, such as the highly aggressive behavior of an autistic child in a special classroom. The teachers of both of these children, however, encounter extreme frustration in attempting to help each child realize his potential.

Teachers often say, and rightly so, that they have for the most part been poorly prepared to cope with many of the student difficulties that arise in the classroom. There has been little effort made to provide teachers with useful classroom techniques which would enable them to carry out their professional teaching responsibilities in as effective a manner as possible.

Within the past five years, however, an increasing number of psychologists and educators have made great strides in improving classroom behavior by training teachers in a very specific set of basic learning principles, those of operant conditioning. By systematically applying these principles, teachers have successfully promoted underdeveloped positive behavior and altered undesirable behavior of children in their classrooms. Of major significance is the fact that the procedures have been carried out by teachers rather than researchers or psychologists. The fact that personnel who are relatively untrained in the discipline of psychology can quickly and effectively learn to use such techniques has important and widespread implications for education.

The title given to the application of laboratory-derived learning principles to behavior problems is behavior modification, behavior therapy or behavior management. Operant conditioning principles, though, form only one of several sets of techniques that can be considered behavior modification procedures. Other methods include the use of respondent conditioning techniques and principles of imitative learning. For over a decade, the practice of behavior modification has achieved considerable success in alleviating those maladjustments which are generally included under the heading of clinical disorders. To date, however, it has primarily been the operant principles which have experienced widespread use in the classroom, with some very recent attempts to introduce respondent techniques as well.

The major portion of this book of readings is devoted to a sampling of articles which illustrate the rationale behind and the utilization of operant principles in classroom behavior modification. The operant section has been specifically divided into four chapters. The introduction provides a brief summary of basic operant conditioning principles and the methodological procedures used to implement these principles in the classroom. The next three chapters contain studies which are direct applications by teachers of preschool children, schoolage children and children in special education classes. An attempt has been made to classify the studies according to the broad area of behavior which is being modified (e.g. academic behavior, social behavior). Although the categories are not always mutually exclusive, it was believed that a more organized presentation could be made by using such a classification. The operant section is followed by a section on respondent principles in education. An introductory paper is presented which briefly explains basic respondent techniques and suggests various ways in which they apply to the classroom. Also included in this section are several studies which deal with the treatment of emotional behavior, such as test anxiety and stage fright in school settings. The final two sections, respectively, are concerned with the training of educators in the application of learning principles and a discussion of problems and ethical issues related to the use of these principles.

CONTENTS

Section Three
Teacher Training

Section Four
Issues and Problems

Behavior Modification

in

Educational Settings

Section One

Operant Principles in Education

I
INTRODUCTION

In the first article, Ross describes the rationale behind the use of operant techniques by classroom teachers. He emphasizes that within a behavior modification framework, all behaviors, whether appropriate or maladaptive, are considered to be learned, with the basic premise being that behavior is a function of its consequences. He states that teachers can be readily taught elementary operant principles and can then begin to serve as "therapeutic educators." This role would include measuring the observable overt behaviors of students and then making decisions involving the use of appropriate modification procedures based on such observations.

By having the teacher focus only on those behaviors which can be seen and recorded, Ross dismisses the more traditional psychoanalytic theories, which, with their emphasis on nonobservable unconscious conflicts and dynamic forces, have proven to be of little practical value for educators.

The second article, by Haring, suggests how teachers can begin to view the total classroom situation in behavioral terms. He indicates that by carefully specifying the major dependent and independent variables operating in the classroom, the teacher can start to obtain a more accurate scientific picture of his educational procedures.

After introducing several operant principles, Haring outlines some of the systematic procedures necessary for teachers to follow in order to effectively and predictably change student behavior. Two brief accounts are then offered on the use of operant techniques to modify various academic and social behaviors.

It should be clearly noted here that although both the Ross and Haring articles are directed towards special education, the rationale and principles set forth in these two papers are equally applicable to the regular classroom, as will be seen in many of the papers which follow.

In the next article, Bijou *et al.* discuss a methodology for conducting experiments in the natural environment and approaches to analyzing data in such settings. They emphasize the careful specification, definition and recording of behavioral events. Examples are given of how data can be collected and analyzed, and they suggest that the most useful analyses of behavior can be made when the data are recorded as frequency-of-occurrence measures. The recording forms and the reliability procedures described are similar to those used in the studies which follow. The importance of the article is not to encourage teachers to hire observers to perform experiments but rather to show how classroom procedures can be examined empirically.

While Bijou *et al.* emphasize the use of frequency counts and transformation of data into percentage form, Lovitt *et al.* argue that rate (e.g. number of problems completed over time) is an extremely useful method for analyzing pupil performance. They stress the fact that pupils complete similar tasks in varying lengths of time and that simple frequency counts or percentages do not reveal this important information. Once rate is examined, different teacher-controlled variables such as teacher-pupil contacts, types of reinforcers and reinforcement contingencies can be examined to determine their effect upon rate. Such analyses, Lovitt *et al.* point out, can help to determine whether these variables or inadequate programing materials are responsible for learning difficulties. Analyzing group data in terms of rate ranges is also encouraged in order to discover the influence of various environmental changes (i.e. substitute teacher, physical rearrangement of the room, new textbooks) upon performance.

1

The Application of Behavior
Principles in Therapeutic Education

ALAN O. ROSS

THERE IS A RAPIDLY accumulating literature suggesting that the application of behavioral principles is as relevant to education as it is to the treatment of patients with psychological disorders. This makes it possible to speak of a *therapeutic educator* with training in the application of behavioral principles that can be brought to bear on the teaching of children with psychological problems. Behavioral principles indeed have already been successfully applied in a variety of areas where modification of behavior is sought. These include the training of the mentally retarded, the rehabilitation of the physically handicapped and the treatment of children and adults with psychological disorders. This last application has come to be known as *behavior therapy*.

Behavior therapy differs from traditional psychotherapy in that it starts from the premise that psychological disorders represent *learned* behavior and that known principles of learning can be applied to their modification. Unlike traditional psychotherapists who view a disorder as symptomatic of some underlying disease process that must be uncovered before the symptoms will change, the behavior therapist views the manifest *behavior* as the problem

NOTE: This paper is based on a lecture delivered at the Special Evaluative Techniques with Handicapped Children, Columbus, Ohio, March 13, 1967. The contribution of Mrs. Minnie G. Hubbard to its development is gratefully acknowledged.

From *The Journal of Special Education*, 1:275–286, 1967. Copyright 1967, Buttonwood Farms Inc. Reprinted with permission of author and publisher.

with which he must deal, and although he would not deny that this behavior may have lengthy and complicated antecedents in the individual's past, he does not believe that it is necessary to reconstruct this past in order to effect a change in the behavior.

Once one accepts this premise, the exploration of an individual's past with a view toward "understanding" his present behavior becomes largely an academic excercise that may well have relevance to the prevention of disorders in others but little bearing on the treatment of the disorder manifested by the individual who has come for help.

Behavior therapy takes a variety of forms and finds its theoretical base in both Hullian drive-reduction theory and Skinnerian operant conditioning. The nature of the patient's problem seems to determine whether respondent or operant conditioning provides the treatment of choice, although there are those who would argue that in most instances the former is but a special case of the latter. Ignoring this issue, one can say that a patient whose difficulties focus on autonomic responses can be treated by respondent conditioning, while someone whose difficulties are primarily in the skeletal-motor-verbal realm is probably most efficiently treated by operant methods. A patient whose difficulties cover both the autonomic and the skeletal-motor systems will probably respond best to a combination of the two approaches.

Because the behaviors that are most easily observed and hence modified in the classroom are those in the skeletal-motor-verbal realm, we shall concentrate on behavior modification based on operant conditioning, mentioning only that the respondent work is probably best known through the application described by Joseph Wolpe as *desensitization or reciprocal inhibition therapy* (Wolpe, 1958).

The basic principle of behavior therapy based on operant conditioning is elegant in its simplicity and therefore easily taught. Its basic principle is that behavior is a function of its consequences. That is to say, the probability of a certain behavior recurring depends on what has followed that behavior when it has previously occurred. Behavior can thus be strengthened or weakened by manipulating its consequences, and the efficiency of such behavior modification depends on the degree to which we can control the consequences. Behavior can be strengthened if the consequences are positive—if it is followed by a positive reinforcer (reward) or by the cessation of a negative reinforcer (aversive stimulation). Behavior will be weakened if it has no consequence—if it has no effect on the environment—or it it is followed by a negative reinforcer or by the termination of a positive reinforcer.

The idea that reward and punishment regulate behavior is, of course, nothing new, and the recognition that people seek pleasure and avoid pain goes back to the Greek philosophy of hedonism. The new and highly significant contribution of operant conditioning is its stress on the importance of the temporal relationship between the response and the reinforcement. This relationship is called the *contingency*, and the basic principle of operant conditioning demands that the consequences be contingent upon the occurrence of a specified behavior. Positive reinforcers, for example, are presented if, and only if, the behavior one is seeking to strengthen has occurred.

Beyond this basic principle, certain technical considerations—such as the nature of reinforcers used, the behaviors to be modified and the scheduling of the reinforcement contingencies—require advanced specialized training for full utilization, but one person with such specialized training can give the necessary instructions to a great many people with considerably less training who then can do the direct work of managing the contingencies. The implications for the manpower problem in the mental health field are obvious!

Because there are great individual differences among children in their available response repertoire, their responsiveness to stimuli, the relevance of particular reinforcers to their behavior and their rate of acquiring new responses or extinguishing old ones, the application of operant techniques to behavior modification requires a highly individualized approach. There is nothing automatic or routine about this work. What is more, it calls for the very active participation of the child in his own treatment, and anyone who considers behavior therapy as an authoritarian method of controlling people without their knowledge has not taken the trouble to learn what this approach is about.

Discussion of behavior therapy at times becomes confounded by certain preconceptions or misconceptions that get in the way of rational discussion. It may be well to touch on these in the hope of removing potential obstacles to comprehension.

Our culture gives us a compelling set to seek for explanations of current events in the antecedents of these events. Telling people that antecedent events are irrelevant to a child's problem frequently offends them because it frustrates their legitimate intellectual curiosity about how things have come to be the way they are. We want to know the cause of what we experience and invariably look for it in what has gone before. Thus, when we observe a child sitting by himself in the corner of a room we tend to wonder, "What makes him do that?" The behavior we observe is seen as purposive and goal-oriented, and we think that we can understand it if we can define the purpose or goal. Guessing that the child is in the corner because he feels insecure, we join him in the corner, hoping to increase his security by talking to him, only to find to our surprise that this only makes him seek his corner more frequently.

An example from everyday life may serve as illustration of this important principle: The telephone rings and a man picks up the receiver and says "hello." If we ask him why he has engaged in this behavior he is very likely to answer that he picked up the phone because it rang; that is, he views the stimulus of the ringing bell as having elicited his response of picking up the receiver. This "obvious" answer is unfortunately the wrong answer as we can see in the case where after repeated ringing and answering sequences, the man finally stops lifting the receiver because no one ever responds to his "hello." At this point the phone will ring but he will not lift the receiver, and if we ask him why he will probably tell us, "Why should I, there's nobody at the other end."

This demonstrates that the man has lifted the receiver in the first place, not because the bell somehow "drove" him to it but because he has learned in the past that *if* he lifts the receiver and says "hello" *when* the bell rings, he is rewarded by hearing a human voice with a message at the other end. It is the consequence of the receiver-lifting that has maintained the behavior. The *antecedent* (the ringing bell) in and of itself has not "made him" do anything; it has merely signaled the potential availability of a reinforcing consequence.

The same logic holds in analyzing all operant behavior. The child remains in his corner not *in order* to gain increased security but *because* it is in the corner that he receives our attention. Behavior is maintained by its consequences, and the modification of these consequences will change the behavior. It can be shown that a child such as the one in our example will cease to sit in the corner once we ignore his sitting there and attend instead to any response that approximates moving out of the corner. Why he originally began sitting in the corner and all the historical reconstructions we can muster are quite irrelevant to the problem he presents and its resolution. It may in fact have been an accidental event that initiated his behavior. What is important is what happens once he is in the corner.

Behavior therapy is sometimes accused of being impersonal, mechanical, manipulative and authoritarian. Some of this is no doubt due to the rather unfortunate terminology that derives from the psychological laboratory. Words like "control," "contingency," "schedule," "program" and "conditioning" do indeed sound prohibitive, but as soon as one substitutes "learning" for "conditioning," "planning" for "programming," and "handling" for "control," one finds that the concepts as such are not at all objectionable. As far as the supposed manipulative, authoritarian aspects are concerned, behavior therapy does things *for* people and not *to* people; the subject is very much involved in carrying out his own treatment and the behavior that is changed is defined by the subject, not determined by the therapist. Every subject is treated according to a program based on his own needs and problems. The treatment procedures and rationale can be clearly spelled out and explained to him; there is nothing he need take on faith or on the basis of the therapist's authority.

Because behavior therapy deals with observable and therefore measurable behavioral events, both therapist and subject are at all times aware of the progress or lack of progress that is being made. Lack of progress can bring about immediate changes in the treatment procedures so that the subject is protected from being exposed to interminable groping for ill-defined improvements.

The principle that a response is made more likely and thus learned when its consequence is a positive reinforcer carries the implication that reinforcement must be forthcoming only if—and soon after—the appropriate response has been made. In child rearing and training, this means, of course, that the child must make the required response before he is reinforced; the reinforcement is thus conditional and must be earned. This often leads to the objection that reinforcement is a "bribe" and that making reinforcement conditional is "not nice," particularly if reinforcement is in the form of maternal affection. However, calling contingent reinforcement a bribe misses the entire point. The word "bribe" carries ethical implications because by definition a bribe is used to corrupt the conduct or pervert the judgment of someone in a position of trust. It is thus a form of reinforcement for a response the individual should *not* be making. In childrearing and other educational efforts, we are, hopefully, trying to establish responses that the child *should* be making. If someone tries to corrupt a child's conduct by using reinforcement principles, the immorality lies with the person doing this and not with the principles he employs. The analogy to the use of atomic energy is all to obvious.

Those who object to the use of reinforcement principles in childrearing because they view it as a form of bribery tend to forget that a quarter paid to a child as reinforcement for doing his homework is no more a bribe than the paycheck they themselves collect at the end of a certain period as reinforcement for the work they have performed. To ask whether a child should be doing his homework simply because that is the right and proper thing to do is like asking whether a school teacher should be teaching simply because doing a socially useful thing is in and of itself rewarding. It may not suit our idealism but it is a fact of life that no one performs work unless it is followed by some meaningful pay-off, and if we have no meaningful reinforcer other than a quarter, then this is what we must use to reinforce the behavior called doing homework. One hopes that homework will eventually generate consequences that are of secondary reinforcement value and are rewarding on less concrete levels, such as achieving success, getting praise or being promoted, but until that stage is reached, material reinforcers may be the most effective tools at our disposal.

The general objection to making maternal affection conditional upon specific behavior is based on misguided, misplaced kindness. If consistently applied in an across-the-board fashion, this kindness would result in making child rearing a much more complicated and hazardous process than it already is.

A potentially reinforcing event that occurs as a consequence to some desired behavior can be effective only if the child can discriminate that the occurrence of this event is contingent on his response. Furthermore, any reinforcer loses its effectiveness when the child is satiated with it. Take, for example, a mother's show of appreciation expressed in the words "Good boy!" Assuming that these words have acquired secondary reinforcement value, they will be effective in reinforcing a particular response only when they are contingent on the occurrence of that response. A mother who is unconditionally appreciative—that is, one who indiscriminately proclaims, "Good boy!"—will quickly make these words into meaningless sounds as far as their reinforcement value is concerned.

The same principle holds when we substitute the words "I love you" for "Good boy." When the complex pattern of behavior we call mother-love is unconditionally and indiscriminately present, it will lose its effectiveness as a reinforcer. It may not be a coincidence that statements of unconditional love are often made by parents who must resort to punishment in order to change the behavior of their child. Because they do give love unconditionally, they have lost the use of this powerful positive reinforcer and must therefore resort to negative reinforcement to control behavior, paradoxically assuring the child that they hurt him because they love him so much. A parent who makes his display of love contingent upon desired performance and who uses withdrawal of love to weaken undesired behavior may never have to resort to the questionable device of inflicting pain that often teaches the child many things other than what we hope him to learn.

So much for the underlying principles and some of the misunderstandings and distortions. We shall now refer briefly to some recent work in which responsible investigators have modified deviant behavior in children in ways pertinent to education.

The highly deviant, disruptive and self-destructive behavior of autistic children has been modified by the selective reinforcement of desirable responses and the systmatic extinction of undesirable responses. While these modifications do not represent a "cure," the ability to provide a 4½-year-old nonverbal autistic child with a basic speaking vocabulary in a period of six months (Hewett, 1965) represents a dramatic achievement.

A variety of troublesome behaviors displayed by nursery school children have been modified by the application of operant principles under the general direction of Wolf *et al.* Excessive crying, regressed crawling and isolate behavior have been dealt with in this manner, and one of the most interesting aspects of this work is that the treatment was conducted by nursery school teachers who had learned systematic techniques involving the withdrawal of attention from undesired behavior and providing attention to desired behavior. Thus a child who spent most of her nursery school periods crawling on hands and knees was ignored whenever she was on the floor but given adult attention and approval as soon as she even approached a standing position. In order to demonstrate the effectiveness of these techniques, Wolf had the teacher reverse the procedure, clearly showing how the undesirable behavior returned as soon as it was once again reinforced by the teacher's attention. This, of course, also illustrates the fact that attention, praise and other social reinforcers can be used with children for whom these consequences have become effective secondary reinforcers. Relationships are indeed important in human affairs, but they are effective tools only when used in a systematic fashion.

Another case is that of a nine-year-old brain-damaged boy whose marked hyperactivity had not only disrupted the class but also interfered with his capacity to learn (Patterson, 1965). The technique used here was to install a small light and the dial of an electric counter on the child's school desk. The light and counter were controlled by an observer, and the child was told that whenever he sat still the light would flash on and the counter click, indicating that he had earned a piece of candy. He was then reinforced for every ten-second interval during which "attending behavior" occurred, and at the end of the session he collected the candy thus earned. Note the child's fully aware participation in his own treatment program. He was not "being conditioned"— he was taught!

An interesting aspect of the above approach is that the rest of the class was told that the boy in question would divide the candy he earned among his classmates. The class not only desisted from distracting him but also cheered for him, thus adding social reinforcement to the situation. Patterson reports a significant decrease in the number of hyperactive responses for the boy, and both teacher and parents reported some generalization of this "settling down" to situations outside the classroom.

It has already been pointed out that one of the major attractions of behavior therapy approaches is that they can be readily taught to and applied by individuals other than mental health professionals—nursery school teachers, for example. This would mean that treatment could eventually be carried out by individuals not trained to conduct psychotherapy. One well-trained professional psychologist could conceivably work out the details of a treatment program that could then be carried on by teachers or technical personnel with relatively little training.

Indeed, there is no reason why parents should not also be able to carry out behavior modification techniques. A group of psychologists at the University of Washington (Wahler, *et al.*, 1965) report an attempt to modify the deviant behavior of three children by systematically producing specific changes in the behavior of their mothers. Viewing the mother's behavior as a powerful class of reinforcers for the child's behavior, they taught the mothers to make discriminations between desirable and undesirable behaviors and to respond selectively to these behaviors. In two of three cases reported, the mothers' reactions to behavior were simply attending or ignoring, but in the third case punishment of the child by isolating him in an empty room immediately following undesired responses was added to the contingencies. Again, as is fortunately becoming routine practice in much of the research on behavior modification, the contingencies were reversed during one phase of the procedure in order to demonstrate that the experimental manipulation was indeed responsible for the behavior change.

One might ask why a mother must learn to modify the behavior of her child, and the answer to this seems to be that many mothers are unable to discriminate between desirable and undesirable behavior in its incipient form, so that they often attend to undesirable behavior and ignore desirable behavior—the exact opposite of what the logic of reinforcement theory demands. In the study here referred to, the initial teaching of when to respond and when not to respond was done by signal lights operated by an observer in an adjacent room, but in more recent work, a small FM receiver somwhat like a hearing aid has been used to give mothers verbal instruction. Treatment along the lines just described has also been carried out effectively in private homes. (Hawkins *et al.*, 1966).

BEHAVIOR THERAPY AND EDUCATION

By now, words like "learning" and "teaching" have been used several times, and it may have become apparent that behavior therapy is much more closely related to education than it is to traditional psychotherapy. There is basically no difference between learning arithmetic and learning how to control one's temper, between practicing one's multiplication table and practicing one's interpersonal skills. The principles underlying the teaching of academic subjects are the same principles that underlie the teaching of how to live one's life adaptively and constructively.

Indeed, the behavioral point of view rejects the "disease" notion that psychological disorders are symptomatic, distorted discharges of accumulated tensions, derivative of unconscious conflicts between defensive forces and repressed impulses striving for discharge. From this point of view, it is meaningless to speak of an illness that must be diagnosed, an etiology that must be established, a nosologic category that must be determined or a therapy that must be prescribed so that a patient can be cured. Such terms are irrelevant to an approach that stresses the learning, unlearning and relearning of behavior.

What can the behavioral approach contribute to the field of special education in general and to the education of the emotionally disturbed in particular?

With the establishment of special programs and classes for the so-called emotionally disturbed child, the question of role definition for the teacher of such classes has become topical. Questions are being asked about the differences between the task of the teacher and the task of the therapist. Such questions reflect the assumption that there is an essential difference between teaching and therapy—a point of view which derives from the disease model of psychological disorders mentioned above. One of the principal consequences of a behavioral approach, however, is a merging of the roles of teacher and of therapist into what might be called a therapeutic educator and a new orientation toward the role of teachers in helping children with psychological problems. For when psychological disorders are seen as learned maladaptive responses or as a failure to have learned adaptive behavior patterns, the management of such disorders becomes a process of unlearning or relearning, with the focus on modifying behavior that is interfering with the child's effectiveness.

As soon as one views treatment as a process of unlearning and relearning, it becomes an activity closely related to education, and when we speak of therapeutic education, it is with the conviction that all good therapy is education and that all good education is therapeutic in the sense that it enhances human effectiveness and increases social competence. In this light, questions regarding the differences between the roles of therapist and teacher are resolved in terms of differences in focus, for the methods used are basically the same. The teacher will be primarily concerned with teaching academic subject matter, while the therapist will be primarily concerned with teaching personal and social behavior; but the teacher at times must be concerned with behavior just as the therapist at times may have to teach factual material.

A primary requirement of the behavioral approach is a continuous and objective assessment of each child in which the following questions should be considered: What desirable behavior and skills does a child exhibit, and how can these be developed? What are the child's behavior deficits and undesirable behaviors, and how can these be changed or eliminated? What new skills and behavior patterns is the child capable of learning? What environmental forces are supporting the undesirable behavior or preventing the child from acquiring more appropriate patterns? What reinforcers are effective for the child and how can these be used to modify behavior?

Implicit in these questions is the need for careful, systematic observations and for an individually designed program that takes the child's present educational, psychological and environmental conditions into account. When these are carefully studied, there is no need to explore the historical origin of the child's disorder, and questions of etiology become of primarily academic interest.

One of the implications of the behavioral approach lies in its facilitating the identification of disturbed children in regular classes. The best available estimates suggest that 5 to 10 percent of all children in our schools are psychologically disturbed and that at present most of them sit in the typical classroom where the typical teacher tries to maintain them, although their behavior disrupts the classroom and their performance is far below acceptable standards. Much of their fidgeting, fighting, instigating and crying is viewed as "bad" or "immature," but, as a rule, since this kind of behavior is typically considered to be the responsibility of mental health professionals, nothing is done to help these children until someone "diagnoses" their "emotional disorder" and refers them to an outside facility.

As long as disturbed behavior is seen as a symptom of an underlying disease, that "disease" will have to be identified before treatment for the child can be sought. A child is not referred for help just because he isn't sitting still; he is referred if someone raises questions as to whether he "has" a disorder—neurosis or brain injury, for example. This very qestion-raising is a form of labelling, however—a form of diagnosis that many teachers feel unqualified to enter into. The introduction of a behavioral approach frees the teacher of the necessity and responsibility for this quasidiagnostic questioning and labelling imposed by the disease model of mental illness. When the emphasis is on behavior, the teacher need only report what he sees and, freed from an esoteric mental health nomenclature, he should be able to make more extensive and more accurate observations. He no longer needs to wonder what a behavior means. That it occurs, how frequently it occurs and with what intensity it occurs are far more important data to him than any presumed underlying etiology.

By abandoning the disease analogy and viewing behavior as behavior, the problem of screening and identification of pupils' problems comes to revolve around the question of which behaviors can be modified by the teacher in the regular classroom; which are so intractable or disruptive as to require handling in a setting permitting greater contingency control, such as a special class or residential setting; and which are of such a nature that intermittent intervention at a clinic, in combination with the work of the teacher, can be successful.

Questions such as whether brain-damaged and emotionally disturbed children should be in the same special class become meaningless when the focus shifts from etiology to manifest behavior. A soundly based behavioral approach to the question, "Identification for what?" can instead be answered in terms of specific programs of intervention that may not only reduce the number of children who are presently not receiving adequate help but may also give a specific task to the special educators who are now being trained to work in classes for children with psychological disorders.

THE THERAPEUTIC EDUCATOR

The behavioral approach to the education of disturbed children has exciting implications for breaking the vicious cycle of mutual distrust and lack of collaboration that often exists between the educator and the mental health worker. As long as teacher and psychotherapist have labored on different problems, their relationship has often been strained because each has seen the other as interfering with his task. One of teachers' most frequent complaints about child guidance clinics has been the clinic's failure to tell the teacher what to do. Asking a teacher to bear with a child while he is undergoing the lengthy process of treatment, requesting her to understand the child's difficulty and often making her feel that an insistence on rules, limits and controls might harm the child or retard his progress in therapy are not ways in which a clinic endears itself to the school. As Sarason and his co-authors have pointed out in their book describing exciting pioneer work at the Yale Psycho-Educational Clinic (Sarason *et al.,* 1966), a teacher who knows that a certain child is being seen in a child guidance clinic often takes a "hands off" policy that has frequently been antitherapeutic for child, teacher and other children.

With the basic assumption that negative responses can be modified or eliminated and desirable responses established and strengthened, the teacher is challenged to become immediately and actively involved with what she perceives as important— behavior. She is challenged to use her skills and training to observe and teach with a specified goal and explicit program in mind. The imposed passivity and the frustrations of the clinic waiting list are eliminated. The teacher is now actively participating to help the pupil.

The introduction of a behavioral approach with its focus on problem behavior makes it possible for teacher and clinician to talk about the same thing. When the teacher, for example, is concerned about a given child's stealing, the clinician, after carefully assessing the situation, is able to tell the teacher quite specifically what he can do to reduce the incidence of this behavior. The teacher no longer needs to be told that the child has unconscious dependency conflicts that manifest themselves in stealing and to be asked to understand this problem and to bear with the child while the clinic attempts to "get at" and resolve these conflicts.

In by-passing the outdated disease model of psychological disorders, according to which a "cure" could be achieved only if the underlying problem was discovered and done away with, and replacing it with a psychological model, which holds that disturbed behavior represents inappropriate learning or failure to have learned, we are placing the treatment of disturbed children squarely within the province of the educator and removing the mystique of psychotherapy. This makes the "treatment" process no more than teaching and learning—and with these the school has long been familiar. The teacher becomes a therapeutic educator who, working hand in hand with her psychological consultant, brings about change in the child's behavior where it counts most, namely in the classroom and the real world. If a teacher approaches the child's problems as faulty techniques of living—that is, as a learning problem that she proposes to work on together with the child—the potential for developing a positive classroom climate is tremendously enhanced. With rational tools at her disposal, the teacher can develop a relationship with the child that is enhanced by a behavorial approach because the emphasis is on health rather than illness, on teaching rather than treatment, on learning and the pupil's involvement rather than fundamental personality reorganization. The behavioral approach with its assumption that maladaptive behavior is learned and that it can be modified or eliminated through techniques related to teaching involves the teacher in a mental health program not by sufferance but by design.

CONCLUSION

At present, most teachers are poorly prepared to participate actively in the promotion and protection of the mental health of the children they teach. While this problem has many roots, the primacy of psychoanalytic theory and of what Sarason has called "professional preciousness" have contributed strongly to its perpetuation if not to its cause. Teachers and administrators sensitive to the emotional needs of children, whose experience and interaction with children have reinforced their interest in their emotional well-being, have been forced to pursue their interest and concern in an academic climate not entirely receptive to this interest. To be sure, teaching educators how to do psychotherapy has been inappropriate for an education curriculum, and what students' psychology courses have taught them about children's emotional disorders has been largely a watered-down version of psychoanalytic jargon that has only underscored their view of therapy as something esoteric that they could never hope to learn, a high-priced procedure that is taking place somewhere outside the schools where they would be teaching.

With special classes for emotionally disturbed children being established all over the country, we are now training teachers to serve in them, but as long as the disease model predominates as a basis for helping these children, these classes can be little more than holding areas where children spend their time so that they will not disrupt the regular class while they await the magic hour of precious psychotherapy that takes place in some other building at some other time. Under such circumstances, the teacher will have little more than a caretaking role, and what training one might concoct for him might include more paraphrastic psycho-analysis and an acquaintance with the various diagnostic classi-fications so he can label the children in his room.

A special class will become a therapeutic experience when the teacher is prepared and expected to be a therapeutic educator. While the behavioral approach is no panacea for the ills of the world, it does provide a framework in which the needs of children can be studied and met in school classrooms. It also lays the foundation for professional rapprochement and cooperation be-tween educator and mental health professional that is long overdue.

REFERENCES

Allen, K. E., Hart, B. M., Buell, J. S., Harris, F. R. and Wolf, M. M.: Effects of social reinforcement on isolate behavior of a nursery school child. In L. P. Ullmann and L. Krasner (Eds.): *Case Studies in Behavior Modification.* New York, Holt, Rinehart and Winston, 1965, pp. 307–321.

Hawkins, R. P., Peterson, R. F., Schweid, E. and Bijou, S. W.: Be-havior therapy in the home: amelioration of problem parent-child relations with the parent in a therapeutic role. *Journal of Experi-mental Child Psychology,* 4:99–107, 1966.

Hewett, F. M.: Teaching speech to an autistic child through operant conditioning. *American Journal of Orthopsychiatry, 35:*927–936, 1965.

Patterson, G. R.: An application of conditioning techniques to the control of a hyperactive child. In L. P. Ullmann and L. Krasner (Eds.): *Case Studies in Behavior Modification.* New York, Holt, Rinehart and Winston, 1965, pp. 370–375.

Sarason, S. B., Levine, M., Goldenberg, I. I., Cherlin, D. and Bennett, E. M.: *Psychology in Community Settings: Clinical Educational, Vocational, Social Aspects.* New York, Wiley, 1965.

Ullmann, L. P. and Krasner, L. (Eds.): *Case Studies in Behavior Modification.* New York, Holt, Rinehart and Winston, 1965.

Wahler, R. G., Winkel, G. H., Peterson, R. F. and Morrison, D. C.: Mothers as behavior therapists for their own children. *Behavior Research and Therapy,* 3:113–124, 1965.

Wolpe, J.: *Psychotherapy by Reciprocal Inhibition.* Stanford, Stanford University Press, 1958.

2

Behavior Principles in Special Education

NORRIS G. HARING

WHEN WE WALK into a classroom for observation and are met with the almost overwhelming task of rearranging the environment to establish conditions which promote more effective instruction, solutions are hardly comprehensible. Solutions not only seem difficult to envision but are probably impossible in one effective step. That multitudes of teachers have been taught to approach the classroom behavior of children through an underlying causal frame of reference makes the task of changing the behavior of children toward improved patterns of performance difficult, if not impossible.

An alternative to viewing behaviors as representing some underlying cause, however, is a strategy which encompasses procedures to identify, measure and change systematically the events and conditions arranged to affect performance within the classroom. This strategy for changing behavior, involving a number of specific responsibilities, incorporates established principles of learning that define lawful relationships between behavior and the immediate environment.

There are two views of the behavior problem: the view of the disordered behaviors observable in the child and the view of the disorder caused by these behaviors. One must begin with the premise that no behavior problem is totally unresolvable with a formidable strategy and with the cooperation of the administra-

NOTE: Presented at 17th Annual Series of Lectures in Special Education and Rehabilitation, University of Southern California, July, 1968. Published by permission of the author.

tion and supporting school personnel. The strategy of this article is designed to guide the way, tactic by tactic, to modify behavior toward concisely defined objectives. To facilitate clarity of direction as well as content, several basic teaching premises and a set of terms will be presented.

BASIC TEACHING PREMISES

With the incorporation of four basic premises into the teachers' procedures, behavior modification within an educational setting can become an established fact, observable in the performance of the child.

1. The teacher holds within her classroom all the power to change these behaviors from the inappropriate and disturbed behaviors she observes to any behavior she wants, if she makes the correct responses in planning procedures and conducting the program.
2. Correct teacher responses in planning the conducting programs for behavior modification require the systematic arrangement and presentation of classroom events, that is, stimuli temporally related to the child's specified performance.
3. Behavior modification requires the use of scientific procedures for measuring the performance of the pupil in order to evaluate the effectiveness of procedures arranged for the specific program for learning.
4. Teachers can be more scientific.

CLASSROOM VARIABLES

These premises suggest that the teacher must become accustomed to a different, or possibly just a more accurate, view of the child in her classroom. She must observe with a more refined view his behaviors and performances and all the things that happen in her classroom in order to gain an awareness of the effect of these happenings on the child's performance.

Dependent Variables

Everything the child is observed to do in the classroom can be listed as his classroom *behavior*. Writing spelling words or arithmetic answers, pointing to a choice of letters following auditory cues, picking up the correct object following verbal or written directions, talking to the teacher or to another child or to the class, jumping out of his seat, sharpening his pencil, throwing a paper plane, hitting another child or staring out the window are all movements he makes—behaviors he exhibits in the classroom.

Any instance of behavior observable from the child is a *response*. For example, writing an answer, hitting a child, pronouncing a word or cranking the handle of the pencil sharpener each represent *one unit of behavior*, one response. Turning a page in a book, raising one hand, pointing to the correct answer, smiling at another child are also each an example of a unit of behavior, i.e. one response. Each unit of behavior has specific definable characteristics and the characteristics defined represent the *topography* of that unit.

Any one of these types of responses can be made a number of times during an interval. During an arithmetic assignment, for example, a child can be observed to write many answers. If each of these writing responses is similar in that they are made to the same type of arithmetic problem, they can be grouped into a *response class* because they have similar topographies, similar definable physical characteristics. For instance, all answers to three-column, two-digit addition problems might be considered as one response class. All hitting responses might be grouped into one response class, though hitting responses that vary in topographies could be considered different response classes.

Independent Variables

The child's classroom *environment* is everything in the room that can be observed: the teacher and what she says and is observed to do, the children individually and in various group arrangements, the words the children say, their observable behavior, the books and materials, assignments on the board, signs and posters and posted work, display equipment, noises from inanimate objects, and furniture, closets and cupboards.

Some things in the child's environment are always constant. For instance, the color of the walls is always the same, as are

the lighting and temperature of the room. The closets and cupboards are always in the same place, and in some school rooms
the desks and chairs maintain immovable positions.

Easily outnumbering the constants in the classroom, however,
are the things that vary, that change in any number of ways any
number of times. Think of the number of times a teacher speaks
to a child, a small group, or the whole class. Think, too, of the
number of movements she makes around the room each day, from
child to child, from cupboard to desk, from child to group, and
innumerably more. Think of the number of times a child says
or does something in the classroom or the number of times a
group of children make a verbal or physical movement. Every
time a different book is put before the child or a different piece
of paper is given him to write on or a piece of display equipment
offers a new presentation, the child's environment has varied.
These are all variables, rather than constants, in the classroom
environment.

Any physical event or condition within the classroom environment can be a *stimulus* to a child; all constants and variables
within the room, including the child's own behavior, are stimuli
to that child as well as to any other child and the teacher.
Stimulus events can be viewed from many degrees of identifiable
scope, from very microscopic to very macroscopic. Each single
action of the teacher, each arithmetic problem or printed letter,
each musical note, each tick of the clock, is a microscopic stimulus
event. Each schoolbook, assignment, musical recording or workbook page are viewable as more macroscopic stimulus events.

All classroom events can be viewed as temporal events, since
by occurring either before or after a specified response, they are
related in time to that response. An arithmetic book placed on
the child's desk before he begins to write arithmetic answers or
instructions given to the child before he begins reading a para-
graph are stimuli which temporally occur before the writing or
reading responses. Similarly, the teacher's reprimand following
the child's hitting another child is a stimulus which temporally
follows the hitting response, just as a spelling assignment following an art lesson is a stimulus which temporally follows the art
lesson.

Any such stimulus which is presented before the child makes the specified response an antecedent stimulus event. Antecedent stimuli can be observed in many degrees of refinement. They can be observed grossly, as the type of material presented to the child before he begins a task (an arithmetic book, a workbook page in reading, or a list of spelling words). An antecedent event may also be viewed microscopically, as when defining the precise stimulus event which occurs before each single response observed. When identifying a microscopic antecedent event, the observer may note that many times this event may simply be the previous response of the child.

Any event which occurs immediately after the child makes a response is viewed as a subsequent stimulus event. For example, a "look from a peer" following the dropping of a pencil is a subsequent event to the child who dropped the pencil. Or again, a frown from the teacher is a subsequent event to whatever the child was doing immediately prior to the frown. As with antecedent events, observation of subsequent events can also range from a gross to a microscopic view, depending on one's purpose and/or skill. A gross view might be observation of the stimulus event which occurs when the child has completed an assignment. For example, if an art lesson immediately follows an English assignment, the art lesson is the subsequent stimulus event for the responses the child made during the English assignment. As another example, losing the opportunity for physical education class tomorrow because of too much screaming during the class today is the subsequent event which followed a half hour of screaming. A subsequent event may also be view microscopically, as when identifying the precise stimulus event which occurs immediately after each response emitted. Here again, as when microscopically identifying antecedent stimulus events, the observer may note that the subsequent event following any response within a series of responses is simply the next response. For example, with the child who is writing answers to arithmetic problems at a rapid rate, the subsequent event to one answer written is simply the next problem.

Further, each stimulus event actually has two temporal relationships to each of the child's responses. Each stimulus event is (a) subsequent to the response just made and (b) antecedent to the next response to be made.

The child's total classroom performance, as well as all the many specific types of responses he makes each day, are *dependent variables* that result from the temporal arrangement of classroom stimulus events, the *independent variables*. Measurement of the dependent variables (a specified type of response or performance from the child) is *the index* of the effect of the independent variables (stimulus event) used to facilitate performance.

This discussion of terms presented has been an attempt not only to promote a common base from which to proceed but also to point to the predictable relationships which become established between the child and the events and conditions within the environment that occur in time with it. These inter-relationships have been examined and have come to be defined as principles of behavior.

As we examine the variables relevant to instruction, it is necessary to consider the principles of behavior as the basic source of reliable information which can serve as a guide for the improvement of instruction in special education. The application of behavior principles in the classroom requires incorporating systematic procedures of instruction. The refinements and improvements of instruction implicit in special education can come from increased precision made possible through the utilization of procedures applied systematically with an instructional environment based in behavior principles.

PRINCIPLES OF BEHAVIOR AS OBSERVED IN THE CLASSROOM

Principles of behavior are statements of the lawfulnes of behaviors observed under specific conditions. All the principles of behavior to be mentioned will be relevant to reinforcement of behavior—to the consequences which follow a response or pattern of behavior. Behavioral psychology has shown that the consequence for making a response, that is, the event which temporally follows the behavior of interest, is a critical variable in behavior acquisition.

Through specific arrangements of consequences following a

specified response, the rate of occurrence of these responses can be increased, decreased, maintained or extinguished predictably. By presenting systematically a pleasant experience or event following a specific response or pattern of responses, the probability of the occurrence of that response increases. Such *positive reinforcement* has the effect of strengthening the probability of the occurrence of the response it follows. If the teacher's attention or her smile or her statement of "good job" is a pleasant event for a child, the teacher can react to the child in one of these ways following a pattern of academic performance and predictably accelerate the child's rate of performance. The principle of positive reinforcement, then, is a statement of the types of consequence which should follow a specific behavior and a description of the effects on behavior this arrangement will have.

The principle of positive reinforcement can be viewed as a very general principle which incorporates a number of *subprinciples*, all of which are descriptions either of conditions which bring about precise patterns of behavior or are descriptions of types of consequences which function as positive reinforcers generally. Precise patterns of behavior are brought about through specific arrangements in presenting reinforcement. It is not enough simply to present a pleasant event sometime after a pattern of behavior or a set of responses occur, in order to establish the behavior efficiently. When a pattern of behavior is just becoming established, reinforcement needs to occur frequently, so that responding will occur at a high, accurate rate. When a high rate has become established, then reinforcement of these responses is only necessary intermittently. For example, when a child rarely makes any reading responses, almost every response he makes correctly to reading material should be reinforced if we want to increase his probability of reading more material. When he is reading at a high, accurate rate, then reinforcement need occur only intermittently. This, as yet, appears to be the most efficient pattern of reinforcement for establishing and maintaining an efficient, steady rate of accurate performance.

Specific types of events or conditions come to acquire strength as positive reinforcers and can be described in terms of the strength they predictably acquire and how they come to influence behavior. The principles of *conditioned reinforcement* and *generalized reinforcement* explain the environmental arrangements which establish a wide variety of objects, events, conditions and our own responses as pleasant events which can be used to increase the probability of responding. The human smile, the pat on the back, the gold star on a chart, the words in a book, are not initially events which strengthen behavior, although for most people they gain this strength when paired systematically with consequences already pleasant. Consequently, they come to have enough strength to maintain most of our adult behavior.

Negative reinforcement is a principle of behavior describing conditions which strengthen the probability of the occurrence of a pattern of responses through removal of an aversive stimulus, arrangements which lawfully produce escape and avoidance behaviors. Too many children in the classroom never begin working on an assignment until the teacher becomes very stern. For these children, scolding nagging or some other aversive act redirects them back to work. Consequently, the teacher stops her prodding and quite soon many of these children are again observed not to be working. This is a predictable effect of negative reinforcement. Children predictably respond to remove an aversive stimulus and when it is removed the necessity to respond is also removed.

The principle of *extinction*, which describes environmental conditions that predictably eliminate a pattern of behavior, is the final principle to be mentioned. Arranging events so that a positively reinforcing consequence no longer follows a particular response pattern will lead to the elimination of that behavior. For example, if the teacher will cease to attend to the child when he is shouting out or leaving his seat for no useful purpose or whispering to his neighbor, these behaviors will decrease in number and eventually almost disappear if it is the teacher's behavior that is maintaining it. At the same time, the most efficient procedure for the elimination of those behaviors inappropriate to the classroom is concurrent positive reinforcement of another pattern of behavior incompatible with responding inappropriately. Consequently, using positive reinforcement for responses made to academic materials is a good counterprocedure along with those applied to extinguish a behavior.

Systematic Procedures

Behavior principles offer clear prescriptions for arranging conditions in the environment to change behavior predictably. However, to effect a predictable change in behavior with these prescriptions, it is necessary to use a set of systematic procedures. As we concern ourselves with observable behavior and observable conditions in the environment, it is necessary to use systematically procedures of direct observation, continuous measurement of the behavior of concern and systematic manipulation of the environmental events thought to be effective for changing the behavior. These procedures will be described only briefly.

Direct Observation

Systematic observation of behavior involves stepping through several degrees of refinements in observation procedures which may first begin with describing narratively the behaviors observed and identifying specific behaviors of interest. Then, once the behavior selected as the target for further observation is identified, it is defined by its precise topography so that units or cycles of its occurrence can be counted. The occurrences of these units of behavior are then counted over time in order to determine the rate of occurrence.

Continuous Measurement

Measurement of these responses requires that a response topography be selected which will maintain its comparability during changes in environmental conditions, even though response requirements increase in difficulty as academic materials naturally become more complex. This facilitates the sensitivity of measurement necessary for precise evaluation of the effects of changes in contingencies and reinforcers.

Systematic Changes in Environmental Conditions

Event changes lead to the establishment of prescribed behavior patterns or sets of responses. Because behavior is lawful, because it develops lawfully from environmentally arranged conditions, the conditions which influence behavior can be determined if condition changes are introduced one at a time and held constant while measurement of performance is taken. A pattern of behavior may not initially register the effect of the temporally arranged conditions. Thus, to obtain a reliable measure of the degree of influence of one particular environmental condition, that condition must remain as introduced over a period of time.

Contingency Management

Applying behavior principles in the classroom using a systematic set of procedures is commonly referred to as contingency management, defined most precisely in terms of the systematic utilization of reinforcing events in relation to specified behavior. Wide agreement has been reached on the observation that a child learns by the effect he has upon his environment—on both the change he produces in his physical environment and on the temporal arrangement of events in his environment. The systematic application of contingencies of reinforcement to change behavior in a specified direction relatively recent in its systematic application, finding its way into the classroom only within the past three or four years (O'Leary and Becker, 1967; Birnbrauer *et al.*, 1965; Nolen *et al.*, 1967; Quay, 1966; Haring and Hauck, 1969; Zimmerman and Zimmerman, 1962; Lovitt and Curtiss, 1968). In terms of the classroom, there are three variables relevant to the contingencies responsible for changing behavior: (a) the occasion upon which behavior occurs, (b) the performance of concern and (c) the consequence of behavior. Armed with this important information, the teacher can have a strong and predictable influence upon behavior by arranging conditions which facilitate the establishment of appropriate classroom behavior. She accomplishes this responsibility first by making certain that consequences occur and that they occur under conditions which are optimal for producing the changes known as learning. Once certain events can be seen to reinforce behavior, behavior can be changed by the teacher quite predictably.

A pattern of behavior is concurrently influenced not only by the reinforcing consequence but also by the adjustment of the schedule (Ferster and Skinner, 1957) upon which the reinforcing events are presented. Attention to scheduling of reinforcement is critical to the acquisition of a new pattern of behavior as well as to the maintenance of a strong and stable behavior pattern over long periods of time. The many investigations of reinforcement schedules have demonstrated several principles. As mentioned earlier, certain schedules, presenting reinforcement intermittently, have been found to maintain a high and stable rate of responding, observable in the classroom as a child hard at work. It is this important principle that promotes behavior appearing to be intrinsically motivated, while actually it is the specific schedule of reinforcement. Many observations of children cause teachers and other adults to make statements, such as, "He's just a good boy," "He is certainly conscientious about his work," or "He naturally enjoys reading." These statements serve to conceal the reinforcement histories of the children which have established the materials they respond to as conditioned reinforcers and have made it possible to use more powerful reinforcers only once in a while. For most children in almost all classrooms, acceptable rates of academic responding have been shaped and are maintained by the natural occurrences of reinforcing events from the classroom. There are other children, however, who exhibit a different reinforcement history. These are children described as lazy or apathetic or who dislike reading or hate school. As with the children whose behavior looks very acceptable, these behaviors could be explained if a record were retrievable of the effects of the child's behavior upon the environment.

Maximizing Conditions for Learning

There are certain very basic steps the teacher can take in setting up the most efficient, individualized program to apply to a group of children. Here, the teacher must attend to two major variables of learning: (a) to the instructional materials and (b) to the consequences for responding to the task. Instructional materials to present at the child's level of responding may be anything from sand blocks to basal readers to spelling books to programmed reading materials. They are introduced in order to bring out a specific response from the child, such as writing a word for spelling, printing a letter in a programed reading book, writing a number under an arithmetic problem or feeling a sand block to determine its shape. Instructional materials provide the cues to which the child must respond. They are a major variable in learning.

The second major variable for learning has been observable throughout our discussion of behavior principles in the classroom—that is, the consequences for responding. A program for the acquisition of any series of academic responses must move through a number of successive approximations toward the desired behavior pattern. In order to reach this objective, an extended series of reinforcing events must be handled by the teacher initially, followed later by procedures which bring the child to managing his own contingencies.

Both of these major variables require effective sequencing in their presentation in the classroom. It is extremely important to sequence academic materials to the child which permit him to respond accurately. Materials should be sequenced which guide him to making responses that successively approximate the terminal skills expected of him. At no time under these conditions is he expected to make a response too difficult for him. It is just as important to sequence reinforcement to the child, and it becomes more critical for the teacher as she is less prepared to respond. When both of these variables are attended to systematically, we come closer to maximizing accurate and efficient learning.

PRACTICAL EXAMPLES OF THE APPLICATION OF BEHAVIOR PRINCIPLES IN THE REMEDIAL SETTING

Over the next several years, many classroom programs in which behavior principles are systematically applied will become evident. At the present time, only a few programs have developed to serve as models, models which at best are crude approximations to the refinements which should materialize.

Individualized Reading Program

An individualized reading program (Hauck and Haring, 1968) for 24 students in a regular classroom provides an early example of the application of behavior principles to the classroom. Within this program, the teacher carried out the responsibilities involved with cueing and reinforcing responses, and with measuring performances and managing contingencies. Several features of this program hold particular interest in these developmental stages of contingency management. First, basal readers were used rather than programed material. Second, students from the reading program were trained as pupil monitors to measure and record a reinforcing consequence having broad reinforcing strength and response information from each child. Third, the teacher selected one that was easy to dispense. Fourth, a package program was introduced with which the teacher initially could obtain a reliable baseline measurement of performance from which further program evaluation could commence.

Each student was provided a basal reader at his own reading level, with assignments programmed to allow measurement of reading responses in observable, comparable units. The 30-minute reading session included silent and oral reading of a word list, emphasizing discrimination of word parts, silent reading of sets of pages, oral reading of lines of print and comprehension questions. Reading assignments were framed in equal response units, so that the student silently read three pages of text, answered a comprehension question, orally read eight lines of print to the pupil monitor and then turned to the next set of pages to respond to.

Students were assigned to pupil monitors who read at least several stories ahead of them, and during the course of the program each student served as a pupil monitor. Most of the monitor's responsibilities involved response measurement, such as measuring and recording the rate and accuracy of oral reading and the accuracy of comprehension and word discrimination. Thorough training of the monitor was the critical feature of the program.

Following each session, students determined their own reading rate and accuracy, then plotted the data on graphs displayed on the wall. Performance rate exhibiting improvement or maintenance of a previously high rate earned the opportunity for extra recess or physical education.

The role of the classroom teacher in this program was to provide information on unknown words to individual students upon request during silent reading to check on the accuracy of pupil monitors as they conducted their responsibilities and to use performance data for making decisions about the effectiveness of contingencies for each child.

Results of performance data for this large group of children clearly exhibited the feasibility and effectiveness of group management (a) for individualizing instruction and rate of progress, (b) for evaluating effectiveness of conditions through direct performance measurement and (c) for establishing a reading program which was obviously reinforcing to the children involved. Marked changes in the patterns of reading performance were observable when contingencies required average or better performance. Variable rates of performance were stabilized, low rates of performance were improved and high rates were maintained. Performance became so efficient that students typically progressed through several basal readers in less than a month. Long-term retention of content was almost 100 percent.

Maxfield Summer Program

The summer program (Haring *et al.*, 1968) in remedial reading and math at Maxfield Elementary School, primarily for regular-class children, serves as an example of a total school program designed to incorporate the principles of behavior and is a second approximation of the application of necessary systematic procedures. This program, again, should be viewed as an early approximation to the type of school program that should be functioning for each child. Generally, the description can proceed in terms of the application of principles of behavior, utilization of systematic procedures, refinements in modification procedures introduced during the program and performance data of the children.

The summer program for 200 children in grades kindergarten through eight was designed to provide programmed sequencing of reading and math materials to facilitate a low rate of error. Positive reinforcement was presented for correct responses in each of three different materials for strengthening and maintaining patterns of responding. The principle of extinction was applied to inappropriate behavior by withholding positive reinforcement for behaviors that should not recur. In other words, talking out, out-of-seat and other similarly inappropriate behaviors were ignored, short of allowing damage to others or to performance data. Negative reinforcement was avoided. The classrooms were arranged in two basic areas: a work area and an activity area containing many pleasant games, crafts and art supplies. Children earned the opportunity to engage in these activities following performance which showed improvement in rate or maintenance of a high accurate rate.

Each teacher applied the systematic set of procedures described earlier to the observable behaviors and conditions for learning in the classroom. Correct and incorrect academic responses were counted and recorded and rate was determined and graphed. Children assumed responsibilities of recording as soon as they acquired the skill. Performance was continuously measured as conditions changed in the classroom to evaluate the effects of these changes on the evident changes in child performance. After observing child performance for a week under conditions which specifically cued and reinforced responses, the teacher, using the response data of the child, made decisions about necessary changes in contingencies. That is, she decided which children were well motivated to work accurately and efficiently under present conditions and which children would require revision in kind or amount of reinforcement.

As precise contingencies became established between performance and the opportunity for time to engage in self-chosen activities within the summer program, many children exhibited marked changes in performance patterns. Changes in social behaviors were just as evident—behavioral changes which were the first to give great relief to the teacher. Children who left the room at a high rate, walked the ledges of the coat racks in the hall, dropped articles from the window, and shouted loudly in class at the beginning of the program showed remarkable changes in behavior when classroom conditions made it more reinforcing to respond to reading material than to respond to something else. Marked changes in behavior management skills also became very evident in the teachers, a change they were the first to admit.

SUMMARY

Both the Bellewood Reading Program and the Maxfield Summer Program provide significant and interesting implications for extensions and refinements of the procedures used as well as for the educational growth of the child. The programs themselves; the efforts such programming requires, especially in the early stages; and the results obtained in terms of performance and skill development underscore the importance of *Three P's of Education.* For effective instruction and for respectable growth in the field of education, educators must come to recognize and incorporate into their instructional routine: (a) systematic procedures (b) professional ethics and (c) pride of teaching.

Systematic Procedures

The importance of systematic procedures, especially as they adhere to the application of behavior principles in the classroom, has already been discussed and examples of their application provided. Further discussion is not necessary, except to emphasize that systematic procedures provide the educator with effective instruction, reliable information and significant skill development.

Professional Ethics

Professional ethics, although not yet described, are inherent in the conduct of these procedures and the principles they apply. Professional ethics are facilitated and observable when promoting or incorporating procedures which facilitate learning. To see that children learn is the ultimate responsibility of educators. This responsibility requires effective program planning in the classroom and effective training in the colleges as well as in-service training in the schools. The lawfulness of behavior has been demonstrated a thousandfold. It is, therefore, our ethical responsibility to insure that these results materialize in extensions to the classroom and to professional preparation. If educators do not accept their professional responsibility for maximizing the effects of conditions which can be brought to bear on performance, the door is left open for haphazard learning experiences and deficits in skill development.

It is the further ethical responsibility of educators to make educational decisions based on the performance data of the child. Reliable data must be collected and interpreted objectively. Information sent out for public consideration must especially be based on behavioral data from the child. This emphasis does not in any way lessen the importance of educational decision making in the classroom with response data from the child. Education as a system is ethical, and if an educator is adhering to procedures which facilitate effective learning, he is professionally ethical.

Pride of Teaching

Pride of teaching can be described by each of us in many ways, but primarily it comes through effort, planning and progress which has already been discussed. When effort is taken for effective instruction and the observable results are child progress in learning, we have before us four representations of pride in teaching: the planning, effort, evaluation and effectiveness.

REFERENCES

Birnbrauer, J. S., Wolf, M. M., Kidder, J. D. and Tague, C. E.: Classroom behavior of retarded pupils with token reinforcement. *Journal of Experimental Child Psychology, 2:*219–235, 1965.

Ferster, C. B. and Skinner, B. F.: *Schedules of Reinforcement.* New York, Appleton-Century-Crofts, 1957.

Haring, N. G. and Hauck, M. A.: Improved learning conditions in the establishment of reading skills with disabled readers. *Exceptional Children, 35:*341–352, 1969.

Haring, N. G., Hauck, M. A. and Starr, R. T.: School-wide contingency management in remedial reading and math: Maxfield summer program. Final Report, St. Paul Board of Education, St. Paul, Minnesota, Summer, 1968. Unpublished manuscript, University of Washington.

Haring, N. G. and Kunzelmann, H. P.: The finer focus of therapeutic behavioral management. In Hellmuth, J. (Ed.): *Educational Therapy,* vol. 1. Seattle, Bernie Straub, 1966.

Hauck, M. A. and Haring, N. G.: Individualized reading program with continuous evaluation of progress. Paper presented at Washington Organization for Reading Development Conference, Lynnwood, Washington, April, 1968. Unpublished manuscript, University of Washington.

Lovitt, T. C. and Curtiss, K. A.: Academic response rate as a function of teacher and self-imposed contingencies. Unpublished manuscript, University of Washington, 1968.

Nolen, P. A., Kunzelmann, H. P. and Haring, N. G.: Behavioral modification in a junior high learning disabilities classroom. *Exceptional Children, 34*:163–168, 1967.

O'Leary, D. K. and Becker, W. C.: Behavior modification of an adjustment class: a token reinforcement program. *Exceptional Children, 33*:637–642, 1967.

Quay, H. C.: Dimensions of problem behavior in children and their interaction in the approaches to behavior modification. *Kansas Studies in Education, 16*:6–12, 1966.

Zimmerman, E. H. and Zimmerman, J.: The alteration of behavior in a special classroom situation. *Journal of the Experimental Analysis of Behavior, 5*:59–60, 1962.

3

A Method to Integrate Descriptive and Experimental Field Studies at the Level of Data and Empirical Concept

SIDNEY W. BIJOU, ROBERT F. PETERSON and MARION H. AULT

It is the thesis of this paper, that data from descriptive and experimental field studies can be interrelated at the level of data and empirical concepts if both sets are derived from frequency-of-occurrence measures. The methodology proposed for a descriptive field study is predicated on three assumptions: (a) the primary data of psychology are the observable interactions of a biological organism and environmental events, past and present; (b) theoretical concepts and laws are derived from empirical concepts and laws, which in turn are derived from the raw data; (c) descriptive field studies describe interactions between behavioral and environmental events; experimental field studies provide information on their functional relationships. The ingredients of a descriptive field investigation using frequency measures consist of (a) specifying in objective terms the situation in which the study is conducted, (b) defining and recording behavioral and environmental events in observable terms and (c) measuring observer reliability. Field descriptive studies following the procedures suggested

NOTE: The formulation presented here was generated from the research conducted under grants from the U.S. Public Health Service, National Institute of Mental Health (M-2208, M-2232, and MH-12067), and from the United States Office of Education, Handicapped Children and Youth Branch (Grant No. 32-23-1020-6002, Proposal No. R-006).

From the *Journal of Applied Behavior Analysis, 2*:175–191, 1968. Copyright 1968 by the Society for the Experimental Analysis of Behavior Inc. Reprinted with permission of the authors and publisher.

here would reveal interesting new relationships in the usual ecological settings and would also provide provocative cues for experimental studies. On the other hand, field-experimental studies using frequency measures would probably yield findings that would suggest the need for describing new interactions in specific natural situations.

Psychology, like the other natural sciences, depends for its advancement upon both descriptive accounts and functional analyses of its primary data. Descriptive studies answer the question "How?" They may, for example, report the manner in which a Bantu mother nurses her child or the way in which the yellow-shafted flicker mates. Experimental studies, on the other hand, provide the "Why?" They might discuss the conditions which establish and maintain the relationships between the mother and infant, between the male and female birds.

It has been claimed that progress in the behavioral sciences would be enhanced by more emphasis on descriptive studies. This may be true, but one may wish to speculate on why descriptive accounts of behavior have been deemphasized. One possibility is the difficulty of relating descriptive and experimental data. For example, a descriptive study of parent-child behavior in the home may have data in the form of ratings on a series of scales (Baldwin *et al.*, 1949), while an experimental study on the same subject may have data in the form of frequencies of events (Hawkins *et al.*, 1966). Findings from the first study cannot reasonably be integrated with the second at the level of data and empirical concepts. Anyone interested in relating the two must resort to imprecise theory or concepts like "permissive mother," "laissez-faire atmosphere," "controlling child," "negativism," etc. This practice is unacceptable to psychologists who believe that all concepts must be based on, or linked to, empirical events.

It is the thesis of this paper that descriptive field studies (which include cross-cultural, ecological, and normative investigations) and experimental field studies can be performed so that the data and empirical terms in each are continuous, interchangeable and mutually interrelatable.

Barker and Wright (1955) state that one of the aims of their ecological investigations is to produce data that may be used by all investigators in child behavior and development. Their study of "Midwest" and its children (1955) is in part devoted to the development of a method which provides raw material (which they compared to objects stored in a museum) amenable to analyses from different theoretical points of view. There are two considerations which make this doubtful. First, their data consist of "running accounts of what a person is doing and his situation on the level of direct perception or immediate inference" with "minor interpretations in the form of statement *about* rather than descripions *of* behavior or situations" (Wright, 1967). It would seem that the material they collect would be serviceable only to those who accept nonobservables in the raw data defined according to their prescription. Investigators who prefer to define their hypothetical variables some other way or who wish to exclude nonobservables will find it difficult to intergrate their data with those in the Barker and Wright studies. Second, final data in the form of running narrations cannot readily be transformed into units describing interactions between behavioral and environmental events, such as duration, intensity, latency or frequency. Any attempt to convert such verbal accounts into one or more of the interactional dimensions would require so many arbitrary decisions that it would be doubtful whether another investigator could even come close to producing the same operations and results.

If, however, frequency-of-occurrence measures of environmental and behavioral events were used in both descriptive and field experimental studies, data and empirical concepts could be made congruous. The measure of frequency is preferable to that of duration, intensity and latency for several reasons (Skinner, 1953). First, this measure readily shows changes over short and long periods of observations. Second, it specifies the amount of behavior displayed (Honig, 1966). Finally, and perhaps most important, it is applicable to operant behaviors across species. Hence, a methodology based on frequency of event would be serviceable for both experimental and descriptive studies of both human and infrahuman subjects. This versatility has been illustrated by Jensen and Bobbitt in a study on mother and infant relationships of the pigtailed macaques (Jensen and Bobbitt, 1967).

With the use of frequency measures, the work of the ecological psychologist and the experimental psychologist would both complement and supplement each other. Descriptive studies would reveal interesting relationships among the raw data that could provide provocative cues for experimental investigations. On the other hand, field experimental studies would probably yield worthwhile leads for descriptive investigations by pointing to the need for observing new combinations of behavioral classes in specified situations. Ecological psychologists would show in terms of frequency of events, the practices of a culture, subculture, or an institutional activity of a subculture; experimental investigators working with the same set of data terms and empirical concepts would attempt to demonstrate the conditions and processes which establish and maintain the interrelationships observed.

Before considering the procedures for conducting a descriptive study using frequency measures, it might be well to make explicit three basic assumptions. The first: for psychology as a natural science, the primary data are the observable interactions between a biological organism and environmental events, past and present. These interrelationships constitute the material to be recorded. This means that the method does not include accounts of behavior isolated from related stimulus events ("Jimmy is a rejected child." "Johnny is a highly autistic child." "First Henry moved about by making swimming movements, later he crawled, now he can walk with support.") Furthermore, it means that it excludes statements of generalizations about behavior and environmental interactions. ("This is an extremely aggressive child who is always getting into trouble.") Finally, it means that it excludes accounts of interactions between behavioral and environmental events intertwined with hypothetical constructs. ("The preschool child makes errors in describing the water line in a jar because of his undeveloped cognitive structure.")

The second assumption: concepts and laws in psychology are derived from raw data. Theoretical concepts evolve from empirical concepts and empirical concepts from raw data; theoretical interactional laws are derived from empirical laws and empirical laws from relationships in the raw data.

The third assumption: descriptive studies provide information only on events and their occurrence. They do not provide information on the functional properties of the events or the functional relationships among the events. Experimental studies provide that kind of information.

We move on to consider the procedures involved in conducting a descriptive field investigation. They include (a) specifications of the situation in which a study is conducted, (b) definitions of behavioral and environmental events in observable terms, (c) measurements of observer reliability and (d) procedures for collecting, analyzing and interpreting the data. We terminate the paper with a brief illustration of a study for the behavior of a four-year-old boy in a laboratory nursery school.

SPECIFYING THE SITUATION IN WHICH A STUDY IS CONDUCTED

We define the situation in which a study is conducted in terms of its physical and social setting and the observable events that occur within its bounds. The physical setting may be a part of the child's home, a hospital or residential institution, a store or a playground in the city park. It may be a nursery school, a classroom in an elementary school or a room in a child guidance clinic.

The specific part of the home selected as a setting may consist of the living room and kitchen if the design of the home precludes flexible observation (Hawkins *et al.*, 1966). In a hospital it might be the child's bedroom, the dining room, or the day room (Wolf *et al.*, 1964). In a state school for the retarded, it may be a special academic classroom (Birnbrauer *et al.*, 1965); in a regular elementary school, a classroom (Becker *et al.*, 1967); and in a nursery school, the schoolroom and the play yard (Harris *et al.*, 1964).

During the course of a study, changes in the physical aspect of the situation may occur despite efforts to keep them constant. Some will be sufficiently drastic to prevent further study until restoration of the original conditions (e.g. power failure for several days). Others will be within normal limits (e.g. replacement of old chairs in the child's bedroom) and hence will not warrant disrupting the research.

The social aspect of the situation in a home might consist of the mother and the subject's younger sibling (Hawkins *et al.*, 1966); in a child guidance clinic, the therapist and the other children in the therapy group. In a nursery school it might include the head teacher, the assistant teacher and the children (Johnston *et al.*, 1966).

Sometimes the social situation changes according to routines and the investigator wishes to take records in the different situations created by the changes. For example, he may wish to describe the behavior of a preschool child as he engages in each of four activities in the morning hours of the nursery school: show and tell, music and games, snack and preacademic exercises. Each would be described as a field situation and data would be taken in each as if it were a separate situation. The events recorded could be the same for all the activities (*e.g.*, frequency of social contacts), or they could be specific to each depending upon the nature of the activity. They could also be a combination of both (*e.g.*, frequency of social contacts and sum of total of prolonged productive activity in each pre-academic exercise).

Major variations in social composition in a home study that would be considered disruptive could include the presence of other members of the family, relatives or friends. In a nursery school, it might be the absence of the head teacher, presence of the child's mother or the absence of many of the children. These and other events like them would probably call a halt to data collection until the standard situation is returned.

Temporary social disruptions may take many forms. For example, in the home the phone may ring, a salesman may appear, a neighbor may visit; and in the nursery school it might be a holiday preparation or a birthday party for a member of the group.

In summary, the physical and social conditions in which an ecological study is conducted is specified at the outset. Whether the variations occurring during the study are sufficient to disrupt data collection depends, in large measure, on the interactions to be studied, practical considerations, and the investigator's experience in similar situations in the past. However, accounts of changes in physical and social conditions, whether major or minor, are described and noted on the data sheets.

Defining Behavioral and Stimulus
Events in Observable Terms

In this method, we derive definitions of behavioral and stimulus events from preliminary investigations in the actual setting. Such pilot investigations are also used to provide preliminary information on the frequencies of occurrences of the event of interest and the feasibility of the situation for study.

A miniature episode in the life of a preschool boy, Timmy, will serve as an example. We start with having the observer make a running description of Timmy's behavior in the play yard in the style she would use if she were a reporter for a magazine.

> Timmy is playing by himself in a sandbox in a play yard in which other children are playing. A teacher stands nearby. Timmy tires of the sandbox and walks over to climb the monkeybars. Timmy shouts at the teacher, saying, "Mrs. Simpson, watch me." Timmy climbs to the top of the apparatus and shouts again to the teacher, "Look how high I am. I'm higher than anybody." The teacher comments on Timmy's climbing ability with approval. Timmy then climbs down and runs over to a tree, again demanding that the teacher watch him. The teacher, however, ignores Timmy and walks back into the classroom. Disappointed, Timmy walks towards the sandbox instead of climbing the tree. A little girl nearby cries out in pain as she stumbles and scrapes her knee. Timmy ignores her and continues to walk to the sandbox.

To obtain a clearer impression of the time relationships among antecedent stimulus events, responses and consequent stimulus events, the objective aspects of the narrative account are transcribed in to a three-column form and each behavioral and stimulus event is numbered in consecutive order.

Setting: Timmy (T.) is playing alone in a sandbox in a play yard in which there are other children playing. T. is scooping sand into a bucket with a shovel, then dumping the sand onto a pile. A teacher, Mrs. Simpson (S.), stands approximately six feet away but does not attend to T.

Time	Antecedent Events	Response	Consequent Social event
9:14		1. T. throws bucket and shovel into corner of sandbox.	

2. T. stands up.

3. T. walks over to monkeybars and stops.

4. T. turns toward teacher.

5. T. says, "Mrs. Simpson, watch me."

6. Mrs. S. turns toward Timmy.

6. Mrs. S. turns toward Timmy

7. T. climbs to top of apparatus.

8. T. looks toward teacher.

9. T. says, "Look how high I am. I'm higher than anybody."

9:16

10. Mrs. S. says, "That's good, Tim. You're getting quite good at that."

10. Mrs. S. Says, That's good, Tim. You're getting quite good at that."

11. T. climbs down

12. T. runs over to tree.

13. T. says, "Watch me climb the tree, Mrs. Simpson."

14. Mrs. S. turns and walks toward classroom.

14. Mrs. S. turns and walks toward classroom.

15. T. stands, looking toward Mrs. S.

9:18   16. Girl nearby trips and falls, bumping knee.

17. Girls cries.

18. T. proceeds to sandbox.

19. T. picks up bucket and shovel.

20. T. resumes play with sand.

Note that a response event (e.g. 5. T. says, "Mrs. Simpson, watch me.") may be followed by a consequent social event (e.g. 6. Mrs. S. turns toward Timmy.) which may also be the antecedent event for the next response (e.g. 7. T. climbs to top of apparatus.) Note, too, that the three-column form retains the temporal relationships in the narration. Note, finally, that only the child's responses are described. Inferences about feelings, motives and other presumed internal states are omitted. Even words like "ignores" and "disappointed" do not appear in the table.

On the basis of several such running accounts and analyses, a tentative set of stimulus and response definitives are derived and criteria for their occurrence are specified. This material serves as a basis for a provisional code consisting of symbols and definitions. Observers are trained to use the code and are tested in a series of trial runs in the actual situation.

Consider now the problems involved in defining behavioral and stimulus terms, devising codes and recording events. But first let us comment briefly on the pros and cons of two recording methods.

When discussing the definitions of events and assessing reliability of observers, we refer to observers who record with paper and pencil. In each instance, the same could be accomplished by electromechanical devices. The investigator must decide which procedure best suits his purpose. For example, Lovaas used instruments to record responses in studies on autistic behavior. He and his co-workers have developed apparatus and worked out procedures for recording as many as 12 responses in a setting. The following is a brief description of the apparatus and its operation (Lovaas, Freitag, Gold and Kassorla, 1965b).

> The apparatus for quantifying behaviors involved two units: an Esterline-Angus 20-pen recorder and an operating panel with 12 buttons, each button mounted on a switch (Microswitch: "Typewriter pushbutton switch"). When depressed, these buttons activated a corresponding pen on the Esterline recorder. The buttons were arranged on a 7 by 14-in. panel in the configuration of the fingertips of an outstretched hand. Each button could be pressed independently of any of the others and with the amount of force similar to that required for an electric typewriter key (p. 109).

An electromechanical recording device has certain advantages over a paper-and-pencil system. It requires less attention, thus allowing the observer to devote more of his effort to watching for critical events. Furthermore, instruments of this sort make it possible to assess more carefully the temporal relationships between stimulus and response events, as well as to record a large number of responses within a given period. On the other hand, paper-and-pencil recording methods are more flexible. They can be used in any setting, since they do not require special facilities, such as a power supply.

DEFINING AND RECORDING BEHAVIORAL EVENTS

The main problem in defining behavioral events is establishing a criterion or criteria in a way that two or more observers can agree on their occurrences. For example, if it is desired to record the number of times a child hits other children, the criteria of a hitting response must be clearly given so that the observer can discriminate hitting from patting or shoving responses. Or if it is desired to count the number of times a child says, "No," the criteria for the occurrence of "No" must be specified to discriminate it from other words the child utters, and from nonverbal forms of negative expressions. Sometimes definitions must include criteria of loudness and duration. For example in a study of crying behavior (Hart *et al.*, 1964), crying was defined to discriminate it from whining and screaming and it had to be (a) "loud enough to be heard at least 50 feet away and (b) of 5-seconds or more duration."

The definitions of complex behavioral events are treated the same way. Studies concerned with such intricate categories of behavior as isolate behavior, fantasy-play, aggressive behavior and temper-tantrums must establish objective criteria for each class of responses included in the category. We shall elaborate on defining multiple-response classes in the following discussion on recording behavioral events.

There are two styles of recording behavioral events in field situations: One consists of logging the incidences of responses (and in many situations, their durations); the other of registering the frequencies of occurrences and nonoccurrences within a time interval. Sometimes frequencies and their durations are recorded (Lovaas, Freitag, Gold and Kassorla, 1965b).

Recording the frequencies of occurrences and nonoccurrences in a time interval requires the observer to make a mark (and only one mark) in each time interval in which the response occurred. It is apparent that in this procedure, the maximum frequency of a response is determined by the size of the time unit selected. If a 5 second interval were used, the maximum frequency would be 12 per min.; if a 10-second interval were employed, the maximal rate would be 6 per minute, and so on. Thus, in studies with a high frequency of behavioral episodes, small time intervals are employed to obtain high correspondence between the actual and recorded frequencies of occurrences.

There are several approaches to defining and recording single and multiple class responses. One method consists of developing a specific observational code for each problem studied. For example, in studies conducted at the Child Behavior Laboratory at the University of Illinois, codes were prepared for attending-to-work behavior, spontaneous speech and tantruming. The attending-to-work or time-on-task code was employed with a distractible seven-year-old boy. It included: (a) counting words, (b) looking at the words and (c) writing numbers or letters. When any of these behaviors occurred at any time during a 20-second interval, it was scored as an interval of work. In a second study involving a six-year-old boy with a similar problem, this code was used with one additional feature: in order for the observer to mark occurrence in the 20-second interval, the child had to engage in relevant behavior for a minimum of 10 seconds. The reliability on both codes averaged 90 percent for two observers over 12 sessions. (See Section 3 for our method of determining reliability).

A code for spontaneous speech was developed for a four-year-old girl who rarely spoke. Incidences of speech were recorded whenever she uttered a word or words which were not preceded by a question or a prompt by a peer or teacher. Although this class of behavior was somewhat difficult to discriminate, reliability averaged 80 percent for two observers over 15 sessions.

Tantrum behaviors exhibited by a six-year-old boy were defined as including crying, whining, sobbing and whimpering. The average reliability for this class of behavior was 80 percent for two observers over 11 sessions.

In contrast to this more or less vocal form of tantrum behavior, a code developed in another study on temper-tantrums centered around gross motor responses of an autistic child (Brawley *et al.*, 1968). Here a tantrum was recorded whenever the child engaged in selfhitting in combination with any one of the following forms of behavior: (a) loud crying (b) kicking or (c) throwing himself or objects about.

Another method of defining and recording responses is to develop a general observational code, one that is inclusive enough to study many behaviors in a given field situation. An example of such a code is the one prepared by the nursery school staff at the University of Washington. In essence, verbal and motor responses are recorded in relation to physical and social events using a three- or four-track system. Tables 3-1 and 3-2 show

1	2	3	4	5	6	7	8	9	10	11	12	13	14	15	16	17	18	19	20	21	22	23	24
															V	V	V				V		
	P	P	P				P		P	P	P				P	T	T	P		P			P
					E	E			E	E	E				E	C	C						

TABLE 3-1
SAMPLE LINE FROM A DATA SHEET OF NURSERY SCHOOL
GIRL WHO CHANGED ACTIVITIES WITH HIGH FREQUENCY

1	2	3	4	5	6	7	8	9	10	11	12	13	14	15	16	17	18	19	20	21	22	23	24	25	26	27	28	29	30
V					V						(V)				V	V	V	V	V	(V)	(V)							V	
P	P				P	P	P	P							P	P	(T)	(T)	P		P	P	P	P	P	P	T	P	
C	C		C	C	C	C	C	C	C	C	A	A	A	A	A	A	A	A	A	A	A			A	A	C	C		
					B	B	B	B	B	B	B					B	B	B	B	B	B	B	B	B	B	B	B	B	

TABLE 3-2
SAMPLE LINE FROM A DATA SHEET OF NURSERY SCHOOL
BOY DISPLAYING AGGRESSIVE BEHAVIORS

sample lines from data sheets. Each box represents an interval of 15 seconds.

In Table 3-1, which is a segment of a data sheet for a nursery school girl who changed activities with high frequency, entries were made in the boxes in the top row to indicate occurrences of vocalization (V). Entries were made in the middle row to show proximity (P) or physical contact (T) with another person, and in the bottom row to indicate contact with physical objects (E) or with children and whether the interaction was parallel play (A) or shared play (C). Other marks and symbols are added in accordance with the problem studied. For example, each single bracket in Table 3-1 indicates leaving of one activity and embarking on another. During the 6-minute period in which records were taken (twenty-four 15-second intervals), the child changed her activity 12 times. During that time, the teacher gave approval five times contingent upon her verbal or proximity behavior as indicated by X's above the top line (10, 11, 16, 17 and 18). A tally of the data indicated that she spent most of the 6-minute period alone or in close proximity to another child, sometimes on the same piece of play equipment. During three intervals (16, 17 and 18) she talked (V), touched (T) and engaged in physical interaction with another child (C). Even though rate of activity change, and not peer interaction, was the subject of the study, the other data on social behavior provided interesting information: decline in rate of activity change was related to an increase in rate of appropriate peer behavior.

This code can be readily modified to handle more complex interactions. For example, it was used to record the behavior of a nursery school boy who shouted epithets, kicked and hit other children. Ordinarily these aggressive acts would appear in the record sheets undifferentiated from a nonaggressive interaction. To differentiate them from other behaviors the symbol letter was circled if the behavior met the criteria of an aggressive act. As shown in Table 3-2, intervals 13, 22 and 23 contain a "V" with a circle, Ⓥ, which indicates aggressive verbalizations while intervals 19 and 20 contain a "T" with a circle, T, which indicates physical "attack" (actual hitting, kicking, or pinching). Another bit of information was incorporated in the recording system. The letter "B" was entered in the fourth row to indicate that the child was playing with or being aggressive to a specific nursery school boy named Bill. This additional notation was made midway in the study when teachers observed that the subject and Bill usually behaved aggressively toward each other. Data collected before this change served as a baseline against which to judge the effects of changing social contingencies. Subsequently, teachers gave approval contingent on nonaggressive interactions between these boys as shown by the X's above intervals 6, 7, 8, 11, 12, 17, 18, 26, 27 and 29.

Another general observational code, tailored for analysis of pupils' behavior in the elementary school classroom has been devised by Thomas and Becker (1967). Like the nursery school code, it consists of symbols and definitions designed to cover the range of interactions that may take place in the field situation defined by the classroom.

DEFINING AND RECORDING STIMULUS EVENTS

The ease or difficulty of defining a stimulus class is related to its source. It has been pointed out (e.g. Bijou and Baer, 1961) that some stimuli originate in natural and man-made things, some in the biological make-up of the subject himself and some in the behavior of people and other living organisms. Consider briefly each source in turn.

Defining stimuli from physical things does not pose a difficult problem, since physical objects are usually available for all to see. All that is required is that these stimuli be described in the usual physical dimensions of space, time, size, velocity, color, texture and the like.

Defining stimuli which originate in the biological make-up of the subject is beset with difficulty, mostly because of their obscurity under any circumstance and particularly under field conditions. Consider what must be available to an observer if he is to record in objective terms the duration, intensity or frequency of stimuli involved in a toothache, "butterflies" in the stomach, general bodily weakness, dizziness and hunger-pangs. Instruments would be needed to make visible all sorts of internal biological events, and for the most part, these are not yet available in practical forms. It seems clear that at present, field methods of research, especially with human beings, are not appropriate for describing biologically anchored variables. Research on these variables must be postponed until it is practical to monitor physiological actions through cleverly designed telemetric devices. But it should be stressed that the exact role of specific biological variables *must* be studied at some time for a thorough functional analysis of psychological behavior (defined here as the interaction of a total functioning biological individual with environmental events).

Defining social stimuli, or stimuli which evolve from the action of people, ranges in difficulty between physical and biological events. This is so because social events, like physical and biological events, must in many instances be described in terms of their physical dimensions, and as is well known, the components of social stimuli can be terribly subtle and complex. For the reader interested in a further analysis of social event within the framework of a natural science, Skinner's discussion is recommended (1953, pp. 298–304).

In field studies, the procedure for defining and recording social stimuli is the same as that for defining and recording response events, since social events are treated as the responses of people in antecedent or consequent relationships to the behavior of the subject. Therefore, the entire previous section on defining and recording behavioral events pertains to defining and recording social events.

Some social stimuli, like response stimuli, may consist of a single class of behavior on the part of an adult or a child and may be recorded on the basis of frequency or its occurrence or non-occurrence within a time interval. Examples of single-class antecedent stimuli are simple commands and requests, e.g. "Start now," "Gather around in a circle," "Come, let's ride the trikes." Examples of single-class consequent stimuli are confirmations ("Right"), disconfirmations ("Wrong"), approval ("Good") and disapproval ("You play too rough.")

Other social stimuli may be composed of several classes of behavior stemming from one person or several in concert. As in the case of defining multiple response classes, criteria for each subclass in the group may constitute a code. A specific observational code may be developed to describe social events in a specific situation for a specific study. For example, in a study of autistic behavior, adult attention was defined as: "(a) Touching the child; (b) being within two feet of and facing the child; (c) talking to, touching, assisting or going to the child" (Brawley *et al.*, 1968). With such criteria, the investigator catalogued the types of behaviors which constituted social interaction involving attention and excluded other stimuli originating in the behavior of an adult in contact with the subject.

General observational codes for social events, like those for response events, have also been devised to study many problems in a general type of field setting. For example, Becker and Thomas (1967) have developed a comprehensive code for recording the teacher's behavior in an elementary classroom situation.

Which classes of behavior-environmental interactions will be selected for study will depend on the purpose of the investigation; the maximum number, however, will be limited by the practical considerations. Studies requiring detailed analyses of many response classes may be planned as a series, with the first dealing with grossly defined classes and others with more and more progressively refined categories. For example, the first study may be concerned with the frequency of social contacts with adults and peers and the second with specific verbal and motor responses directed to specific adults (teachers and parents) and peer (boys and girls).

ASSESSING OBSERVER RELIABILITY

Disagreements between observers may be related to inadequacies in (a) the observational code, (b) the training of the observers or (c) the method of calculating reliability.

The Observational Code

Problems of defining and recording behavioral and stimulus events have been discussed previously. Observer reliability is directly related to the comprehensiveness and specificity of the definitions in the observational code. Generally it is advisable to devise codes with mutually exclusive event categories, with each definition having criteria that do not occur in any other definition.

Training of Observers

Even when a code is completely serviceable, two observers may not necessarily record the occurrence of the same event at the same time unless each has been adequately trained in using the code and in controlling his behavior while observing and recording.

For example, training might begin by familiarizing the observer with the tools for recording, e.g. the clipboard, stopwatch and data sheets. This might be followed by an orientation to the code and exercises in recording behavioral events. A film or videotape of sequences similar to those in the actual situation might be used to provide supplementary experiences.

It is often helpful to have a second observer to record along with the first observer. During trial recordings, the observers can indicate to each other the behaviors being scored and uncover misunderstandings regarding the nature of the code or ambiguities in the definition of particular responses. Such a procedure reduces interpretation on the part of the observer and can contribute to an improved code.

Since it is relatively easy for the observers to slip an interval in the course of a long recording session, they should be instructed to note the beginning of certain activities, e.g. storytime, snack, nap, etc. This allows them to determine easily when they are out of phase with one another. Slips may also result from inaccurate stopwatches. Watches should be periodically tested by starting them simultaneously and checking them a few hours later.

After being trained on the proficient use of the code, the observer might then be given instruction on how to conduct himself while observing and recording. Thus, he might be told how to refrain from interacting with the subject, e.g. ignore all questions, avoid eye-contact and suppress reactions to the subject's activities as well as those associated with him. He might also be instructed in moving about to maintain a clear view of the subject, yet not make it obvious that he is following him.

Method of Calculating Reliability

The reliability index is to some degree a function of how it is calculated. Suppose we have data from two observers showing the frequency of a class of events taken over 1 hour. Unless the sums obtained by each observer are equal, the smaller sum is divided by the larger to obtain a percentage of agreement. If the sums are identical, the reliability index would be 100. This method is often used when the investigator is interested in frequencies per se, since the measure obtained gives only the amount of agreement over the total number of events observed. It does not indicate whether the two observers were recording the same event at exactly the same time. Thus, it might be possible that one observer was recording few behaviors during the first half hour and many during the second, while the second observer was doing just the opposite. To ascertain whether this is the case, one could divide the period of observation into small segments and calculate the reliability of each. Agreements over progressively smaller segments give confidence that the observers are scoring the same event at the same time. One may asses the agreement over brief intervals such as 5 or 10 seconds. Reliability is calculated by scoring each interval as agree or disagree (match or mismatch) and dividing the total number of agreements by the number of agreements plus the number of disagreements. Note that one may score several agreements or disagreements in an interval if a number of events are being recorded simultaneously, as shown in Tables 3-1 and 3-2. In this case, the interval is broken down according to the number of different events recorded, with each event scored as a match or mismatch.

The reliability index may also be influenced by the frequency of response under study. When a behavior is displayed at a very low rate, the observer will record few instances of occurrence and many of nonoccurrence. In this situation, the observers could disagree on the occurrence of the behavior yet still show high reliability due to their agreement on the large number of intervals where no behavior was recorded. A similar problem exists with regard to high-frequency behaviors. Here, however, the observers may disagree on the nonoccurrence of the behavior and agree on occurrence, because of the frequency of the latter. The problem may be resolved by computing not one but two reliability coefficients, one for occurrence and one for nonoccurrence.

In some cases, the requirement of perfect matching of intervals may be relaxed slightly. Thus, behaviors recorded within one interval (especially if the interval is short) may also be considered as instances of agreement for reliability purposes. A technique of noncontinuous observing may also increase reliability (O'Leary *et al.*, 1967). In this procedure, the observers record for shorter portions of time. For example, instead of taking continuous 10-second observations, the observer might record for 10 out of every 15 seconds or for 20 out of every 30 seconds. During the period in which the observer is not attending to the child, he should be recording the behaviors just observed.

The use of a second observer does not insure high reliability of recording; it is possible for both observers to agree on the scoring of certain events and at the same time be incorrect (Gewirtz and Gewirtz, 1964). Both observers might record some events which should not be noted and ignore others which should. Hence, a third observer might be used on occasion to determine if this possibility exists.

COLLECTING, ANALYZING, AND INTERPRETING DATA
Data Collection

Final data collection is begun as soon as it is evident that the observers are adequately trained, the field situation is feasible and the subject has adapted to the presence of the observers.

Whether the investigator collects data during all of the time available for observation or takes time samples will depend upon many factors, including the purpose of the study, the nature of the data and the practical considerations. Regardless of the frequency with which observations are made, it is recommended that the data be plotted at regular intervals to provide a kind of progress chart. A visual account of the fluctuations and trends can help the investigator make important decisions *e.g.* setting up the time for the next reliability evaluation or establishing the termination time for a phase of the study.

Data Analysis

Up until now, we discussed the investigators' activities in relation to the interactions between the observer and the field events.

The investigator was viewed as a critic, watching the observer record the events in a natural ecology. Thus, in the data collection phase of a study, the investigator's role is somewhat similar to that of a motion picture director evaluating what the camera is recording in relation to the scene as he sees it. In this section on data analysis and in the next on interpretation, we shall consider what the investigator does, not in relation to the recording equipment and field events, but in relation to the data collected.

Basically, in data analysis, the investigator looks at the data collected to "see what is there." Usually he finds that making one or several transformations in the raw data helps him to see more clearly the relationships among the events observed. Transformational procedures might consist of converting the frequency counts into graphic, tabular, verbal, arithmetical or statistical forms. Exactly which operations he performs on the data will depend on the purpose of the study, the nature of the data, and his theoretical assumptions about what can or cannot be demonstrated by a descriptive field study.

Usually data analysis begins when data collection ends. However, as noted previously, an investigator might graph the data while the study is in progress. Under these circumstances, data analysis might consist of revising and refining the graphs and making other transpositions to show the relationships among the subparts of the data.

Data collected in terms of rate are usually plotted in a graphic form with responses on the vertical axis and time on the horizontal axis. Points on the chart may represent either discrete or cumulative values. Discrete values are the sums or means for each successive session; cumulative values are the sums or means for all previous sessions. Therefore, curves with discrete values might go up, stay at the same level or go down; cumulative curves might also go up or stay at the same level. Cumulative curves do not go down. A decrease in the frequency of a response is shown in the curve as a deceleration in rate (bends toward the horizontal axis); an increase in frequency as an acceleration (bends toward the vertical axis); a constant frequency as no change in rate; and a zero frequency as a horizontal line.

In most instances, graphic presentations are made more mean-ingful when accompanied by percentage values. In addition, it is often advantageous to show percentages of occurrences in the different conditions and subconditions of the field situation.

Viewing the interactions in selected time periods (early morn-ing, and late morning) or around certain events (before and after mealtime) as populations, statistical analyses may be made to assess the nature of and the reliability of differences observed.

Interpretation of Findings

Essentially, interpretation of findings consists of the investiga-tor's statements on what is "seen" in the data together with his conception of their generality. Such statements are the *raison-d'être* of an investigation.

Obviously, an investigator is free to interpret his findings in any way he chooses. The investigator who accepts the assump-tions of a natural science approach to psychology seeks to limit his interpretations to empirical concepts and relationships consis-tent with his observations and the analytical operations made upon the products of his observations. Hence, in a descriptive field study, his interpretations would usually consist of a discus-sion of what was found in the situation with comparisons to other findings obtained under functionally similar conditions. Conclu-sions on the similarities and differences between his findings and others would be incorporated in his argument for the generality of his findings. Interpretations in an experimental field study would depend on the number and type of manipulations employed and would usually be limited to describing the functional relation-ships obtained.

ILLUSTRATIVE STUDY

Using the procedures previously described, a study was under-taken to obtain a descriptive account of a boy in a laboratory nursery school at the University of Illinois. The nursery school curriculum and the practices of the teaching staff of this school were based on behavioral principles (Skinner, 1953; Bijou and Baer, 1961).

Subject and Field Situation

The subject (Zachary) was typical of the children in the nursery school in the judgment of the teachers. He was 4.5-years-old, of high average intelligence (Peabody IQ, 116) and from a middle socioeconomic-class family. On the Wide Range Achievement Test, he scored kindergarten 3 in reading, pre-kindergarten 5 in spelling, and kindergarten 6 in arithmetic.

The nursery school consisted of a large room, approximately 21 by 40 feet. Evenly spaced along one wall were three doors which led to three adjacent smaller rooms. One of these rooms was a lavatory; the second contained paints, papers and other equipment; and the third a variety of toys. Nearby was a large table and several chairs used for art activities and snack. Opposite these rooms, along the other wall, were several tables separated by brightly colored, movable partitions. In these booths, the children worked on academic subjects.

The school was attended by 12 children, six boys and six girls, between four and five years of age. The teaching staff consisted of a full-time teacher, an assistant teacher and, depending on the time of day, one to three undergraduates who assisted in administering new programs in reading, writing and arithmetic.

In general, the morning program was as follows:

9:00–10:00	Art, academic, and preacademic work.
10:00–10:30	Free play.
10:30–11:00	Snack.
11:00–12:00	Academic work, show-and-tell, and storytime.

A typical morning might begin with art. At this time, eight to ten children sat around a large table, working with various materials. During this activity, each child in turn left the group for 10 to 20 minutes to work on writing or arithmetic. While engaged in writing or arithmetic, the child worked with a teacher in one of the booths. After completing his assigned units of work, he returned to his art activity and another child left the group to work on his units of writing or arithmetic. After all the children had participated in these academic subjects, the art period was terminated and was followed by play. During play, the children were free to move about, often spending much of the time in either of the smaller nursery school rooms playing with blocks or other

toys. After approximately 30 minutes of play, the youngsters returned to the large table for a snack of juice and cookies. While
eating and drinking, they talked spontaneously and informally
with their teachers and peers. Following snack time, some of the
children participated in reading, while the others gathered for
show-and-tell or storytime. During storytime, the children sat on
the floor in a group while the teacher read and discussed the story.
In show-and-tell, instead of the teacher leading the group, each
child had a chance to stand by the teacher in front of the group
and show an object he had brought from home and tell about it.
As they did during the art period, the children left the group one
at a time for a period of reading. Because of variations in the
amount of time a child spent on academic subjects, a child did not
engage in all of these activities every day.

Behavioral and Stimulus Events Recorded

The behaviors recorded were of two general categories: social
contacts and sustained activities. Social contacts included verbal
interchanges and physical contacts with children and teachers.
Sustained activities involved behaviors in relation to the school
tasks. The specific observational code developed for the study is
presented in Table 3-3.

Observation began 3.5 weeks after the start of the school year
and covered a three-hour period in the morning. The observations
were taken on 28 school days. The observer sat a few feet from
the subject and discretely followed him as he moved from one
activity to another in the nursery school room. Every 10 seconds,
the teacher recorded the occurrence or nonoccurrence of events
defined in the code. The data sheet was similar to that shown in
Table 3-1; however, only the first and second rows were used.

Observed Reliability

The reliability of observation and the adequacy of the behavioral code was evaluated several times throughout the study
by having a second observer record stimulus and response events.
Reliability was calculated by scoring each interval as a match or
mismatch and dividing the total number of agreements by the

TABLE 3-3

OBSERVATIONAL CODE FOR DESCRIBING THE BEHAVIOR OF A BOY
IN A LABORATORY NURSERY SCHOOL

Symbol	Definition
	First Row (Social Contacts) *S* verbalizes to himself; includes any verbalization during which he does not look at an adult or child or does not use an adult's or child's name. Does not apply to a group situation.
	S verbalizes to adult. *S* must look at adult while verbalizing or use adult's name.
	S verbalizes to child. *S* must look at child while verbalizing or use child's name. If in a group situation, any verbalization is recorded as verbalization to a child.
S	Child verbalizes to *S*. Child must look at *S* while verbalizing or use *S*'s name.
△	Adult verbalizes to *S*. Adult must look at *S* while verbalizing or use *S*'s name.
∽	Adult gives general instruction to class, or asks question of class, or makes general statement. Includes storytelling.
	S touches adult (physical contact with adult).
	S touches child with part of body or object (physical contact with child).
V	Adult touches *S* (physical contact with adult).
T	Child touches *S* with part of body or object (physical contact with child).

TABLE 3-3 CONTINUED

Symbol	Definition
▫	**Second Row (Sustained Activity)** *Sustained activity in art.* S must be sitting in the chair, facing the material and responding to the material or teacher within the 10-second interval. Responding to the material includes using pencil, paint brush, chalk, crayons, string; scissors, paste or any implement on paper; or working with clay with hands on clay or hands on implement which is used with clay; or folding or tearing paper. Responding to the teacher includes following a command made by an adult to make a specific response. The behavior must be completed (child sitting in his chair again) within two minutes.
▫	*Sustained activity in storytime.* S must be sitting, facing the material or following a command given by the teacher or assistant. If the S initiates a verbalization to a peer, do not record sustained activity in the 10-second interval.
▫	*Sustained activity in show-and-tell.* S must be sitting, facing the material or following a command given by the teacher. If the S initiates a verbalization to a peer, do not record sustained activity in that 10-second interval.
▫	*Sustained activity in reading.* S must be sitting in the chair, facing the material and responding to the material or the teacher within the 10-second interval.
▫	*Sustained activity in writing.* S must be sitting in the chair, facing the material and responding to the material or the teacher within the 10-second interval. Responding to the material includes using the pencil (making a mark) or holding the paper or folder. Responding to the teacher includes responding verbally to a cue given by the teacher.
▫	*Sustained activity in arithmetic.* S must be sitting in the chair, facing the material and responding to the material or the teacher within the 10-second interval. Responding to the material or teacher includes using the pencil or eraser or holding the paper or folder or responding verbally to cue.
◺	Sustained activity did not occur in interval.

number of agreements plus disagreements. Four checks on social contacts showed agreements of 75, 82, 85 and 87 per cent. Three checks on sustained activity yielded agreements of 94, 95 and 97 per cent. Thus, average agreement on social contacts exceeded 82 per cent, while average agreement of sustained activity exceeded 95 per cent.

ANALYSIS OF DATA
Social Contacts

Data were gathered on Zachary's social behaviors in informal activities of art, play, snack, storytime and show-and-tell. They will be described, and samples of the detailed accounts in art and snack will be presented in graphic form. The youngster's most dominant behavior during the art period, shown in Figure 3-1, was talking to others (14% of the time).

Teachers and peers talked with him about equally, an average of 8 and 7 per cent respectively. Physical contacts between Zachary, teachers, and peers were low, around 1 to 2 per cent.

The child's verbal behavior to peers during the play period was higher than in the art period. He talked to his friends on an average of 38 per cent; they talked to him on an average of only 10 per cent. Verbal exchanges with teachers were low (an average of 2.5%). Zachary touched other children 7 per cent of the time on the average and they reciprocated on an average of 3 per cent. Physical contacts with teachers were relatively infrequent.

As in the art and play periods, Zachary's social interactions during snack time, shown in Figure 3-2, consisted mostly of talking to his classmates, an average of 21 per cent. They, in turn, talked to him only an average of 7 per cent. During this period, the teacher's general commands (instructions addressed to the group) were relatively high, averaging 7 per cent in contrast to the 2 per cent during art and play. Physical contacts with other children were low, as in art and play, about 3 per cent.

Compared to the art, play and snack periods, Zachary's verbalizations to peers and to teachers were low (8% and 4% respectively), and the number of times he touched children (10%) and children touched him were also relatively low (2%). Story-

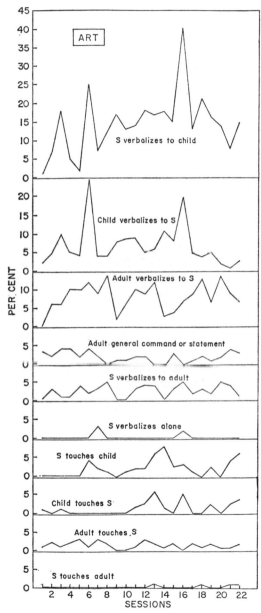

Figure 3-1. Social contact during art.

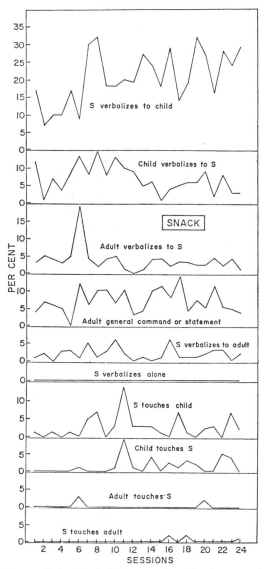

Figure 3-2. Social interaction during snack.

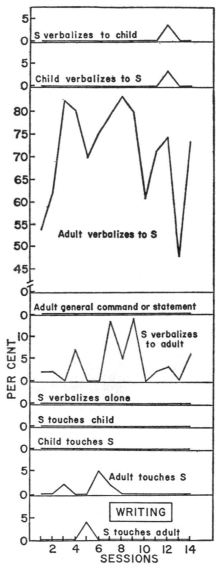

Figure 3-3. Social behavior during writing.

time had a high frequency of teacher's general commands and statements (average of 73%), since this category was scored when the teacher read and discussed the stories.

In show-and-tell, Zachary's social behavior was similar to that during storytime. He talked to other children 14 per cent of the time and touched them 9 per cent of the time. Zachary physically contacted teachers about 1 per cent of the time and they reciprocated about 3 per cent of the time.

In respect to Zachary's social behavior during the academic periods, these data clearly indicate that the teacher talked to Zachary a great deal during the reading (an average of 69%), writing (an average of 71%) and arithmetic periods (an average of 58%); and the child talked to the teacher with high frequency, particularly in reading (an average of 44%) and arithmetic (an average of 41%). In writing, he talked to the teacher only 3 per cent of the time. There were also a few instances in which the teacher touched Zachary and rare occasions in which Zachary interacted socially with other children. Figure 3-3 is a detailed graphic account of his social behavior during the writing period.

Sustained Activity

For the observer to mark the occurrence of sustained activity. Zachary had to respond in a manner appropriate for a particular school activity (see second part of Table 3-3). For example, during art, the child had to be sitting in his chair, facing the art materials and manipulating them during each 10-second interval. Similar definitions were used for other situations and periods. Given these definitions, the results show a generally high level of sustained activity in all phases of the morning program. Daily rates of sustained activities in art, storytime and show-and-tell range between 70 and 99 per cent with an average of 89 per cent for art, 95 per cent for storytime and 88 per cent for show-and-tell. See Figure 3-4 for variations from session to session in Zachary's sustained behavior during art. Sustained activity in reading, writing and arithmetic range from 90% to 100 per cent over the days observed, with an average of 97, 95, and 96 per cent respectively. See Figure 3-5 for variations in the child's sustained

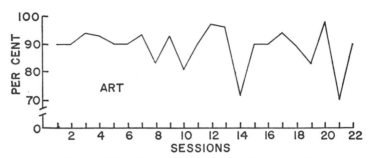

Figure 3-4. Sustained activity during art.

behavior in writing. Due to the limited availability of the observer and the fact that not every activity occurred every day, the number of observations on each activity varied.

DISCUSSION

A descriptive account of the behaviors of a boy during the morning hours in a laboratory nursery school was obtained in terms of the frequency of occurrence of objectively defined stimulus and response events. The account shows rates of changes in social interactions (verbal and physical contacts) and sustained activities during eight periods of the school morning.

In the informal activities of the nursery school, in which the youngster performed on an individaul basis, as in art, free play, and snack time, the subject talked to his peers and teachers to a moderate degree. His peers and teachers responded to him verbally to a lesser extent. He talked more than he listened and over

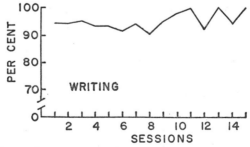

Figure 3-5. Sustained activity during writing.

the period of the study, his verbal output increased. Physical interactions with peers and teachers in these situations were at a relatively low level. Finally, the youngster's sustained activity in the art period was high (between 70 and 98%) and became more variable, on a day-to-day basis, during the second half of the study. In the other two informal activities, storytime and show-and-tell, the child participated as a member of a group in which the teacher's verbal behavior was prominent, especially during storytime. In these two situations, the child talked to others less, but as in art, free play, and snack time, he talked more than he listened. In storytime and show-and-tell, he engaged in some body contacts with peers and teachers, yet his sustained activity on nursery school tasks was high, with a range of 90% to 99 per cent for the former and 70 to 95 per cent for the latter.

In the more structured activities of reading, writing and arithmetic, the teacher's verbal behavior to the child was high and his verbal behavior to her was correspondingly high, particularly in reading and arithmetic. During academic exercises, all other social interactions were zero or near zero, and the child's sustained activities were consistently higher over days, ranging from 90 to 100 per cent of the time.

The data gathered in this study can serve two main purposes. First, they can provide normative information on behavior in a laboratory preschool. Thus, it might be interesting to compare this child's rates of response obtained in this study after 3.5 weeks of school with his rates during the last month of the school year. It might also be interesting to compare this child's behavior with another child's in the same nursery school. Such a comparison might be especially valuable if someone claimed that the second child's behavior was deviant. In addition, it might be informative to compare this child's behavior with a comparable child in a community-operated nursery school. Second, the data suggest certain relationships between the behavior of the subject, the teacher, and other children. Thus, the investigator might use the data as a baseline for an experimental study in which conditions are manipulated to test for possible functional relationships.

REFERENCES

Baldwin, A. L., Kalhorn, J. and Breese, F. H.: The appraisal of parent behavior. *Psychological Monographs, 63,* No. 299, 1949.

Barker, R. G. and Wright, H. F.: *Midwest and Its Children: the Psychological Ecology of an American Town.* New York, Harper and Row, 1955.

Becker, W. C., Madsen, C. H., Jr., Arnold, Carole R. and Thomas, D. R.: The contingent use of teacher attention and praise in reducing classroom behavior problems. *Journal of Special Education, 1:*287–307, 1967.

Becker, W. C. and Thomas, D. R.: A revision of the code for the analysis of a teacher's behavior in the classroom. Unpublished manuscript, 1967.

Bijou, S. W. and Baer, D. M.: *Child Development: A Systematic and Empirical Theory,* vol. 1. New York, Appleton-Century-Crofts, 1961.

Birnbrauer, J. S., Wolf, M. M., Kidder, J. D. and Tague, Cecilia: Classroom behavior of retarded pupils with token reinforcement. *Journal of Experimental Child Psychology, 2:*219–235, 1965.

Brawley, Eleanor R., Harris, Florence R., Allen, K. Eileen; Fleming, R. S. and Peterson, R. F. Behavior modification of an autistic child. *Behavioral Science,* 1968.

Gewirtz, Hava and Gewirtz, J. L.: A method for assessing stimulation behaviors and caretaker-child interaction. Unpublished manuscript, 1964.

Harris, Florence R., Wolf, M. M. and Baer, D. M.: Effects of adult social reinforcement on child behavior. *Young Children, 20:*8–17, 1964.

Hawkins, R. P., Peterson, R. F., Schweid, Edda and Bijou, S. W.: Behavior therapy in the home: Amelioration of problem parent-child relations with the parent in a therapeutic role. *Journal of Experimental Child Psychology, 4:*99–107, 1966.

Honig, W. K. Introductory remarks. In Honig, W. K. (Ed.): *Operant Behavior: Areas of Research and Application.* New York, Appleton-Century-Crofts, 1966.

Jensen, G. D. and Bobbitt, Ruth A.: Implications of primate research for understanding infant development. In Hellmouth, J. (Ed.): *The Exceptional Child,* vol. 1. Seattle, Special Child Publications, 1967.

Johnston, Margaret S., Kelley, C. Susan, Harris, Florence R. and Wolf, M. M.: An application of reinforcement principles to development of motor skills of a young child. *Child Development, 37:*379–387, 1966.

Lovaas, O. I., Freitag, G., Gold, Vivian J. and Kassorla, Irene C.: Experimental studies in childhood schizophrenia: analysis of self-destructive behavior. *Journal of Experimental Child Psychology,* 2:67–84, 1965a.

Lovaas, O. I., Freitag, G., Gold, Vivian J. and Kassorla, Irene C.: Recording apparatus and procedure for observation of behaviors of children in free play settings. *Journal of Experimental Child Psychology,* 2:108–120, 1965b.

O'Leary, K. D., O'Leary, Susan G. and Becker, W. C.: Modification of a deviant sibling interaction pattern in the home. *Behaviour Research and Therapy,* 5:113–120, 1967.

Skinner, B. F.: *Science and Human Behavior.* New York, Macmillan, 1953.

Wolf, M. M., Risley, T. R. and Mees, H. L.: Application of operant conditioning procedures to the behavior problems of an autistic child. *Behaviour Research and Therapy,* 1:305–312, 1964.

Wright, H. F.: *Recording and Analyzing Child Behavior.* New York, Harper and Row, 1967.

4

The Dimensions of Classroom Data

THOMAS C. LOVITT, HAROLD P. KUNZELMANN,
PATRICIA A. NOLEN and WILLIAM J. HULTEN

Behavioral modification techniques have become quite widely utilized. Numerous instances exist where teachers, therapists and others in the field of rehabilitation have effectively used operant techniques to alter behavior. However, the majority of reports from classroom settings describe how these techniques have been used to attenuate a variety of socially inappropriate behaviors. Few investigations have attempted to accelerate academic responses. Indeed, while many teachers see the use of behavioral management practices as effective with deceleration targets, they do not see it as effective with acceleration targets.

The intent of this chapter is to describe how behavioral modification techniques may be employed to increase academic performance through a three-phase procedure of data diagnosis, data programming and data decisions. Initially described is a method of obtaining pupil performance data and information concerning relevant variables of the teacher-pupil dyad. A second method is presented whereby pupil and teacher data may empirically enable the teacher to evaluate curricular materials. Lastly, a discussion is provided pertaining to the use of data in making classroom managerial decisions.

NOTE: This paper was presented as a symposium at the Association for Children with Learning Disabilities Annual Convention in Boston, Massachusetts, February, 1968.

From the *Journal of Learning Disabilities, 1*:20–31, 1968. Copyright 1968 by the Professional Press Inc. Reprinted with permission of authors and publisher.

MANY CHILDREN FAIL to attain academic skills at rates which permit them to remain in the mainstream of education. Often these children are labeled "learning disabled," implying that failure is inherent in the child rather than in the teaching situation. Whether a given failure stems from a learning disability or a teaching disability is a question for which final answers are not readily available. However, guidelines toward solving this problem can be found in the rates of a child's academic performance and in an investigation and rearrangement of possible controlling variables. Such an investigation of these possible controlling classroom variables through analysis of changes in children's rates of performance constitutes educational diagnosis through data.

Traditionally, many classroom teachers have analyzed pupils' performances by percentage. While a percentage score reveals how many correct answers a child has completed in relation to the total number attempted, it reveals little about how long the child has taken to do the work. One child may have taken two days to do 25 problems, and another, five minutes. How long the child requires to do his academic work must be incorporated into the teacher's strategy. Responses divided by the time factor can be termed simply "rate."

Rate evaluations of pupil performance first require a specification of the performance to be assessed. In written work, for example, each word is counted as one response and the total is reported in relation to time, usually in the form of responses per minute. However, while these statements of academic performance rates as problems completed per minute or words written per minute provide a more detailed analysis of pupil performance than gross percentage statements, they do not take into account the variance in the number of letters in words or digits in a mathematics problem.

In past research at the Experimental Education Unit of the Mental Retardation and Child Development Center at the University of Washington, one answer to a mathematics problem was counted as one response and the child's rate of completing the problems as the dependent measure, regardless of the movements required to arrive at the answer. For example, the written solution "4" to the stimulus "2 + 2" was counted as one response, just as was the written answer "749" to the stimulus "312 + 437." However, as a child moved to higher-level mathematics, there were continuously more steps and more time involved in completing answers to problems. Questions then asked were, Do these additional steps, inherent in a curriculum of sequential complexity, affect the child's response rate? And if a rate is slowed by more steps, does the data so indicate?

Figure 4-1 is an example of a 14-year-old boy's response rate on simple addition problems. Each plot represents a group of problems, divided by the number of minutes it took to do those problems, yielding a rate of response per minute. During Condition A, the subject performed one-place addition. During Condition B, he did two-place addition; and during Condition C, three-place addition. One response was defined as one complete problem, regardless of the number of places involved in the addition.

As visual inspection of the graph indicates a substantial re-

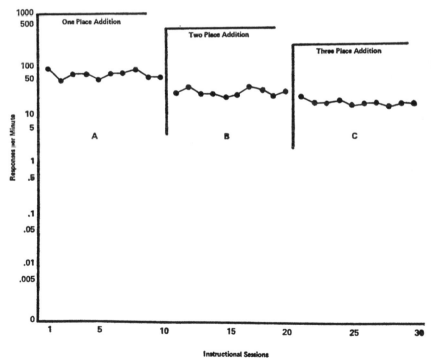

Figure 4-1. Decrease in rate from 50 responses per minute under Condition A to 14 responses per minute under Condition C when each complete problem was defined as one response unit.

duction in response rate, an immediate question is why this child's response rate has dropped. If the increased movements involved in constructing the answers in Conditions B and C are not considered, it might be erroneously concluded that the child's rate has greatly decelerated.

What is needed then is a means of defining equivalent responses in an academic setting. It appears that the closest approximation of equivalent response units in a written response topography is a written letter or numeral. The letter "A," the numeral "2," or a symbol "?" each represent one response cycle and as such may be considered approximately equal. On the other hand, if each word were counted as a response, "cat" would be measured as an equal response with the word "supercalifragalisticexpealidocious."

Figure 4-2 records the same data as Figure 4-1, but instead of

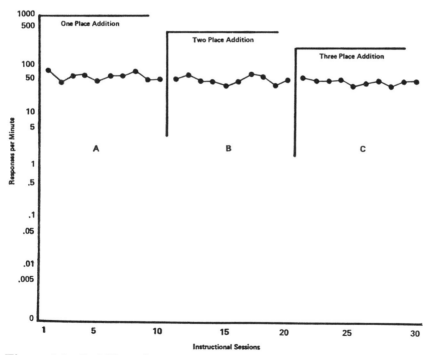

Figure 4-2. Stability of rate from Condition A to Condition C when each numeral was defined as one response unit.

counting each complete answer as a response unit, each numeral constructed was counted as one response unit. The data indicate the child has maintained a fairly stable response rate, in contrast to the declining rate which appears to have taken place in Figure 4-1 when entire answers were counted as a response.

Once criteria of what to count have been established, how to record what is counted is the next concern. However, recording re-

	Time	Contact Initiation	Subject	Error	Correct	Points	Consequence (Cash–In's)	No. Taken
					EEU Hourly Event Sheet			
	1							
	2							
	3	P	M	2	39	4		
	4							
	5	P		0	2		Art	3
	6							
	7	T						
	8							
	9	P		4	47	5	Volleyball	5
	59							
	60	T		6	89	10		
TOTAL	TIC 2 PIC 3		—	E 12	C 177	P 19	C – I's 2	No. 8

Figure 4-3. Hourly Event Sheet used for determining contingency relationships between a pupil's behavior and the teacher's management. The final row indicates the total for each column. For example, a total of two teacher-initiated and three pupil-initiated contacts were made in this hour.

sponses is a simple matter of a written notation on a special form. Figure 4-3 is an example of an Event Sheet (Haring and Kunzelmann, 1966) used at the Experimental Education Unit. Many different kinds of data are recorded on the event sheet, such as the number of responses the child has emitted, both correct and incorrect, and at what time these events occurred within any instructional hour. These two bits of data form the basis for calculating the child's rate of response. All other data are considered as to how they may be affecting the particular child's rate of response.

The numerals on the outer edge indicate at what time the contact with the child occurred. There is one sheet for each hour of the instructional day, with a different color representing each hour. The first entry is on line three, indicating that the contact occurred at three minutes after the hour. The column headed "Contact Initiation" indicates whether the teacher or the pupil first initiated the contact. The "Subject" column is for indicating by subject area the curriculum assignment. The next two columns, "Error" and "Correct," are for recording the number of responses the child made. Under "Points" is recorded the number of contingency units the child received as a consequence of correct responses made. Beneath "Consequence" the activity selected by the child is indicated. The column "Number Taken" indicates how many minutes the child elected to take, the maximum permissible being determined by how many points the child accumulated. The total taken is subtracted from 60 to give the number of minutes the child spent working on his academic program for that particular hour.

Computation of rates of responses from event sheet data is shown in Figure 4-4. To get response rate per minute, the 177 correct responses made were divided by the number of minutes spent on the program. In this case, the child took a total of eight minutes of free-time activity, leaving 52 minutes spent on the program. The 177 correct responses divided by 52 yields a rate of 3.4 correct mathematic responses per minute, while 12 error responses divided by 52 minutes on the program gives a rate of .23 error responses per minute.

At least five variables under teacher control can be identified from the event sheet data: (a) the curriculum material assigned

Totals	TIC 2 PIC 3	—	E 12	C 177	P 19	C–I's 2	No. 8

Time on program — 60 — 8 = 52

CORRECT RESPONSE RATE = $\dfrac{\text{Correct Responses}}{\text{Time on Program}}$

$\dfrac{177}{} = \boxed{3.4}$ Correct Responses Per Minute

ERROR RESPONSE RATE = $\dfrac{\text{Error Responses}}{\text{Time on Program}}$

$\dfrac{12}{} = \boxed{.23}$ Error Responses Per Minute

Figure 4-4. Computation of correct and error response rates from the totals row of the Hourly Event Sheet.

to a child, (b) the ratio of pupil responses to the number of teacher-initiated contacts, (c) the ratio of pupil responses to the number of pupil-initiated contacts, (d) the ratio of pupil responses to the number of points received as a consequence and (e) the ratio of pupil responses to the number of cash-ins (points exchanged for an activity). All of these variables are looked at in the light of what happens to the correct and error rates of the child when these variables are manipulated. Prior to any data analysis, however, teacher-pupil contacts, points given the child or his selection of an activity can only be considered as events that occur in the child's learning environment. An examination of the child's rate of response must be made before any conclusions can be drawn regarding value as possible reinforcers. When these variables are analyzed and controlled, an infinite number of What would happen to the child's response rate if . . . ? qustions could be asked and answered empirically for any child.

Figure 4-5 represents an attempt to examine the function of points received for correct responses. The student was new to the program, and manipulation of the schedule of points was made to see if points were a reinforcing consequence. The median correct rate per minute during Condition A was 2.8 responses per minute. During Condition A, the child was on an incontingency basis; that is, no points were given him. During Condition B, when one point was given for approximately each eight responses,

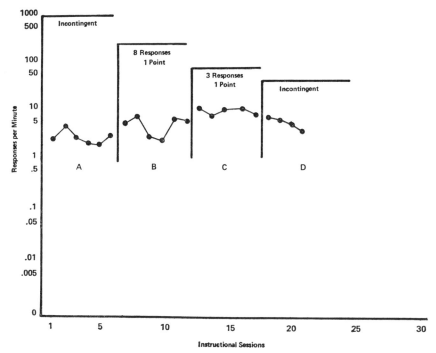

Figure 4-5. Changes in academic response rate under Condition A (incontingent), Condition B (contingent 8:1), Condition C (contingent 3:1) and Condition D (incontingent). Median changes between A and C show an accelerated rate change of approximately 200 percent.

his median rate of response rose to 5.1. During Condition C, in which the child received one point for approximately each three responses, his median rate was 8.2 responses per minute. To check whether the trend would continue under a contingency system of no points, points again were not given. Each of the following four sessions successively declined.

The data indicate that for this child, under certain conditions, points seemed to be a contributing factor to his rate of response. There are no indications about what would happen to any other child under similar circumstances. It might be shown, for example, that manipulation of the number of points for another child had little or no effect on his response rate.

It is not important whether a point contingency system works, but what procedures are available allowing the classroom teacher to assess his techniques. As data diagnosis procedures are available, the classroom teacher need not rely on generalizations made from children other than the one with whom he is concerned. He can examine his teaching procedures in his own classroom and determine their effectiveness.

DATA PROGRAMING

Where teaching is considered data diagnosis, it follows that the programing of subject matter content must be submitted to an equally fine analysis, based on the data of the learner's responses. Ordering content within such a framework is no simple task, for to program beginning reading skills, stimuli must be arranged in a certain sequence to promote acquisition and maintenance. First in order is the eliciting stimulus with which certain behavior operations are already associated. Next, the contextual stimulus is provided in order that the desired behaviors will occur in those situations in which it will be demanded at a later time. Finally, the new stimulus to which the original behavior is to be associated is placed in the teaching sequence. In beginning reading, for example, the eliciting stimulus may be a picture of a cat; the contextual stimulus may be a workbook or a series of frames in book or machine format; and the cue stimuli may be the letter sequence c, a and t. The desired response, of course, is the linguistic behavior already associated with the sight of a cat, that of an orally produced word, "cat."

A completed program awaits only the pupil response data for confirmation of this approach to teaching reading. Usually programers analyze response data in terms of the placement and number of errors in order to identify particular sequences that need rewriting or reprograming. Where errors occur with some pattern of regularity, the programmer will redesign his cues, prompts, methods of fading and number of practices or feedback resources, and hope that the corrected program will produce errorless or near-errorless learning on subsequent trials. Occasional errors are usually evaluated as particular to an individual learner or the learner's rate, rather than particular to the individual program.

These tryout, rewriting and second tryout stages have become traditional programming procedures. Traditionally, program data is completed prior to the marketing of a program. Traditionally the programer has been given an error allowance of ten percent for an average population of learners in a "completed" program. And traditionally, once the program has been tried in the field and placed in the hands of the teacher, the programer has fulfilled his obligations.

Currently, however, the educational staff making decisions based on response data view errors in any program or sequence teaching as unnecessary, as such errors expose either programming or teaching failures. This view of pupil response deficits occurring as the result of teaching or programming deficits has been analyzed further as either a lack of coordination of stimulus and response functions (Cook and Adams, 1966), inadequate prior learning or inefficient schedules of reinforcement contingencies. Whether errors are to be attributed to stimulus-response coordination, to past learning or to scheduling of reinforcing stimuli is a question for which classroom response data can provide answers.

For example, inadequate contingencies of reinforcement, either within the teaching procedure or within the program, are exposed in the manner explained herein. If the learner's errors are on material previously mastered, the new frames that have produced inadequate responses may be presented again with a more generous schedule of reinforcement. This schedule may be provided either within the program (a "good," "100%," the child's marking himself correct, or a smile rather than just confirmation of the response) or as an adjunct to the program (an increase in negotiable points or tokens) (Haring and Kunzelmann, 1966; Lovitt, 1967). This enriched schedule, always defined for the individual learner, may make a difference between learning with or without error. It may also speed a rate slowed by error or slow a rate where speed has produced errors. In the classrooms of the Experimental Education Unit, it has been found that approximately 75 percent of response deficits in both rate and error are amenable to the more stringent control of reinforcing stimuli.

Figure 4-6 is an example of a commercial reading program. Frames 110 through 121 reveal that errors have occurred in a

Name	A			B			C			A			C		
Frame	Date	Rate	Error	Date	Rate	Error	Date	Rate	Error	Date	Rate	Error	Date	Rate	Error
110	1–7	2.1	a/i					.07			1.8				
111															
112					1.0										
113			a/i			a/i			a/c						
114							1–6								
115															Begin
116									c/t						
117			c/t												
118															
119															
120			b/t	1–4					c/a						
121			c/a		.09			Rerun							
122	Revise						Contingency Change			Return			Return		

Figure 4-6. Frame analysis of a commercial reading program recording pupil errors in letter discrimination and rate of response. For example, in frames 110 and 113, child A responded with the letter "i" on a frame in which "a" was requisite. Subsequent programing decisions are also recorded on the sheet.

pattern particular to the program itself. Figure 4-7 shows the same pattern of errors as units of child A's inattention to the reading task, with the plateaus indicating the child's failure to attend at the regular-interval times of observation. It is interesting to note that the pause in the cumulative observation records, as shown in Figure 4-7, occur in a pattern roughly corresponding to the program error data. While the two are not in precise correspondence, there is, nevertheless, an inattention zone suggesting error areas charted as to frame. Notice also that the reinforcement contingencies established on the original presentation of the program are in a ratio of 5:2. For every five correct responses made by the learner, two points negotiable for a certain number of minutes of free time in an activity of the child's own choosing were allotted (Haring and Kunzelmann, 1966).

The same frame sequence for Child A was assigned the next day, this time with more stringent control of the consequences of the child's responding. The errors have largely disappeared, as

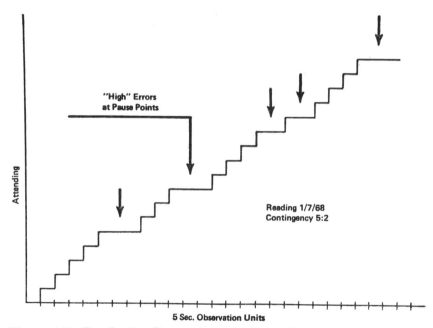

Figure 4-7. Pupil attending under initial contingencies of 5:2 where high errors are noted at pause points.

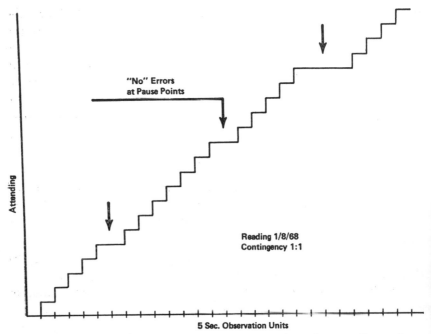

Figure 4-8. Pupil attending under contingencies of 1:1, where there is no correspondence between pause points and error.

shown by the frame records under Trial II in Figure 4-6 (Column 4). Further, the second plot of the child's attention to task (Figure 4-8) seems to show no corresponding relation to errors. This difference appears to be attributable to the change in reinforcement contingencies. Whereas on the first record the ratio was 5:2, on the re-presentation of the program, the schedule was 1:1.

A second presentation of a particular sequence of frames, together with a change in schedule of contingencies, however, may mask inadequate prior learning. If the programmer sees that an already generous schedule is in effect and has been effective in the past, he looks to the internal design of the frame rather than to a new contingency schedule. If a further detailed analysis of the program suggests that the original presentation included an optimal schedule of prompts and a number of practices and fading devices, a second presentation without change may take place. However while merely representing a program does increase the practice effect and may preclude response deficits the second time around, this situation has seldom occurred in experience. It is included to emphasize that proliferation of frames is not always the solution to response deficits. As the data in the last column of Figure 4-6 attest, Child C with the same program two days in a row was able to continue without error.

In approximately one fourth of the patterned error instances, however, response deficits appear that are attributable not to reinforcement contingencies or inadequate practice but to failures in the programming of stimulus-response coordination. In beginning reading, analytic reference is made to the original associations among eliciting, contextual and cue stimuli. When the child's data show a second presentation of a particular program with increased reinforcement ratios still providing sources for error, program redesign is mandatory. In this case, it is clear that neither the program nor the teacher gained discriminative control over the pupil's emission of appropriate reading responses.

In either programed or traditional reading, a common source of error is found in the stage immediately beyond that of the simpler sound-symbol association. This is the area of mediating associations, the fusing or blending process. Little is known about this process. It seems either too covert or too complex for anything other than some reinforcement grossly applied to the integrated and completed process after it occurred. The mediating association is made up of separate elements; however, as it is largely covert, it does not appear to lend itself to programming principles. For most early readers, blending occurs at some stage, largely through self-initiated trial and error. For a child with reading disability, however, the acquisition of blending is much more arduous. The programer is then tempted to either proliferate frames similar to the original program or re-present a new set of contextual and cue stimuli with the assumption that eventually, practice will produce the second-order association.

Such an impasse has been reached several times at the Experimental Education Unit with children who seemingly would not or could not blend sounds into a meaningful word. A redesign of simple programmed sequences, as those shown in Figure 4-9, has allowed many learners to maintain their rates of respond-

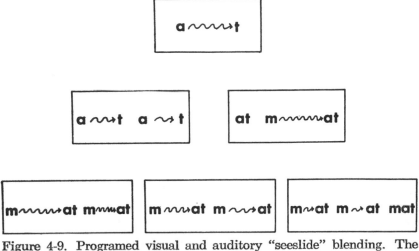

Figure 4-9. Programed visual and auditory "seeslide" blending. The visual stimulus is synchronized with the corresponding sounds, presenting the auditory and visual stimuli simultaneously.

ing beyond the primary association of sound and symbol. These frames have been presented by means of a device which compounds an auditory stimulus with a visual stimulus. Both sound and sight stimuli are foreshortened in time of presentation by adjusting the visual arrow and accelerating the speed of the recorded speech sound. This simple sequence of an arrow of changing proportions coupled to compression of speech sounds appears to correspond to a deceleration of pauses in students' attention to task records, as well as allow the maintenance of rate and errorless responding.

The simultaneous attenuation of an oral and a graphic symbol undoubtedly is not highly original. However, when reliance is placed not on the "arrow" method but on the data and the direction in which the data point, it appears that something new in programming has occurred. The claim is not that a mediating response has been programmed but only that a coordination of stimulus and response functions has appeared to take place within the program. This coordination may be an antecedent cue stimulus; it may be the response itself. The data does not answer this question. The data show only whether or not the desired behavior occurs, at what rate and under what conditions.

Data programing continues to explore response deficiencies, not as a function of the child but as a function of insufficient reinforcement schedules, inadequate prior learning or failure to incorporate psychological principles in the program. Data programming considers each one of these areas relative to the data, not gathered from a large n in tryout stages, removed in time and place, but taken from daily charts of an "n of one" in the individual's present learning stage.

DATA DECISIONS

Data decisions, equally applicable to both individual and group performance, are specific environmental changes that the teacher makes in the classroom to affect performance rates of pupils. Included herein are illustrations of the use of data to build rate ranges from individual pupil data and, subsequently, illustrations of how the median score of the rate range reflects teacher control in the classroom.

Preliminary studies at the Experimental Education Unit show that response range for individuals and rate range for groups supply sensitive measures for such questions as What happens when a substitute teacher takes over?, What happens when a teacher uses deceleration tactics to reduce undesirable behaviors? or What happens when avoidance tactics such as keeping pupils after school are used? Rate ranges, as they can detect changes due to new textbooks or different arrangements of subject matter, can also supply concrete recommendations to the curriculum specialist. Indeed, rate-range sensitivity seems to reflect small changes in most variables considered relevant at the present time.

Figure 4-10 charts the procedures and components of rate ranges. The first two weeks, Section A, focus on one child's correct and error rates. The correct rate is 1.5 responses per minute, while the error rate is approximately .12. When a teacher wishes to consider all the children within a class, he may group the individual plots into a range. Section B illustrates the individual data of three children placed into ranges for correct and error responses. Week three of Section B illustrates a wide range in correct and error rates, while week four of Section B illustrates a narrow correct rate range and a wide error rate range.

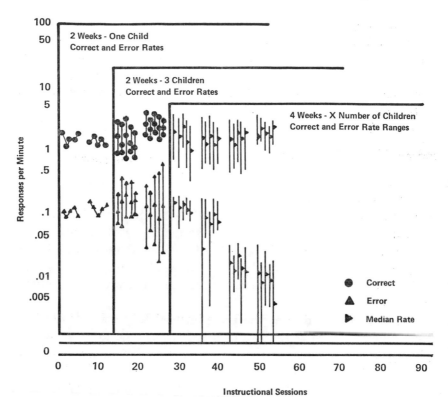

Figure 4-10. Sample data, showing correct and error rates, progressing from one child to a group of children. Section A shows correct and error rates for one child. Section B presents correct and error rates for three children, while Section C shows correct and error ranges and median points for a large group of children.

Section C shows rate ranges with only median points. The median rate point for the class demonstrates to the teacher where she had the maximum control of pupil performance. Although a teacher may have an individualized program, he may find the majority of the pupils at one or the other end of the range. Week seven of Section C illustrates such a broad expanse. According to this graph, children are performing at a rate of .8 responses per minute for correct work, while errors are occurring at a rate of .02.

Figure 4-11 shows data recorded over approximately ten weeks from a primary class where the teacher selected the median rates

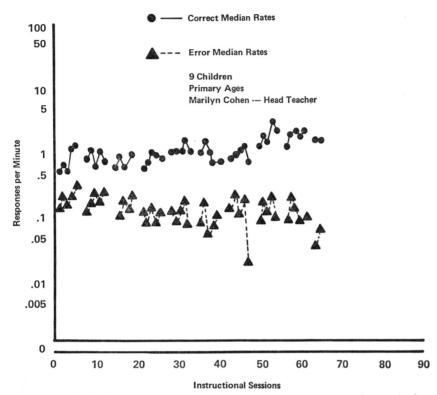

Figure 4-11. Primary class median correct and error rates in math for one teaching quarter, showing 150 percent increase in correct rate and 50 percent decrease in errors.

of all nine of her primary pupils in arithmetic. For each day of instruction, the teacher placed two data points on the graph, each point representing the most typical rate for her group. The mid-median for the correct response rate is .97, while the percent of change in correct rate between the first and last week is 150 percent. Notable also in Figure 4-11 is the decrease in error rate. The mid-median score for errors is .08, and the errors drop approximately 50 percent between weeks one and nine.

A median plot representing correct and error rates under teacher control can be the basis for decisions illustrated in Figures 4-12, 4-13, 4-14 and 4-15. Basic decisions that have evolved at

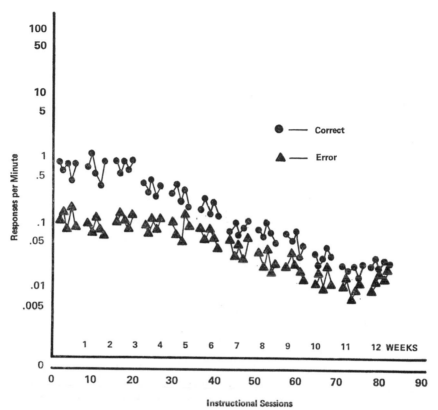

Figure 4-12. Sample data showing extreme drops in correct and error rates, where the teacher's decision is to change consequences.

the Experimental Education Unit while looking at data from the classroom have taken four directions:

1. Discover a consequence that will accelerate a child's performance rate.
2. Change the program of instructional materials to facilitate correct performance.
3. Differentially correct by increasing the reinforcers available for accurate performance and deduct the same reinforcers at a reduced level for error performance.
4. Move instructional decisions, such as correction and establishment of reinforcer values, to the child.

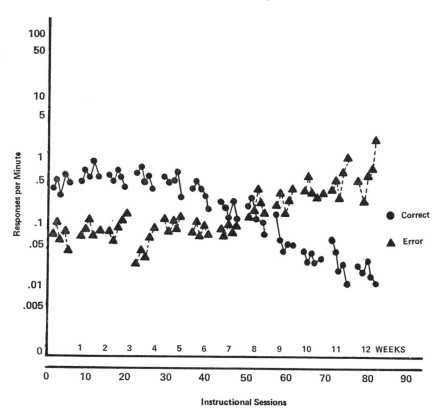

Figure 4-13. Sample data showing error rate increases above correct rate, where the teacher's decision is to make a curriculum change.

Figure 4-12 illustrates consistent deceleration over a period of 12 weeks. As evidenced from the data, the teacher viewing this performance probably would attempt to find better reinforcers. The reduction in response rate noted during weeks 10, 11 and 12 might be analogous to a satiation period, as described in the laboratory findings of operant conditioners. It should be observed that a teacher would not allow as many weeks to elapse as in the illustrated data but rather would attempt to change the consequences in the classroom the first few days of week four. Such a decision to accelerate correct performance by changing consequences is a direct manipulation of the classroom environment.

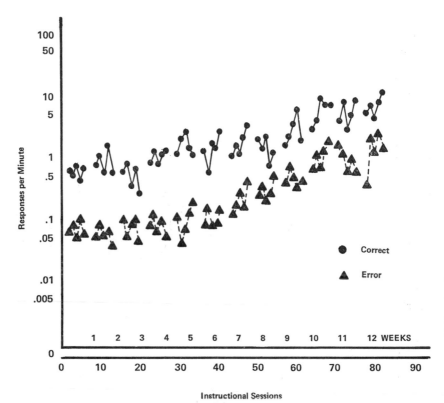

Figure 4-14. Sample data showing acceleration of both correct and error rates, where the teacher decides to correct differentially.

The effects of the decision upon the pupil's performance will be known immediately when data plots are made each day.

Figure 4-13 illustrates data with a reverse trend. The teacher has managed to keep the correct rate higher than error rate during the first six weeks. During the fourth and fifth weeks, the teacher would probably attempt to discover a curriculum or program variable accounting for the correct and error trend. However, during weeks 7 through 12, the error rate is higher than the correct rate. Therefore a program change, different materials or materials at a less complex level would be utilized. These data might also serve to describe an initial contact of teacher and pupil. Assume that the teacher found in the first few days working with

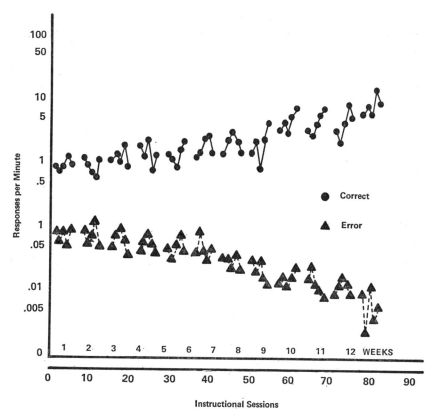

Figure 4-15. Sample data showing correct rate acceleration and error rate deceleration, where the teacher's decision is to allow self-management.

the child that the correct rate was systematically lower than the error rate. The teacher would then change the prescribed curriculum design for that particular child until a time that the correct rate of performance would exceed the errors.

Figure 4-14 pinpoints through weeks four, five and six an acceleration pattern for both correct and error rates. When correct and error rate are highly correlated, it is necessary for the teacher to differentially correct the child's performance. The data shows that the teacher has an excellent reinforcement system in operation and a program that allows for high correct rate. Again during weeks four, five and six, the teacher would probably decide to increase the consequence for correct rates and take away reinforcement for errors. The lack of a discernible contingency system has commonly been found to maintain similar correct and error rates.

Figure 4-15 illustrates the ideal classroom condition, a high and accelerating correct performance rate and a low and decelerating error rate. The teacher has obviously programed appropriately, managed contingencies well and discovered an excellent consequence system. Therefore, since control of the learning situation to the child is the uppermost educational goal of the teacher, under the conditions described, the decision would be made to allow the child to manage his own programing. For example, the child may be allowed to decide what subjects he prefers during various times of the day, and at what levels. He may correct much of his own work, using teacher manuals and programed instruction, or he may determine use of his free time for extracurricular activities and decide upon many of his own consequences. Such a learner is at a position described as self-management in the classroom.

While it is not yet known what the total utility of rate ranges may be, the technique appears to display the effects of any changes in a learning environment, whether they are changes in pupils, programs or systems for making either effective. This technique further appears to offer a means for replicable analysis from which teaching and administrative decisions can be made—not for all time, but for the present and the child presently labeled disabled in learning.

REFERENCES

Cook, C. and Adams, H. E.: Modification of verbal behavior in speech deficient children. *Behavior Research and Therapy, 4:* 265–271, 1966.

Haring, N. G. and Kunzelmann, H. P.: Finer focus of therapeutic behavioral management. In Hellmuth, G. (Ed.): *Educational Therapy.* Seattle, Special Child Publications, 1966, pp. 225–251.

Lovitt, T. C.: Assessment of children with learning disabilities. *Exceptional Children, 14:*233–239, 1967.

Luria, A. R. and Vinogradova, O. S.: An objective investigation of the dynamics of semantic systems. *British Journal of Psychology, 50:*89–105, 1959.

II

PRESCHOOL CHILDREN

Much of the initial research carried out in classroom behavior management was conducted in laboratory preschools. One of the advantages of working in such an environment was that a more precise control and examination of the variables to be manipulated and studied could be achieved if several adults and only a limited number of children were present. The extension of the basic operant principles into more typical classrooms awaited their validation in these relatively restricted settings.

In the first study, Allen *et al.* demonstrate how teacher attention can increase the attending behavior of a young child who displayed a very high frequency of changing activities. Since the methodology employed by these investigators is typical of behavior modification experiments in general, it will be used to illustrate these procedures as well as to provide the basis for a brief discussion of several related issues.

After carefully specifying the desired terminal behavior, prior to any experimental treatment, one of the first tasks in any modification program is to collect data on the behavior being studied. This has been termed *baseline* data, and in the study by Allen *et al.*, it meant recording how many activity changes were made by the child each day for a period of several days. The length of the baseline period, as well as any other phase of the experiment, is usually determined by waiting until a relatively stable picture is obtained of the behavior being modified. When this is achieved, the second phase begins, in which some reinforcement procedure is initiated. In the Allen *et al.* study, teachers began to socially reinforce the child for attending to an activity for at least one minute. This was maintained until it was evident that a stable and lower frequency of changing activities had been established.

If this were an investigation employing more traditional experimental methods, data might also have been collected on other children in the class who changed activities quite frequently. They could have served as a control group. The present experiment would then have been considered a success if the reinforcement procedures had *not* been applied to them and if their high rate of activity change had been maintained.

One might argue, however, that the improvement in the attending behavior of only one child might be due to chance alone. Perhaps he finally found some aspect of the activities interesting and this just happend to coincide with the introduction of reinforcement techniques. Or perhaps the child had simply matured. As a result of these possibilities, most behavior modification studies tend to use the subject as his own control. Essentially, this means removing and then reintroducing the experimental variable which supposedly was responsible for the change in the child's behavior. In this study, the experimental variable was teacher attention. One of the purposes of the study was to show that when the teachers no longer systematically reinforced attending behavior, the high frequency of activity changes seen in the original baseline condition would reappear. Similarly, if they then reversed the process by again giving social approval for attending behavior, the frequency of activity changes would decrease. In effect, the teachers were asked to replicate the experiment with the same subject in order to empirically show that changing activities was, for the child, a function of teacher attention. Allen *et al.* were able to demonstrate such effects.

The basic process of recording a baseline, introducing a treatment, reversing back to the baseline condition and then reintroducing the treatment has been termed a *reversal* design. Each of the four phases of such a study has been labeled with a letter, and since the first and third stages are essentially identical, as are the second and fourth stages, the entire method is referred to as an ABAB reversal design.

Actually, the last phase of the Allen *et al.* study was not really a return to the first B stage. The teachers, in this final phase, now reinforced the child for every two minutes of attending, a slightly more realistic schedule of reinforcement. Thus, technically the design was ABAC and is a minor offshoot of the ABAB variety.

A legitimate teacher reaction might be: "If I use operant techniques, collect baseline data and institute successful modification procedures, why should I perform a reversal? I'm not interested in seeing maladaptive behavior reappear." The answer to such a question is not simple. The argument against doing experimental reversals has recently been supported not only by teachers but by some researchers in the area as well. The researchers believe that a sufficient number of empirical demonstrations have been performed to obviate the need for continued control procedures, even in scientific investigations. Continuing with such a stand, it should be said that the sole purpose of a reversal design is to scientifically prove that the experimental treatment is, in fact, the cause of the behavior change. Some investigations include more than one such replication simply because the more often a treatment is introduced and removed, the more reliable the procedure is said to be—that is, provided the expected results are obtained.

Teachers, however, are not in the field of education for the purpose of either validating a concept scientifically or publishing articles in journals which require proof that a modification treatment is empirically reliable. In fact, some teachers who have willingly participated in modification experiments have balked at the idea of using an experimental reversal. Teachers are interested, though, in using already well-established scientific psychological methods. Hence, most educators, it could be argued, should be content with the knowledge that the reinforcement techniques they have introduced have improved the classroom environment, without feeling obligated to verify the issue by removing the treatment.

On the other hand, it is strongly believed by some individuals that teachers need to function as applied researchers and should therefore use scientific methods of analysis. Several other arguments in favor of reversal designs include: (a) they help to convince nonbelievers of the power of such techniques when undesirable behaviors reappear during the reversal phase and (b) they suggest that teachers discontinue complicated or time-consuming treatment procedures that are no longer necessary (i.e. during the reversal phase, the teacher may notice that the maladaptive behavior does *not* return) (Axelrod, 1971).

In our experience, we have encountered teachers who have refused to do reversals as well as those who were eager to prove a
hypothesis. Our own bias is towards the continued use of such
reversal designs when the teacher is modifying a complex series
of behaviors or is undertaking a relatively novel modification procedure. If, however, the process involves a simple technique and
the modification of a specific behavior which has been repeatedly
demonstrated to be readily altered, we see no pressing need to use
a reversal design. The only exception might be in a teacher training course where the use of such a procedure would enable the
teacher-student to see a dramatic behavioral change.

Recently, however, use has been made of an alternative methodological design which does allow a scientific determination of
those variables controlling behavior without using a reversal design. For example, if a teacher is faced with a student who has
a high error rate in several academic subjects (e.g. mathematics,
spelling and reading), the following technique may be used to
validate the modification procedure. A baseline rate can be calculated simultaneously for all three subject areas. Then a reinforcement program is applied to the behavior of the child in only *one*
of the academic areas (e.g. mathematics). Baseline data are still
collected in spelling and reading. When a stable improvement is
found in mathematics, the modification program can then be
applied to both mathematics and spelling behavior. Finally, after
spelling improves, the reinforcement techniques are used in all
three subject areas. If improvement over baseline performance
occurs in each area only as the treatment is specifically applied
to behavior in that subject matter, increased performance can be
said to be a function of the reinforcement procedures. Since baseline data is collected simultaneouly in several subject areas, the
method is called a multiple baseline technique.

The question may immediately arise as to why improvement
occurs only in the academic area to which the modification is
applied. In other words, when the child's mathematics behavior
is initially modified, why do these effects not generalize to spelling
and reading? Most behavior modification studies demonstrate
that one finds improvement only in those areas in which modifica-

tion procedures are applied. If you want the child to perform better in mathematics, reading and spelling, it is usually necessary to set up a modification program in all three subjects. Similarly, if a teacher modifies a child's talking-out behavior, will a reduction also occur automatically in his rate of out-of-seat behavior? Probably not.

This is not to say, however, that behavior modification is so "behavior-specific" that changes never occur in any responses other than those being altered. There have been instances of more general improvement. Such findings have been reported most frequently when the original behavior under study has been a positive social behavior which the child displayed very infrequently. For example, if a child had a very low rate of peer verbal interaction and these interactions were then selectively reinforced, an increase might also be observed in the closely related behaviors of playing games and group motor activities. In this example, peer verbal interaction itself becomes so reinforcing, independent of teacher procedures, that other activities which involve such behavior also show a higher rate of participation.

Far fewer cases have been documented in which the deceleration of a specific negative behavior has resulted in a corresponding decrease in the frequency of related maladaptive behaviors.

Another question concerns the extent to which the effects of behavior modification generalize to different settings. If, for example, a teacher modifies calling-out behavior in a child in her classroom, will he continue to call out in other classes where behavior management has not been in effect? Most research indicates that he will continue to call out. This, however, is probably more true for the generalized elimination of a negative behavior than it is for the generalization of a positive behavior which has itself become reinforcing or which introduces the child to reinforcing events. A good example of the latter case might be modifying the behavior of a child who refuses to dance. If this is done successfully in school, dancing behavior will probably be readily extended to other situations, partly because it is found to be fun and relaxing and partly because it introduces the child to other potentially more reinforcing events—members of the opposite sex.

As with the study by Allen *et al.*, the next study by Jacobson *et al.* also examines frequency of changing activities. The interesting aspects of this latter report include the fact that the modification procedures were successfully carried out with an entire class of Head Start children, with the teachers being the mothers of the children who attended. It was demonstrated that the frequency of switching activities could be reduced by making switching contingent upon the correct completion of a simple academic task. Thus, instead of giving social approval for attending, a somewhat difficult procedure to apply to an entire group of students, changing activities was permitted if a requirement was fulfilled. Since the required task was one which the teacher considered important, but one which many of the students ordinarily refrained from doing, the modification procedure served both the purpose of getting students to switch activities less frequently as well as having them complete a specific academic problem.

The next three articles are concerned with social behaviors. Hart *et al.* provide data which indicate that an increase in reinforcement alone, without regard to whether it is given contingent upon the desired behavior, is not sufficient for improvement to be seen in the selected behavior. This paper supports an earlier statement by Ross which maintains that while reinforcement is certainly not a novel concept, it is most effectively used when applied systematically and contingently.

The paper by Wahler is one of only a few existing publications that attempts to examine the effects of peer reinforcement upon a child's behavior. Teachers are often made aware of the fact that many classroom behaviors are maintained through the reinforcement these actions receive from other students. Wahler's study substantiates this belief and has implications for the effective treatment of classroom problems by students as well as teachers.

The modification of aggressive and fantasy behavior are reported by Sloane *et al.* The procedures are amplified by the use of a time-out room into which the child was placed when his behavior became severe. In addition, the investigation attempted to make the treatment maximally effective by having the child's parents apply the same techniques at home.

In the final paper of this chapter, Johnston *et al.* report the functional relationship between teacher attention and climbing behavior. This chapter has enabled us to present some of the numerous types of behavior that have been altered by classroom teachers as well as several of the different procedures that have been employed. With the exception of the study by Jacobson *et al.,* the reports in this chapter were conducted in highly controlled laboratory preschools. Many of the remaining papers attempt to show the effectiveness of operant techniques in more representative classroom settings.

REFERENCES

Axelrod, S.: Education and science: Compatible endeavors. Paper presented at the University of Kansas Symposium on Behavior Analysis in Education, Lawrence, May, 1971.

5

Control of Hyperactivity by Social Reinforcement of Attending Behavior

K. Eileen Allen, Lydia B. Henke, Florence R. Harris, Donald M. Baer, and Nancy J. Reynolds

A 4½-year-old boy with an excessively short span of attention was helped to acquire more extended attending behavior through the systematic programming of contingencies for adult social reinforcement. When the child remained with a single activity for one continuous minute, teachers immediately gave attention and approval for as long as he remained with that activity. Teachers withheld their attention consequent upon all other behavior. Within seven days, the number of activity changes decreased markedly. Reversal of these procedures reinstated the hyperactive behavior. When original reinforcement contingencies were reintroduced, there was again a marked decrease in number of activity changes. The study gives evidence that adults can help a child to increase his attending behavior, a crucial aspect of learning.

THERE EXISTS now a series of experimental field studies applying reinforcement principles to problem behaviors of preschool children. These studies have dealt with crying (Hart *et al.*, 1964, regressive crawling (Harris *et al.*, 1964), isolate play (Allen *et al.*, 1964), passivity (Johnston *et al.*, 1966), noncoopera-

NOTE: From the *Journal of Educational Psychology,* 58:231–237, 1967. Copyright 1967 by the American Psychological Association. Reprinted with permission of authors and publisher.

tive behaviors (Hart *et al.*, 1966), self-multilative scratching (Allen and Harris, 1966), autistic behavior (Brawley *et al.*, 1966; Wolf *et al.*, 1964) and classroom disruptiveness (Allen *et al.*, 1966). In each instance, the behavior under examination was highly responsive to adult social reinforcement. The present study was conducted to ascertain whether similar social reinforcement procedures could alter the hyperactivity of a four-year-old boy who tended to flit from activity to activity.

Attending behavior, commonly referred to as "attention span," has long been recognized as a crucial and desirable alternative to hyperactivity. What has not always been clear is the extent to which attending is a behavior which teachers can help a child to develop, although Patterson (Patterson, Jones, Whittier and Wright, 1965) has done work in this area with older children. Thus it is of interest to determine if systematic social reinforcement can increase the duration of a young child's attending to an activity, and also to analyze the successive steps a teacher might take in helping a child to maintain his attention to an activity for increasingly long periods.

One of the ultimate objectives of preschool education is, of course, to develop a child's skills in using materials constructively and creatively. An essential first step toward this objective sometimes must be to increase the time the child spends engaging in each activity. Fortunately, duration of attention can be defined, observed and reliably recorded in the field situation.

METHOD
Subject

James was one of 16 normal children of middle-socioeconomic status who comprised the four-year-old group in the laboratory preschool. At the inception of the study, he was four years, six months old and had been attending school for three months.

James was a vigorous, healthy child with a well-developed repertoire of motor, social and intellectual skills. Although he made a comfortable adjustment to school during the first few weeks, a tendency to move constantly from one play activity to another, thereby spending little time in any one pursuit, was noted early.

Since such behavior is common to some young children in a new situation, his teachers merely continued their friendly efforts to engage him in more prolonged and concentrated use of materials.

After 12 weeks, James showed no diminution in number of activity changes during play periods. An observer then was assigned to record his behavior, noting his activities and the time spent in each. Records kept over five school mornings showed that although occasionally James stayed with an activity for 1, 2 or 3 minutes, the average duration of an activity was less than one minute. The parent reported that the same kind of "flightiness" had long caused concern at home. It was agreed that a study be made of ways of helping James to increase his attending behavior.

Procedure

The procedure for increasing the duration of time spent in any activity was to make adult social reinforcement contingent solely on the subject's (*S*'s) emitting attending behavior for a specified minimum period of time. Attending behavior was defined as engaged in one activity. This included play activity (*a*) with a single type of material, such as blocks or paint, (*b*) in a single location, such as in the sandbox or at a table or (*c*) in a single dramatic role, such as sailor or fireman. Adult social reinforcement (Bijou and Baer, 1965) was defined as one or more of the following teacher behaviors: talking to *S* while facing him within a distance of three feet, or from a greater distance, using his name; touching *S*; and giving him additional materials suitable to the ongoing activity. Withholding or withdrawing social reinforcement consisted of turning away from *S*; not looking or smiling at him; not speaking to him; and directing attention to some other child or activity.

One teacher was assigned major responsibility for maintaining reinforcement contingencies. However, since the two other teachers might at times also deliver or withhold reinforcement, each had to remain constantly aware of the conditions in force.

The design of the study required four successive experimental stages, as delineated by Harris (1964).

Base Line

The existing rate, or operant level, of activity changes prior to systematic application of adult social reinforcement was recorded for several play sessions.

Reinforcement

Social reinforcement was presented immediately when attending behavior had been emitted for one unbroken minute. Reinforcement was maintained continuously until S left the material or the area or verbalized a change in his play role. Immediately consequent upon such a shift in play activity, social reinforcement ceased until one minute of attending behavior had again been emitted. The procedure was continued until attending behaviors had materially increased.

Reversal

Then, to ascertain whether social reinforcement was in fact the determining factor in modifying the behavior under study, reinforcement was again delivered on a noncontingent basis such as had been in effect during the baseline period. This reversal of contingencies was carried out long enough to yield a clear assessment of the effects of the changed conditions.

Reinstatement

During this period, the procedures in effect during the second stage, "Reinforcement," were reinstituted. After attending behaviors had again increased in duration, the criterion for presenting social reinforcement was raised to 2 minutes.

Recording

The S's attending behavior and adult social reinforcement, as previously defined, were coded and recorded in successive 10-second intervals by an observer using a stopwatch and a red flashlight with a magnet attached. The recording system was similar to that described by Allen *et al.* (1964). Each period of attending to one activity was enclosed in brackets. Since an increase in attending behavior brought a corresponding decrease in the number of activity changes, data on attending behavior were counted and graphed in terms of the number of activity changes occurring within successive 50-minute time units. In general, but not necessarily, two 50-minute periods indicated 1 day of recording of play time exclusive of teacher-structured or teacher-directed activities.

During the two reinforcement stages, the observer used a flashlight to inform teachers when S reached criterion for social reinforcement. The cue consisted of placing the flashlight on top of the metal clip of the clipboard as soon as S had emitted one minute and later two minutes, of attending behavior. When the behavior stopped, the observer removed the flashlight and placed it under the clipboard, where it remained out of sight until criterion attending behavior had again been emitted. Teachers were instructed to maintain awareness of the flashlight position and to check it before giving S any social reinforcement.

Periodically throughout the study, observer reliability on attending behaviors, activity changes and adult social reinforcement was checked by an independent observer. Agreement of records ranged between 97 percent and 100 percent. No post checks of attending behavior could be made because the study was terminated by the close of the school year, at which time the family moved to another city.

In addition to the behavior under study, some assessment of whether social aspects of S's behavior were affected by changes in his attending behavior seemed desirable. Therefore, S's verbalizations, proximity to, and cooperation with, other children were defined, coded and recorded. The quality of the child's social behavior was estimated by considering cooperative behavior as high-level social behavior and mere proximity as low-level social behavior, in contrast to isolate behavior, which was considered nonsocial. Interrater reliability on these parameters ranged between 84 per cent and 92 per cent.

RESULTS
Base Line—Stage 1

The number of activity changes that James made in each of 21 successive 50-minute periods of free-choice play, both indoors

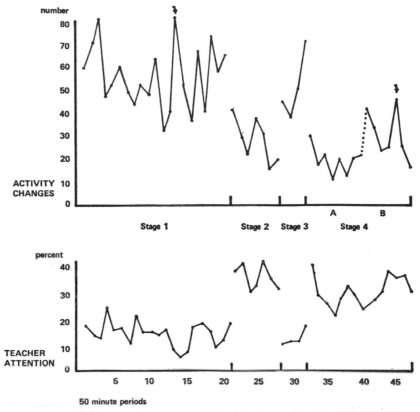

Figure 5-1. Number of activity changes of S during 50-minute periods throughout study, compared with concurrent percentage of time S received teacher attention. (Stage 1, baseline of activity change under noncontingent attention; Stage 2, attention contingent on 1 minute of attending; Stage 3, base-line condition; Stage 4, contingent attending as in Stage 2; at dotted line, criterion for attending raised to 2 minutes. Arrows indicate days S's mother visited.)

and out, is shown in Figure 5-1. The fewest number of activity changes were 33 during Period 12, with an average duration of 1 minute, 29 seconds per activity. The greatest number of activity changes occurred in Period 14, with 82 changes and an average duration of 37 seconds per activity. The overall average for the baseline stage (the operant level of the behavior under study) was 56 activity changes per 50-minute period, with an average duration of 53 seconds per activity.

The amount of teacher reinforcement presented to James on a random, noncontingent basis averaged 16 per cent of each session. This rate was within the normal range in this preschool of amount of teacher attention per child.

Reinforcement—Stage 2

This stage comprised seven 50-minute periods, as shown in Figure 5-1. Activity changes ranged from a high of 41 in Period 22 (the first period of experimental procedures) to a low of 19 in Period 28 (the last period of experimental procedures). The overall average of activity changes for the seven periods was 27, with an average duration of 1 minute, 51 seconds per activity, or twice that of the base-line stage. Teacher reinforcement during Stage 2 averaged 38 per cent of each period.

Reversal—Stage 3

During the four-period reversal stage (Figure 5-1, Stage 3), activity changes rose markedly. An average of 51 activity changes per period occurred, with an average duration of 59 seconds per activity. Both measures (number of changes and average duration) were comparable to the baseline stage. During the reversal, teacher attention averaged 14 per cent of each period.

Reinstatement—Stage 4-A and B

Reinforcement contingencies during Stage 4-A, Figure 5-1, were the same as those in effect during Stage 2. Under these conditions, the rate of activity changes again dropped markedly, with a high of 31 and a low of 12 (Periods 33 and 36, respectively). The overall average of activity changes for the eight periods of Stage 4-A was 20, with an average duration of 2½ minutes per activity. Teacher reinforcement during Stage 4-A averaged 31 per cent of each period.

In Period 41 (Figure 1, Stage 4-B), the criterion for delivery of social reinforcement was raised to 2 minutes of attending behavior. Some increase in number of activity changes occurred during Period 41, with a subsequent leveling off. During this part of Stage 4, the greatest number of activity changes was 45, occurring in Period 45; the fewest number, 16, occurred in Period 47. The average number of activity changes during Stage 4-B was 32 per period, with an average duration of 1 minute, 34 seconds per activity. Teacher reinforcement averaged 33 per cent of each period.

The overall average for Period 4 (A and B combined) was 27 changes per session, with an average duration of 1 minute, 51 seconds per activity.

Social Behavior

The quality of social behavior was defined and measured as high, low and isolate. Although not under experimental manipulation, it merits remark for its constancy throughout the experimental procedures. The averages per session were as follows:

	High	Low	Isolate
Stage 1	45%	37%	16%
Stage 2	50%	38%	12%
Stage 3	48%	40%	13%
Stage 4-A	49%	39%	13%
Stage 4-B	41%	44%	15%

These figures were well within the range of the preschool's normative social behavior.

DISCUSSION

The data presented in Figure 5-1 give strong support to the hypothesis that attending behavior is "teachable," in the sense that it can be shaped and maintained by teachers. Moreover, adult social reinforcement again appears to be a powerful instrument for this purpose. When adult social reinforcement was given in a systematic fashion, solely as an immediate consequence of continuing attending behavior, the number of activity changes diminished to half the number that occurred under the more usual, nonsystematic adult procedures of the baseline and reversal stages.

The continuing fluctuation of the data which occurred during each of the experimental periods may merit comment. Behavior does, of course, vary somewhat from day to day. The factors responsible for this variability were not brought under experimental control. Many of them are inherent in the field setting of a preschool and could hardly be controlled in that setting. It is apparent, though, that systematic control of adult social reinforcement, which is readily achieved, is sufficient to override these factors (Baer and Wolf, 1966).

Two of the high points in activity changes, Periods 14 and 45, suggest possible examples of such uncontrolled factors. During Periods 14 and 45, James's mother was present for the entire morning. She interacted with him freely each time he contacted her and went with him frequently when he requested her to come and look at a particular object or play situation. In addition, she made frequent suggestions that he "settle down" and paint her a picture, build with blocks, or "tend to his own business." The mother appeared to have more reinforcing value than the teachers on these novel occasions, a fact not surprising in itself. The fact that the mother was often reinforcing behaviors incompatible with the behavior that teachers were shaping strengthened the original hypothesis that the child's short attention span was in fact a function of adult social reinforcement.

No formal attempt was made to secure data on the quality of James's attending behaviors. In the judgment of the teachers, however, the quality improved steadily. During Stage 4, James frequently spent 15 to 20 minutes pursuing a single activity such as digging, woodworking or block building. Within these activities, he made frequent excursions to get additional materials relevant to his project, such as a wheelbarrow or a dirt sifter. By definition, such departures were recorded as activity changes, even though he returned and continued with the same play. Such occasions, clearly delineated in the data, teachers considered evidence of improved quality of attending, for the side trips were relevant to a core activity, rather than a series of unrelated activity changes as were typical of Stages 1, 2 and 3. The data thus are probably a conservative estimate of the degree of change produced in James's attention span.

The data on social behavior are of particular interest, for they answer in part the often-asked question regarding peripheral effects on overall behavior patterns when one aspect of behavior is under intensive treatment. As was indicated, there was no change in the quality of James's social interaction, already deemed satisfactory by teachers at the start of the study, though the number of separate contacts did decrease, as was predicted. These data add to the evidence that only the behavior specifically being worked on increases or decreases as a function of the reinforcement contingencies.

Throughout the study, the child's mother was informed of procedures and progress in frequent parent conferences. However, no systematic attempts were made to program presentation of social reinforcement from the family. For one thing, the mother worked, and there were frequent changes of babysitters. Nevertheless, the mother reported that James had "settled down" considerably at home. She kept no data to substantiate these statements but did relate several incidents which indicated that there was some generalization from preschool to home. Both the mother and the teachers judged that James was eminently more ready for kindergarten at the end of the study than he had been prior to it. The importance of intensive attending behavior to future learning is obvious. The ease of socially altering attending behavior in *either* direction while perhaps less obvious, is no less important to an analysis of children's intellectual, perceptual and social development.

REFERENCES

Allen, K. E., Hart, B. M., Buell, J. S., Harris, F. R. and Wolf, M. M.: Effects of social reinforcement on isolate behavior of a nursery school child. *Child Development, 35*:511–518, 1964.

Allen, K. E. and Harris, F. R.: Elimination of a child's excessive scratching by training the mother in reinforcement procedures. *Behaviour Research and Therapy, 4*:79–84, 1966.

Allen, K. E., Reynolds, N. J., Harris, F. R. and Baer, D. M.: Elimination of disruptive classroom behaviors of a pair of preschool boys through systematic control of adult social reinforcement. Unpublished manuscript, University of Washington, 1966.

Baer, D. M. and Wolf, M. M.: The reinforcement contingency in preschool and remedial education. Paper presented at the meeting of the Carnegie Foundation Conference on Preschool Education, Chicago, January, 1966.

Bijou, S. W. and Baer, D. M.: *Child Development.* New York, Appleton-Century-Crofts, 1965, vol. 2.

Brawley, E. R., Harris, F. R., Peterson, R. F., Allen, K. E. and Fleming, R. E.: Behavior modification of an autistic child. Unpublished manuscript, University of Washington, 1966.

Harris, F. R., Wolf, M. M. and Baer, D. M.: Effects of adult social reinforcement on child behavior. *Young Children, 20:*8–17, 1964.

Harris, F. R., Johnston, M. K., Kelley, C. S. and Wolf, M. M.: Effects of positive social reinforcement on regressed crawling in a preschool child. *Journal of Educational Psychology, 55:*35–41, 1964.

Hart, B. M., Allen, K. E., Buell, J. S., Harris, F. R. and Wolf, M. M.: Effects of social reinforcement on operant crying. *Journal of Experimental Child Psychology, 1:*145–153, 1964.

Hart, B. M., Reynolds, N. J., Brawley, E. R., Harris, F. R. and Baer, D. M. Effects of contingent and non-contingent social reinforcement of the isolate behavior of a nursery school girl. Unpublished manuscript, University of Washington, 1966.

Johnston, M. K., Kelley, C. S., Harris, F. R. and Wolf, M. M.: An application of reinforcement principles to development of motor skills of a young child. *Child Development, 37:*379–387, 1966.

Patterson, G. R., Jones, R., Whittier, J. and Wright, M. A.: A behavior modification technique for the hyperactive child. *Behaviour Research and Therapy, 2:*217–226, 1965.

Wolf, M. M., Risley, T. and Mees, H.: Application of operant conditioning procedures to the behavior problems of an autistic child. *Behaviour Research and Therapy, 1:*305–312, 1964.

Switching Requirements in a Head Start Classroom

JOAN M. JACOBSON, DON BUSHELL, JR., AND TODD RISLEY

Two experiments were conducted by the mothers of the children in a Head Start classroom. Both examined the effects of a switching task on the frequency with which children moved from one activity area of the classroom to another. The results indicated that the rate at which the children changed activities could be adjusted by varying the difficulty or magnitude of the switching task and that the task itself could be used to introduce academic subjects which would be poorly attended if initially presented in an activity area.

THERE ARE OCCASIONS when the staff of a preschool classroom judges it desirable to exert some degree of control over the movement of children from one activity area to another. Excessive switching from one task to the next may detract from an atmosphere conducive to instruction and may also set the occasion for teachers to deal with the children more abruptly than necessary. In the laboratory, the frequency of switching between stimulus conditions can be controlled by manipulating the "response require-

NOTE: The authors express appreciation to Dr. R. Vance Hall and to Mrs. Barbara Hughes for their invaluable assistance in all aspects of these studies and to Michael Kellerman for his assistance during Exp. I. This research was supported by Grants (CG-8474) from the Office of Economic Opportunity, Head Start Research and Demonstration, and (HD 03144) from the National Institute of Child Health and Human Development to the Bureau of Child Research and the Department of Human Development at the University of Kansas.

ment" for switching (Findley, 1958). This suggests that an analogous procedure might similarly control the frequency of physically "switching" from one place to another. This report describes the effects of a switching task on the frequency with which children moved from one activity area of a preschool classroom to the next.

Setting

The study was conducted in the Parent Cooperative Preschool of the Juniper Gardens Children's Project in Kansas City, Kansas (cf. Risley, 1968). The co-op class was conducted in the gymnasium of the Community Center from 8:30 A.M. to 11:30 A.M. four days each week. The large undifferentiated room was divided into activity areas with 4-foot high movable partitions; the materials for the areas were stored in movable boxes so the entire classroom arrangement could be folded out of the way at the end of each day's session, thus allowing the space to be used for other purposes in the afternoon.

The classroom operated much like other Head Start classes except that it was staffed by the mothers of the children who attended. The mothers were divided into three groups of 10, and each group participated in operating the program on a three-week rotation basis. The children, of course, attended regularly. The mothers supervised the activity areas, conducted group instruction, tutored individual children, and assumed responsibility for moving the children through each day's program. The present study was concerned with the effects of a classroom management procedure executed by the mothers during that period of each morning when the children were free to enter and leave any or all of the five activity areas. Mothers and children involved in this study met Office of Economic Opportunity guidelines of poverty necessary for enrollment in Head Start.

Switching System

The essentials of this system were (a) the explicit definition of the boundaries of each activity area (e.g. block area, manipulative toy area, creative materials area, climbing area, pre-reading area), and (b) the use of a switching task as a requirement for moving from one area to another. At the beginning of each session, the children were free to enter any area they might choose. When the switching task was employed, movement from the first area to another required that the child stop at a centrally located table and complete a simple matching problem (Exp. I) or academic task (Exp. II). Completion of this task enabled the child to select a ticket to enter an activity area of his choice. The child could stay in that area as long as he wished. Each move to another area required a stop at the central table and the completion of another task to obtain the appropriate ticket.

EXPERIMENT I
Procedures

During the initial year in which the switching requirement was employed, the switching task consisted of matching colored pegs on a pegboard. One or more "sample" rows of ten pegs of assorted colors (red, yellow, blue, green) were arranged in the pegboard in a different sequence each day. For a child to enter an activity area, he was required to fill in the lower, adjacent rows with pegs that matched the color of these pegs. Any peg that did not match the color of the corresponding peg in the sample row was simply removed by the supervising mother without comment. When a child completed the task and selected a ticket, his name was written on it and the ticket was stamped in a time clock. When the child subsequently left that activity area, his ticket was again stamped and retained by the teacher. The data on frequency of switches per hour were compiled from these tickets by dividing the number of tickets for each child each day by the total time he spent in the activity areas, as indicated by the times stamped on each ticket.

A switching requirement of one row of pegs was inserted for all children on the fourth day of the preschool year and was maintained at this level for most children throughout the year. During the last two months of the preschool year, the level of the switching requirement was individually altered for five children by varying the number of rows on the pegboard matching task.

TABLE 6-1
AVERAGE FREQUENCY OF SWITCHING

Child	Rows in Task	Days	Average Switches Per Hour
HW	1	9	3.6
	3	8	1.1
	1	13	3.2
DK	1	9	3.5
	3	8	1.6
	1	12	2.5
PS	1	9	2.3
	0	14	3.9
CW	1	9	1.3
	0	13	2.6
	1	2	0.9
	0	7	3.7
MM	1	18	2.8
	0	16	5.5
	5	6	1.4

Results

The average frequency of switches for the entire group of 30 children declined steadily from 5.5 per hour on the first day of the one-row switching requirement to 2.0 per hour by the thirteenth day, and remained at that level for the next 100 days of preschool. The average frequency of switches of each of the five children under various levels of the switching requirement is presented in Table 6-1. Daily switching rates of two of these children during various levels of the switching requirement are shown in Figure 6-1. With all five children, rate of switching from area to area was an inverse function of the number of rows in the switching task; the more rows in the task, the lower the rate of switching.

EXPERIMENT II
Procedures

During the second year, the switching procedure was evaluated in three phases. During the first and third phases, the children were allowed to switch freely from one area to another with no intermediate stops. During the second phase, the switching task required that area tickets be earned at the central table by placing 10 to 30 individual letters or 3 to 4 individual short words along-

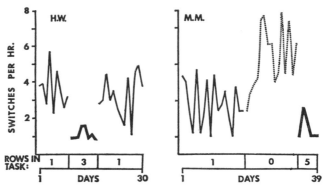

Figure 6-1. Daily switching rates of two children during periods of different switching requirements. The switching task consisted of matching 0, 1, 3 or 5 rows of colored pegs on a pegboard.

side matching letters or words on a sheet of paper. Observation and record keeping was accomplished by mothers seated at the entrance to each of the five areas. The observation and recording instruments consisted of a class roster and a 60-minute kitchen

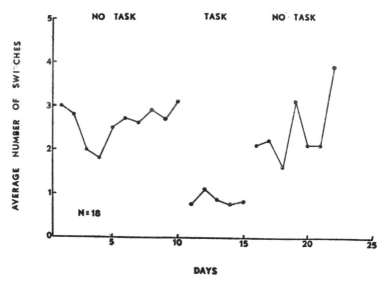

Figure 6-2. Average number of switches per hour from one activity area to another under task and no-task conditions. The task consisted of matching letters or combinations of letters.

timer. As each child entered or left an area, the entry and exit times were recorded beside the appropriate name on the roster by noting the number showing on the timer.

Reliability was checked in two ways. A second observer was occasionally stationed at the entrance to an activity area to make a duplicate record of arrivals and departures. Another check resulted from the fact that two independent notations were made each time a child moved from one area to another. The exit time from one area was checked for correspondence with the entry time to another area or to the switching table so that a complete minute-by-minute record was produced showing the activity of each child throughout the observation hour each day.

RESULTS

Reliability across all conditions was essentially 100 per cent, presumably because the entry or exit of a child from an area required him to pass immediately in front of the observers. For one month the mothers recorded the movement of the children from area to area when there was no switching task requirement. Their records during that time indicated that the children averaged approximately three switches per hour (average time in an area was 23 min). Seventy-seven percent of the children averaged two or more (up to 11) switches per hour.

When the switching requirement was introduced, the rate of switching immediately dropped to approximately 1 per hour and remained at that level. For the five days of this phase, an average of only 18 percent of the children switched areas two or more times. Figure 6-2 shows that the removal of the switching requirement on Day 16 corresponded to an immediate increase in the amount of switching. During the seven days of the final phase, 64 percent of the children averaged two or more switches per hour.

The effects of the switching requirement varied from child to child. The greatest effect was observed for a child who averaged 5.4 switches per hour during the first phase, 2.2 during the second phase, and 5.9 during the third phase. The median effect was, respectively, 2.0, 0.6, 2.6; and the smallest effect was 3.0, 1.4, 1.3.

For two children out of 18, the level of Phase-1 switching was not recovered during the third phase, although all children switched less during the second phase than during the first.

DISCUSSION

These investigations were conducted in order to determine the effects of several types and magnitudes of "response requirements" on the level of switching activity in the classroom. The results indicated that the rate of switching could be adjusted by varying the difficulty or magnitude of the switching task. Findley (1958) found that the average rate of switching between stimulus conditions could be controlled by the response requirements for switching. This study indicated that preacademic learning tasks could be similarly used to control the frequency of preschool children physically moving from one activity area to another. Premack has suggested that "of any two responses, the independently more probable one will reinforce the less probable one" (1963, p. 81). These effects might be interpreted in terms of the reciprocal of the "Premack Principle" (Premack, 1959), in which a presumed high-probability behavior (switching between activity areas) is reduced by requiring the child to engage in a presumed low-probability behavior (the switching task) contingent upon the high-probability behavior. However, in the absence of data on the independent probabilities of the various behaviors involved, this interpretation can only be suggested.

The results also suggest that the switching task itself may be used to introduce academic subjects which would be poorly attended if initially presented in an activity area. In a situation where children are allowed to choose between playing with blocks and learning how to print letters, a number of factors may influence a preference for blocks. By inserting printing as the switching task, it may be possible to bring the children in contact with the instructional activity without having to plead and coax that they stay and finish the assignment before running off to another area. Further, success at the switching task immediately results in a consequence determined by the child's preference. Consequently, this management procedure allows access to the various materials and events in the preschool classroom to become subject-selected back-up reinforcers (Whitlock and Bushell, 1967) for academic behavior instead of reinforcers contingent only on physical movement from one place to another. Hart and Risley (1968) and Reynolds and Risley (1968) have similarly found such materials and events to be effective and convenient reinforcers in preschool classrooms.

REFERENCES

Findley, J. D.: Preference and switching under concurrent scheduling. *Journal of the Experimental Analysis of Behavior, 1:*123–144, 1958.

Hart, Betty M. and Risley, T. R.: Establishing use of descriptive adjectives in the spontaneous speech of disadvantaged preschool children. *Journal of Applied Behavior Analysis, 1:*109–120, 1968.

Premack, D.: Toward emperical behavior laws: I. Positive reinforcement. *Psychological Review, 66:*219–233, 1959.

Premack, D.: Rate differential reinforcement in monkey manipulation. *Journal of the Experimental Analysis of Behavior, 6:*81–89, 1963.

Reynolds, Nancy J. and Risley, T. R.: The role of social and material reinforcers in increasing the talking of a disadvantaged preschool child. *Journal of Applied Behavior Analysis, 1:*253–262, 1968.

Risley, T. Learning and lollipops. *Psychology Today,* Dec., 1968, pp. 28–31.

Whitlock, C. and Bushell, D.: Some effects of "back-up" reinforcers on reading behavior. *Journal of Experimental Child Psychology, 5:*50–57, 1967.

7

Effect of Contingent and Noncontingent Social Reinforcement on the Cooperative Play of a Preschool Child

BETTY M. HART, NANCY J. REYNOLDS, DONALD M. BAER,
ELEANOR R. BRAWLEY and FLORENCE R. HARRIS

The effect of adult social reinforcement on the cooperative play of a five-year-old girl in a preschool setting was assessed under two conditions: (1) presented randomly throughout the school day, and (2) presented contingent on cooperative play. Only in the latter condition was a significant change in cooperative play observed.

A SERIES OF recent studies has shown that adult social stimulation, presented as a consequence of various behaviors of preschool children, successfully increased those behaviors (Allen *et al.*, 1964, 1967; Harris, *et al.*, 1964; Baer and Wolf, 1968). In each case, the child's behavior was modified by making this teacher reinforcement both frequent and contingent upon the behavior, whereas previously reinforcement had been intermittent and noncontingent. In this study, a simple comparison was made of the

NOTE: This research was supported by PHS grants MH-02208 and MH-11768, National Institute of Mental Health, entitled An Experimental Analysis of Social Motivation.

From the *Journal of Applied Behavior Analysis, 1*:73–76, 1968. Copyright 1968 by the Society for the Experimental Analysis of Behavior Inc. Reprinted with permission of the authors and publisher.

separate roles of frequent reinforcement and contingent reinforcement in developing the cooperative play of a preschool child.

METHOD
Subject

Martha, aged five years, four months, was enrolled in a group of 15 normal children in a university preschool. The group attended school five afternoons per week for approximately 2.5 hr each day. Most of Martha's time at school was spent in nonsocial tricycle-riding, sand play, swinging, "cooking" and playing with animal toys. Her contacts with other children, though frequent, tended to be brief and noncooperative. Her refusals to play when invited, her taunts and competitive statements ("I can do that better than you") and her foul language and rambling accounts of violent accidents perhaps made her aversive to other children. These behaviors, her frequent upsetting of materials and her typical delay in fulfilling routines seemed to have a similar effect on teachers.

Procedures
General Procedures

The general plan of study was built upon a "reversal" design incorporating two different contingencies of reinforcement. The baseline consisted of normal preschool practices, composed essentially of intermittent attention to Martha, in no particular contingency. The first type of reinforcement consisted of greatly increased and carefully noncontingent [1] social reinforcement from teachers. There then followed a period of decreased reinforcement presented contingent upon cooperative play or approximations to it. Following clear evidence of behavioral change, this condition was discontinued and a return to the prior condition, frequent noncontingent reinforcement, was instituted. This was done to

---

[1] In this report, the term "noncontingent reinforcement" means reinforcement presenting according to random intervals of time, without regard for what behavior might be occurring at those times. It is to be distinguished from the term DRO (differential reinforcement of other than cooperative behavior).

demonstrate experimental control of the behavioral change, thus validating the functional nature of the contingent reinforcement used to bring it about and again demonstrating the previously noted lack of function in frequent but noncontingent reinforcement. As soon as this was clear, decreased but contingent reinforcement was again instituted, and a more intermittent schedule was approached.

Approximations to cooperative play were reinforced when necessary in the first stages of shaping the behavior. These approximations were typically verbal responses to children who had been prompted by the teachers to approach Martha with an idea for play. Verbal response was a minor component of cooperative play (as defined below), but was judged a good behavioral route to the cooperative behaviors ultimately sought.

The major behavior observed and treated experimentally was cooperation between Martha and any other children. In addition, a second class of behavior, Martha's proximity to other children, was observed and recorded. Proximity was studied in part because it is often taken as evidence of a social orientation in a child, and in part because it existed at a considerable rate in Martha from the outset, and could easily be mistaken for a cooperative social orientation when in fact it need not be.

Specific Procedures

For 10 days, Martha's teachers maintained their ongoing pattern of responding to her intermittently and without regard for her immediately preceding behavior. Objective records were taken of Martha's rates of cooperative play and of maintaining simple proximity to other children. This constituted the baseline period of the study.

Cooperative play was defined specifically as any of the following activities: pulling a child or being pulled by a child in a wagon; handing an object to a child, or pouring into his hands or into a container held by him; helping a child by supporting him physically, or bringing, putting away or building something verbalized as expressly for him; sharing something with a child by digging in the same hole, carrying the same object, painting on the same paper or from the same paint pot, or adding to the same structure or construction (such as a chain of manipulative toys, or a block house).

Proximity was defined as being within 3 feet of another child indoors and within 6 feet outdoors.

For the next seven days, the teachers displayed attention and approval in close proximity to Martha at random intervals throughout the school session, so that approximately 80 percent of each session involved such interaction. This constituted the first period of noncontingent reinforcement.

Teacher reinforcement consisted of remaining near Martha and attending closely to her activities, sometimes supplying her with equipment or materials, and sometimes smiling, laughing, conversing and admiring her.

Subsequently, for a period of 12 days, Martha received the same teacher reinforcement only as a consequence of cooperative play or behavior conducive to cooperative play. This constituted the first reinforcement of cooperative play.

Since Martha emitted cooperative play at a very low rate initially, it was necessary to use priming and shaping procedures. Priming meant that other children were prompted to speak to Martha or initiate potentially cooperative situations with her. (No such promptings were ever given to Martha herself.) Shaping meant that Martha was initially reinforced for all responsive verbalizations in proximity to children, subsequently only for such verbalization in potentially cooperative situations, and finally (by the seventh day of this 12-day period) only for full-blown cooperative play.

After these 12 days, noncontingent stimulation was resumed for four days, the second noncontingent reinforcement period. Again, teachers interacted with Martha for approximately 80 percent of each school session.

Finally, over an eight-day period (the last eight days of the school year), the teachers again resumed contingent reinforcement of cooperative play, constituting the second reinforcement of cooperative play. During the last four days of this period, the teachers steadily decreased their rate of reinforcing cooperative play and correspondingly increased their attention to desirable behaviors other than cooperative play, to regain a more typical reinforcement schedule for the girl and to see if the rate of co-operative play would be maintained nevertheless.

Recording

Data on Martha's behavior were recorded daily in consecutive 10-second intervals by an observer. Observation was continuous during the school-day session, except for a teacher-structured group-activity period of 20 to 30 minutes daily. In recording Martha's behavior, the observer used the categories of proximity, cooperative play and teacher reinforcement. The child's scores for any day were the percentages of the 10-second intervals marked as involving proximity or cooperative play.

Observer reliability was checked on five separate days by having a second observer record Martha's behavior in the same fashion as the first. Comparison of total incidences of proximity, co-operative play and teacher reinforcement yielded 92 percent or better agreement on each of the five days.

RESULTS AND DISCUSSION

The percentage of each session involving proximity and cooper-ative play is graphed in Figure 7-1. It can be seen that during the baseline period, Martha was in proximity to children roughly 50 percent of the day; at the same time, her rate of cooperative play was 5 percent or less of the day, and on five of the ten days, 0 percent. Teacher reinforcement averaged about 20 percent of the school day.

When Martha was then given continual, noncontingent teacher reinforcement for about 80 percent of each session (Days 11 through 17 in Fig. 7-1), her rate of proximity to children varied sporadically between about 40 percent and 90 percent of the day, the average rising to about 65 percent. Probably this was due in part to the attraction of other children to a situation in which a teacher was giving close and continual attention. The decline in the rate of proximity to children after Day 15 might indicate the adaptation of the other children to a teacher always being some-where near Martha. Except for Day 14 (when Martha's favorite

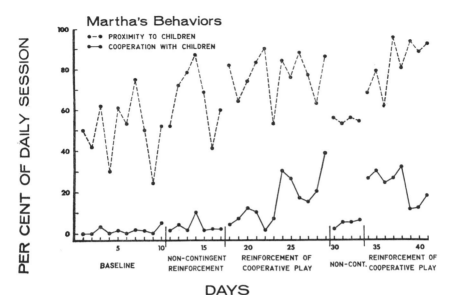

Figure 7-1. Daily percentages of proximity and cooperative play over sequential experimental conditions.

companion returned from four days of hospitalization and she spent some time pulling him in a wagon), there was no overall change in Martha's rate of cooperative play, which still averaged less than 5 percent of the day.

After the eighteenth day, when teacher reinforcement of Martha was made contingent on cooperative play or approximations to it, the rate of teacher reinforcement dropped to its baseline level, and frequently amounted to less than 20 percent of the day; yet at the same time Martha's rate of cooperative play increased from 4 percent of the day to almost 40 percent. In the course of developing this increase, teachers found that their verbalizations to Martha frequently drew her out of cooperative play with a child and into interaction with them; therefore, reinforcement was given with increasing frequency to the entire cooperating group rather than to Martha as an individual.

Figure 7-1 shows that during the period of reinforcement of cooperative play, Martha's proximity to children increased to about 75 percent of the day and was maintained at approximately that level. When Martha was again given almost continual noncontingent teacher reinforcement for any and all behavior (beginning on Day 30), both proximity to children and cooperative play dropped almost to their baseline levels. Martha again spent about 55 percent of the school day in proximity with children and only 5 percent in cooperation with them; yet teacher reinforcement had increased from near 20 percent of the day to about 80 percent. During this time, cooperative play was not ignored; like any of the rest of Martha's behaviors, it might be reinforced if it occurred while a teacher was present. However, teachers during this period went to Martha immediately upon her arrival to school rather than waiting for a cooperative behavior to occur and thus tended to reinforce behaviors sometimes incompatible with cooperative play at the start of each school day.

When teacher reinforcement was again made contingent upon cooperative play, a high rate of the behavior was immediately recovered and was maintained for four days (Days 34 to 37) at 25 percent or more of the day. In this process, teacher reinforcement again decreased to about 20 percent of the day. Martha's proximity to children (not reinforced as such) rose again to a 75 percent average.

When teachers began on Day 38 to generalize reinforcement from specifically cooperative behaviors to broader categories of play, there were only four days of school remaining. As can be seen in Figure 7-1, teacher reinforcement of cooperative behaviors was decreased too quickly during the first three days, and Martha's rate of cooperative play declined, though not to its baseline level. During this time, however, Martha was spending approximately 90 percent of the day in proximity to children. Her interactions with them appeared to be not only of much longer duration, but of a more positive nature than had characterized baseline interactions. Teachers judged that Martha had changed from an "obnoxious" girl to one who was "sometimes unpleasant." A high rate of "obnoxious" behavior could hardly co-exist with a high rate of cooperative play, of course, but many preschool children are capable of alternating between the two repertoires.

It can be seen in Figure 7-1 that noncontingent reinforcement, whether continual or intermittent, did not appreciably develop cooperative play. Only when reinforcement was made contingent upon the behavior did any reliable change in rate appear. Hence, the data indicate that the behavior change was less a function of teacher attention (whether "a lot" or a "little") than it was a function of teacher attention made contingent on the behavior. Yet it is frequently assumed that children display hostile or angry (noncooperative) behaviors as a result of too little positive attention from the adults in their environment. In this case, at least, abundant positive attention from all involved adults had no power to develop a cooperative replacement for Martha's unpleasant behaviors as long as it was presented as a noncontingent gift. Yet a much smaller amount of reinforcement could drastically alter her behavior, so long as it occurred in contingency with that behavior. Furthermore, it is to be noted that abundant but noncontingent attention could not maintain Martha's newly shaped cooperative repertoire when contingent reinforcement was discontinued early in that development. It would seem, then, that to whatever extent Martha's behavior can serve as a guide, deliberate behavior modification is likely to proceed more effectively when it is based upon contingent, rather than abundant, stimulation.

REFERENCES

Allen, K. Eileen, Hart, Betty M., Buell, Joan S., Harris, Florence R. and Wolf, M. M.: Effects of social reinforcement on isolate behavior of a nursery school child. *Child Development, 35:*511–518, 1964.

Allen, K. Eileen, Henke, Lydia B., Harris, Florence, R., Baer, D. M. and Reynolds, Nancy J.: Control of hyperactivity by social reinforcement of attending behavior. *Journal of Educational Psychology, 58:*231–237, 1967.

Baer, D. M. and Wolf, M. M.: The reinforcement contingency in preschool and remedial education. In Hess, R. D. and Baer, Roberta M. (Eds.): *Early Education: Current Theory, Research, and Practice.* Chicago, Aldine, 1968.

Harris, Florence R., Johnston, Margaret K., Kelley, C. Susan and Wolf, M. M.: Effects of positive social reinforcement on regressed crawling of a nursery school child. *Journal of Educational Psychology, 55:*35–41, 1964.

Hart, Betty M., Allen, K. Eileen, Buell, Joan S., Harris, Florence R. and Wolf, M. M.: Effects of social reinforcement on operant crying. *Journal of Experimental Child Psychology, 1:*145–153, 1964.

8

Child-Child Interactions in Free Field Settings: Some Experimental Analyses

Robert G. Wahler

This study was concerned with investigating peer group variables which may control the social behavior of children in free play settings. Five preschool children and their peers served as subjects. Methodologically the experimental procedure followed an intrasubject replication design which involved repeated manipulation of the same experimental variables to insure reliability. The results demonstrate that the preschool child's behavior in free field settings may be subject to the reinforcement control of his peers. In four of five subjects studied, the data show that peer social attention can act as a set of positive reinforcers and control the social behavior of other children.

CHILD-CHILD INTERACTIONS have recently received the attention of several reinforcement theorists who are concerned with laboratory investigations of child behavior (Hartup, 1964; Horowitz, 1962; Patterson and Anderson, 1964; Tikten and Hartup, 1965). These investigators have conceptualized the child, not only as a behaving organism but also as a source of reinforcement for the behavior of other children. For example, Hartup (1964) and Patterson and Anderson (1964) have shown that a child's behavior in the laboratory can be controlled through social approval dispensed by a member of the child's peer group.

NOTE: This study was supported by research Grant MH11759-01 from the National Institute of Mental Health. The author is grateful to Dennis Freeman and Wesley Morgan, who served as observers in the study.

From the *Journal of Experimental Child Psychology,* 5:278–293, 1967. Copyright 1967 by Academic Press Inc. Reprinted with permission of authors and publisher.

The above studies have provided some interesting experimental analyses of child-child interactions within laboratory environments. As of yet, however, there have been no experimental studies on this topic within free or naturalistic environments. While volumes of naturalistic data on child-child interactions have been generated by psychological ecologists such as Barker and Wright (1949, 1954, 1963, 1965), these researchers have preferred to limit their procedures to systematic observation. As a result, only correlational and normative data are available, making it difficult to specify the effects which children have on each other. If experimental procedures are applicable to this problem, it should prove possible to demonstrate these effects with little ambiguity.

Given a group of preschool children in a naturalistic setting, extended observation would probably reveal that some responses of any one child are frequently correlated in time with certain responses of the other children (Parten, 1932, 1933; Shure, 1963). For example, on those occasions when a child screams and stamps his feet, the other children may watch him or walk over to him. Or when a child begins a block-building project, other children may ask his permission to help. On the basis of such observations, it would be assumed from a reinforcement theory viewpoint that some of the child's behavior in these settings may be controlled or maintained by the contingent behavior of his peers. If this assumption can be shown to be valid, further information would be added to the currently known picture of those naturalistic events which may control the preschool child's social behavior. Thus far it has been demonstrated that parents and teachers may function in natural settings as powerful sources of reinforcement and thus control a variety of the child's social actions (Harris *et al.*, 1964; Wahler *et al.*, 1965). As the earlier-cited laboratory and observational analyses suggest, preschool peer groups probably add a further component to these sources of control. The present study was designed to yield data relevant to this possibility.

METHOD
Subjects and Apparatus

Subjects were five children and members of their preschool peer group, all ranging in age from five to six years. All children were enrolled in the University of Tennessee Nursery School.

The apparatus involved an Esterline-Angus twenty-pen event recorder and two operating panels, each containing ten microswitches arranged in a horizontal row. When depressed, these microswitches activated selected pens on the event recorder.

General Procedure

At the beginning of the study, when procedural problems were expected to be greatest, it was decided to place some restrictions on the free-field setting in which the children were observed. This involved E placing S and two randomly selected peers in a large playroom and instructing them to play in one section of this room until E returned 15 minutes later. These restrictions were in effect for the first three S's. The last two S's were studied in their natural nursery school environment, composed of a large playroom with approximately twelve peers and three or four teachers. These S's were observed for 15-minute intervals, scheduled three times weekly at the same time of day.

Behavior Classification Sessions

For the first few sessions, two observers, operating in a concealed observation booth, obtained written records of S's verbal and nonverbal behavior, plus any peer behavior which was contingent upon S's behavior. For the last two S's, who were observed in a setting composed of teachers as well as peers, teacher contingent behavior was also recorded. These sessions were terminated when the observers decided that they had obtained a stable picture of S's most frequently occurring responses and their usual contingencies. At this point, S's responses were grouped into classes on the basis of topographic similarities among the separate responses. Contingent peer and teacher responses were initially classified in the same way until a later analysis of the data revealed that the observers were unable to record reliably multiple response classes for both S and peers and teachers. It was then decided to consider peer and teacher contingencies as two stimulus classes, namely peer social attention and teacher social attention. These classes included, "looking at S, physical contact with *S*, and verbal or nonverbal behavior which clearly involved *S*."

Observer Reliability and Baseline Observations

In further sessions, the observers made their recordings via the multichannel event recorder. A timing device was also introduced which produced an audible click in the observation booth every 10 seconds. The observers were instructed to quickly depress and release selected microswitches upon hearing the click if members of any of the previously defined response classes or contingent stimulus classes occurred during the preceding ten-second interval. Thus, for any response class or contingent stimulus class, the maximum rate of occurrence was one event per ten-second interval.

In obtaining observer reliability, *E* monitored the event recorder and called out disagreements to the observers immediately after they occurred. When a disagreement occurred, the observers stopped recording and discussed the problem. Discussion generally involved a review of the component members of the class or classes which were involved in the disagreement. After each of the observer training sessions, the event recorder records were analyzed for reliability. For each class, an agreement or disagreement was tallied for every ten-second interval and the percentage of agreements for observers was then computed for each class. Once the agreement percentage for all the classes reached 90 percent or better, the baseline sessions were begun. At this point, one of the observers was arbitrarily chosen to record the data, and the other observer served as a reliability check. In all cases, reliability checks showed observer agreement of 90 percent or better on all classes.

The length and number of baseline periods varied for the five *S*'s. For *S*'s one, two and three, the baseline period lasted 5 minutes and was immediately followed by two 5-minute experimental manipulation periods. Longer baseline periods were not deemed necessary with these *S*'s, since their behavior and that of their peers was remarkably consistent in earlier sessions. For *S*'s four and five, who were seen in much less restricted settings, several 15-minute sessions were devoted to baseline observations.

Experimental Manipulation of Peer Contingencies

Following the baseline period, one of S's response classes was selected for experimental analysis. The selection procedure was based on response rate; a class was selected if its baseline rate was exceptionally high compared with other classes or exceptionally low. It was hoped that this selection would increase the chances of detecting peer reinforcement control through maximizing the possible rate changes following manipulation of peer contingencies.

When a response class was selected, E met with S's peers for a short session while S played alone. With S's four and five, who were in the large group, only those peers who frequently provided contingencies for S's behavior were seen by E. In these sessions, E told the peers that they were to "play a new game" with S. The instructions then differed, depending on whether the response class under analysis was one of low rate or of high rate. For a high-rate class the peers were told to play with S in any way they wished, except when he emitted members of the predetermined response class; then they were to ignore him until he did something different. Several examples of the to-be-ignored response class were given to them through E's imitation of the specific responses involved. In addition, E "pretended" that he was S and played the game with the peers. During the game, E made approving comments to the peers following their appropriate responses to E's behavior.

For a low-rate class E told the peers to be selectively responsive to this class. In other words, they were instructed to ignore S completely unless he emitted members of this class; then they should play with him as long as he continued to produce this behavior. As in the high-rate class instructions, E gave examples of this behavior and imitated S's behavior in a game.

After the peer instruction sessions, the peers were returned to S and the observers continued their recording. When the observational records revealed that the peers were behaving appropriately and when S's selected response class showed a change in its baseline rate, the next procedural step was attempted. This step involved a second manipulation of peer behaviors in an effort to reinstate the baseline contingencies between the selected response class and peer behavior. This step was attempted through use of the previously described manipulation sessions with the peers.

RESULTS
Subject No. 1

Sally, a five-year-old girl, was randomly selected to serve as the first *S*. Two other five-year-olds, a boy and a girl, were randomly selected as her peers. Prior to the first session, *E* told the three children that they were going to play in a "special room with new toys" and that they must remain in a designated part of the room. *E* then left them alone for 15 minutes, after which they were returned to their regular preschool group. This trio was seen for a total of four 15-minute sessions; three of the sessions were used for behavior classification purposes and the fourth served as baseline and experimental manipulation periods.

During the classification sessions, three kinds of behavior appeared to be consistent parts of Sally's repertoire: doll play (playing with dolls, doll furniture, etc.), instructions (commands or suggestions) and other toy play (with guns, cars, etc.). Of the three, doll play was by far the most frequent, followed by instructions and play with other toys. Only the female peer member was responsive to these classes. The boy ignored both girls and played with building blocks during the sessions.

Figure 8-1 shows cumulative records of Sally's three response classes and peer social attention to these classes during the fourth session. Notice that the baseline response rate of doll play was higher than the rates of the other two classes, and peer attention to doll play was continuous during the baseline period. As in the classification sessions, attention was provided by the girl only.

Following the baseline period, doll play was selected for experimental analysis. In an instruction session, Sally's peers were treated to a brief manipulation procedure described in the general procedure section of this paper. Essentially they were told to ignore doll play but to remain responsive to other classes of behavior. Reference to the first manipulation period shown in Figure 8-1 indicates their success in following these instructions;

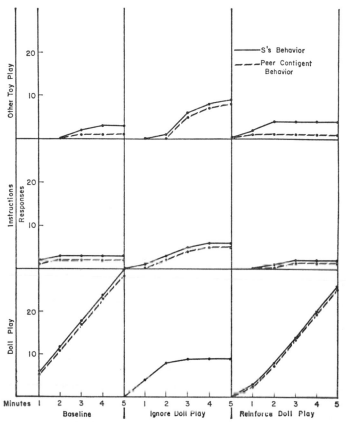

Figure 8-1. Cumulative records of doll play, instructions, other toy play and peer contingent attention for one baseline and two experimental manipulation periods.

peer attention (from the female peer alone) was contingent only upon instructions and other toy play. Correlated with this shift in peer contingencies, doll play decreased in rate compared with the baseline period, and the two other classes increased.

Following the manipulation period, a second peer manipulation was attempted in an effort to reinstate the baseline contingencies for Sally's response classes. In a brief session with *S*'s peers, *E* carried out the previously described manipulation procedure, in which the female peer was told to resume her attention to Sally's doll play. As the last manipulation period in Figure 8-1 shows, they were again successful in following instructions, and as expected, doll play increased in rate compared with the second manipulation session, while the other two classes decreased. Thus the finding that doll play could be weakened when peer contingencies were removed and strengthened when they were reinstated points with some certainty to the fact that Sally's doll play was under the reinforcement control of her peers (in this case the female peer).

Subject No. 2

Dick, a five-year-old boy, was selected randomly along with two girls, also five years of age. All were given the same instructions as were the first three. The trio was seen for a total of four 15-minute sessions, three of which were used for behavior classification purposes and the fourth as baseline and experimental manipulation periods.

During the classification sessions, four kinds of behavior appeared to be consistent parts of Dick's repertoire: aggressive behavior (shouting, running, and throwing toys), passive behavior (sitting, quiet talk and slow, methodical play with toys), instructions (commands or suggestions) and stuttering (speech impediment). Both peers responded to these classes, usually by laughing, smiling or running with Dick.

Figure 8-2 shows cumulative records of Dick's four response classes and peer social attention contingencies during the fourth session. Examination of the baseline period reveals that Aggressive Behavior occurred at a higher rate than the other three classes, and peer attention to this class was continuous.

Following the baseline period, aggressive behavior was selected for experimental analysis. Dick's peers were treated to the manipulation procedure which was used for S No. 1. The first manipulation period shown in Figure 8-2 shows the peer's general success in following instructions; only one peer response was made contingent upon aggressive behavior during this period. Correlated with this shift in peer contingencies, aggressive behavior decreased in rate compared with the baseline period, but passive behavior and instructions increased.

Figure 8-2 also shows E's success in reinstating peer contingencies during the second manipulation period. After instructions

CHILD-CHILD INTERACTIONS

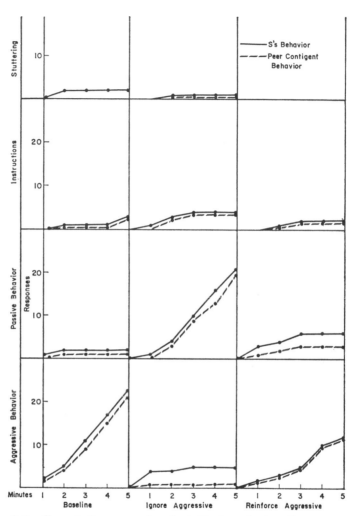

Figure 8-2. Cumulative records of stuttering, instructions, aggressive behavior, passive behavior and peer contingent attention for one baseline and two experimental manipulation periods.

to resume their attention to Dick's aggressive behavior, the peers produced their attention on a continuous schedule following the aggressive behavior. As the second manipulation period of Figure 8-2 indicates, aggressive behavior increased in rate compared with the first manipulation period, and other response classes decreased. As was true for *S* No. 1, peer reinforcement control was demonstrated, this time for an aggressive class of behavior.

Subject No. 3

Eddie, a five-year-old boy, was selected randomly along with two other five-year-old boys. All were given the same instructions as were the first two trios of children. This trio was seen for a total of three 15-minute sessions, two of which were used for behavior classification purposes and the third for baseline and experimental manipulation periods.

During the classification sessions, three kinds of behavior appeared to be consistent parts of Eddie's repertoire: cooperative behavior (playing a game initiated by peers), solitary play (playing alone at a nonpeer initiated game) and shouting. Peer responses were about equally divided between the two boys and were mainly contingent upon cooperative behavior. Their contingent responses usually involved verbal comments to *S* as he played the games.

Figure 8-3 shows cumulative records of Eddie's three response classes and peer social attention contingencies during the third session. Cooperative behavior showed higher baseline rates than the other two classes, and peer attention was contingent upon this class.

Following the baseline period, cooperative behavior was selected for experimental analysis. Eddie's peers were treated to the same manipulation procedure which was used for *S*'s No. 1 and 2. As the second manipulation period of Figure 8-3 indicates, peer contingencies were not eliminated for cooperative behavior but were markedly reduced compared to the baseline period. Correlated with the drop in peer contingent attention, cooperative behavior dropped in rate compared with the baseline period. Solitary play and shouting increased in rate during this period.

Figure 8-3 also shows *E*'s success in reinstating peer contingencies for cooperative behavior during the third manipulation period. Following *E*'s instructions to resume their attention to Eddie's cooperative behavior, the peers were continuously atten-

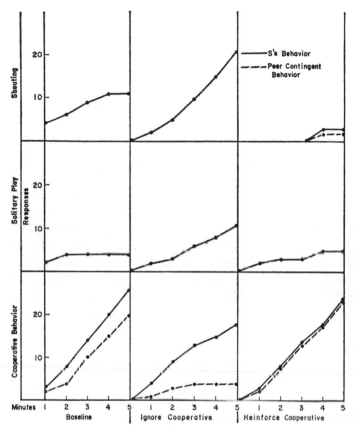

Figure 8-3. Cumulative records of cooperative behavor, solitary play, shouting and peer contingent attention for one baseline and two experimental manipulation periods.

tive to this class and, as expected, cooperative behavior increased in rate, while other response classes decreased. Thus, like *S*'s No. 1 and 2, Eddie's behavior showed evidence of peer reinforcement control.

Subject No. 4

Jimmie, a five-year-old boy, was selected because of *E*'s interest in reports that Jimmie was unusually isolated from the other children. According to his teachers, Jimmie seldom interacted with the other children, usually preferring to play alone or watch the others. Jimmie was studied in his natural nursery school environment, composed of twelve to fifteen peers and three or four teachers. At the beginning of the baseline sessions the teachers were instructed to ignore Jimmie completely during all sessions.

Jimmie was observed for a total of nine sessions, three of which were used for behavior classification and six for baseline and experimental manipulation purposes. All sessions were 15 minutes long and scheduled every other day during the nursery school free play time.

During the classification sessions, three kinds of behavior appeared to be consistent parts of Jimmie's repertoire: speech (mainly directed to peers), looking (interactions restricted to observing others) and cooperative behavior (playing a game initiated by peers). Peer and teacher social attention was seldom contingent upon any of these classes.

Figure 8-4 shows frequency counts of Jimmie's three response classes and peer social attention contingencies during the three baseline sessions. Examination of response classes during these sessions reveals a remarkable intersession consistency in rate for

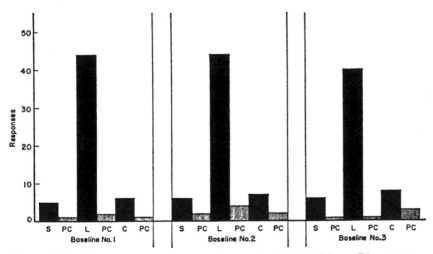

Figure 8-4. Frequency measures of speech (S), looking (L), cooperative behavior (C) and peer contingent attention (PC) for three baseline sessions.

the various classes. Looking was by far the most frequently occurring response class, followed by cooperative behavior and speech. Peer contingencies were infrequent for these classes.

Following the last baseline session, speech was selected for experimental analysis. Since two peers (boys) provided most of the baseline contingencies, they were selected for manipulation purposes. In a brief session they were treated to the "low-rate" manipulation procedure described in the general procedure section of this paper. Essentially they were told to be selectively attentive to Jimmie's speech; if he talked to them they were to respond to him immediately and frequently in any approving way.

Figure 8-5 describes the same response classes and their contingencies during three manipulation sessions. Reference to the first of these sessions reveals that speech and cooperative behavior increased in frequency compared with the baseline sessions, while looking dropped markedly. The increase in peer contingencies for cooperative behavior as well as for speech indicates the peer's failure to accurately follow instructions during those sessions, plus the fact that peers other than those instructed by *E* added their contingencies to these response classes. According to the teachers, Jimmie's "status" with the group as a whole seemed to increase during the session.

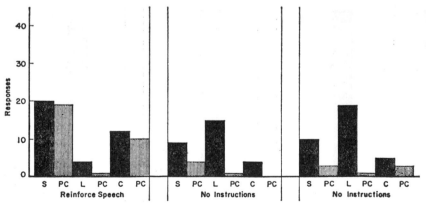

Figure 8-5. Frequency measures of speech (S), looking (L), cooperative behavior (C) and peer contingent attention (PC) for three experimental manipulation sessions.

The last two sessions shown in Figure 8-5 represent *E*'s efforts to reinstate baseline contingencies for Jimmie's response classes. It was anticipated that *E*'s instructional effects on *S*'s peers would probably diminish rapidly with time, and since the sessions were each separated by almost 24 hours, *E* expected that peer baseline contingencies could be reinstated by simply eliminating further instructions to the peers. As the last two sessions of Figure 8-5 indicate, this expectation was borne out. Peer contingencies for all response classes are similar to their baseline frequencies. In addition, Cooperative Behavior and Speech dropped in frequency compared with the first manipulation session, and Looking increased, thus supporting the assumption of peer reinforcement control of Jimmie's speech and cooperative behavior.

Subject No. 5

Betty, a six-year-old girl, was selected because of *E*'s interest in teacher reports that her behavior had changed markedly over a 2-month period of time. When Betty entered the preschool group 6 months prior to this study, she immediately presented problems for the teachers through her hyperactivity, oppositional behavior and hitting or pushing the other children. Then, after about 4 to 5 months, these behavior patterns began to decline in frequency until she was considered to be a problem on periodic occasions only. The teachers attributed these changes to their "tightened control" of her and "greater peer acceptance."

Betty was studied in her natural nursery school environment, composed of twelve to fifteen peers and three to four teachers. She was observed for a total of nine sessions, three of which were used for behavior classification and six for baseline and experimental manipulation purposes. All sessions were 15 minutes long and scheduled every other day during the nursery school free play time.

During the classification sessions, four kinds of behavior appeared to be consistent parts of Betty's repertoire: spontaneous behavior (changing interactions with objects or peers with no observable cue), cooperative behavior (playing a game initiated by peers), aggressive behavior (shouting, running and hitting) and passive behavior (quiet speech, sitting and slow, methodical play with toys). Peer and teacher social attention was frequently contingent upon all of these classes.

Figure 8-6 shows frequency counts of Betty's four response classes and peer and teacher contingencies during two of the four baseline sessions. Examination of response classes during these sessions reveals good intersession consistency in rate for the various classes. Passive behavior was by far the most frequently occurring response class, followed by spontaneous behavior, cooperative behavior and aggressive behavior. Social attention contingencies were provided frequently by both peers and teachers.

Figure 8-7 describes the same response classes and their contingencies during baseline sessions three and four. For these sessions, the teachers were instructed to ignore Betty completely.

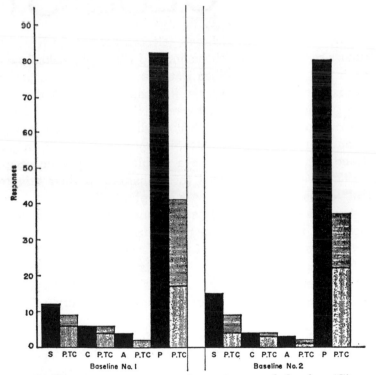

Figure 8-6. Frequency measures of spontaneous behavior (S), cooperative behavior (C), aggressive behavior (A), passive behavior (P), and peer and teacher contingent attention (PTC) for two baseline sessions.

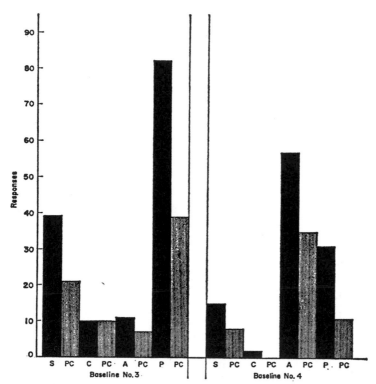

Figure 8-7. Frequency measures of spontaneous behavior (S), cooperative behavior (C), aggressive behavior (A), passive behavior (P), and peer contingent attention (PC) for two baseline sessions.

Moderate rate changes occurred in spontaneous and aggressive behavior during the third session, and during the fourth session marked rate changes occurred; aggressive behavior increased dramatically in rate while passive behavior and cooperative behavior dropped. Peer social attention was frequently contingent on all classes. At this point, it would have been interesting to assess the effect of teacher social attention by reinstating earlier contingencies. However, since E was more interested in peer influence this was not done.

Following the dramatic increase in Betty's aggressive behavior during the fourth baseline session, E intended to schedule further baseline sessions to assess the reliability of this change. However, because of general concern over Betty's aggressive behavior it was decided to manipulate peer contingencies in further sessions. Passive behavior was selected for the analysis. Since two children (a boy and a girl) provded most of the later baseline contingencies, they were selected for manipulation purposes. In brief sessions they were treated to the "low-rate" manipulation procedure, essentially instructing them to be selectively attentive to Betty's passive behavior.

Figure 8-8 describes response classes and peer contingencies during two manipulation sessions. Prior to each session, the "low-rate" peer manipulation procedure was carried out by E, and the teachers were instructed to continue ignoring Betty. As Figure 8-8 reveals, the peers were fairly successful in following these in-

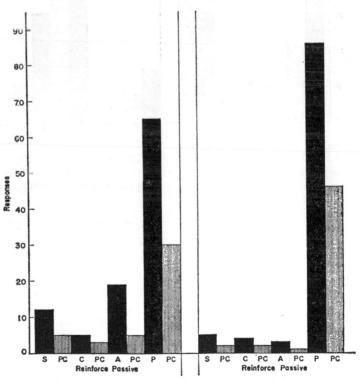

Figure 8-8. Frequency measures of spontaneous behavior (S), cooperative behavior (C), aggressive behavior (A), passive behavior (P), and peer contingent attention (PC) for two experimental manipulation sessions.

structions; the majority of their social attention was contingent upon Passive Behavior, although a few contingencies were also provided for other behavior. As expected, passive behavior dramatically increased in frequency and aggressive behavior decreased.

It would have been desirable from an experimental design standpoint to further demonstrate peer reinforcement control of Betty's passive behavior by performing other peer contingency manipulations for this response class. However, since the teachers were becoming increasingly worried about the effect of the experimental interventions on Betty, it was decided not to conduct further manipulations. Thus, evidence of peer reinforcement control cannot be considered as reliable for this S as it was for the other four S's.

DISCUSSION

The data reported in this study indicated that the preschool child's behavior in free field settings may be subject to the reinforcement control of his peers. Experimental analyses of several child-peer interactions revealed that peer social attention could control a variety of S's' social behaviors, such as cooperative behavior, aggressive behavior, and speech. That is, through E's instructions, the peer groups were able to predictably alter the strength of these response classes by manipulating their social attention contingencies.

The above findings are consistent with laboratory data on peer reinforcement control of child behavior (Hartup, 1964; Horowitz, 1962; Patterson and Anderson, 1964; Tikten and Hartup, 1965). Further support is thus given to the contention that the peer group may influence significantly the behavior of its individual members. While several free field studies have demonstrated adult control of child behavior (Harris *et al.*, 1964; Wahler *et al.*, 1965), this investigation provides the first experimental evidence that the peer group may serve a similar function in naturalistic settings.

Although the behavioral control demonstrated in this study was of a short-term nature, it was rather dramatic in most of the groups studied. If this degree of peer reinforcement control could be maintained by adult directions over longer periods of time, practical implications would follow. For example, the child who presents social problems in the classroom and other child group situations might be most effectively treated by procedures which allow control of peer social attention contingencies as well as those provided by adults.

REFERENCES

Barker, R. G. (Ed.): *The Stream of Behavior.* New York, Appleton-Century-Crofts, 1963.

Barker, R. G.: Explorations in ecological psychology. *American Psychologist., 20*:1–14, 1965.

Barker, R. G. and Wright, H. F.: Psychological ecology and the problem of psychosocial development. *Child Development, 20*:131–143, 1949.

Barker, R. G. and Wright, H. F. *Midwest and Its Children: the Psychological Ecology of an American Town.* New York, Rowe Peterson, 1954.

Harris, F. R., Wolf, M. M. and Baer, D. M.: Effects of adult social reinforcement on child behavior. *Young Children, 20*:8–17, 1964.

Hartup, W. W.: Friendship status and the effectiveness of peers as reinforcing agents. *Journal of Experimental Child Psychology, 1*:154–162, 1964.

Horowitz, F.: Incentive value of social stimuli for pre-school children. *Child Development, 33*:111–116, 1962.

Lovaas, O. I., Freitag, G., Gold, V. J. and Kassorla, I. C.: Recording apparatus and procedure for observation of behaviors of children in free-play settings. *Journal of Experimental Child Psychology., 2*:108–120, 1965.

Parten, M. B.: Social participation among preschool children. *Journal of Abnormal Social Psychology, 27*:243–269, 1932.

Parten, M. B.: Social play among preschool children. *Journal of Abnormal Social Psychology, 28*:136–147, 1933.

Patterson, G. R. and Anderson, D.: Peers as social reinforcers. *Child Development, 35*:951–960, 1964.

Shure, M. B.: Psychological ecology of a nursery school. *Child Development, 34*:979–992, 1963.

Tikten, S. and Hartup, W. W.: Sociometric status and the reinforcing effectiveness of children's peers. *Journal of Experimental Child Psychology, 2*:306–315, 1965.

Wahler, R. G., Winkel, G. H., Peterson, R. F. and Morrison, D. C.: Mothers as behavior therapists for their own children. *Behavior Research Therapy, 3*:113–124, 1965.

9

Successive Modification of Aggressive Behavior and Aggressive Fantasy Play by Management of Contingencies

HOWARD N. SLOANE, MARGARET K. JOHNSTON and
SIDNEY W. BIJOU

INTRODUCTION

THIS REPORT is an account of a field study involving the treatment of a highly aggressive nursery school boy with excessive fantasy play. Conventional clinical treatment of a behavior problem of this intensity is usually based on the assumption that it is a symptom of hidden emotional disturbance. Hence most therapies are aimed at removing hypothetical "underlying causes." Client-centered play therapists stress allowing the child to express and "act out" aggressive "feelings" and the importance of acceptance of these feelings by the therapist. This relationship, together with the alleged cathartic effect, is said to provide an opportunity for the child to experience growth and self-insight with a resultant reduction in the aggressive behavior (Haworth, 1964). Psychoanalytically oriented therapies also stress accep-

NOTE: The research reported in this study was supported by grant MH 12067-01 from the National Institutes of Health, United States Public Health Service, and grant 32-23-1020-6002 from the United States Office of Education. The assistance of Herbert Huckle in preparing the data is gratefully acknowledged. We are particularly grateful to Mrs. Florence R. Harris, director of the nursery school, for her advice and assistance in conducting this study.

From the *Journal of Child Psychology and Psychitary*, 8:217–226, 1967. Copyright 1967 by Pergamon Press. Reprinted with permission of authors and publisher.

tance of aggressive behavior by the therapist (Rosenthal, 1956; Schiffer, 1952), although some of these therapists give greater emphasis to the importance of setting "limits" than others (Haworth, 1964). Regardless of the extent of the concern with limits, psychoanalytic therapies view the treatment of aggression in children in the context of "resistances," "defenses," "transference" and "interpretations" (Finch, 1960).

The sparse literature on the treatment of aggressive behavior based on principles derived from behavior theory emphasizes the role of stimulus consequences in developing and maintaining aggressive behavior. One treatment approach has been to modify parental behavior by training parents to provide social reinforcement for appropriate behavior and to withhold or withdraw social reinforcement following aggressive acts (Hawkins *et al.*, 1966; Wahler *et al.*, 1965; Russo, 1964). Such training has taken place in the context of actual parent-child interaction in the clinic and home. Differential reinforcement procedures to modify aggressive behavior in children have also been used in institutional, school, nursery and summer camp settings (Burchard and Tyler, 1965; Brown and Elliott, 1965; Quay *et al.*, 1966; Richard and Dinoff, 1965). In these environments, treatment involved changing the behavior of the staff rather than that of the parents. Similar approaches have been used with self-destructive behavior in disturbed children (Wolf *et al.*, 1964; Lovaas *et al.*, 1965). These behavior therapists all attempted to modify aggressive behavior in the environment in which it normally occurred, and treatment was relatively independent of historical considerations.

The procedures used in this report are based upon the modification of problem behavior through the systematic manipulation of its consequences.

SUBJECT

The subject, Denny, was a 4½-year-old boy whose behavior in a day-care center, at home and in the neighborhood, was characterized by extreme aggressiveness, temper tantrums and excessive fantasy play. His parents had been asked to withdraw him from the day-care center which he had been attending for a year. The social worker at the center described the child as "not knowing reality from fantasy," and stated that he was frequently quite aggressive while engaging in fantasy roles. At home he used role-behaviors to get his parents to do as he wished. When they would not respond to him in a manner compatible with his fantasy role, he would have a violent temper tantrum. The parents reported that they were not consistent in the ways in which they responded to Denny and were unable to handle him.

Denny was described by his teachers as an alert youngster with normal physical development. He had good motor coordination and well-developed speech patterns, and he was an articulate child. His attention span was described as short, and his skills with nursery school materials were said to be below average. He also lacked serviceable social skills; he did not play with other children other than in the context of some fantasy play in which he dominated the whole play sequence.

Denny's parents were young university students who were anxious to obtain help for their child and expressed eagerness to cooperate in the treatment program.

Denny was enrolled in a small experimental remedial guidance school group for children with behavior problems, which met for 2½ hours a day during the school year. The general objective was to modify the child's behavior to enable him to participate in the activities of a normal school group. This goal was divided into the following specific components: (a) to reduce aggressive behavior; (b) to strengthen appropriate (non-fantasy) play and (c) to teach other acceptable social skills.

PROCEDURE

During the first phase of the study, attention was devoted to attenuating aggressive behavior; during the second, to modifying fantasy play behavior. The procedure for reducing aggressive behavior was continued during the second part of the study, and instructions in the development of acceptable social skills were given throughout the entire treatment period.

Aggressive Behavior
Period A—Baseline

To determine the level of aggressive behavior before systematic procedures to modify it were introduced, the following frequencies of aggressive acts were recorded over a five-day period:

1. Physical assault: hits, with hands or object; kicks, bites or attempts to bite; scratches, pushes, grabs, or pulls at, jumps on, or throws objects at, other child or adult.
2. Destructive behavior toward physical surroundings: knocks materials off shelves, overturns furniture, throws materials or equipment, kicks doors, walls or furniture.
3. Verbal assault: verbally threatens physical assault (as defined above), or threatens violent action against child or adult. Example: "I'm going to kill you," or "I'll cut your scalp off." Verbally resists instructions, saying, "I don't like you," or "go away."

The baseline period was limited to 5 days out of consideration for the other children's safety. Even under close supervision, there was a possibility that Denny would suddenly throw a heavy object or attack another child, resulting in serious injury. During this baseline period, teachers followed procedures normally practiced by nursery school personnel, including talking to child about not hurting others, giving verbal instruction to stop undesirable behavior and using physical restraint. The data were obtained by a trained observer assigned to Denny throughout the study. The recording technique, developed by Allen *et al.* (1964), involved recording the number of aggressive acts during ten-second intervals.

Period B—Contingencies for Aggressive and Cooperative Behavior

The treatment procedure consisted of withdrawing positive reinforcement following physical assault or destructive behavior and presenting positive social reinforcement for cooperative and friendly behavior. Social reinforcement, defined in terms of the behavior of a teacher, consisted of watching, speaking to, smiling at, touching, or offering play material, equipment, or special privileges or activities. Reinforcement was not withdrawn for verbal aggression.

The withdrawal of positive reinforcement consisted of removing Denny from the school room and placing him in a "time-out" room immediately following each aggressive act which was not terminated after verbal instructions to stop. Teacher attention was minimized at such times, consisting only of the brief statement, "You can't stay in the school room when you hurt people." The child was left alone in the time-out room, observed through a one-way screen and intercommunication system, until he was quiet for 2 minutes. At the end of the time-out period, he was returned to the school room without further comment about his behavior. This procedure lasted for 47 class sessions, beginning on session 6 and ending on session 52.

Period C—Participation in a Normal Nursery Group, and Withdrawal from the Group Contingent upon Aggressive Behavior

Denny participated in the regular four-year-old nursery group in which three teachers worked with 16 children. He was returned to the remedial group when an act of physical aggression was not immediately terminated after a verbal instruction. As before, no particular consequences were programmed for verbal aggressive behavior. Intermittent social reinforcement from teachers was given for all cooperative, friendly and appropriate social interaction with others on a nonsystematic basis. Period C was continued for 29 class days (from session 53 to session 81), at which point the study terminated.

Fantasy Play

Period A—Baseline

The baseline rate of Denny's fantasy play was recorded for 19 days. The first day coincided with the first day of Period B for aggressive behavior in which differential contingencies were attached to aggressive and cooperative behaviors. Fantasy play was defined as explicit verbal statements referring to himself or to others as imaginary characters, or actions which carried out such a role once it had been verbalized. For example, if Denny made the statement that he was an Indian and carried around a drum, beating it, the time intervals during which he was using the drum were scored for fantasy play. (Fantasy play during music period, which normally included imaginary role-playing, was not scored as fantasy play.) Data were recorded in the same manner as for aggressive behavior described above.

Period B—Differential Contingencies for Fantasy and Appropriate Play

Beginning on the 20th day, no social reinforcement or attention was given when Denny engaged in fantasy play. Adults interacting with Denny or in close proximity to him left when he started to engage in it. On the other hand, he was reinforced with attention for each observed instance of appropriate play. These conditions were in effect for 28 sessions (Sessions 20 to 37).

Period C—Reinforcement of Appropriate Play in the Normal Group

As previously mentioned, near the end of this study, Denny was gradually admitted to the four-year-old group. Social reinforcement for appropriate play was informally programmed in this group on an intermittent schedule, both for Denny and the other children, and coincided in time with Period C of the analysis of aggressive behavior, except that data were collected for one additional day.

Social Skills

An informal program to teach Denny better social skills was instituted during the time Denny spent in the regular four-year-old group. The teacher took Denny to the play yard of the four-year-old group and led him around by the hand, instructing him to say "Hello" or "Hi" to individuals and groups of children. This was repeated for several days. Denny was then told to ask the other children what they were playing, and in the next step was also instructed to ask if he could play. He was returned to the remedial group when an act of physical aggression was not immediately terminated following a verbal warning. No particular consequence followed verbal aggressive behavior alone. Each time Denny followed the teacher's instructions, he was praised by her. If he was accepted into the group, the play was allowed to continue. This procedure was extended over 10 days. The time that he spent with the regular group was gradually increased.

Denny's imminent entrance into public kindergarten did not allow sufficient time to institute control periods. A "reversal" condition during which the procedures in effect during the baseline periods were reinstated, or a period during which social reinforcement was delivered on a nonresponse-contingent basis, would have clarified the role of the contingencies programmed.

RESULTS

The reliability of recordings was evaluated by having a second observer record the occurrence or nonoccurrence of aggressive and fantasy play behavior in ten-second intervals. Reliability checks made on four days early in the study and three days near the end of the study showed an average agreement of 93 percent.

Aggressive Behavior

In period A (baseline), there was an average of 15 acts of physical assault a day (Figure 9-1). Ninety percent of these were directed at teachers and included hitting, kicking, biting and throwing objects. During this same period, 24 instances of verbal assault were recorded. On the second day following the institution of contingencies (session 7), the frequency of physically aggressive acts dropped to 2. Each time Denny was taken to the time-out room is indicated by an arrow in panels B and C. The frequency of aggressive responses (physical assault) for the following 17 days averaged three a day. As is shown in panel B (differential contingencies), the rate of verbal aggression decreased after the fifth day of this period, closely paralleling the decrease in physical aggression. Increased physical aggression occurred on day 30. Other than that, there was a low and stable rate throughout the remainder of the study, with a daily average of three such aggressive acts.

The relative infrequency of time-outs indicates that on most days when several aggressive acts occurred, the behavior was quickly terminated by verbal warnings. The longest time that Denny spent in the time-out room was 18 minutes; more typically he stayed there for 5 minutes. The first two or three times that

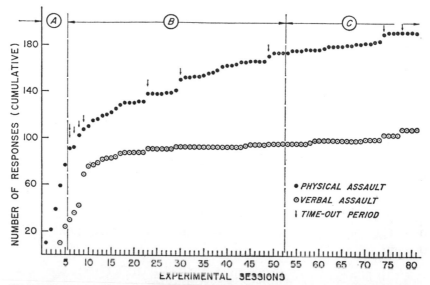

Figure 9-1. Aggressive behaviors. Cumulative errors of the frequency of physical and verbal assault during period A (baseline), period B (planned contingencies) and period C (planned contingencies and participation in normal group). Each arrow indicates an instance in which Denny was placed in the time-out room.

he was escorted into the room, he engaged in tantrum behavior, shouting, screaming and kicking. On those rare occasions that the room was used in the latter part of the study, Denny quickly settled down and waited until the teacher came to return him to the school room.

Both physical and verbal aggression remained at a constantly low rate, averaging not more than three such incidents a day when Denny was participating in the regular four-year-old group, as indicated in panel C of Figure 9-1.

Fantasy Play

As shown in Figure 9-2, baseline data (period A) recorded over 19 sessions indicated that Denny initially engaged in fantasy play on an average of about 35 percent of his time at school. His rate of appropriate play averaged 39 percent during this time. On session 20 and on all following days (period B), social reinforcement was given for appropriate play and withheld contingent on fantasy play. Under this procedure, Denny's frequency of fantasy play decreased rapidly during the first 11 days. By the eleventh treatment session, Denny engaged in fantasy behavior about 5 percent of the time. During the remainder of this period, as well as during period C (experimental contingencies, plus participation in normal four-year-old group), covering sessions 31 to 77, fantasy play remained at about 4 percent, and appropriate play increased to about 60 percent of his time at school, averaging 51 percent for the entire period after the baseline. Since Denny spent some time each school day moving between the remedial and the regular four-year-old group, as well as contributing 20 minutes each day towards the standardization of a laboratory procedure, he had fewer opportunities to engage in appropriate play activities. Therefore, the measure of time spent in appropriate play during the later phase of the study is conservative.

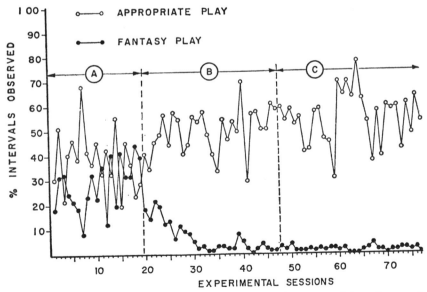

Figure 9-2. Fantasy play. The frequency of appropriate play and fantasy play for period A (baseline), period B (differential contingencies) and period C (differential contingencies and participation in normal group).

When Denny was admitted to the normal four-year-old group to spend most of his school day, fantasy play continued at the low rate of about 3 percent, as shown in panel C.

Social Skills

Although the variability of conditions in the natural setting of the group situation precluded gathering formal data on the success of these procedures, the written records show that Denny did use the techniques that had been systematically taught him in his subsequent play with these children. During the last weeks of the study, Denny spent almost his entire school session in the four-year-old group. Fantasy play and aggressive behavior remained low in the regular group. Denny was warmly accepted by the other children, though he was younger than most, and he made several friends who consistently welcomed him as a playmate.

He participated in the dramatic and imaginative play which were normally part of the activities of the four-year-olds without resorting to his favorite power roles, and on many occasions explicitly verbalized the distinction between "being" an imaginary person and "pretending" to assume a role appropriate to the play of the others.

DISCUSSION
Aggressive Behavior in School

The procedures used in this study, planned to modify the subject's aggressive behavior before attempting to change the fantasy play with which it appeared to be closely associated, provided an opportunity to determine whether aggressive behavior could be treated independently of the fantasy play and to investigate any possible relationship between the two behaviors. This plan of treatment represents a departure from the traditional clinical approach to behavior problems associated with "confused reality concepts," often assumed to be symptomatic of severe "emotional" disturbances. The results are of interest, since they show that the child's rate of aggressive behavior was reduced in a short period by maintaining consistent consequences for aggressive behavior, while fantasy play still continued at a high rate. It is significant that when the procedures to modify fantasy play were implemented, aggressive behavior stayed at a low rate. As Figures 9-1 and 9-2 show, consistently low and stable rates of both aggressive behavior and fantasy play were maintained throughout the duration of the study in both the remedial and the normal nursery school environment.

One provocative result of this study is the fact that the rate of verbal aggressiveness was positively correlated with the rate of physical aggression, although verbal aggressive behavior was not subject to systematic contingencies. This suggests that for this child, the three classes of aggressive acts were not functionally separate behavioral classes.

The definition of aggressive behavior did not allow for differential classification of aggressive acts according to their intensity, so that qualitative changes in the nature of Denny's aggressive acts are not shown in the recorded data. However, observers and teachers noted a marked diminution in the intensity and duration of aggressive behaviors as the study progressed. Many of the aggressive incidents recorded during the second quarter of Denny's enrollment consisted of mild, brief episodes of striking at others, in contrast to the baseline behavior which was characterized by severe hitting, kicking, biting and throwing things.

Fantasy Play in School

The rapid rate at which fantasy play diminished in strength when it was no longer reinforced with adult attention indicates the degree to which social consequences influence this behavior. During the baseline period, Denny consistently involved adults in his play, assigning them roles and dictating details of their participation. The types of roles that he played were almost always "power figures" such as an "Indian chief," "leader of the people," or "Superman." His aggressive acts were almost always accompanied by statements explaining his actions in terms of his role. When teachers addressed him as "Denny," he demanded that he be addressed as the character he was playing.

Since the remedial group offered very few opportunities for Denny to interact with children in play activities geared to his age, contact with children from the regular four-year-old group was initiated during the sixth week of the study. A teacher from the regular group brought three or four children at a time for a short visit to the play yard used by the remedial group. Denny's approach to these children was frequently bizarre and inappropriate; he often attempted to play with them by making threatening statements related to a role that he was playing. On one occasion when he had painted his face like an Indian, he charged menacingly at the visiting children, and they laughed at him. This was immediately followed by a sudden attack on the nearest teacher. This incident accounts for the high rate of aggressive behaviors noted on the thirtieth day.

Aggressive Behavior and Fantasy Play at Home

At the end of the first month of this study, Denny's parents were asked to carry out the same procedures at home as were being implemented at school, and this consistent treatment at home and at school was probably an important factor in the rapid change observed in Denny's behavior in the 42 months of the study.

During the course of the study, no new problem behaviors were observed in the nursery school or reported to be occurring in the home.

Social Skills

Without experimental data, it is difficult to estimate the significance of the training in social skills which Denny received. It certainly is possible that Denny would develop new ways of interacting with other children as a function of the different manner in which they might respond to him following the reduction in his aggressive and role-playing behavior. Other more socially desirable behaviors which were already part of his repertoire but competed out of existence by the problem behaviors might have emerged without explicit tutoring. As the consequences of behavior are usually maintained more consistently in a treatment environment than in home or school, occasional reinforcement for aggressive or fantasy behavior is likely to occur with any child at home or school. The development of socially acceptable skills which compete strongly with these problem behaviors seems one way of decreasing the probability of a so-called "relapse," and developing acceptable behavior in strength after extinguishing undesirable behavior seems recommended as a general strategy in many such situations.

Follow-up

Informal follow-up data were obtained by consulting with Denny's teachers in kindergarten, which he entered 3 months after this study terminated, and by having the observer-recorder who obtained data in the study observe Denny in this kindergarten. Formal data were not obtained, as it was felt that the different conditions would invalidate them.

In the first several months of Denny's attendance in kindergarten, his progress looked good, but then teachers reported an increase in aggressive behavior, and transferred him from one class to another. Ten months after termination of the study, the observer-recorder reported no fantasy play and moderate agressive behavior. The observer-recorder stated that the aggressive behavior was of a much lower rate and intensity than before the study but certainly higher than most adults consider desirable in a child this age. She also reported that the teachers in kindergarten provided a great amount of attention for aggressive behavior and little attention for "constructive behaviors.

SUMMARY

Extremely high rates of aggressive acts and excessive fantasy play in a young boy were treated by systematic manipulation of their consequences in a remedial nursery school setting. In the first phase of the study, only the subject's aggressive behavior was treated. In the second phase, fantasy play was modified while the procedures for controlling aggressive behavior were continued. In both phases, tutoring in acceptable social skills was part of the treatment. Throughout the study, continuous frequency counts of the several kinds of behavior were obtained by trained observer-recorders.

After a baseline period, in which the frequency of aggressive behavior before systematic treatment was recorded, positive reinforcement (social) was withdrawn after occurrences of aggressive behavior which did not terminate after one brief warning, and positive social reinforcement was delivered contingent upon friendly, cooperative contact with others. Participation in a non-remedial group was then made contingent upon nonaggressive behavior. Aggressive behavior declined quickly when social reinforcement was made contingent upon its nonoccurrence.

Fantasy play, defined in terms of explicit verbal statements referring to himself or others as imaginary characters, was similarly treated and quickly dropped to a very low frequency.

In the latter part of the study, an informal program of tutoring in social skills was instituted.

REFERENCES

Allen, K. E., Hart, B., Buell, J. S., Harris, F. R. and Wolf, M. M.: Effects of social reinforcement on isolate behaviour of a nursery school child. *Child Development,* 35:511–518, 1964.

Brown, P. and Elliott, R.: The control of aggression in a nursery school class. *Journal of Experimental Child Psychology,* 2:103–107, 1965.

Burchard, J. and Tyler, V.: The modification of delinquent behaviour through operant conditioning. *Behavior Research and Therapy,* 2:245–250, 1965.

Finch, S. M.: *Fundamentals of Child Psychiatry.* New York, Norton, 1960.

Hawkins, R. P., Peterson, R. F., Schweid, E. and Bijou, S. W.: Behaviour therapy in the home: Amelioration of problem parent-child relations with the parent in a therapeutic role. *Journal of Experimental Child Psychology,* 4:99–107, 1966.

Haworth, M. R. (Ed.): *Child Psychotherapy.* New York, Basic Books, 1964.

Lovaas, O. I., Freitag, G. Gold, V. J. and Kassorla, I. C.: Experimental studies in childhood schizophrenia: analysis of self-destructive behaviour. *Journal of Experimental Child Psychology,* 2:67–84, 1965.

Quay, H. C., Werry, J. S., McQueen, M. and Sprague, R. L.: Remediation of the conduct problem child in the special class setting. *Exceptional Children,* 32:509–515, 1966.

Richard, H. C. and Dinoff, M.: Shaping adaptive behaviour in a therapeutic summer camp. In L. P. Ullmann, and L. Krasner (Eds.): *Case Studies in Behaviour Modification*. New York, Holt, Rinehart and Winston, 1965.

Rosenthal, L.: Child and guidance. In S. R. Slavson (Ed.): *The Fields of Group Psychotherapy*. New York, International University Press, 1956.

Russo, S.: Adaptations in behavioural therapy with children. *Behavior Research and Therapy*, 2:43–37, 1964.

Schiffer, M.: Permissiveness versus sanction in activity group therapy. *International Journal of Group Psychotherapy*, 2:255–261, 1952.

Wahler, R. C., Winkel, G. H., Peterson, R. F. and Morrison, D. C.: Mothers as behaviour therapists for their own children. *Behavior Research and Therapy*, 3:113–134, 1965.

Wolf, M. M., Risley, T. R. and Mees, H. L.: Application of operant conditioning procedures to the behaviour problems of an autistic child. *Behavior Research and Therapy*, 1:305–312, 1964.

10

An Application of Reinforcement Principles to Development of Motor Skills of a Young Child

MARGARET K. JOHNSTON, C. SUSAN KELLEY,
FLORENCE R. HARRIS, and MONTROSE M. WOLF

An unusually low rate of vigorous physical activity of a preschool child was changed to a normal rate through systematic social reinforcement of climbing behavior on a specific piece of play-yard equipment. Initially, a high rate of climbing was developed by a teacher's giving her attention contingent upon contact with the piece of equipment and withholding her attention for other behaviors as far as possible. A reversal of these contingencies reduced the climbing behavior, and later reinstatement again produced a high climbing rate. Climbing behavior was then generalized to other play-yard equipment by reinforcing the subject's use of this equipment.

THIS CHAPTER PRESENTS a study that was part of a program of research in the experimental application of reinforcement principles to the guidance of nursery school children. Some of the problem behaviors worked with to date include regressed crawling (Harris *et al.*, 1964), social isolation (Allen *et al.*, 1964) and operant crying (Hart *et al.*, 1964). Results indicated that rein-

NOTE: The authors gratefully acknowledge the frequent counsel of Sidney W. Bijou, Donald M. Baer and Jay S. Birnbrauer. We are indebted also to Robert G. Wahler for his cooperation in developing observation techniques. This investigation was supported in part by Public Health Service Research Grants MH-02208 and MH-02232, from the National Institute of Mental Health.

From *Child Development*, 37:379–387, 1966. Copyright 1966 by the Society for Research in Child Development. Reprinted with permission of authors and publisher.

forcement techniques could be effectively applied in field conditions to change the kinds of behaviors studied.

The purpose of the present study was to determine whether similar procedures could be used to induce a three-year-old boy to engage in vigorous play activity on a piece of climbing equipment. Interest was also focused on maintaining and generalizing such behavior. Increasing the child's use of one piece of climbing equipment seemed an appropriate step toward the ultimate objective of fostering the development of the child's physical skills. It also met the practical requirements of an experimental analysis under field conditions, since it focused on a behavior that could be readily observed and recorded.

METHOD

Subject

Mark was one of the 12 children enrolled in the three-year-old group at the Laboratory Preschool and was three years and eight months old when the study began. It was apparent during the first 6 months of school that he spent very little time engaging in physical activity of any kind. His limited behavioral repertoire included few skills with materials or equipment, or in play with children. Much of his behavior during the first half of the year consisted of random wandering from one activity to another. Occasional attempts to join other children in play resulted in disruption of the ongoing activities. He avoided most of the climbing equipment, such as boards, ladders and boxes; and he almost never used the piece of outdoor equipment referred to as the "large climbing frame."

Procedures

The procedures for getting the child to play on the climbing frame consisted of making adult social reinforcement contingent solely upon his use of this piece of equipment. Using the climbing frame, hereafter called "climbing-frame behavior," was defined as follows: physical contact with the frame or with the auxiliary boards, blocks, ladders or ropes temporarily attached to it for the purpose of enlarging any play possibilities the climber presented. Social reinforcement was defined as follows: a teacher standing within 10 feet (the length of the climber) of the subject and watching, speaking to, smiling at or touching the child, or bringing him supplementary equipment to amplify his play on the climber. Withdrawing or withholding social reinforcement consisted of the teacher's turning away, not looking or smiling at the child or speaking to him, and focusing her attention and activity elsewhere. One of the two teachers who were regularly in charge of the group was assigned the task of reinforcing the child to make sure that the above procedures were carried out consistently and promptly. Concurrently, this teacher included under her supervision any other children who came to the climber. The other teacher, who assumed major responsibility for guidance of the rest of the group, followed identical procedures in reinforcing the subject child whenever his proximity to her made it appropriate. No other adults interacted with the children. The study was carried out in five phases.

Baseline

The subject's behavior during the outdoor play period, before reinforcement procedures were systematically applied, was recorded to ascertain the operant level of his climbing-frame behavior. Recording was carried on for nine days.

First Reinforcement

Continuous social reinforcement was given whenever the subject was using the climbing frame and was withheld whenever he engaged in other activities. Since initially Mark had no climbing-frame behavior for teachers to reinforce, it was necessary at first to reinforce successive approximations to his behavior. The reinforcing teacher, stationed near the climbing frame, smiled and spoke to him when he approached or walked by, terminating her attention to him when he moved away. As he came closer and stayed longer, she narrowed her criteria for reinforcement; that is, at first she gave attention to him when he came within about 6 feet of the climber, then not until 5 feet, and so on. Eventually, he touched the frame and was soon climbing on it. From this point on, the teacher gave him attention only for climbing-frame behavior as previously defined. Only the amount of time he actually engaged in climbing-frame behavior over a period of nine days was recorded.

Reversal

Contingencies for delivery of reinforcement were reversed; that is, adults withheld attention to climbing-frame behavior but gave continuous attention to all other activities. Although the reinforcement teacher assumed the major responsibility for giving this attention, the other teacher also reinforced the subject for activities away from the climbing frame. This procedure was followed for five days to ascertain whether the contingency employed (adult attention) was a significant variable in any change in climbing-frame behavior observed in the first reinforcement period.

Second Reinforcement

Continuous social reinforcement for climbing-frame behavior was again instituted for five days with no reinforcement contingent upon other behaviors.

Generalization

The reinforcement schedule for climbing-frame behavior was gradually shifted from continuous to intermittent, and all other physical activity was likewise intermittently reinforced. This procedure was carried on for four days. In effecting this change in reinforcement procedures, teachers could vary their reinforcement with respect to the number of instances of climbing-frame activity and with respect to the duration of time that the ongoing behavior was reinforced. On a schedule of continuous reinforcement, the teacher gave Mark attention every time and for as long as he played on the climbing frame. When he left it, the teacher immediately turned to other children or duties. When an intermittent schedule was instituted, the teacher first attempted to reinforce approximately every other incidence of this behavior for as long as it continued. Next, she gradually reduced the duration of the reinforcement by staying only a few minutes. Slowly then, the teacher increased the number of responses required for reinforcement and varied the duration of reinforcement in the direction of shorter periods, flexibly adjusting her two-way leaning of the schedule so that the child's climbing-frame behavior was maintained. In the final stages of this phase, teachers reinforced Mark on an intermittent schedule consistent with that given to any child in the group.

Changes in the above procedures were to be instituted whenever the behavior reached a consistently stable rate, showing no extreme variation for 3 days. However, no changes were to be made on a Monday or a Friday, so that possible effects of the weekend holidays might be minimized.

Recording

An observer recorded in ten-second intervals the subject's climbing-frame behavior, using a stopwatch with recording sheet that had been developed in previous studies (Allen *et al.*, 1964). The observer was unobtrusively seated on the sidelines of the play area, never closer than ten feet from the climber. During the baseline and generalization periods, climbing behavior on outdoor equipment other than the climbing frame was also recorded. Social reinforcement by teachers was likewise recorded. Observer reliability on the subject's climbing-frame behavior was checked on 3 different days by a second independent observer. These records showed over 90 percent interobserver agreement. No reliability measures were taken on the adult social reinforcement behavior. Recording took place only during outdoor play periods. Approximately 1½ hours of each morning were spent in outdoor play.

RESULTS

As Figure 10-1 shows, the operant level of climbing-frame behavior (days 1–8) averaged less than 1 percent, with one episode of touching the frame occurring on the seventh day. Concurrently, the data indicated that about 25 percent of Mark's time was spent in desultory activities such as standing still and walking around, and 75 percent of the time in sedentary activities such as sandbox play.

Climbing-frame behavior rapidly increased in response to continuous reinforcement (see Figure 10-1, Reinf. 1). By the second

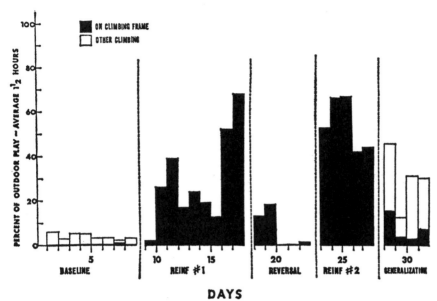

DAYS

Figure 10-1. Percentages of each morning spent by a nursery school boy in using a climbing frame apparatus.

day, this behavior occupied 25 percent of Mark's time outdoors. By the ninth day of this schedule, climbing-frame behavior comprised 67.4 percent of his outdoor play time.

On the first day of the reversal phase, Mark approached the climber briefly several times during the morning. On the second day, 17 percent of the play period was spent in using the climbing frame; on the third day, the percentage dropped to zero and remained at that level during the next 2 days. The overall percentage of time spent on the climbing frame during the reversal phase was 12.3 percent (see Fig. 10-1, Reversal).

Reinforcement for climbing-frame behavior was then reinstituted. The behavior reconditioned rapidly, reaching a high rate of over 50 percent on the first day of the phase. Figure 10-1, Reinforcement 2, shows that an average of 54 percent of Mark's time was spent on the climbing frame during the five-day period. At this point, it was considered that the increase in climbing-frame behavior (vigorous physical activity) had been achieved, and an attempt was made to generalize it to other equipment and other kinds of play.

During the generalization phase, reinforcement for climbing-frame behavior was gradually made more intermittent. At the same time, all vigorous physical use of other play materials and equipment was continuously reinforced. Climbing behavior spread to all the climbing equipment in the yard, that is, ladders, suspended and inclined boards, packing boxes, trees and other frames. An average of 30 percent of the time during the four-day phase, Mark used this equipment (see Fig. 10-1, Generalization).

When Mark returned to school the following fall as a member of the four-year-old group, observers' records showed that he spent 50 to 60 percent of his time in vigorous climbing activity and used all climbing equipment freely. This contrasted with the baseline data (of the previous year) on all climbing, which averaged less than 10 percent.

DISCUSSION

The baseline data showed that Mark was engaging in very little vigorous motor activity. The observers' records of teachers' attending behavior, although not evaluated for reliability and not as dependable as data, nevertheless indicated that he was receiving attention from teachers for an average of about 40 percent of his time during the baseline period. Almost 100 percent of the attention was for behaviors other than climbing-frame behavior. The teachers evidently gave Mark considerable attention because of the inappropriate play patterns that he exhibited. Lacking both physical and social skills, Mark often pushed his way into group play, disrupting ongoing activities. At such times, teachers would attend to him and attempt to redirect his activity. Teachers also appeared to respond to his random behavior by going to him and trying to encourage him to participate more purposefully in the many activities available to him. Giving attention under these circumstances, while in accordance with customary teaching methods, may have maintained both his social ineptitude and his physical inactivity.

During the first reinforcement phase, Mark spent an average of 28 percent of his time in using the climbing frame. While practically 100 percent of this behavior was reinforced by the teacher, the record indicated that approximately 30 percent of the total daily social reinforcement he received was for behaviors other than climbing. Most of the attention was in relation to assisting him with routine matters, such as putting on boots and wraps and on occasions of his inept approaches to other children. Such behaviors were difficult, if not impossible, for the teachers to ignore.

It was apparent during the first reinforcement phase that reinforcing climbing-frame behavior also provided recognition and encouragement for the verbal and social behaviors occurring simultaneously with climbing. Furthermore, a teacher and a child pleasurably engaged in activity at the climbing frame presented an occasion which attracted many of the other children. Mark's social interaction with children was, of course, reinforced, being an integral part of his climbing play. The teachers reported an increase in his social play during this phase of the study.

During the reversal phase, Mark spent 7 percent of the time (on the average) climbing on the frame and was reinforced for only about 1 percent of this behavior. However, he received attention for approximately 45 percent of his time at school. Ninety-nine percent of the attention, of course, was directed toward his other activities. Procedures involved in the reversal phase proved to be most beneficial to Mark through extending his active play to a wide range of equipment and varied play situations. The activities he engaged in therefore seemed to be closely related to the amount of social reinforcement given. Other investigators have reported a similar relation between adult social reinforcement and children's interest in an activity. For example, Gilmore and Zigler (1964) found in an experimental setting that the amount of adult social reinforcement given significantly influenced the length of time that children would play a repetitious game.

While the reversal phase was in effect, the climbing frame was used very little by any of the children, although other climbing equipment was popular. A similar effect had been observed in the course of the other studies conducted in this setting. Activities reinforced in the course of modifying the behavior of a particular child tended to become more popular with all the children and to attract fewer children when this activity was no longer being reinforced.

During the second reinforcement phase, Mark spent an average of 54 percent of his time on the climbing frame. The rapid rate at which climbing-frame behavior was reinstated following a period of withdrawal of social reinforcement for this activity is similar to that found in previous field studies of the behavior of nursery school children. Following the reversal phase in the regressed crawling study (Harris *et al.*, 1964), upright walking was reestablished on the first day that reinforcement of walking was resumed. In the operant crying study (Hart *et al.*, 1964) extinction of this crying, after a reversal phase during which it had been reinforced, also took effect on the first day of shifting the reinforcement contingencies. In the social isolation study (Allen *et al.*, 1964), involving a more complex constellation of behaviors, the same rapid return to the levels of social interaction achieved in the initial reinforcement phase was observed.

In all of these studies, the behavior that had been originally reinforced, once reestablished, remained stable after the studies were terminated, as shown by postchecks made of the subjects under study. A study on the training of nursery school children reported by Keister in 1938 demonstrated both a similar application of social reinforcement and similar long-range effects of this training. Her subjects were reinforced with praise and encouragement for the completion of a series of carefully graded tasks without specific help or directions being given to them. The performance of these children in subsequent related problem-solving situations was significantly improved, a finding related to the modifications of behavior that occurred in the nursery school field studies.

The records indicated that during the second reinforcement phase, about 85 percent of Mark's climbing-frame behavior was reinforced. He continued to receive a high rate of total adult reinforcement, about 50 percent of his time at school. It is of interest that there seemed to be less reinforcement, either inadvertent or "essential," given to him for behaviors other than climbing, during this reinforcement period (about 10% of the reinforcement given). This lower rate may have reflected his increased appropriate participation in group activities. During this phase, the teachers observed a marked improvement in the subject's climbing skills, although no program for teaching these skills was undertaken. Although this improved skill may have been primarily the result of almost continuous practice in climbing, it may also have been partly due to the fact that teachers tended to reinforce Mark's more skillful climbing with greater enthusiasm.

During the generalization phase, Mark engaged in play on the climbing frame an average of 7 percent of his time at school but spent an average of 23 percent of his time in other climbing activities. Approximately 60 percent of the climbing-frame play and 85 percent of the other climbing behavior was reinforced. The total percentage of social reinforcement averaged about 30 percent of the four sessions. This lower rate of social reinforcement reflected the gradual shift from continuous reinforcement to the intermittent rate usual in the school situation. Even though the total amount of adult attention was reduced, apparently his new achievements with the play-yard equipment and his improved relation with other children were sufficiently reinforcing to maintain and even to amplify his new patterns of activity.

The average amount of social reinforcement given in the five different phases of the study was consistently high and did not vary more than about 13 percent from one phase to the next. This suggests that the significant variable influencing the subject's behavior was the systematic nature of the presentation and withholding of teacher attention. Such a finding opens to question the commonly held view that merely increasing the amount of adult attention to a child will effect desirable behavior changes.

It appeared that, along with the planned manipulation of Mark's climbing-frame behavior, desirable modifications had occurred in two other classes of behavior over which no control had been attempted and no data recorded. These behaviors were (a) improved skill with all the active play equipment and (b) an increase in social and verbal behaviors that enabled him to interact more effectively with his peers. A similar improvement in verbal and social behaviors accompanying changes in motor activity had been observed in the regressed crawling study (Harris *et al.*, 1964).

The results of this study indicate that overcoming avoidance behavior in relation to a play activity on a piece of equipment can be added to those behaviors modifiable by operant conditioning techniques. They also suggest that the interests of a group of children in one type of activity can be influenced by the amount of adult social reinforcement directed toward this activity. Equally provocative is the implication that systematic reinforcement of a specific activity can develop interests and skills that may be generalized to other related activities.

REFERENCES

Allen, K. Eileen, Hart, Betty M., Buell, Joan S., Harris, Florence R. and Wolf, M.: Effects of social reinforcement on isolate behavior of a nursery school child. *Child Development, 35:*511–518, 1964.

Gilmore, J. B. and Zigler, E.: Birth order and social reinforcer effectiveness in children. *Child Development, 35:*193–200, 1964.

Harris, Florence R., Johnston, Margaret K., Kelley, C. Susan and Wolf, M.: Effects of positive social reinforcement on regressed crawling of a nursery school child. *Journal of Educational Psychology, 55:*35–41, 1964.

Hart, Betty M., Allen, K. Eileen, Buell, Joan S., Harris, Florence R. and Wolf, M.: Effects of social reinforcement on operant crying. *Journal of Experimental Child Psychology, 1:*145–153, 1964.

Keister, Mary E.: The behavior of young children in failure: an experimental attempt to discover and modify undesirable responses of preschool children to failure. *University of Iowa Studies on Child Welfare, 14:*27–82, 1938.

III

SCHOOL-AGE CHILDREN

Most classroom behavior modification investigations have been concerned with demonstrating that teachers can reduce the frequency of specific disruptive behaviors exhibited by their students. Far less attention, however, has been focused on improving academic performance. The first three papers in this chapter describe attempts to modify academic behavior and have been selected in order to contrast the student behaviors examined, as well as to present some interesting findings about teacher variables.

The report by Hall *et al.* indicates that inexperienced teachers are able to readily improve study behavior in children. In view of the fact, as Hall *et al.* point out, that these new teachers received only a minimal amount of training in operant concepts, strong arguments can be made in favor of introducing these techniques on a widespread basis to new and potential teaching personnel. While this paper is novel in terms of the individuals being trained, the type of academic behavior which was altered—study behavior—is typical of that which has been changed in many other academically oriented modification investigations. Study behavior has generally been equated with attending to work materials or to the teacher and is often referred to as on-task behavior. Although we would agree that it is probably more conducive to education to have children oriented towards their work materials than it is for them to be highly disruptive, little data is available to indicate that increases in "study" behavior are accompanied by corresponding changes in more direct measures of learning such as task completion, error rate and test performance. Although it is commonly assumed that if a child is "attending" to his task, he is probably learning, the extent to which he actually is learning or the degree to which attending is a component of learning is not known. Since the functional relationship between attending and other academic variables has not been determined, we should evaluate investigations such as Hall *et al.* on the basis of the behavior changes they have documented and be careful not to expect more than just that.

The study by Reynolds *et al.* is especially valuable for several reasons. It examines changes in the rate of test passing for an entire class of children and empirically demonstrates that these changes are functionally related to the content of the reinforcing statements made by the teacher. After determining that the majority of positive academic comments made by the teacher concerned the quality or accuracy of the students' work, Reynolds *et al.* requested that the teacher exclusively reinforce quantity of work, rather than quality. The result was a decrease in the frequency of tests passed. A subsequent increase occurred when the teacher reverted back to reinforcing quality. While other investigations have made it clear that the teachers' social behavior can effectively modify student responses, this is one of the first attempts to show the differential effects of a specific type of teacher attention.

The study by Lovitt *et al.*, demonstrates in a very brief report how a single classroom teacher readily increased the spelling performance of most of his students simply by making free time contingent upon a perfect spelling paper. The authors emphasize how the application of these procedures forced the teacher to look at his children individually, not only in terms of reinforcers but also with regard to the appropriateness of their academic assignments.

Many examples are available of the modification of disruptive behavior in public school classrooms. The next three papers have each made a significant contribution towards expanding the basic applications to more complex situations.

Barrish *et al.* show how the classroom teacher might use a simple game to reduce incidences of disruptive behavior. The procedure involved dividing the class into two teams and providing a reward to the team which earned fewer negative points for inappropriate behavior. A group reward was thus made contingent upon the behavior of the individual team members. Results indicated that the game markedly lowered the frequency of disruptive behavior for the class as a whole, although the procedure was not completely effective for every student. The rewards used in the study are readily available to all classrooms. The authors emphasize the point that teachers should investigate all potential reinforcing activities in the school before purchasing rewards. Children are frequently reinforced by activities that the teacher might never believe to be rewarding. Teachers are thus encouraged to ask children for suggested reinforcers. It should be kept in mind, however, that when modifying the behavior of a group of children, several rewards of equal value should be available to account for individual preferences. In addition, teachers should be aware of the need to change reinforcers periodically as the demand for a particular one subsides.

With the exception of the papers by Sloane *et al.* and Barrish *et al.*, the studies presented thus far have concentrated exclusively on showing how positive consequences can affect behavior. Generally, teachers have dispensed social or tangible reinforcers while attempting to ignore undesirable responses. Little, however, has been said about the use of teacher consequences which can be categorized as negative reinforcers. The time-out procedure discussed by Sloane *et al.* and effectively used in other classroom situations has certain limitations, one of which is the very real possibility that the teacher does not have an easily accessible or manageable time-out location. One other technique which will be elaborated upon in a later paper is concerned with the loss of rewards (points) already earned. All of these procedures, however, are somewhat external to the teacher in the sense that they consist either of removing a child from a desired activity, the earning of "negative points" or the loss of some tangible reward or points. The use of teacher verbal reprimands is a more direct teacher-child negative interaction. Although throughout the history of education teachers have most certainly used this procedure at least as often, if not more so, than positive reinforcement techniques, there have been few attempts to analyze the effects of verbal reprimands. The next two papers in this chapter illustrate the beginning of such analyses.

O'Leary *et al.* report that soft reprimands, ones directed quietly and solely to the student being reprimanded, tend to reduce that student's disruptive behavior more effectively than when the student receives reprimands audible to the entire class. It was also demonstrated that fewer soft than loud reprimands were needed in order to achieve such results. The former findings were replicated with six additional children in three separate classrooms. In a fourth classroom, soft reprimands did not seem to be more effective than loud ones for the two children observed. Although some procedural difficulty was encountered with the fourth teacher, such results should again caution teachers to the continued need for individualizing reinforcement techniques. Quite conceivably, as the authors point out, soft reprimands may function for some students as a positive reinforcer merely because of the proximity of the teacher when the reprimand is delivered.

Working at the secondary school level, McAllister *et al.* demonstrate that verbal reprimands, when combined with praise statements, can effectively reduce disruptive behavior. The results are presented for an entire class of high school students, thus showing that a single teacher can have a marked effect upon a relatively large group of secondary students, using only social reinforcement. Since McAllister *et al.* did not introduce praise and reprimands separately, it is not possible to tell from the study which of these two variables was of primary importance in determining the change. Earlier studies, however, have noted that with highly disruptive elementary school students, praising and ignoring led to increased disruption. To the extent that praise was also used in the McAllister *et al.* paper, the main difference was the substitution of verbal reprimands for ignoring, and thus it might be concluded that reprimands were the most effective element. However, it is also possible that the reprimands functioned only to set the stage whereby praise would be most effective. Hence, no conclusions other than the fact that the two variables were useful in combination should really be made until further research is conducted.

It should also be carefully noted that the reprimands used in the McAllister *et al.*, study were loud statements. This is not in accord with the preceding paper by O'Leary *et al.* and might point to the need for reprimands of varying intensity depending upon the age of the student. Again, however, such conflicts emphasize the need for additional investigations in this area.

This chapter concludes with an article by Ayllon *et al.*, who successfully eliminated school phobia through the use of operant procedures. The typical behavioral approach to such a problem has been to use techniques of systematic desensitization (procedures based largely upon principles of classical conditioning—see paper by Roden and Hapkiewicz) until the phobic reactions have been extinguished. Ayllon *et al.*, however, first redefine school phobia in terms of school attendance and then proceed to experiment with different contingencies until an increase occurs in the frequency of school attendance. Importantly, the child's mother is used as an effective agent of change. She administers both positive and negative consequences to the child based upon improved attendance versus nonattendance at school.

11

Instructing Beginning Teachers in Reinforcement Procedures Which Improve Classroom Control

R. Vance Hall, Marion Panyan, Deloris Rabon
and Marcia Broden

Systematic reinforcement procedures were used to increase study behavior in the classrooms of three beginning teachers experiencing problems of classroom control. Classroom study rates were recorded during a baseline period. During subsequent experimental periods, the teachers changed one or more reinforcement contingencies (teacher attention, length of between-period break, a classroom game) to bring about increased study rates and concomitant reductions in disruptive behaviors. A brief reversal period, in which these contingencies were discontinued, again produced low rates of study. Reinstatement of the contingencies resulted once again in marked increases in study behaviors.

NOTE: The authors wish to express appreciation to Dr. O. L. Plucker, Dr. Bertram Caruthers, Alonzo Plough, Curtis Reddic, and Barbara Gaines of the Kansas City, Kansas Public Schools and Kenneth Tewell, Robert Clark, and John Beougher of the Bonner Springs, Kansas Public Schools without whose cooperation and active participation these studies would not have been possible. We are also indebted to Dr. R. L. Schiefelbusch, Director, and R. H. Copeland, Associate Director of the Bureau of Child Research, who provided essential administrative support and counsel. The research was carried out as a part of the Juniper Gardens Children's Project, a program of research on the development of culturally deprived children and was partially supported by the National Institute of Child Health and Human Development: (HD 03144-01) and the Office of Economic Opportunity: (CG 8190) Bureau of Child Research, University of Kansas.
From the *Journal of Applied Behavior Analysis, 1*:315–322, 1968. Copyright 1968 by the Society for the Experimental Study of Behavior Inc. Reprinted with permission of the authors and publisher.

Previous studies (Hall *et al.*, 1968; Evans and Ozwalt, 1968; Thomas *et al.*, 1968) have shown that teacher-applied contingencies could be used to increase or decrease study rates and academic performance of dawdling or disruptive pupils in regular school classrooms. These studies, like almost all of those which have demonstrated that teacher-applied contingencies can be effective in special education classrooms (Wolf *et al.*, 1968; Clark *et al.*, 1968; O'Leary and Becker, 1967; Hall and Broden, 1967; McKenzie *et al.*, 1968), were carried out by experienced teachers. Often, the teachers had been selected because of their excellent classroom management skills and the high probability that they could carry out the experimental procedures successfully.

These demonstrations have been important, but they have not addressed themselves to one of the most significant aspects of classroom management in education: the training of beginning teachers in the principles and procedures which will bring about classroom control.

The present studies were carried out in the classrooms of 3 first-year teachers. Not only were these teachers initially unfamiliar with learning theory principles and the systematic application of contingencies, but each was experiencing significant problems of general classroom control.

TEACHER ONE

The first teacher had received his B.A. in education the previous year. His first teaching assignment was a class of 30 sixth-graders in a public school located in a low socioeconomic area of Kansas City, Kansas. His class was selected for study on the principal's recommendation because of continued high rates of disruptive and other student nonstudy behaviors. In the principal's words, the class was "completely out of control."

Data were recorded every day during the first hour of the school day during the reading period. The recording system was essentially that used in previous studies with individual pupils in which an observer recorded pupil behavior every 10 seconds during a 30-minute observation session, except that instead of observing the same pupil throughout the session, each was observed for 10 seconds on a consecutive rotating basis. If the pupil being observed was out of his seat or if he talked without being recognized by the teacher any time during the 10-second interval, an "N" for nonstudy was scored for the interval. Otherwise, the student's behavior at the end of the 10 seconds determined the rating. If he was looking out the window, playing with cards, fighting or poking a classmate, tapping pencils on books, cleaning out his desk or engaging in any of a variety of other such behaviors, an "N" was recorded. If there was no "N" behavior, an "S," indicating study, was scored for the interval. Study behaviors included writing the assignment, looking in the book and answering the teacher's questions.

When every class member had been observed in turn, recording began again with the first child, until all were observed again in the same order. From this time-sampling procedure the percent of study for the entire class was computed by dividing the number of study intervals by the total number of observation intervals and multiplying by 100.

The teacher's verbal attention, defined as a verbalization directed to a pupil or pupils, was also analyzed. The teacher's comment was recorded as a "$+$" if it followed appropriate study behavior and a "$-$" if it followed an instance of nonstudy behavior. These comments were recorded when they occurred. Almost without exception, those that followed study behavior were approving and those that followed nonstudy behavior were in the form of a verbal reprimand. See Broden (1968) for a more detailed description of these interval recording procedures.

Periodically, and at least once during every experimental condition, a second observer made a simultaneous observational record. Correspondence of the two records, interval-for-interval, yielded the percentage of interobserver agreement. For this study, the percentage of agreement for class study behavior and for teacher attention ranged from 87 to 93 percent.

Figure 11-1 presents the class study rates for the various phases of the experiment and the frequency of teacher comments following study and nonstudy behaviors. The broken horizontal lines indicate the mean study rates for each experimental condition.

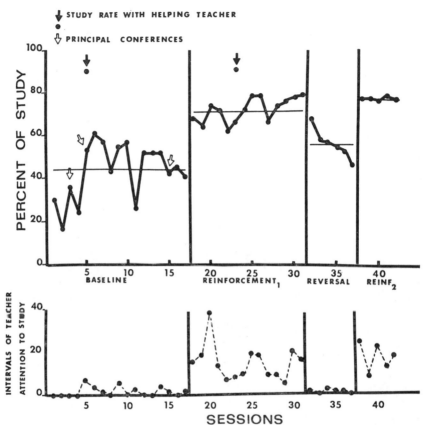

Figure 11-1. A record of class study behavior and teacher attention for study behavior during reading period in a sixth-grade classroom: baseline, before experimental procedures; reinforcement₁, increased teacher attention for study; reversal, removal of teacher attention for study; reinforcement₂, return to increased teacher attention for study; post–follow-up checks up to 20 weeks after termination of experimental procedures.

During baseline, the mean class study rate was 44 percent. The mean number of intervals in which the teacher made comments following study behavior was 1.4 per session. The class study rate rose to 90 percent when the helping teacher presented a demonstration lesson. The points at which the teacher met with the principal to discuss organizational procedures are indicated. After the first meeting, the teacher began writing all assignments on the board. After the third, he changed the class seating arrangements. As can be seen, these counseling procedures seemed to have some beneficial effects, but the improvement was not enough to eliminate concern.

Before the first day of the second phase, reinforcement principles and procedures used in other studies which had been effective in increasing study behavior of individual pupils were discussed with the teacher. He was shown the class baseline study record and the record of the frequency of teacher comments following study behavior. He was instructed to increase the frequency of positive comments for appropriate study. Each day he was shown the records of the class study rates and the frequency of his comments following appropriate study. Under these conditions the mean frequency of teacher comments following study behavior increased to 14.6 per session. There was a dramatic and sustained concomitant increase in study behavior to a mean rate of 72 percent. According to the subjective observations of the teacher, principal and the observers, the class was under better control and classroom noise had decreased significantly.

During a brief Reversal phase, the teacher provided almost no reinforcement for study behavior. This resulted in a sharp decrease in study, which by the sixth session was well within the baseline range. According to the subjective judgments of the teacher, principal and observers, disruptive behaviors and high noise levels also returned.

During the Reinforcement$_2$ phase, an immediate sustained increase in study to a mean rate of 76 percent accompanied an increase of "+" teacher comments to a mean frequency of 14 per session. In the final nine sessions (43 to 52) of the Reinforcement$_2$ phase, the teacher was instructed to continue reinforcing study behavior but to discontinue making comments following nonstudy behaviors. Up to that point, the level of these "−" comments had remained fairly constant, occurring in about 12 intervals per session. When the teacher decreased "−" comments so that they occurred in only 4.5 intervals per session, there was no significant change in the class study rate. Therefore, study behavior seemed to be unaffected by comments (usually reprimands) following nonstudy.

Continuous observation was terminated at the end of the Reinforcement$_3$ phase when the primary observer, who was a student intern, returned to her university classes. Postchecks taken at one-, three- and five-month intervals, however, indicated that the relatively high rates of study and teacher attention for study were being maintained.

TEACHER TWO

The second teacher was also a recent college graduate and in her first year of teaching. She had been assigned to teach a first-grade class of 24 pupils in the same Kansas City, Kansas school. Again the principal and helping teacher had recommended and demonstrated procedures to the teacher for improving classroom management. The results were deemed unsatisfactory because both principal and teacher felt nonstudy behaviors were still too high.

Data were recorded every day the first 30 minutes of the morning reading period. This time was selected at the request of the teacher because of her concern about the low study rate of pupils at their desks doing "seatwork" while she was working with one or another of the three classroom reading groups in a circle at the front of the room.

The recording procedures were essentially those used with Teacher One. The percentage of agreement between observers for class study behavior and teacher attention ranged from 85 to 88 percent.

Figure 11-2 presents the class study rates for the various phases of the experiment. Mean rates for each condition are shown by a broken horizontal line. During the baseline phase, the mean study rate of pupils at their desks not participating in reading circle was 51 percent. The mean frequency of intervals of teacher attention following study behavior was 1.6.

Before the first experimental phase (Reinforcement$_1$) reinforcement principles and procedures were explained to the teacher and she was shown the baseline study record and the record of her verbal attention following study behavior. She was asked to increase the frequency of her attention for appropriate study of pupils working at their desks. As a result of these instructions,

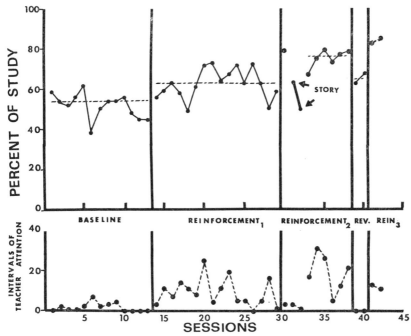

Figure 11-2. A record of study rates and teacher attention for study of pupils at desks during a first-grade reading period; baseline, before experimental procedures; reinforcement₁, increased teacher attention for study; reinforcement₂, study game following reading period; reversal, removal of study game and attention for study; reinforcement₃, reinstatement of study game and attention for study.

the frequency of teacher attention following appropriate study was increased to nine per session. The mean rate of appropriate study increased to 62 percent. The teacher, however, was still not satisfied with this study rate. So a second condition, the study game, was introduced as a contingency.

The study game was the simple classroom game, familiar to many teachers, commonly called "7 Up." In it, the teacher selects seven pupils, in this case the seven best studiers, to go to the front of the room. Then the rest of the class members put their heads down on their desks and close their eyes. The seven tiptoe around the room, touch one of the seated pupils lightly on the head and return to the front of the room. The seated pupils then open their eyes. The seven who were touched stand and in turn attempt to guess which of those who are up in front touched them. If they succeed they get to go to the front of the room and be "it" on the next round. "Seven Up" was renamed the "study" game. It was used because it is a favorite of elementary pupils up through the sixth grade, it is quiet, and it requires little or no teacher supervision.

The "study" game was introduced to the children before reading period on the first day of the Reinforcement$_2$ phase. This was a priming procedure similar to that described by Allyon and Azrin (1968). Teacher judgment was the sole criterion as to whether or not pupils studied enough to play the "study" game.

When the "study" game followed the reading period in the Reinforcement$_2$ phase, study rose to 79 percent. An unplanned reversal effect was observed in the next two sessions of Reinforcement$_2$ when the teacher read a story to her students after the reading period in lieu of the "study" game. By the second session, study had dropped to 50 percent. When the "study" game was reinstituted as a contingency for study, the class study rate rose to higher levels.

The next phase was a planned reversal in which the teacher was instructed not to reinforce study and told the pupils they could not play the "study" game. The mean study rate for Reversal was 63 percent.

The mean rate of study during the two days of the Reinforcement$_3$ phase, when the "study" game was again used as reinforcement for appropriate study was 82 percent. Since these last two sessions were during the last week of the school year, the teacher was particularly pleased at the high study rate achieved and the almost complete lack of disruptive behavior in the class.

TEACHER THREE

In the third study, the teacher taught a class of 30 seventh graders enrolled in an afternoon unified studies (English and social studies) class in the small town of Bonner Springs, Kansas, which is just outside Kansas City. The class met daily for 40 minutes with a 5-minute break and then met for another session of 45 minutes.

The class was selected on the principal's recommendation because the teacher was in his first year and there was concern because of the high rate of disruptive behaviors. These included the students' talking without permission, being out of their seats, fighting and throwing paper. The noise level was so high and so constant that the teacher kept the classroom door closed and the shade over the door window pulled at all times.

Observations were made daily during the first 30 minutes of the period before the 5-minute break.

The recording system was essentially that used in the first two experiments, except that the recording interval was 5 seconds rather than 10. Thus, the recorded behavior for the first pupil was that which was occurring after the first 5 seconds of observation, the behavior of the second pupil was recorded after the next 5 seconds of observation, and so on, so that the behavior of a different pupil was recorded at each 5-second interval until the entire class had been observed. Then the observation sequence was repeated. Teacher attention for both study and nonstudy was also recorded as it occurred. Reliability checks made during each phase of the study showed an interobserver agreement which ranged from 80 to 90 percent.

Figure 11-3 shows that the mean class study rate for the baseline period of 25 days was 47 percent. The mean frequency of teacher attention following study behavior was six times per session. The frequency of attention for nonstudy was over 20 per session; most often this attention was in the form of the command "Let's have it quiet in here."

During the first Reinforcement phase, the teacher was asked to try to increase the amount of attention to study and decrease the amount of attention for nonstudy. As a result, teacher attention for study increased to nine times per session while attention for nonstudy decreased to about nine per session. The study rate under these conditions increased to 65 percent. According to the subjective judgment of the teacher, principal and the experimenters, however, the classroom noise still remained at a disruptive level.

In the next phase (Reinforcement$_2$), the teacher added an additional condition. He placed a chalk mark on the chalkboard

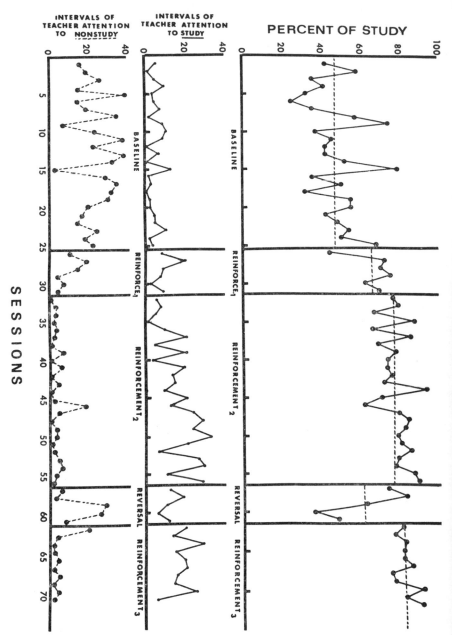

Figure 11-3. A record of class study rates and teacher attention for study and nonstudy during a seventh-grade unified study period: baseline, before experimental procedures; reinforcement₁, increased attention for study; reinforcement₂, increased attention for study and shortened between-period break for disruptive behavior; reversal, removal of punishment for disruptive behavior; reinforcement₃, reinstatement of punishment for disruptive behavior.

if any student got out of his seat without permission or disturbed the class. For each mark placed on the board, 10 seconds were deducted from the 5-minute between-period break. If as many as 24 marks were accumulated, there was to be no break. The teacher paused about 5 seconds before placing a mark on the board. If the class became quiet and the disruptions stopped within the 5-second period, no mark was put on the board.

Under these conditions, study increased to 76 percent. A marked decrease in classroom noise was noticed by the observers and the teacher began to leave the door to the room open. He also, for the first time, left the room for brief periods without losing control.

After the first two days of Reversal, when punishment of noisy behavior was discontinued, the rate of study behavior dropped sharply. At the same time, teacher attention for nonstudy behaviors increased, as did the high level of classroom noise, according to the judgment of the observers.

During the final reinforcement phase, the study behavior rose immediately to 81 percent and was maintained at that level to the end of the study.

DISCUSSION

The beginning teacher faces a formidable challenge. Except for a brief exposure to student teaching, where the classroom is organized and supervised by an experienced teacher, he or she has had no pedagogical experience. Often the practice teaching is at a different grade level than the one assigned the new teacher when he gets his own classroom. Thus, on the first day of school the teacher suddenly finds himself alone, facing a classroom of 30 or so pupils with responsibility for providing them an effective learning environment. All too often he finds that he is ill-prepared to cope with the management and control problems which face him, for his professors have not specified precisely enough what procedures should be followed to bring about classroom control.

Most teachers do learn over time the techniques which are effective in getting pupils to study, rather than to engage in non-study behaviors. Often another teacher, the principal or, in some districts, a helping teacher, suggest or demonstrate ways for achieving classroom control. Even this help, however, is often ineffective. Sometimes it is well into the year before a semblance of good classroom control has been achieved. Some new teachers never make it and drop out during or after that first year. Those that do succeed often look back and realize that both they and their pupils wasted a great deal of time and energy that first year until they "caught on" on how to manage a class.

The results of the present experiments showed that beginning teachers of three different grade levels experiencing problems of classroom control could be taught to use systematic reinforcement procedures to increase classroom study behavior even when previous attempts at assistance by principals and helping teachers had been relatively ineffective.

In the first experiment, before the changes brought about, the principal had termed the sixth-grade teacher's status as "precarious." He had contemplated replacing him during the year and certainly could not have offered him a contract for a second year if considerable improvement in control had not occurred. The teacher's awareness of his situation was reflected in a remark made to the observer after the third day of the first reinforcement phase, when an improved classroom atmosphere was already evident. He said: "You know, I think I'm going to make it." He did make it and was offered and accepted a contract to continue teaching.

In the cases of the first- and seventh-grade teachers, there was less immediate concern about imminent failure. Even so, both the teachers and the principals reported that the improvements seen in class control were dramatic.

One notable aspect of all three studies is that the teachers were able to carry out the procedures after an initial explanatory session of between 15 and 30 minutes at the beginning of each experimental period and daily feedback of the results. The feedback sessions were also used to provide social reinforcement to the teacher for carrying out the procedures. It seems likely that for all three teachers, the fact that their classes became more manageable served to reinforce and thus maintain the changes in the teacher's reinforcement behavior. They reported it was actually less work to teach using the procedures than when they had not used them. In the case of the seventh-grade teacher, this was borne out by the fact that whereas he provided attention (mostly verbal reprimands) almost once a minute during baseline, he was able to maintain a much higher study rate during the reinforcement phases with about half as much total teacher attention.

We are well aware that good teachers (who had "caught on") had been using these same techniques effectively long before B. F. Skinner formulated the principles of operant conditioning. Even these teachers, however, had not looked at behavior closely enough and with enough understanding to be able to specify precisely what they had done and what the ineffective teacher needed to do to bring about desired pupil behavior. These studies indicate that a behavior analysis approach will allow educators, including principals and helping teachers, to help the beginning teacher who otherwise may have been doomed to failure or at least to a fumbling and frustrating trial and error period, quickly to learn to manage his clasroom through systematic use of the reinforcing contingencies available to him.

Furthermore, college instructors should now be able to give prospective teachers functional information regarding the relationship of their behavior to that of their pupils. This information can be specific and precise enough so that the new teacher can apply it in the classroom.

Finally, it should be noted that the procedures were carried out with telling effect within the existing school structure. Teacher attention, a classroom game and access to a between-period break were used rather than reinforcers extrinsic to the situation. The procedures described (or others that are similar) which use the reinforcers already available in the schools can be employed by teachers in any classroom without added expense and without major administrative revision.

REFERENCES

Allyon, T. and Azrin, N. H.: Reinforcer sampling: a technique for increasing the behavior of mental patients. *Journal of Applied Behavior Analysis, 1*:13–20, 1968.

Broden, Marcia: Notes on recording. *Observer's Manual for Juniper Gardens Children's Project*, Bureau of Child Research, 1968.

Bushell, D., Wrobel, P. A. and Michaelis, M. L.: Applying "group" contingencies to the classroom study behavior of preschool children. *Journal of Applied Behavior Analysis, 1*:55–61, 1968.

Clark, M., Lachowicz, J. and Wolf, M. M.: A pilot basic education program for school dropouts incorporating a token reinforcement system. *Behavior Research and Therapy, 6*:183–188, 1968.

Evans, G. and Ozwalt, G.: Acceleration of academic progress through the manipulation of peer influence. *Behaviour Research and Therapy, 5*:1–7, 1967.

Hall, R. Vance and Broden, Marcia: Behavior changes in brain-injured children through social reinforcement. *Journal of Experimental Child Psychology, 5*:463–479, 1967.

Hall, R. Vance, Lund, Diane and Jackson, Deloris: Effects of teacher attention on study behavior. *Journal of Applied Behavior Analysis, 1*:1–12, 1968.

McKenzie, Hugh, Clark, Marilyn, Wolf, Montrose, Kothera, Richard and Benson, Cedric: Behavior modification of children with learning disabilities using grades as token reinforcers. *Exceptional Children, 34*:745–752, 1968.

O'Leary, K. D. and Becker, W. C. Behavior modification of an adjustment class: a token reinforcement system. *Exceptional Children, 33*:637–642, 1967.

Thomas, Dan R., Becker, Wesley C. and Armstrong, Marianne: Production and elimination of disruptive classroom behavior by systematically varying teachers' behavior. *Journal of Applied Behavior Analysis, 1*:35–45, 1968.

Wolf, Montrose M., Giles, David K. and Hall R. Vance: Experiments with token reinforcement in a remedial classroom. *Behaviour Research and Therapy, 6*:51–64, 1968.

12

Mathematics Performance as a Function of the Differential Reinforcement of Quality or Quantity

LARRY J. REYNOLDS, JUDY A. LIGHT and FAYE MUELLER

As INTEREST HAS GROWN in the use of reinforcement techniques in the classroom, teacher attention has been shown to be an effective reinforcer in a variety of classroom settings. Early research has focused on the effects of teacher attention contingent on disruptive behavior. A series of studies have demonstrated that systematic use of teacher praise for appropriate behavior results in relatively low frequencies of disruptive behavior in the normal classroom (Becker *et al.*, 1967; Madsen *et al.*, 1968; and Thomas *et al.*, 1968).

Thus far, there is little reported evidence that teacher attention, as a reinforcer, is functionally related to academic achievement. Hall *et al.* (1968) studied the effects of teacher attention on the "study behavior" of selected children in normal classrooms. Contingent teacher attention resulted in a dramatic increase in the amount of time children were observed attending to their tasks. Reinforcers other than teacher attention or in combination with teacher attention have been shown to facilitate both "study behavior" (Bushell *et al.*, 1968) and academic achievement (Wolf *et al.*, 1968).

A recent unpublished study we have conducted demonstrated

NOTE: A portion of this paper was presented at a meeting of the American Educational Research Association, New York, February, 1971, under the title "The Effects of Reinforcing Quality or Quantity on Academic Performance." Published by permission of the authors.

that academic performance decreases as a function of a reduction in contingent teacher attention. In that study, the teacher attended to children who were performing their tasks, accurately completing their work and passing tests on the materials under study. Teacher attention was accompanied by praise. During an experimental period, the teacher continued to contact the children, but attention was no longer exclusively contingent on appropriate behavior nor did the teacher praise children for their accomplishments. As a result of this change, the accuracy and rate of the children, as they progressed through the curriculum, was reduced. A return to baseline conditions led to an increase in performance which was quite similar to the baseline data.

Since teacher attention appears to be functionally related to academic performance, one concern is with the specific parameters of the phenomenon. For example, what is the effect of the teacher attending to various aspects of student behavior? One generalizable conclusion which might be drawn from earlier studies is that the specific behavior reinforced is the behavior which becomes dominant. However, reinforcement which increases attention to task (or studying) may not have any effect on academic achievement. Attention to task is a necessary but not sufficient condition for learning. In fact, an interesting result of our earlier study is that a decline in academic performance was not correlated to a decline in observed attention to task. It appears that the change in academic performance was due to decline in the reinforcement of "academic behaviors" not "attention to task behaviors."

In our present study, we sought to examine the effects of specific teacher comments on academic performance. It was expected that a shift in the type of behavior reinforced would result in a change in performance. The classes of behavior selected for differential reinforcement were the quality of performance and the quantity of performance. These dimensions were selected because they were the two major aspects of academic performance as measured by tests. For example, children can pass or fail tests (quality) and they can progress by passing tests at various rates (quantity). A "good" student is frequently characterized as one who works accurately and progresses rapidly. A student whose work is accurate but who does not progress rapidly is rarely referred to as a "good" student. Of course, it is impossible to progress rapidly without accuracy if progress is measured in terms of the tests passed.

Having determined that the teacher in the present study primarily reinforced children for quality or accuracy, it was decided that the effects of that emphasis could be assessed by changing the emphasis to quantity. Essentially accuracy, as a behavior, would be systematically extinguished and quantity of output would be reinforced. One would expect a decline in accuracy which would ultimately result in a decline in the quantity of tests passed.

METHOD
Subjects

The subjects were a class of sixth-grade children. There were 13 boys and 10 girls. They had a mean intelligence of 105.5 with a standard deviation of 15.34 on the Otis-Lennon Mental Abilities Test. The neighborhood from which the students were drawn was judged to be a middle-income area. The class was under continuous observation throughout the school year in which this study took place. The students were subjects in another study early in the school year. That study examined the effects of reduced contingent attention on academic performance (unpublished).

Teacher

The teacher had four years of teaching experience. She taught at the school for two years prior to this study. During her fourth year of teaching, she was trained in the principles of operant behavior analysis and the techniques of behavior modification. She worked with the first two authors throughout the school year in which this study was conducted.

Setting

The class was held in an elementary school, grades K through 6. The school is a demonstration school for the Instructional Design and Evaluation Program of the Learning Research and Development Center, University of Pittsburgh. The experiment was conducted during the mathematics period in the last two months of the school year. The period extended from 10:35 to 11:15 A.M. each day of the school week. An individualized curriculum, Individually Prescribed Instruction (IPI),[1] was employed for mathematics instruction.

In the IPI curriculum, each student is given a pretest to determine the skills he must learn. The pretest identifies the instructional needs of a child, and he is "prescribed" instructional tasks determined to be appropriate by the pretest results and the teacher's judgement. Upon completion of a prescribed task, the child takes a test on that skill. If he passes the test, he is allowed to continue to another objective. If he fails a test, he prepares for another test on the same objective. Once a child has completed the tasks and passed the tests for all the skills in an area (e.g. addition, subtraction, etc.), he takes a posttest covering all of the skills in the area. The criterion for passing a test was 85 percent of the items correct. For those tests with six or less items, a child could err on no more than one item.

Virtually every child in the class is doing something different. By the time the children reach the sixth grade in IPI, they are working in widely different parts of the curriculum. This is in terms of both the difficulty and the subject area.

In the context of this curriculum, the teacher's main responsibilities are to (a) assist children having difficulty with their prescribed tasks, (b) prescribe instructional tasks to those having difficulty (the students wrote the first prescriptions based on a standard guide) and (c) evaluate pretest results.

The Traveling Teacher

Throughout the study, the teacher employed a "style" of teaching which allowed her to quickly circulate around the classroom, reinforcing children at a high frequency. This style of teaching was named "traveling" due to the mobile dimension of the role.[2]

---

[1] Individually Prescribed Instruction is the product of the Learning Research and Development Center, University of Pittsburgh.

[2] The early work on the traveling teacher role was carried out between the first author and Mrs. Dorothy Buchanan. Mrs. Buchanan coined the term "traveling teacher."

The teacher circulated around the room following a pattern that insured she would come into contact with every student many times each period. However, the pattern was not easily predicted, since requests for attention frequently resulted in a change in direction of travel. As she traveled, the teacher specifically avoided long interactions with any one student. If the student needed extensive help, the teacher would solicit the aid of another student, prescribe an alternate task or frequently return to the desk of the troubled student to evaluate his work and provide short specific instructions.

As mentioned, the teacher was trained in behavior modification techniques. Specifically, the teacher learned to manage and motivate the children through the use of attention and praise. The teacher sought to attend only to children who were "working." Attention was contingent on the children attending to their tasks, following correct procedures or doing well on their prescribed tasks and tests. The teacher also responded to children who appropriately requested her attention by placing a piece of construction paper in the form of a miniature tent on top of their desks. In addition to only interacting with appropriately behaving students, the teacher frequently praised those children.

Children who were moving around the room, talking to their neighbors about something other than mathematics or doing something unrelated to mathematics were specifically ignored. Punishing comments were rarely made.

Experimental Conditions

The study employed a modified repeated measures design which used the subjects as their own experimental control. Data were collected on successive days for each experimental condition. The unique feature of this design is that data for any one day are representative of only a portion of the class membership; that is, data were recorded for only those students who happened to take a test on a skill. Previous research had shown that these data form an extremely stable baseline despite their apparent lack of representativeness. Since an earlier study in the same classroom showed that changes in teacher behavior may have delayed or progressive effects, the duration of the experimental conditions was dependent upon a stabilization of performance following the experimental changes. The criterion for stabilization required that a change in the data had to be consistent for at least five days (representative of a school week). The teacher consistently followed the traveling role described above.

Reinforcement of Quality

During this condition, the teacher reinforced children for the quality or accuracy of their academic performance. She praised them for correct answers, high accuracy on completed tasks and passing tests. Her comments included such statements as: "that's it, you've got that right." "very accurate work," "wow, you passed your test," etc. Tests passed on the first attempt were singled out for special attention. This condition lasted for eight days.

Reinforcement of Quantity

In this condition, the teacher changed from an emphasis on quality to an emphasis on quantity. She specifically reinforced children for the number of problems completed, the number of pages completed and the number of tests passed. The comments now took the form: "you solved that problem in one minute," "very nice, that's three pages already," "oh boy, two tests in two days, you're really passing a lot of tests," etc. Equal praise was given for all tests passed whether or not they were the first attempt. This condition was eight days in duration.

Reinforcement of Quality: Reversal

The teacher reversed to the reinforcement of quality of performance as in the baseline condition.

Teacher Observation

The teacher's verbal behavior was tape recorded for thirty minutes each day of the study. The teacher carried a "wireless" microphone suspended from her neck. A radio receiver placed in the classroom relayed the teacher's comments to a tape recorder. The teacher wore a microphone nearly every day of the school year, and by the end of the year, the children were accustomed to it. Incidentally, the children were quite aware of the microphone's function; however, they did not know why the tape recordings were being made. They never heard a tape recording, and their questions concerning the microphone quickly extinguished early in the school year.

The teacher's comments were evaluated on the basis of the tape recordings. Her comments were categorized by their function. A distinction was made between comments judged to be antecedent or consequential to behavior. The consequential comments were further analyzed into subcategories according to the type of behavior to which they referred. Of particular interest in this study were comments which referred to the quality or the quantity of a child's work. Quality references concerned the accuracy of each child's performance on problems, pages of a task or tests. Quantity references concerned the number of problems completed, pages of the task or tests passed. This category also included references to rate. All other reinforcing comments were combined into a third category.

Each tape recording was analyzed for the frequency of comments in each of the categories. Each phrase of the teacher was judged separately. If the teacher's comments switched categories in the course of a conversation with a child, each comment was recorded in its respective category. If the teacher engaged in an extended conversation with a child, each fifteen-second interval was considered a comment. For example, if the teacher talked to a child for 38 seconds without changing categories, the number of comments was defined as two. Comments of a duration greater than fifteen seconds were separately categorized.

The reliability of the analysis was determined by a comparison of the frequency of the comments in each category, as noted by two independent evaluators. Reliability was computed as the percentage of agreement (lesser number of recorded comments multiplied by 100 and divided by the greater number of recorded comments).

Student Performance

The number of tests on each skill taken, passed and failed was recorded for each class period of the experiment. The skill tests were selected because their relative frequency was about eight per day in contrast to one or two per day for posttests. In IPI, the tests for each skill are the best measure of academic performance, since performance on the prescribed tasks is difficult to evaluate. For instructional reasons, the scoring keys for the *tasks* were openly available to the students.

To assure the accuracy of the test data, the children took their tests in a special area of the classroom. Consequently, the teacher could easily determine which students were taking tests. Talking was not allowed in the testing area. The teacher had the option of removing a test and prescribing an alternate form if a child sought assistance. The skill tests were scored and the results recorded by the students. The scoring keys were provided by a teacher's aide along with special scoring pens. The students left their regular pencils and pens with the aide. In addition to monitoring the test keys and pencils, the aide scored the pretests and posttests. The aide checked the accuracy of the student's scoring after the tests were turned in by the students.

RESULTS

The experimental change from an emphasis on quality to an emphasis on quantity resulted in a decline in both the quality and quantity of the test performance of the class. The reversal to an emphasis on quality was followed by an increase in both the quality and quantity of the tests.

Of particular interest is the performance of the class on their first attempts on tests following the completion of their prescribed instructional tasks. The first test directly reflects the possible effects of teacher-child interactions during the child's preparation for the test. If the child fails a test, he must again prepare for a test on the same skill. It is difficult to predict the interactive effects of failure and teacher behavior. Moreover, the effects of feedback associated with testing are unknown within this context.

The results for the tests taken on the first attempt are graphically presented in Figure 12-1. The three dimensions of the test data presented are (a) the number of tests taken, (b) the number of tests passed and (c) the number of tests failed. The number of tests involved are plotted for each day of the experi-

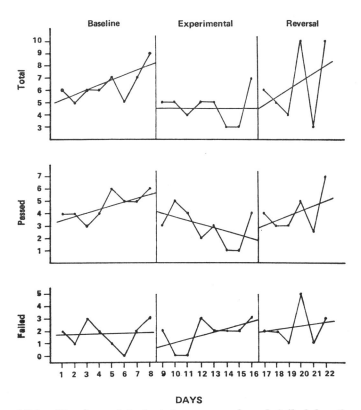

Figure 12-1. Number of tests taken, passed and failed by the class on the first attempt following preparation on instructional tasks.

ment. A line of best fit was calculated for each experimental condition to indicate possible trends in the rate the tests were taken, passed and failed.

During the baseline condition (reinforcement of quality), the number of tests taken appears to be on the increase. This increase appears to be largely the function of an increase in the number of tests passed, since the number of test failures seem to maintain a constant rate throughout baseline. The change to the experimental condition (reinforcement of quantity) resulted in a decline and stabilization in the number of tests taken. The stabilization of the test rate masks a steady decline in the number of tests passed and an increase in the number failed during this phase. For the second and third days of the experimental phase, there is a curious reduction in the rate of test failures to zero; however, an overview of the failure data leads to the general impression that the test failure rate remained stable throughout the experiment. The reversal to the reinforcement of quality resulted in an increase in the number of tests taken and passed. Again there is a steady increase in the rate of testing, as was seen in the baseline condition. The rate of test failure appears stable.

From the point of view of instruction, the most important dimension of test performance is the accuracy of the children. A second important dimension is the rate of progress through the curriculum. This can be interpreted in terms of the number of tests passed per unit time. It seems that the most desirable performance would be one combining a high rate through the curriculum with a low number of failures. This would be the most *efficient* performance. To indicate the efficiency of performance, the data were plotted cumulatively to indicate the rate the class progressed through the curriculum (see Figure 12-2). The steeper the slope, the greater the rate. The effect of failures on class performance is shown by the subtraction of the number of failures from the number of tests passed; thus, each point in Figure 12-2 represents the number of tests passed minus the number failed cumulated for each school day. The data in Figure 12-2 indicate that the efficiency of the class was not immediately affected by the experimental change. A decline in efficiency is not clearly evidenced until the fourth day of the experimental condition. The data in Figure 12-1 indicate that this was a function of a decline in test failures in the second and third days of the experimental condition. It is notable that the efficiency of the class did not immediately increase upon the return to baseline conditions. The acceleration in rate seen in Figure 12-1 can also be seen in Figure 12-2 for the reversal condition.

After failing tests on a first attempt, the students did additional work on instructional tasks related to the tested skill and then they took another test. If a student continued to fail the test, he would have to prepare for the test and take it again until he passed. As indicated above, these data are more difficult to

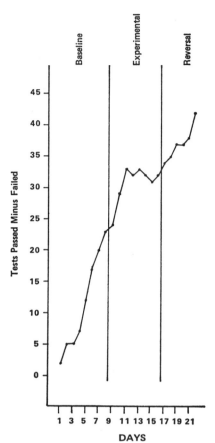

Figure 12-2. Cumulative efficiency of performance of the class on tests taken on the first attempt following preparation on instructional tasks.

interpret; however, they may reveal something about the effects of teacher behavior on general test rate. Figure 12-3 and 12-4 graphically represent the test results for all tests taken before post-testing. These data have been plotted in the same manner as the data in Figures 12-1 and 12-2.

As it was for the tests taken on the first attempt, the number of tests taken was on the increase during the baseline condition, and there was a decrease in the number of tests taken during the experimental condition. It appears that the reversal condition was

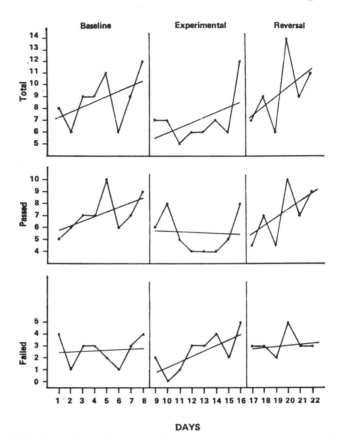

DAYS

Figure 12-3. Number of tests taken, passed and failed by the class on all attempts prior to posttesting.

not entirely different from the experimental condition in the sense that the number of tests taken increased about the same rate as was found in the experimental condition. However, the test-passing rate did not rise during the experimental condition. The rise in the test rate seems to be solely a function of a noticeable rise in the number of tests failed. The efficiency of the class, as indicated by Figure 12-4, recovered much more quickly during the reversal condition than can be seen in Figure 12-2. This can also be seen by comparing Figures 12-1 and 12-3.

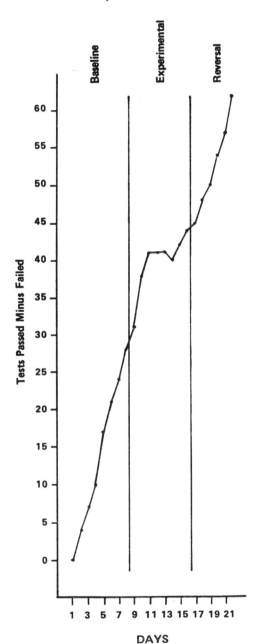

Figure 12-4. Cumulative efficiency of performance of the class on all tests taken prior to posttesting.

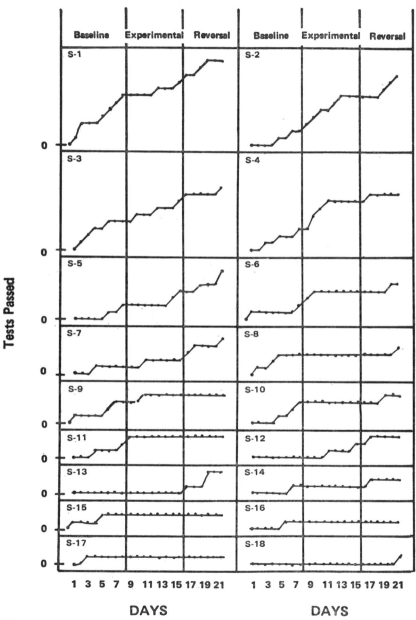

Figure 12-5. Cumulative records of tests passed on the first attempt by each student (S) following preparation on instructional tasks.

Individual Students

The general findings of the study are reflected in the records of the individual students; however, the results are not consistently supported by the records of some students. The cumulative test-*passing* performance for each student appears in Figure 12-5. Eighteen of the 23 students passed tests on the first attempt during the study. Most of the students exhibited a leveling in performance during the experimental period. Subjects 3 and 12 are notable exceptions. The delayed effect of the experimental treatment is most noticeable in the records of subjects 2, 4, 6 and 9. The slow recovery during reversal can be attributed to subjects 4, 6, 8, 9, 10, 11, 15, 16 and 17.

Figure 12-6 shows the test-passing record of 20 of the 23 students who passed tests before taking posttests. The findings are similar to those in Figure 12-5. One feature of these data should be pointed out. Upon failing a test on the first attempt, some students quickly studied for a second test on the same objective. The success of that approach can be seen in the record of student 4; however, it should be noted that that strategy did result in a decline in the slope of his graph during the experimental period. Subjects 19 and 20 never passed their tests on the first attempt. The more rapid recovery evidenced in the class record in Figures 12-3 and 12-4 can be explained by the higher passing rates of subjects 1, 3, 6, 7, 8, 10, 12, 15, 16 and 20. Five of these subjects were in the group of nine responsible for the slow recovery best shown in Figure 12-2.

Teacher Behavior

Analyses of the teacher's verbal behavior indicate that the teacher did substantially change the type of behavior she reinforced. Figure 12-7 shows the percentage of the positive comments which referred to quality or quantity.

It appears that the teacher was able to significantly alter the number of references to quantity in a relatively reliable manner. This is less true for references to quality. Although their frequency was dramatically altered, there is a gradual rise in references to quality during the experimental period. Unfortunately,

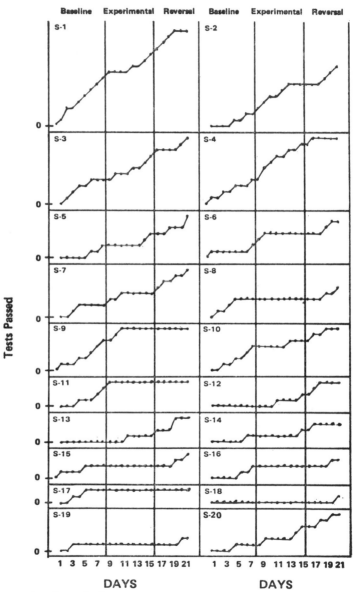

Figure 12-6. Cumulative records of tests passed before posttesting by each student (S).

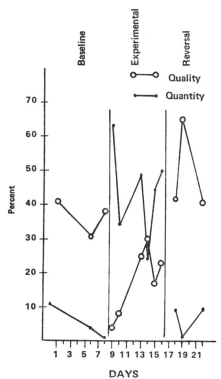

Figure 12-7. The percentage of the positive comments that referred to quality or quantity.

a combination of equipment problems and the theft of some recordings resulted in incomplete teacher data.

The total number of comments for each day (a thirty-minute period) ranged from 113 to 166 with a mean of 130 comments. The average number of comments per child per day was 3.7. The average number of positive comments was 72.9 and the average number of negative comments was only 3. The teacher kept the number of lengthy interactions at a relatively low level. The average number of fifteen second interactions was only 20.3 for the 22 days of the study.

The reliability of the analysis was calculated for 5 of the 12 recordings. For the positive comments referring to quantity, the percentage of agreement ranged from 71 to 94 with a mean agreement of 86 percent. The agreement of the references to quality ranged from 74 to 100 with a mean of 88 percent. The evaluators agreed on the number of positive comments with a percentage ranging from 91 to 97 with a mean of 94 percent. They found a range of agreement on the total number of comments from 79 to 96 with a mean of 92 percent. The two lowest percentages of agreement, 71 and 75, resulted from the low number of comments. The actual difference was only one comment for one and two comments for the other.

DISCUSSION

The experimental change would be expected to result in a decline in the test-passing rate of the children; that is, a decline in quality. Conversely, the reinforcement of quantity would be expected to result in an increase in the number of tests taken. There was a decrease in the number of tests passed throughout the experimental condition, but there was also a sizable drop in the number of tests taken. In the case of the class's first attempts to pass tests, the quantity of tests taken dropped and remained stable; however, this was not true for all attempts on tests. There was a steady increase in the total number of tests failed, which caused a rise in the total number of tests taken. Perhaps the children were attempting to increase their quantity of tests but that increase was at the expense of failure. Therefore, the general effects of extinction and reinforcement are evident. It should be noted that the quantity of tests taken during the experimental condition never achieved the levels of either the baseline or reversal conditions. It appears that to some extent, quantity in performance requires the prerequisite of quality.

There is the interesting possibility that the extinction of quality followed the classic model; that is, the data indicate that there may have been some resistance to extinction in the first three days of the experiment. Most notable is the reduction of the test-failure rate to the lowest levels found for the duration of the study. At the same time, there is a gradual decline in test passing similar to that expected during extinction after a schedule of intermittent reinforcement.

There are a number of factors which may account for the differences found among the students in the study. An individualized curriculum tends to accentuate the differences between children. Each child was working in different levels of the curriculum. It is quite possible for a child to be failing tests while the majority are passing, due to unique difficulties encountered with a particular skill or area of the curriculum. On the other hand, a child might be passing tests while the majority are failing. The curriculum has potential reinforcers built into its structure; for example, student has full feedback on the accuracy of his work on each problem, task and test. That feedback could act as a source of reinforcement for the child. Moreover, a child who has experienced continuous success within the curriculum may be reinforced by that success exclusively. It is equally possible that some students were not affected by teacher attention.

Further research should examine the independent effects of the two reinforcement contingencies. This study serves to point out that the class of behavior reinforced is an important factor, but it would be valuable to know more about the effects of altering one contingency while controlling the other. Perhaps the most important implication is the necessity for further research on the specific contingencies of reinforcement established by the teacher.

This study has a number of implications for the classroom. The class of behavior selected for reinforcement is important. The effects of reinforcing some behaviors may be opposite or less than that desired. A general suggestion that the teacher need only be relatively "positive" and improved behavior can be expected is not likely to be successful when certain classes of behavior are selected for reinforcement. It appears an emphasis should be placed on quality or accuracy before expecting an increase in quantity or rate. This study provides additional evidence that teacher attention is an important factor in the motivation of children.

REFERENCES

Becker, W., Madsen, C., Arnold, C. and Thomas, D.: The contingent use of teacher attention and praise in reducing classroom behavior problems. *Journal of Special Education, 1*:287–307, 1967.

Bushell, D., Jr., Wrobel, Patricia A. and Michaelis, Mary L.: Applying "group" contingencies to the classroom study behavior of preschool children. *Journal of Applied Behavior Analysis, 1*:55–61, 1968.

Hall, R. V., Lund, Diane and Jackson, Deloris: Effects of teacher attention on study behavior. *Journal of Applied Behavior Analysis, 1*:1–12, 1968.

Madsen, C., Jr., Becker, W. and Thomas, D.: Rules, praise, and ignoring: elements of elementary classroom control. *Journal of Applied Behavior Analysis, 1*:139–150, 1968.

Thomas, D. R., Becker, W. C. and Armstrong, Marianne: Production and elimination of disruptive classroom behavior by systematically varying teacher's behavior. *Journal of Applied Behavior Analysis, 1*:35–45, 1968.

Wolf, M., Giles, D. and Hall, R. V.: Experiments with token reinforcement in a remedial classroom. *Behavior Research and Therapy, 6*:51–64, 1968.

13

The Use of a Free-Time Contingency With Fourth Graders to Increase Spelling Accuracy

Thomas C. Lovitt, Tal E. Guppy and James E. Blattner

This investigation was conducted in a fourth grade class of 32 pupils in a public school. The study assessed spelling performances of the group as a function of three conditions: (a) when traditional procedures were in effect, (b) when contingent free-time was individually arranged and (c) when a group contingency, listening to the radio, was added to the individually obtained free-time. As a result of these procedures, the majority of the pupils' spelling performance increased, indicating that the use of contingent free-time and radio-listening were effective reinforcers.

THE PRINCIPLES of contingency management have been widely demonstrated in clinical or therapeutic settings where one investigator manages the behavior of one child (Ullmann and Krasner, 1965; Ulrich *et al.*, 1966; Sloane and MacAulay, 1968; Bijou and Baer, 1967). The majority of these reports describe the efforts of one examiner managing the behavior of a single subject and are generally concerned with the alteration of a social response such as hitting, throwing objects, crying or having temper tantrums.

Other investigations have described the further extension of contingency management procedures. Recent reports have shown how the principles of systematic behavioral management may be applied by the classroom teacher not only to decrease inappropriate

NOTE: From *Behavior Research and Therapy, I,* 151–156, 1969. Copyright 1969 by Pergamon Press. Reprinted with permission of authors and publisher.

social behavior, but also to increase certain types of academic behavior. Clark, *et al.* (1968) demonstrated that when a taken economy was instituted with a group of Neighborhood Youth Corps girls, their academic progress, as assessed by the California Achievement Test, surpassed a control group that functioned on a noncontingent basis. McKenzie *et al.*, (1968) further demonstrated that when parents granted contingent allowances for grades, the academic performance of children in special education classes increased. In both of these studies, where groups of children were involved and where the strategy was to increase some academic behavior, the managerial system was administered by a public school teacher.

The intent of the current report was to contribute further evidence that a single classroom teacher can initiate and administer a contingency system with groups of children for the purpose of increasing academic performance. Furthermore, this investigation attempted to illustrate how the acquisition of regular and continuous behavioral data would enable the classroom teacher to make objective programing decisions.

The current investigation assessed the spelling performances of a group of fourth graders as a function of three conditions: first, when traditional procedures were in effect; secondly, when contingent free time was individually arranged; and finally, when a group contingency was added to the individually obtained free time.

METHOD

Setting and Subjects

This investigation took place in a regular fourth-grade class of 32 pupils in Seattle, Washington. The students in this class were from middle or upper middle class homes and were of normal or above-normal intelligence. The class was conducted entirely by the regular classroom teacher, who administered the spelling program, calculated and graphed the pupils' scores, and managed the contingency system. The teacher was advised by a member of a demonstration project aimed at initiating procedures for continuous measurement in the elementary schools.

Procedure

During the first phase of this study (11 weeks) spelling was scheduled in a rather traditional manner. On Monday of each week, Lesson A from the 4th grade *Spelling For Word Mastery* (1959) text was scheduled. This lesson required the children to read a story containing that week's spelling words, then to say and write the new words. For example, the pupil was required to use one word from a list of new words to fill in a missing blank. On Wednesday, a trial test was given. On Thursday, Lesson D was programed, which involved completing an exercise containing about five answers, similar to Lesson B, and in addition, writing each of the spelling words. Each pupil's grade on the final Friday test was recorded in terms of percentage correct. Throughout this first phase, the only contingencies in effect were report cards and unsystematic social approval from the teacher and peers.

During the second phase of the study, which extended for ten weeks, the spelling procedures were the same—following the suggested plan in the text. Now, however, following the initial presentation of the words on Monday, the children were merely assigned spelling lessons B and D and were required to hand them in by Wednesday. No specific classroom time was allotted for the completion of the work during this phase.

Throughout Phase 2, final tests were given on Tuesday, Wednesday, Thursday and Friday of each week. During this phase, when the pupil received a 100 percent score he was not required to continue taking spelling tests on the remaining testing days of that week. For example, if on the Tuesday test a pupil received a 100 percent score during the Wednesday, Thursday and Friday spelling test period he was allowed to either read a library book or engage in any other school-relevant activity at his desk.

For those students who did not achieve a perfect score on the Tuesday test, their papers, with the corrections, were returned 15 minutes prior to the Wednesday test. This same procedure was practiced prior to the Thursday and Friday tests. The students were not required, however, to write or orally recite the misspelled words after the papers were returned. The returned papers may have simply functioned as a cue or discriminative stimulus that another spelling test was about to be given.

Throughout this phase, the teacher recorded the pupil's score as 100 percent if he returned a perfect spelling paper on Tuesday, Wednesday, Thursday or Friday; otherwise, if the pupil never achieved 100 percent, his Friday score was reported. Furthermore, the teacher recorded which day was represented by the score, 1, Tuesday; 2, Wednesday; 3, Thursday; and 4, Friday.

During Phase 3 of the study, which extended for three weeks, the procedures were the same as those in effect during Phase 2. On Monday, the weekly words were presented; Lessons B and D were assigned to be submitted on Wednesday; and tests were given on Tuesday, Wednesday, Thursday and Friday. The same contingency was in effect—when the pupil achieved a 100 per cent score he was allowed to engage in a free-time pursuit rather than required to continue being tested. An additional contingency was added, however. When on any given testing day all of the pupils received a 100 percent score, the total class was allowed to listen to the radio for 15 minutes.

RESULTS

Figure 13-1 illustrates the group data during the three experimental phases. Depicted in the figure are the total number of

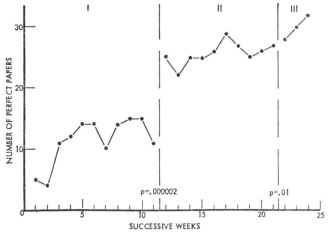

Figure 13-1. Number of 100 percent papers recorded each successive week throughout the three experimental conditions. The *p* values reflect the degree of significance between adjacent conditions.

perfect papers recorded per week. As noted, during Phase 1, where the spelling was taught by traditional techniques, the range of 100 percent scores for the 11 week phase was 11—from 4 perfect papers on the second week to 15 during the ninth and tenth weeks. The median number of perfect papers during Phase 1 was 12.

A median number of 25.5 perfect papers was calculated in the 10-week second phase, when obtaining free time depended upon obtaining a perfect score. The range of perfect papers throughout this phase was 7, from 22 to 29. When the median data from Phases 1 and 2 were subjected to the Fisher Test of Exact Probability, a probability score of 0.000002 was obtained.

During the brief third phase of the study, when a group contingency—listening to the radio—was added to the individually contingent free time, a median of 30 perfect papers was revealed. When this median was related to the median of Phase 2, a probability score of 0.01 was obtained.

Of the 32 members of the class, the median scores of 19 pupils improved in spelling accuracy from Phase 1 to Phase 2. The remaining 13 who did not improve were pupils whose median scores during Phase 1 were already 100 percent. Similarly, the median scores improved for only three pupils from Phase 2 to Phase 3, since the median scores for the 29 others were already at 100 percent during Phase 2.

Figure 13-2 depicts a pupil who improved greatly when the reward of free time was added during the second phase. As noted in the figure, S31's median percent correct throughout Phase 1 was 80 percent, but it increased to a median of 100 percent during Phase 2 and continued to be 100 percent in the final phase. When the data from Phases 1 and 2 were applied to the Fisher Test, a significance of 0.001 was revealed.

Figure 13-3, representing S15, reveals a pupil's record that also improved significantly from Phase 1 to Phase 2. During Phase 1, this pupil's range of scores was from 32–68 percent, whereas his range of scores in the second phase was from 72 to 100 percent. A median of 48 percent was calculated during Phase 1 and 80 percent in Phase 2. These median data, when subjected to the Fisher Test, revealed a probability value of 0.0001. During the three-week third phase the S's three scores were 76, 100 and 100.

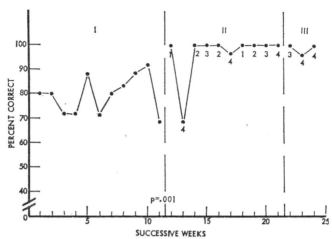

Figure 13-2. *S* 31's percentage scores throughout the investigation. The numbers beneath the data points during conditions 2 and 3 correspond to the day of the week that *S* 31's score was recorded (1 = Tuesday, 2 = Wednesday, 3 = Thursday, 4 = Friday). The *p* value indicates the degree of significance between conditions 1 and 2.

During Phase 1 of this study 125 perfect scores were recorded, an average of 11.4 100 percent papers per week. During Phase 2, however, 257 perfect papers were obtained, an average of 25.7 papers with 100 percent scores from the 32-member class per week. Of these 257 perfect papers, 150, or 59 percent, were recorded on

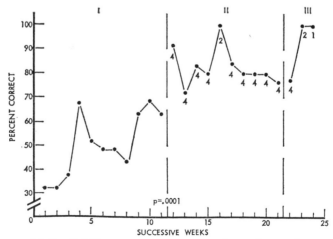

Figure 13-3. *S* 15's percentage scores throughout the study.

Tuesdays, the first day for a spelling test. On Wednesdays, the second day of testing, 69, or 27 percent of the total 100 percent scores, were recorded. Meanwhile, 24 papers (9% of the total) were recorded on Thursday, and 14 (5%) on the final day.

During the final phase of the study, where over a period of three weeks 93 total tests were given, 85 perfect papers were submitted. Of these, 62 percent were recorded on Tuesdays, 28 pecent on Wednesdays, 5 percent on Thursdays and 5 percent on Fridays. Although a group contingency was in effect throughout Phase 3, the class never was allowed to listen to the radio, since the pupils did not all submit perfect papers on any one day. The nearest the class did come to being granted the radio contingency was on Tuesday of the final week, when 21 of the 29 who took the test received 100 percent scores.

CONCLUSION

When teachers are requested to maintain evaluative data and plot graphically the academic performances of pupils, spelling may be the best place to begin. Two reasons might support such a statement. One, spelling performance is probably tested more systematically and regularly than other academic skills. The procedures for testing spelling from week to week are essentially the same—present the words orally and request the pupils to write them. Furthermore, spelling performance is generally assessed at least once each week, whereas evaluations in other academic areas are usually obtained less often. The second reason for using spelling as the basis for graphically and continuously obtaining records of academic performance is that most teachers already record pupil performance in spelling. Many teachers indicate in their record books, in a tabular manner, the weekly percentage scores of the pupils. It becomes a simple matter for the teacher to convert these tabular record book notations to percentage points on a graph.

The contingencies employed in this study represented a natural extension of the classroom environment. Free-time activities, allowing children to undertake an activity of their choosing, are often regularly scheduled classroom events. Many times, however, these activities are provided on a noncontingent basis—not dependent upon prior behavior of the pupils. When contingent leisure time reading was employed during Phase 2 and when the group reinforcement, listening to the radio, was added during the final phase, these were sufficient to alter the majority of the pupils' spelling accuracy. The classroom teacher did not have to resort to reinforcers that were more expensive or less natural to the classrooms to effectively alter the performance of the children.

Of equal importance throughout this study was that not only did pupil performance increase when contingencies were applied but the classroom teacher began to consider individually the children in his class. By viewing the pupil's performance in graphic rather than tabular form, the teacher noted how some children changed dramatically when the consequences were imposed, while others were minimally affected by them. Some children were consistently superior in spelling, while others performed in a less remarkable manner, regardless of the rewards offered. As to the latter children, the teacher speculated that while the initiated contingencies were effective with most pupils, perhaps to increase the performance of some children other individualized rules should be attempted. Further, when viewing the graphic records of certain children, the teacher noted that a program revision was called for. The data suggested to the teacher that perhaps the program was too difficult for some of the pupils and too easy for others.

As a function of this investigation, two rather basic behavioral principles were pointed out to the classroom teacher—one, that the use of systematic contingencies can affect behavior, and two, that data may be used to facilitate the making of classroom decisions. Hopefully, then, this classroom teacher's successful experience in obtaining and using group data regarding spelling will generalize to other academic areas.

REFERENCES

Bijou, S. W. and Baer, D. M.: *Child Development: Readings in Experimental Analysis.* New York, Appleton-Century-Crofts, 1967.

Clark, M., Lachowicz, J. and Wolf, M.: A pilot basic education program for school dropouts incorporating a token reinforcement system. *Behavioral Research and Therapy,* 6:183–188, 1968.

McKenzie, H. S., Clark, M., Wolf, M. M., Kothera, R. and Benson, C.: Behavior modification of children with learning disabilities using grades as tokens and allowances as back up reinforcers. *Exceptional Children, 34:*745–752, 1968.

Patton, D. H. and Johnson, E. M.: *Splling for Word Mastery.* Columbus, Charles E. Merrill Books, 1959.

Sloane, H. N. and Macaulay, B. D.: *Operant Procedures in Remedial Speech and Language Training.* Boston, Houghton-Mifflin, 1968.

Ullmann, L. P. and Krasner, L.: *Case Studies in Behavior Modification.* New York, Holt, Rinehart and Winston, 1965.

Ulrich, R., Stachnic, T. and Mabry, J.: *Control of Human Behavior.* Glenview, Illinois, Scott, Foresman, 1966.

14

Good Behavior Game: Effects of Individual Contingencies for Group Consequences on Disruptive Behavior in a Classroom

Harriet H. Barrish, Muriel Saunders and Montrose M. Wolf

Out-of-seat and talking-out behaviors were studied in a regular fourth-grade class that included several "problem children." After baseline rates of the inappropriate behaviors were obtained, the class was divided into two teams "to play a game." Each out-of-seat and talking-out response by an individual child resulted in a mark being placed on the chalkboard, which meant a possible loss of privileges by all members of the student's team. In this manner, a contingency was arranged for the inappropriate behavior of each child while the consequence (possible loss of privileges) of the child's behavior was shared by all members of this team as a group. The privileges were events which are available in almost every classroom, such as extra recess, first to line up for lunch, time for special projects, stars and name tags, as well as winning the game. The individual

NOTE: This study is based upon a thesis submitted by the senior author to the Department of Human Development in partial fulfillment of the requirements for the Master of Arts degree. The research was supported by a Public Health Service Fellowship IFI MH-36, 964-01 from the National Institute of Mental Health and by a grant (HD 03144) from the National Institute of Child Health and Human Development to the Bureau of Child Research and the Department of Human Development, University of Kansas. The authors wish to thank Drs. Donald M. Baer and Don Bushell, Jr., for helpful suggestions in preparation of the manuscript; Mr. Rex Shanks, Mr. Frank A. Branagan, and Mrs. Betty Roberts for their invaluable help in conducting the study; and Mrs. Susan Zook, Mrs. Sue Chen, and Mr. Jay Barrish for their contributions of time for reliability checks.

contingencies for the group consequences were successfully applied first during math period and then during reading period. The experimental analysis involved elements of both reversal and multiple baseline designs.

RESEARCHERS HAVE recently begun to assess the effectiveness of a variety of behavioral procedures for management of disruptive classroom behavior. Some investigators have arranged token reinforcement contingencies for appropriate classroom behavior (Birnbrauer *et al.*, 1965; O'Leary and Becker, 1967; Wolf *et al.*, 1968). However, these token reinforcers often have been dependent upon back-up reinforcers that were unnatural in the regular classroom, such as candy and money. On the other hand, several investigators have utilized a reinforcer intrinsic to every classroom, *i.e.* teacher attention (Zimmerman and Zimmerman, 1962; Hall and Broden, 1967; Becker *et al.*, 1967; Hall *et al.*, 1968; Thomas *et al.*, 1968; Madsen *et al.*, 1968). Even so, at least one group of investigators (Hall *et al.*, 1968) encountered a teacher who apparently did not have sufficient social reinforcers in her repertoire to apply social reinforcement procedures successfully. The present study investigated the effects of a classroom behavior management technique based on reinforcers natural to the classroom, other than teacher attention. The technique was designed to reduce disruptive classroom behavior through a game involving competition for privileges available in almost every classroom. The students were divided into two teams and disruptive behavior by any member of a team resulted in possible loss of privileges for every member of his team.

METHOD

Subjects and Setting

The study was conducted in a fourth-grade classroom of 24 students. Seven of the students had been referred several times by the teacher to the school principal for such problems as out-of-seat behavior, indiscriminate noise and talking, uncooperativeness and general classroom disruption. Further, the school principal reported that a general behavior management problem existed in the classroom. According to the teacher, she frequently had informed the class of the rules of good classroom behavior.

Definition of the Behavior

One and sometimes two observers visited the classroom for approximately 1 hour each Monday, Wednesday and Friday. Observation took place during the last half of the reading period and the first half of the math period. During both of these periods, similar types of activities, such as individual assignments, oral lessons and discussion, chalkboard work and short quizzes, were assigned to the students; only the subject matter varied—*i.e.* reading or math. Recording was discontinued during the brief transition from the reading to the math period.

Observers sat at the side of the classroom and avoided eye contact and interactions both before and during recording. Observers used recording sheets similar to those used in other studies (Hall *et al.*, 1968). These were divided into rows of squares for each behavior. Each square represented an interval of 1 minute. If any child in the classroom emitted the behavior, a check was made in the row assigned to the behavior, in the square representing that particular interval of time. Teacher attention to inappropriate behavior was marked in the corresponding square by an asterisk.

Interobserver agreement was analyzed by having a second observer periodically (at least once during each of the experimental conditions) make a simultaneous but independent observation record. Agreement was measured by comparing the two records for agreement, interval by interval. The percentage of agreement between the two records was calculated (number of agreements multiplied by 100, divided by the total number of intervals). In addition, by indicating teacher attention to inappropriate behavior by an asterisk, intervals could be compared asterisk against check in the appropriate square to yield a percentage of agreement between the observer and the teacher during the phases that the game was in affect.

While the behavioral definitions were constructed by the experimenter, they were formulated with the help of the principal and the classroom teacher on the basis of what they considered to be the disruptive classroom behaviors.

"Out-of-seat behavior" was defined as leaving the seat and/or seated position during a lesson or scooting the desk without permission. Exceptions to the definition and instances not recorded included out-of-seat behavior that occurred when no more than four pupils signed out on the chalkboard to leave for the restroom, when pupils went one at a time to the teacher's desk during independent study assignment, and when pupils were merely changing orientation in their seat. Also, when a child left his seat to approach the teacher's desk but then appeared to notice that someone else was already there or on his way and consequently quickly returned to his seat, the behavior was not counted. Permission was defined throughout the study as raising one's hand, being recognized by the teacher and receiving consent from her to engage in a behavior.

"Talking-out behavior" was defined as talking or whispering without permission. It included, for example, talking while raising one's hand, talking to classmates, talking to the teacher, calling the teacher's name, blurting out answers or making vocal noises such as animal-like sounds, howls, catcalls, etc., all without permission.

Introduction of the Game

Immediately after the reading period and before the math period in which the system was initially used, a presentation closely following the points listed below was made by the teacher to her class.

1. What they were about to do was play a game that they would play every day during math period only.
2. The class would be divided into two teams. (She then divided the class by rows and seats of the center row.)
3. When a team or teams won the game, the team(s) would receive certain privileges.
4. There were certain rules, however, that the teams had to

follow to win. (These rules were based on the behavior categories as previously defined.)

   a. No one was to be out of his seat without permission (except that four pupils were allowed to leave their seats without permission in order to sign out on the chalkboard to leave for the restroom). Permission could be obtained only by raising the hand and being called on by the teacher.

   b. No one was to sit on top of his desk or on any of his neighbors' desks.

   c. No one was to get out of his seat to move or scoot his desk.

   d. No one was to get out of his seat to talk to a neighbor. This also meant that there was to be no leaning forward out of a seat to whisper.

   e. No one was to get out of his seat to go to the chalkboard (except to sign out for the restroom), pencil sharpener, wastebasket, drinking fountain, sink, or to the teacher without permission.

   f. When the teacher was seated at her desk during study time, the students could come to her desk one at a time if they had a question.

   g. No one was to talk without permission. Permission could again be obtained only by raising the hand and being called on by the teacher.

   h. No one was to talk while raising his hand.

   i. No one was to talk or whisper to his neighbors.

   j. No one was to call out the teachers name unless he had permission to answer.

   k. No one was to make vocal noises.

5. Whenever the teacher saw anyone on a team breaking one of these rules, the team would get a mark on the chalkboard.

6. If a team had the fewest marks or if neither team received more than five marks, the team(s) would get the following privileges.

   a. They would wear victory tags.

   b. The teacher would put a star by each of its members' names on the victory chart.

    c. They could line up first for lunch if one team won, or could line up early if both teams won.

    d. They could take part at the end of the day in a 30-minute free time during which the team(s) would have special projects.

7. The team that lost would not get these privileges, would continue working on an assignment during the last half hour of the day, and members would have to stay after school as usual if they did not do their work during the last half-hour period.

8. If a team or teams had not received more than 20 marks in a week, it would get the extra weekly privilege of going to recess four minutes early.

Whenever the experimental conditions were changed, point "A" was again presented to the class by the teacher with a new explanation about when the game would be played. All the above points were presented before the initial use of the program and then once again after a week-long period of achievement testing during which time the game had not been in effect. The victory tags were commercially prepared circular convention tags. Each tag was of the same color and was threaded with a uniform length of wool yarn of a contrasting color. Tags were worn around the neck. They allowed the teacher to identify easily the winners during the rest of the day. The star chart consisted of a 22-by 28-inch piece of white posterboard labeled "Winners." The chart was divided into two portions designated "Team One" and "Team Two" and ruled off with team members (names) by dates (month and day). The stars were commercially manufactured with gummed backs. The special projects consisted of educational activities in the areas of science or arts which were done as a team or individually.

During the first period in which the game was applied, the teacher stipulated that the team with the fewest marks, or ten or less, would win. The criterion for the second observed session, and for all other sessions except the last one, was set at five marks or fewer. The last session was also the last full day of school. The teacher expected the children to be very excited, and she wanted to be sure that both teams would win, since she had treats planned for the special project period. For this session, the criterion was the fewest marks, or eight or less.

Experimental Phases

The experimental design included both reversal and multiple baseline phases. The data were recorded separately during the reading and math periods providing the two baselines. The study was divided into four corresponding phases. A session in one class period corresponded to a session in the other class period in that they were recorded consecutively and on the same day.

I. Math-Baseline, Reading-Baseline. For ten sessions, the normal (baseline) rates of out-of-seat and talking-out behaviors of the class were recorded during the math and reading periods. The teacher carried out her classroom activities in her usual manner.

II. Math-Game₁, Reading-Baseline. During the second phase, the game was introduced during math but not during reading.

III. Math-Reversal, Reading-Game. In the third phase, the game was introduced during reading and withdrawn during math.

IV. Math-Game₂, Reading-Game. Lastly, the game was reintroduced in math period and remained in effect during reading period. Both periods were treated as one extended period, thus using the same initial criteria of the least number of marks or five or fewer marks.

RESULTS

Figure 14-1 shows the extent to which out-of-seat and talking-out behaviors were influenced by the game. These data indicate that the game had a reliable effect, since out-of-seat and talking-out behaviors changed maximally only when the game was applied. In the math and reading baselines, the median intervals scored for talking-out was approximately 96 percent and for out-of-seat it was approximately 82 percent.

When the game was applied during math period, there was a sharp decline in the scored intervals to medians of approximately 19 percent and 9 percent respectively. Meanwhile, during reading

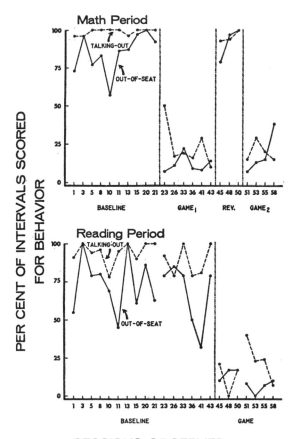

Figure 14-1. Percent of 1-minute intervals scored by an observer as containing talking-out and out-of-seat behaviors occurring in a classroom of 24 fourth-grade school children during math and reading periods. In the baseline conditions, the teacher attempted to manage the disruptive classroom behavior in her usual manner. During the game conditions, out-of-seat and talking-out responses by a student resulted in a possible loss of privileges for the student and his team.

period where the game was not applied, talking-out behavior remained essentially at baseline levels and out-of-seat behavior declined somewhat.

During the third phase, the game was withdrawn during math period, and the baseline rates of the behaviors recovered; in the same phase during the reading period, the game was introduced for the first time, and a decline in the percent of scored intervals for both behaviors resulted. Finally in the fourth phase, the game was applied during math and reading periods simultaneously. The disruptive behaviors again declined during math and continued low in reading.

Both teams almost always won the game. Of the 17 class periods that observations were made, both teams won on all but three occasions, or 82 percent of the time.

The reliability of the measurement procedures was analyzed during the reading and math periods on six occasions. Three different reliability observers were used. Agreement of out-of-seat behavior ranged from 74 percent to 98 percent and averaged 91 percent. Agreement for talking-out behavior ranged from 75 percent to 98 percent and averaged 86 percent.

Agreement between the observer and the teacher was measured during each class period that the game was played. Agreement about the occurrence of out-of-seat behavior ranged from 61 percent to 100 percent and averaged 92 percent. Agreement about the occurrence of talking-out behavior ranged from 71 percent to 100 percent and averaged 85 percent. Thus, the levels of agreement between the observer and the teacher, and the observer and the reliability observers were approximately the same.

DISCUSSION

The game significantly and reliably modified the disruptive out-of-seat and talking-out behavior of the students. The experimental design, involving elements of both multiple baseline and reversal strategies, demonstrated that the effect could be replicated across subject matter periods and that the game had a continuing role in maintaining the reduced level of disruptive behavior. On the other hand, no analysis was carried out to determine the roles of the various components of the game. An analysis of exactly what components contributed to the effectiveness of the procedure is left to future research.

As in the present study, the subject-matter periods of the typical school day lend themselves perfectly to a multiple baseline experimental design. Simultaneous baselines of the behavior of one student or of an entire class can be obtained simultaneously in two or more subject-matter periods. The modification technique can then be introduced successively into each of the periods. If in each instance there is a change in behavior (and the behavior during the remaining baseline periods remains essentially unchanged), the investigator will have achieved a believable demonstration of the effectiveness of his technique. And he will have done so without having depended upon or required a reversal of the behavior (Baer *et al.*, 1968).

Some problems arose which should be noted. The preparation of the special projects required the time and ingenuity of the teacher. This sometimes placed an extra burden on her, since she had also to prepare regular lessons. Another problem that was perhaps not as serious concerned teacher observation of behaviors. No signaling system was used. The teacher had to become alert to out-of-seat and talking-out behaviors in addition to continuing to conduct regular classroom activities. Spotting the target behaviors did not appear to be difficult for the teacher except when she faced the chalkboard or talked with individual students.

The greatest problem with the game involved two students who, before the study began, had been referred to the principal on a number of occasions for disruptive behavior. Both were on the same team and consistently gained a number of marks for their team. Usually they engaged in talking-out behavior. In most instances only one of the students was involved. In one session, one of these students emphatically announced that he was no longer going to play the game. Both the other children and the teacher expressed the opinion that it was not fair to penalize further an entire team because one member would not control himself. The teacher therefore dropped the student from the game and the marks that normally would have been imposed on the entire team were imposed just on him. During the free time, he also refused to work, so he was kept after school. The same individual-consequence procedure was used for one or both students on six occasions. Each time, the marks that they had accumulated were subtracted from the team score. It is possible that the numerous peer comments that appeared to be directed toward these students may have served as social reinforcement for their disruptive behavior. It is important to note, however, that when the students were dropped from their team, the observer continued to record their behavior as before.

Some reactions to the program were gathered from the children, teacher and school officials. The program was apparently popular with students and school officials. Every professional involved in the study who directly observed the classroom situation during the game stated that in general the students seemed to enjoy playing the game. The teacher stated that some students went so far as to request that the game be played every period. After the last session in which the game was played, the teacher requested that each child briefly write whether they liked or disliked the game and why. Of the 21 comments turned in, 14 indicated that they liked the game and seven indicated that they did not. Of those who indicated that they liked the game, some made comments such as: "I like the game because I can read better when it is quiet," "I liked it. Cause it was fun," "You give us free time," "I like the morning game because it helps keep people quiet so we can work" and "I like the team game because we win all the time." Of those who indicated that they disliked the game, some made comments such as: "No I hate being quiet," "I didn't like it because you didn't make good rules," "Because when your team loses the team that won will make fun of your team" and "Its not fair because we have the guys that talk a lot." The teacher stated that she was pleased with the method because "it was an easy program to install since it did not change any of the rules or daily activities in the classroom." All of the back-up reinforcers, with the possible exception of the victory tags, naturally occurred in the classroom setting. Only the structure of the free-time period at the end of the day changed, but it, of course, involved projects of an educational nature.

While game-like techniques are certainly not new to the classroom (Russell and Karp, 1938), an experimental analysis of their effects on behavior is unique. It may follow that an understanding of the mechanisms of the game, e.g. peer competition, group consequences vs. individual consequences, etc., together with research designed to enhance the significance of winning, by pairing winning with privileges could lead to a set of effective and practical techniques of classroom behavior management based on games.

REFERENCES

Baer, D. M., Wolf, M. M. and Risley, T. R.: Some current dimensions of applied behavior analysis. *Journal of Applied Behavior Analysis, 1:*91–97, 1968.

Becker, W. C., Madsen, C. H., Jr., Arnold, R. and Thomas, D. R.: The contingent use of teacher attention and praise in reducing classroom behavior problems. *Journal of Special Education, 1:* 287–307, 1967.

Birnbrauer. J. S., Wolf, M. M., Kidder, J. D. and Tague, C. E.: Classroom behavior in retarded pupils with token reinforcement. *Journal of Experimental Child Psychology* 2:219–235, 1965.

Hall, R. V. and Broden, M.: Behavior changes in brain-injured children through social reinforcement. *Journal of Experimental Child Psychology,* 5:463–479, 1967.

Hall, R. V., Lund, D. and Jackson, D.: Effects of teacher attention on study behavior. *Journal of Applied Behavior Analysis, 1:*1–12, 1968.

Madsen, C. H., Becker, W. C. and Thomas, D. R.: Rules, praise, and ignoring: elements of elementary classroom control. *Journal of Applied Behavior Analysis, 1:*139–150, 1968.

O'Leary, K. D. and Becker, W. C.: Behavior modification of an adjustment class: a token reinforcement program. *Exceptional Children,* May, 1967.

Russell, D. H. and Karp, E. E.: *Reading Aids Through the Grades.* New York, Bureau of Publications, Columbia University, 1938.

Thomas, D. R., Becker, W. C. and Armstrong, M.: Production and elimination of disruptive classroom behavior by systematically varying teacher's behavior. *Journal of Applied Behavior Analysis, 1:*35–45, 1968.

Wolf, M. M., Giles, D. and Hall, R. V.: Experiments with token reinforcement in a remedial classroom. *Behavior Research and Therapy,* 6:51–64, 1968.

Zimmerman, E. H. and Zimmerman, J.: The alteration of behavior in a special classroom situation. *Journal of Experimental Analysis of Behavior,* 5:59–60, 1962.

15

The Effects of Loud and Soft Reprimands on the Behavior of Disruptive Students

K. Daniel O'Leary, Kenneth F. Kaufman, Ruth E. Kass
and Ronald S. Drabman

Two children in each of five classes were selected for a four-month study because of their high rates of disruptive behavior. During a baseline condition, the frequency of disruptive behaviors and teacher reprimands was assessed. Almost all teacher reprimands were found to be of a loud nature and could be heard by many other children in the class. During the second phase of the study, teachers were asked to use primarily soft reprimands which were audible only to the child being reprimanded. With the institution of the soft reprimands, the frequency of disruptive behavior declined in most of the children. Then the teachers were asked to return to the loud reprimand, and a consequent increase in disruptive behavior was observed. Finally, the teachers were asked to again use soft reprimands, and again disruptive behavior declined.

A NUMBER OF STUDIES demonstrate that teacher attention in the form of praise can reduce disruptive classroom behavior (Becker *et al.*, 1967; Hall *et al.*, 1968; Madsen *et al.*, 1968; Walker and Buckley, 1968). In these studies, praising appropriate behavior was usually concomitant with ignoring disruptive behavior. In addition, shaping appropriate behavior or re-

NOTE: The research reported herein was performed in part pursuant to Biomedical Sciences Support Grant No. 31-8200-C, U. S. Public Health Service, 1967–69.

From *Exceptional Children*, 37:145–155, 1970. Copyright 1970 by the Council for Exceptional Children. Reprinted with permission of authors and publisher.

inforcing successive approximations to some desired terminal behavior was stressed. Despite the generally positive results obtained when a teacher used these procedures, a closer examination of the studies reveals that (a) they were not always effective (Hall *et al.*, 1968), (b) the teacher did not actually ignore all disruptive behavior (Madsen *et al.*, 1968) and (c) in one class of disruptive children, praising appropriate behavior and ignoring disruptive behavior resulted in classroom pandemonium (O'Leary *et al.*, 1969).

One might argue that where praising appropriate behavior and ignoring disruptive behavior prove ineffectual, the teacher is not appropriately shaping the children's behavior. Although such an argument is theoretically rational, it is of little solace to a teacher who unsuccessfully attempts to reinforce approximations to desired terminal behaviors. Furthermore, the supposition that the teacher is not appropriately shaping ignores the power of peers to reinforce disruptive behavior. Disregard of disruptive behavior is based on two premises—that it will extinguish if it is not reinforced and that praising appropriate behavior which is incompatible with disruptive behavior will reduce the frequency of the latter. However, even when a teacher ignores disruptive behavior, other children may reinforce it by giggling and smiling. These peer reactions may occur only occasionally, but they may make the disruptive behavior highly resistant to extinction. Thus, the teacher may ask what she can do when praise and ignoring are not effective. The present studies were designed to assess one alternative to ignoring disruptive behavior: reprimanding the child in a soft manner so that other children in the classroom could not hear the reprimand.

The effectiveness of punishment in suppressing behavior of animals has been amply documented (Solomon, 1964). Similarly, the effectiveness of punishment with children in experimental settings has been repeatedly demonstrated (Parke and Walters, 1967). However, experimental manipulations of punishment or reprimands with disruptive children have not often been investigated in applied settings. One attempt to manipulate teacher reprimands was made by O'Leary and Becker (1968) who varied aspects of teacher attention and found that soft reprimands were effective in reducing disruptive behavior of a class of first-grade children during a rest period. Since soft reprimands seemed to have no adverse side effects in the study and since ignoring disruptive behavior is not always effective, further analyses of the effects of soft reprimands seemed promising.

Soft reprimands offer several interesting advantages over loud ones. First of all, a soft reprimand does not single out the child so that his disruptive behavior is made noticeable to others. Second, a soft reprimand is presumably different from the reprimands that disruptive children ordinarily receive at home or in school, and consequently it should minimize the possibility of triggering conditioned emotional reactions to reprimands. Third, teachers consider soft reprimands a viable alternative to the usual methods of dealing with disruptive behavior. Two experiments are presented here which assessed the effects of soft reprimands.

EXPERIMENT I

Two children in a second-grade class were selected for observation because of their high rates of disruptive behavior. During a baseline condition, the frequency of disruptive behaviors and teacher reprimands was assessed. Almost all reprimands were loud, i.e. many children in the class could hear them. During the second phase of the study, the teacher was asked to voice her reprimands so that they would be audible only to the child to whom they were directed. The third phase of the study constituted a return to the teacher's former loud reprimand. Finally, during the fourth condition, the teacher was requested to again use soft reprimands.

Subjects

Child D was described as nervous and restless. He bit his nails, drummed his fingers on his desk and stuttered. He was often out of his seat talking and bothering other children. D avoided any challenging work. He was quick to argue and was known to get into trouble in the neighborhood.

Child S was described as uncooperative and silly. He paid

little attention to his work, and he would often giggle and say things out loud. His teacher said that he enjoyed having other children laugh at him and that he acted in this manner to gain attention.

Observation

Before base period data were collected, college undergraduates were trained over a 3-week period to observe in the classroom. During this time, the observers obtained reliabilities of child observations exceeding 70 percent agreement. There were two undergraduate observers. One observed daily, and the other observed less frequently, serving as a reliability checker. The observers were instructed to neither talk nor make any differential responses in order to minimize their effect on the children's behavior.

Each child was observed for 20 minutes a day during the arithmetic lesson. Observations were made on a 20-second–observe, 10-second–record basis: The observer would watch the child for 20 seconds and then record in 10 seconds the disruptive behaviors which had occurred during that 20-second period. The disruptive behaviors were categorized according to nine classes modified from the O'Leary and Becker study (1967). The nine classes of disruptive behavior and their associated general definitions are:

1. *Out-of-chair.* Movement of the child from his chair when not permitted or requested by teacher. No part of the child's body is to be touching the chair.
2. *Modified out-of-chair.* Movement of the child from his chair with some part of the body still touching the chair (excluding sitting on feet).
3. *Touching others' property.* Child comes into contact with another's property without permission to do so. Includes grabbing, rearranging, destroying the property of another and touching the desk of another.
4. *Vocalization.* Any unpermitted audible behavior emanating from the mouth.
5. *Playing.* Child uses his hands to play with his own or com-

munity property so that such behavior is incompatible with learning.

6. *Orienting.* The turning or orienting response is not rated unless the child is seated and the turn must be more than 90 degrees, using the desk as a reference point.

7. *Noise.* Child creating any audible noise other than vocalization without permission.

8. *Aggression.* Child makes movement toward another person to come into contact with him (exclude brushing against another).

9. *Time off task.* Child does not do assigned work for entire 20-second interval. For example, child does not write or read when so assigned.

The dependent measure, mean frequency of disruptive behavior, was calculated by dividing the total number of disruptive behaviors by the number of intervals observed. A mean frequency measure was obtained rather than frequency of disruptive behavior per day, since the length of observations varied due to unavoidable circumstances such as assemblies. Nonetheless, only three of the 27 observations for child D lasted less than 20 minutes and only four of the 28 observations for child S were less than 20 minutes. Observations of less than 10 minutes were not included.

Reliability

The reliabilities of child observations were calculated according to the following procedure. A perfect agreement was scored if both observers recorded the same disruptive behavior within a 20-second interval. The reliabilities were then calculated by dividing the number of perfect agreements by the number of different disruptive behaviors observed providing a measure of percent agreement. There were three reliability checks during the base period (Loud I) and one during the first soft period for child D. There were two reliability checks during the base period and one reliability check during the first soft period for child S. The four reliability checks for child D yielded the following results: 81,

72, 64 and 92 percent agreement; the three for child S resulted in 88, 93 and 84 percent agreement.

The reliability of the observations of the teacher's loud and soft reprimands to the target children was also checked. On two different days, these observations were taken simultaneously with the observation of the target children. One reliability check was made during the base period and one check was made during the first soft period. A perfect agreement was scored if both observers agreed that the reprimand was loud or soft and if both observers scored the reprimand in the same 20-second interval. The consequent reliabilities were 100 percent and 75 percent during the base period and first soft period respectively.

Procedures

Base Period (Loud I)

During the base period, the teacher was asked to handle the children as she normally would. Since few, if any, soft reprimands occurred during the base period, this period was considered a loud reprimand phase.

Soft Reprimands I

During this phase, the following instructions were given to the teacher:

1. Make reprimands soft all day, i.e. speak so that only the child being reprimanded can hear you.
2. Approximately one-half hour before the observers come into your room, concentrate on using soft reprimands so that the observers' entrance does not signal a change in teacher behavior.
3. While the observers are in the rom, use only soft reprimands with the target children.
4. Do not increase the frequency of reprimands. Reprimand as frequently as you have always done and vary only the intensity.
5. Use soft reprimands with all the children, not just the target children.

Loud Reprimands II

During this phase, the teacher was asked to return to loud reprimands, and the five instructions above for the soft period were repeated with a substitution of loud reprimands for soft ones.

Soft Reprimands II

During this final period, the teacher was asked to return to the soft reprimand procedures.

Results

Child D

Child D displayed a marked reaction to soft reprimands. The mean frequency of disruptive behavior during the four conditions was: Loud I, 1.1; Soft I, 0.8; Loud II, 1.3; Soft II, 0.9. A reversal of effects was evident. When the loud reprimands were reinstated, disruptive behavior increased, while disruptive behavior declined during the second soft period (Figure 15-1). In addition, in order to more closely examine the effects of the two types of reprimands, there was an assessment of the frequency of disruptive behaviors in the two 20-second intervals after a reprimand, when another reprimand had not occurred in one of the two intervals. The results revealed that the average number of disruptive behaviors in these two intervals during the four conditions was: Loud I, 2.8; Soft I, 1.2; Loud II, 2.6; and Soft II, 1.6.

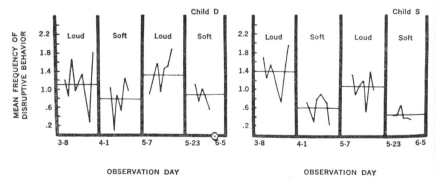

Figure 15-1. Disruptive behavior of children D and S in Class A.

Child S

Child S also displayed a marked reaction to soft reprimands. The mean frequency of his disruptive behavior during the four conditions was: Loud I, 1.4; Soft I, 0.6; Loud II, 1.1; Soft II, 0.5. Again a reversal of effects was evident when the loud reprimands were reinstated. The average number of disruptive behaviors in the two 20-second intervals just after a reprimand was made was as follows during the four conditions: Loud I, 2.9; Soft I, 1.5; Loud II, 2.1; Soft II, 0.9.

Teacher

Although teacher A was asked to hold constant the incidence of her reprimands across conditions, the mean frequency of her reprimands to child D during the four conditions was: Loud I, 7; Soft I, 5; Loud II, 12; Soft II, 6. Similarly, she also had difficulty in holding constant her reprimands to child S across conditions as the following data show: Loud I, 6; Soft I, 4; Loud II, 8; Soft II, 3. Thus, there is some possibility that the increase in disruptive behavior during the second loud phase was a consequence of increased attention to the behavior per se, rather than a consequence of the kind of attention given, whether loud or soft. As the disruptive behavior increased, teacher A felt it impossible to use the same number of reprimands that she had used during the soft period.

Because the frequency of loud reprimands was greater than the frequency of soft reprimands, one could not conclude from Experiment I that the loudness or softness of the reprimands was the key factor in reducing disruptive behavior. It was clear, however, that if a teacher used soft reprimands, she could use fewer reprimands and obtain better behavior than if she used loud reprimands.

EXPERIMENT II

Experiment II was conducted to assess the effects of loud and soft reprimands with the frequency held constant and to test whether all the children's disruptive behavior decreased when the teacher used soft reprimands. Experiment II is divided into three parts. Part I followed the same ABAB paradigm described in Experiment I (Loud, Soft, Loud, Soft), but Parts II and III involved variations which will be described later.

Part I
Subjects

Class B, Grade 2

Child Z was a large boy who said that he wanted to be a bully when he grew up. He was the only child in the class who deliberately hurt other children. He constantly called out answers without raising his hand and his work habits were poor. Child V was extremely talkative. He loved to be with other children and he was always bursting with something to say. He was also mischievous but never intentionally hurt anyone. His work habits were poor and his papers were never completed.

Class C, Grade 3

Child E was an extremely nervous child. When she directed all her energy to her studies, she could perform well. However, she was very undependable and rarely did her work. She was in and out of her seat and talked endlessly. Child W was a disruptive child whose reaction to most situations was to punch, kick, throw things and shove others out of his way. He did little work and devoted his time to such activities as chewing his pencils and punching holes in his papers.

Observation

The observational procedures described earlier in Experiment I were identical to those used in Experiment II. Each target child was observed during a structured academic lesson for 20 minutes each day on a 20-second–observe, 10-second–record basis. The nine classes of disruptive behavior were the same as those in Experiment I with some definitial extensions and a slight change in the definition of aggression. The dependent measure was calculated in the same manner as described in Experiment I.

To minimize the possibility of distance as the key factor in reprimanding the children, the target children in both classes were moved near the front of the room so that the teacher could administer soft reprimands without walking a great distance. This seating arrangement made it easier for the teacher to reprimand the target children either loudly or softly and decreased the possibility of the teacher's serving as a cue for appropriate behavior by her walking to the child.

The occurrence of loud and soft reprimands was recorded throughout the study by a teacher-observer. As mentioned previously, the teachers were asked to hold the frequency of reprimands constant both to the target children and to the class throughout the study. The teacher was also asked to hold other behaviors as constant as possible so that behaviors such as praise, "eyeing down" a child and reprimands to the class as a whole would not confound the results. A graduate student observed almost daily and gave the teachers feedback to ensure adherence to these requirements.

In addition to observations on target children, daily observations of disruptive behavior were taken on all the other children by a sampling procedure for one hour each day. Each nontarget child was observed consecutively for 2 minutes. The observer watched the children in a predetermined order each day, looking for the disruptive behaviors that had been observed in the target children.

Reliability

The reliabilities of child observations for both the target children and the class samples were calculated according to the procedures discussed in Experiment I. There were three reliability checks during the base period for both target children and the class sample. The average reliability for the target children was 84 percent and for the class sample was 79 percent. Nine additional reliability checks of the observations averaged 79 percent for the target children and 82 percent for the class sample.

The reliability of the observations during the base period of loud and soft reprimands used by Teacher B was 79 percent and 80 percent, respectively. The reliability of the observation of loud and soft reprimands used by Teacher C was 82 percent and 72 percent, respectively.

TABLE 15-1

THE AVERAGE OF THE MEAN LEVELS OF DISRUPTIVE
BEHAVIOR DURING THE LAST FIVE DAYS OF EACH
CONDITION FOR THE TARGET CHILDREN

Subjects	Condition			
	Loud I $(\overline{\times}=1.3)$	Soft I $(\overline{\times}=0.9)$	Loud II $(\overline{\times}=1.2)$	Soft II $(\overline{\times}=0.5)$
Child Z	1.0	0.9	1.3	0.8
Child V	1.7	1.4	1.3	0.6
Child E	0.9	0.6	1.1	0.4
Child W	1.6	0.8	0.9	0.3

Results

Because there were definite decreasing trends of disruptive behavior during both soft conditions for three of the four target children, the average of the mean levels of disruptive behavior during the last five days of each condition for the target children are reported in Table 15-1. There were changes in children's behavior associated with changes in teacher behavior (see Fig. 15-2).

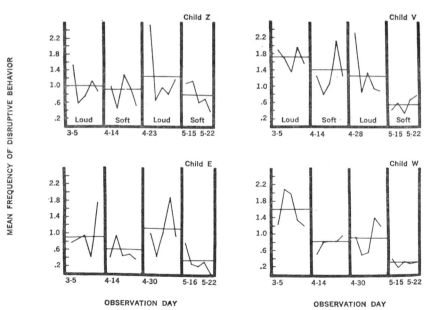

Figure 15-2. Disruptive behavior of children Z and V in Class B and children E and W in Class C.

There was a decrease in the children's disruptive behavior in the soft reprimand phase and then an increase in the disruptive behavior of three of the four children during the reinstatement of loud reprimands. Finally, the second soft period was marked by a decrease in disruptive behavior. Although the disruptive behavior of child V did not increase during the reinstitution of loud reprimands, a reduction of disruptive behavior was associated with each introduction of soft reprimands, particularly during the second soft phase. Consequently, soft reprimands seemed to influence the reduction of disruptive behavior of each of the four children. A mean reduction of 0.4 and 0.7 disruptive behaviors was associated with each introduction of soft reprimands for these children.

In order to demonstrate that the reduction of disruptive behavior was not a function of changes in frequency of reprimands, the frequencies of loud and soft reprimands are provided in Table 15-2. Although there was some slight reduction of reprimands for individual children during the soft reprimand phases, the teachers were able to hold the frequency of reprimands relatively constant across days and conditions, despite an obvious change in the children's behavior. The mean total reprimands, loud and soft, during the four conditions were as follows: Loud I, 5.7;

TABLE 15-2

AVERAGE FREQUENCY OF LOUD AND SOFT
REPRIMANDS PER DAY

Condition	Type of Reprimand to Child Z		Condition	Type of Reprimand to Child V	
	Loud	Soft		Loud	Soft
Loud I	3.8	2.0	Loud	6.8	2.2
Soft I	0.6	2.6	Soft	0.5	6.7
Loud II	3.0	1.7	Loud	3.5	1.0
Soft II	0.1	2.6	Soft	0.1	3.6
Condition	Reprimand to Child E		Condition	Reprimand to Child W	
	Loud	Soft		Loud	Soft
Loud I	3.5	0.6	Loud	3.3	0.7
Soft I	0.4	5.0	Soft	0.4	2.3
Loud II	5.7	0.9	Loud	5.3	0.3
Soft II	0.2	3.4	Soft	0.1	4.6

Soft I, 4.6; Loud II, 5.3; Soft II, 3.7. Also of particular significance was the constancy of praise comments across conditions.
There was an average of less than one praise comment per day
given to each child in each of the four conditions. It can be inferred from these data that soft reprimands can be influential in
modifying classroom behavior of particularly disruptive children.

The data from the class samples taken during the last five
days of each condition did not show that soft reprimands reduced
disruptive behavior for the whole class. Because of the variability
within conditions and the lack of any clear relationship between
type of reprimands and level of disruptive behavior, those data
are not presented here. However, the changes in the behavior of
the target children are evident when one considers that the mean
frequency of disruptive behavior for the class sample B was .9
throughout the experiment and .8 during the second soft condition. The mean frequency of disruptive behavior for the class
sample C was .6 throughout the experiment and .5 during the
second soft condition. Thus one should note that the disruptive
behavior of the four target children during the second soft period
was less than the level of disruptive behavior for the class.

Part II

Two target children and a class sample were observed in the
class of a third-grade teacher. A baseline (Loud I) of disruptive
behavior was obtained in this class during a structured academic
lesson using the procedures described in Experiment I. In the
second phase of the study (Soft I) the teacher was asked to use
soft reprimands, just as the other teachers had done. Because of
the infrequency of her reprimands in the second phase, the teacher
was asked to double her use of soft reprimands in phase three
(Soft II-Double). During phase four (Loud II), she was asked
to maintain her more frequent use of reprimands but to make
them loud. Both child and teacher observations were made in
accord with the procedures described in Part I of Experiment II.

Subjects

Child B was reported to be a happy extrovert who was a com-
pulsive talker. Child R was described by his teacher as a clown
with a very short attention span.

Reliability

The reliability of child observations was obtained for the target children on seven occasions and the reliability of the class sample on five occasions. The resultant average reliabilities were 87 percent and 87 percent, respectively.

The reliability of the observations of teacher behavior was checked on two occasions during the base period and once during the first soft period. The average reliability of the observations of loud and soft reprimands was 82 percent and 72 percent, respectively.

Results

Child B's disruptive behavior declined from 1.6 during the last five days of baseline (loud reprimands) to 1.3 during the last five days of soft reprimands. In contrast, child R's disruptive behavior increased from 1.5 in the last five days of baseline to 1.9 during the last five days of soft reprimands (see Fig. 15-3). With the instructions to increase the use of soft reprimands during phase three (Soft II-Double), child B's disruptive behavior showed a slight drop to 1.1 while child R's increased slightly to 2.0. The return to loud reprimands was associated with an increase to 1.8 for child B and almost no change for child R.

The increase in child R's disruptive behavior from the loud to the first soft condition cannot be attributed to the soft reprimands. In fact, the change appeared to be due to a decrease in both loud and soft reprimands. Even with the instructions to

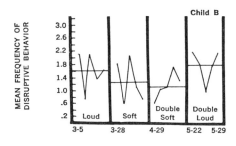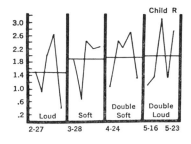

Figure 15-3. Disruptive behavior of children B and R in Class D.

double the use of soft reprimands, the teacher observations reported in Table 15-3 indicate that the frequency of total reprimands during the double soft phase was less than during baseline. However, since child R's disruptive behavior did not increase with the return to loud reprimands, the experimental control over R's behavior was minimal or nonexistent. On the other hand, child B's disruptive behavior appeared to lessen with the use of soft reprimands.

Again, the data from the class sample did not show that soft reprimands reduced disruptive behavior for the whole class. Those data will not be presented here in detail. The mean frequency of disruptive behavior for the class sample throughout the experiment was .62.

Discussion

The failure to decrease child R's disruptive behavior by soft reprimands may have been due to his very deficient academic repertoire. He was so far behind his classmates that group instruction was almost meaningless for him. It is also possible that the teacher felt frustrated because of increases in child R's disruptive behavior when she used soft reprimands; teacher D found them particularly difficult to use. She stated, "It was difficult for me to give soft reprimands, as I feared they were a sign of weakness. The walking and whispering necessary to administer soft reprimands to the disruptive child were especially strenuous for me. As the day wore on, I found that my patience became exhausted and my natural tendency to shout like a general took over." Also of particular note was an observer's comment that when verbal reprimands were administered, whether in a loud or soft phase, they were rarely if ever soft in intensity. In summary, teacher D's data showed that soft reprimands did reduce disruptive behavior in one child. Because of lack of evidence for any consistent use of soft reprimands to the second child, nothing can be said conclusively about its use with him.

Part III

In a third-grade class of a fourth teacher, two target children and a class sample were observed during a structured academic activity. A baseline of disruptive behavior was obtained in the class with procedures identical to those of Experiment I. In the second phase of the study, the teacher was asked to use soft reprimands, just as the other teachers had done. Because of some unexpected results following this second phase, the general nature of the study was then changed and those results will not be presented here. Both child and teacher observations were made according to the procedures described in Part I of Experiment II.

Subjects

Child D was a very intelligent boy (135 IQ) who scored in the seventh-grade range on the reading part of the Metropolitan Achievement Test but he was only slightly above grade level in mathematics. His relations with his peers were very antagonistic.

Child J was occasionally considered disruptive by his teacher. However, he did not perform assigned tasks and would often pretend to be working while he actually was not.

Reliability

The reliability of child observations was obtained for the target children on 15 occasions, and the reliability of the class sample was obtained on three occasions. The resultant average reliabilities were 88 percent for the observations of the target children and 91 percent for the observations of the class sample.

The reliability of the observations of teacher behavior was checked on two occasions during the base period and once during the soft period. The average reliability of the observations of loud and soft reprimands on these three occasions was 78 percent and 79 percent respectively.

Results

Child D's disruptive behavior increased from .9 during the last five days of baseline (loud reprimands) to 1.0 during the last five days of soft reprimands. Child J's disruptive behavior increased from .4 to .8 from baseline to the soft reprimand period (see Fig. 15-4). There was no change in the class sample from baseline to the soft reprimand period. The mean frequency of

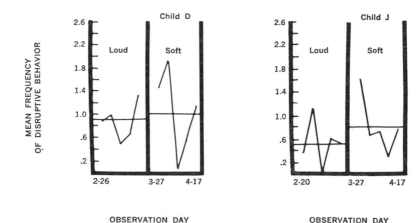

Figure 15-4. Disruptive behavior of children D and J in Class E.

disruptive behavior for the class sample during the loud and soft phase was .6 and .5 respectively.

As can be seen in Table 15-3, teacher E's behavior with child D and child J did appear to have been influenced by the experimental instructions.

Discussion

The reasons that soft reprimands failed to decrease disruptive behavior in this class are not clear. Several factors may have been

TABLE 15-3
AVERAGE FREQUENCY OF LOUD AND SOFT
REPRIMANDS PER DAY

Condition	Type of Reprimand to Child B		Condition	Type of Reprimand to Child R	
	Loud	Soft		Loud	Soft
Loud I	2.0	0.4	Loud	1.5	0.2
Soft I	0.5	1.0	Soft	0.2	0.0
Soft II			Double		
(Double)	1.8	1.1	soft	0.0	0.8
Loud II	3.1	2.3	Loud	2.5	0.0
Condition	Reprimand to Child D		Condition	Reprimand to Child J	
	Loud	Soft		Loud	Soft
Loud	4.5	1.3	Loud	1.3	0.2
Soft	0.2	3.2	Soft	0.0	2.2

important. First of all, teacher E was always very skeptical about the possibility that soft reprimands could influence disruptive behavior, whereas the other teachers were willing to acknowledge the probability of their influence. Second, it is possible that the children learned to control the teacher's behavior since a soft reprimand had to be made while the teacher was close to the child. That is, a child might realize that he could draw the teacher to his side each time he misbehaved during the soft reprimand period. In addition, this teacher tolerated more disruptive behavior than the other teacher, and her class was much less structured. Probably most important, she wished to investigate the effectiveness of various types of instructional programs rather than soft reprimands.

CONCLUSIONS

These two experiments demonstrated that when teachers used soft reprimands, they were effective in modifying behavior in seven of nine disruptive children. Because of a failure to document the proper use of soft reprimands by one teacher (D) to one child, it is impossible to assess the effectiveness on that child. Of particular significance was the finding that soft reprimands seemed to be associated with an increase in disruptive behavior of one—and possibly two—target children in one teacher's class, although the soft reprimands did not influence the level of disruptive behavior for the class as a whole. The results of Experiments I and II lead to the conclusion that with particularly disruptive children a teacher can generally use fewer soft reprimands than loud ones and obtain less disruptive behavior than when loud reprimands are used.

The authors wish to make clear that they do not recommend soft reprimands as an alternative to praise. An ideal combination would probably be frequent praise, some soft reprimands and very occasional loud reprimands. Furthermore, it is always necessary to realize that classroom management procedures such as praise and types of reprimanding are no substitute for a good academic program. In the class where soft reprimands were ineffective for both target children, a type of individualized instruction was later introduced, and the disruptive behavior of both the target children and the class sample declined.

Because soft reprimands are delivered by a teacher when she is close to a child, it is possible that a soft reprimand differs from a loud one in other dimensions than audibility to many children. Although observations of teachers in this study did not reveal that teachers made their soft reprimands in a less harsh, firm or intense manner than their loud reprimands, it might be possible for a teacher to utilize soft reprimands in such a manner. If the latter were true, soft reprimands might require less teacher effort than loud reprimands. Ultimately soft reprimands might prove more reinforcing for the teacher both because of the relatively small expenditure of effort and the generally positive and sometimes dramatic changes in the children's behavior. The inherent nature of the soft reprimand makes its use impossible at all times, particularly when a teacher has to remain at the blackboard or with a small group in one part of the room. As one teacher mentioned, "I had to do more moving around, but there appeared to be less restlessness in the class."

In sum, it is the authors' opinion that soft reprimands can be a useful method of dealing with disruptive children in a classroom. Combined with praise, soft reprimands might be very helpful in reducing disruptive behavior. In contrast, it appears that loud reprimands lead one into a vicious cycle of more and more reprimands resulting in even more disruptive behavior.

REFERENCES

Becker, W. C., Madsen, C. H., Jr., Arnold, C. and Thomas, D. R.: The contingent use of teacher attention and praise in reducing classroom behavior problems. *Journal of Special Education, 1:* 287–307, 1967.

Hall, R. V., Lund, D. and Jackson, D.: Effects of teacher attention on study behavior. *Journal of Applied Behavior Analysis, 1:*1–12, 1968.

Madsen, C. H., Becker, W. C., and Thomas, D. R.: Rules, praise, and and ignoring: Elements of elementary classroom control. *Journal of Applied Behavior Analysis,1:*139–150, 1968.

O'Leary, K. D. and Becker, W. C.: Behavior modification of an adjustment class: A token reinforcement program. *Exceptional Children, 33:*637–642, 1967.

O'Leary, K. D. and Becker, W. C.: The effects of a teacher's reprimands on children's behavior. *Journal of School Psychology, 7:* 8–11, 1968.

O'Leary, K. D., Becker, W. C., Evans, M. B. and Saudargas, R. A.: A token reinforcement program in a public school: A replication and systematic analysis. *Journal of Applied Behavior Analysis,* 2:3–13, 1969.

Parke, R. D. and Walters, R. H.: Some factors influencing the efficacy of punishment training for inducing response inhibition. *Monographs of the Society for Research in Child Development, 32,* (1, Serial No. 109), 1967.

Solomon, R. L.: Punishment. *American Psychologist, 19:*239–253, 1964.

Walker, H. M. and Buckley, N. K.: The use of positive reinforcement in conditioning attending behavior. *Journal of Applied Behavior Analysis, 1:*245–250, 1968.

16

The Application of Operant Conditioning Techniques in a Secondary School Classroom

LORING W. McALLISTER, JAMES G. STACHOWIAK,
DONALD M. BAER and LINDA CONDERMAN

The effects of teacher praise and disapproval on two target behaviors, inappropriate talking and turning around, were investigated in a high school English class of 25 students. The contingencies were applied to all students in the experimental class, utilizing a multiple baseline experimental design in which the contingencies were aimed first at decreasing inappropriate talking behavior and then at decreasing inappropriate turning behavior. Observations were made of both student and teacher behavior. The results demonstrated that the combination of disapproval for the target behaviors and praise for appropriate, incompatible behaviors substantially reduced the incidence of the target behaviors in the experimental class. Observations of these behaviors in a control class of 26 students taught by the same teacher revealed no particular changes. These findings emphasize the importance of teacher-supplied social contingencies at the secondary school level.

NUMEROUS STUDIES have reported the effectiveness of operant conditioning techniques in modifying the behavior of children in

NOTE: This study is based upon a dissertation submitted by the senior author to the Department of Psychology, University of Kansas in partial fulfillment of the requirements for the degree of doctor of philosophy. The authors express appreciation to Mr. William Medley, Principal, and Mr. Max Stalcup, Head Guidance Counselor, at Lawrence (Kansas) Senior High School for their assistance and cooperation in the conduct of the study.

From the *Journal of Applied Behavior Analysis*, 2:277–285, 1969. Copyright 1969 by the Society for the Experimental Analysis of Behavior Inc. Reprinted with permission of the authors and publisher.

various situations. Harris *et al.* (1964), in a series of studies on preschool children, described the effectiveness of contingent teacher attention in modifying inappropriate behavior, Hall and Broden (1967), Patterson (1965), Rabb and Hewett (1967) and Zimmerman and Zimmerman (1962) have demonstrated the usefulness of teacher-supplied contingent social reinforcement in reducing problem behaviors and increasing appropriate behaviors of young children in special classrooms. Becker *et al.* (1967), Hall *et al.* (1968) and Madsen *et al.* (1968) extended these techniques into the regular primary school classroom and demonstrated their effectiveness there. In all of the above studies, only a limited number of children were studied in each situation, usually one or two per classroom.

Thomas *et al.* (1968) studied the effects of varying teachers' social behaviors on the classroom behaviors of an entire elementary school classroom of 28 students. By observing 10 children per session, one at a time, they demonstrated the effectiveness of approving teacher responses in maintaining appropriate classroom behaviors. Bushell *et al.* (1968) also applied group contingencies (special events contingent on earning tokens for study behaviors) to an entire class of 12 preschool children.

There has been an effort to extend the study of teacher-supplied consequences to larger groups of preschool and elementary school subjects in regular classrooms, but no systematic research investigating these procedures has yet been undertaken in the secondary school classroom. Cohen *et al.* (1967) reported the application of various nonsocial contingencies (earning points, being "correct" and taking advanced educational courses) in modifying attitudinal and academic behaviors of adolescent inmates in a penal institution. But there is no record of investigations into the effects of teacher-supplied social consequences on the classroom behavior of secondary-school students in regular classrooms.

At present, the usefulness of contingent teacher social reinforcement in the management of student classroom behaviors is well documented on the preschool and primary elementary school levels, particularly when the investigation focuses on a limited number of children in the classroom. Systematic replication now requires that these procedures be extended to larger groups of students in the classroom and to students in the upper elementary and secondary grades. The present study sought to investigate the effects of teacher-supplied social consequences on the classroom behaviors of an entire class of secondary school students.

METHOD
Subjects

Students

The experimental group was a low-track, junior-senior English class containing 25 students (12 boys and 13 girls). At the beginning of the study, the ages ranged from 16 to 19 years (mean 17.11 years); IQ's ranged from 77 to 114 (mean 94.43). Approximately 80 percent of the students were from lower-class families; the remainder were from middle-class families. The control group was also a low-track, junior-senior English class of 26 students (13 boys and 13 girls). The ages ranged from 16 to 19 years (mean 17.04 years); IQ's ranged from 73 to 111 (mean 91.04). About 76 percent of these students were from lower-class families, 16 percent were from middle-class families and 4 percent were from upper-middle to upper-class families. The experimental class met in the mornings for a 70-minute period and the control class met in the afternoons for a 60-minute period.

Teacher

The teacher was 23-years-old, female, middle class, and held a Bachelor's degree in education. She had had one year's experience in teaching secondary level students, which included a low-track English class. She taught both the experimental and control classes in the same classroom and utilized the same curriculum content for both. She stated that she had been having some difficulties in controlling classroom behavior in both classes and volunteered to cooperate in the experiment in the interest of improving her teaching-management skills. She stated that she had been able to achieve some rapport with these students during the two months that school had been in session. She described the students, generally, as performing poorly in academic work and ascribed whatever academic behaviors she was able to observe in them as being the result of her rapport with them. She stated that she was afraid that she would destroy this rapport if she attempted to exercise discipline over inappropriate classroom behaviors.

Procedures

The basic design utilized was the common pretest-postest control group design combined with the use of a multiple baseline technique (Baer *et al.*, 1968) in the experimental class.

Target Behaviors

Both classes were observed for two weeks to ascertain general occurrence rates of various problem behaviors that had been described by the teacher. Inappropriate talking and turning around were selected as target behaviors because of their relatively high rate of occurrence. Inappropriate talking was defined as any audible vocal behavior engaged in by a student without the teacher's permission. Students were required to raise their hands to obtain permission to talk, either to the teacher or to other students, except when general classroom discussions were taking place, in which cases a student was not required to obtain permission to talk if his statements were addressed to the class and/or teacher and were made within the context of the discussion. Inappropriate turning was defined as any turning-around behavior engaged in by any student while seated in which he turned more than 90 degrees in either direction from the position of facing the front of the room. Two exceptions to this definition were made: turning behavior observed while in the process of transferring material to or from the bookholder in the bottom of the desk was considered appropriate, as was any turning that took place when a student had directly implied permission to turn around. Examples of the latter exception would be when the class was asked to pass papers up or down the rows of desks, or when students turned to look at another student who was talking appropriately in the context of a recitation or discussion.

Observation and Recording

Behavior record forms were made up for recording observed target behaviors in both classes. A portion of the form is illus-

Minute No.	1	2	3	4	5	6	7	8	9	10	11	12	13	14	15	16	17	18	19	20	21
Talking																					
Turning																					

Figure 16-1. Portion of behavior record form used to record incidence of target behavior.

trated in Figure 16-1. The forms for the experimental class contained 70 sequentially numbered boxes for each behavior; the forms for the control class contained 60 sequentially numbered boxes for each behavior (covering the 70- and 60-minute class periods, respectively). The occurrence of a target behavior during any minute interval of time (e.g. during the twenty-fifth minute of class time) was recorded by placing a checkmark in the appropriate box for that interval (e.g. box 25) beside the behavior listed. Further occurrences of that behavior during that particular interval were not recorded. Thus, each time interval represented a dichotomy with respect to each behavior: the behavior had or had not occurred during that interval of time. A daily quantified measurement of each behavior was obtained by dividing the number of intervals that were checked by the total number of intervals in the class period, yielding a percentage of intervals in which the behavior occurred at least once. Time was kept by referral to a large, easily readable wall clock whose minute hand moved 1 minute at a time.

Behaviors were recorded daily during all conditions by the teacher. Reliability of observation was checked by using from one to two additional observers (student teachers and the senior author) who visited the classes twice per week. Students in this particular school were thought to be quite accustomed to observers, due to the large amount of classroom observation done there by student teachers from a nearby university. Except for the senior author and teacher, other observers were not made aware of changes in experimental conditions. Reliability was assessed by comparing the behavior record forms of the teacher and observers after each class period in which both teacher and observers recorded behavior. A percentage of agreement for each target behavior was computed, based on a ratio of the number of intervals on which all recorders agreed (i.e. that the behavior had or had not occurred) to the total number of intervals in the period. Average reliability for talking behavior was 90.49 percent in the experimental class (range 74% to 98%) and 89.49 percent in the control class (range 78% to 96%). Average reliability for turning behavior was 94.27 percent in the experimental class (range 87% to 98%) and 90.98 percent in the control class (range 85% to 96%).

In addition, two aspects of the teacher's behavior were recorded during all conditions by the observers when present: (a) the number of inappropriate talking or turning instances that occasioned a verbal reprimand from the teacher and (b) the number of direct statements of praise dispensed by the teacher for appropriate behaviors. These behaviors were recorded by simply tallying the number of instances in which they were observed on the reverse side of the observer's form. Reliability between observers was checked by computing a percentage of agreement between them on the number of instances of each type of behavior observed. Average reliability for reprimand behavior was 92.78 percent in the experimental class (range 84% to 100%) and 94.84 percent in the control class (range 82% to 100%). Average reliability for praise behavior was 98.85 percent in experimental class (range 83% to 100%) and 97.65 percent in the control class (range 81% to 100%).

Baseline Condition

During the Baseline Condition, the two target behaviors and teacher behaviors were recorded in both the experimental and control classes. The teacher was asked to behave in her usual manner in both classrooms and no restrictions were placed on any disciplinary techniques she wished to use. The Baseline Condition in the experimental class was continued for 27 class days (approximately five weeks) to obtain as clear a picture as possible of the student and teacher behaviors occurring.

Experimental Condition I

This first experimental condition began in the experimental class on the twenty-eighth day when the teacher initiated various social consequences contingent on inappropriate talking behavior aimed at lowering the amount of this behavior taking place. The procedures agreed upon with the teacher for the application of social consequences were as follows.

First, the teacher was to attempt to disapprove of all instances of inappropriate talking behavior whenever they occurred with a direct, verbal, sternly given reproof. Whenever possible, the teacher was to use students' names when correcting them. The teacher was instructed not to mention any other inappropriate behavior (e.g. turning around) that might also be occurring at the time. Examples of reprimands given were: "John, be quiet!" "Jane, stop talking!" "Phil, shut up!" "You people, be quiet!" It was hypothesized that these consequences constituted an aversive social consequence for inappropriate talking.

Second, the teacher was asked not to threaten students with or apply other consequences, such as keeping them after school, exclusion from class, sending them to the assistant principal, etc. for inappropriate talking or for any other inappropriate behavior.

Third, the teacher was to praise the entire class in the form of remarks like: "Thank you for being quiet!" "Thank you for not talking!" or "I'm delighted to see you so quiet today!" according to the following contingencies. (a) During the first 2 minutes of class, praise at the end of approximately each 30-second period in which there had been no inappropriate talking. (b) During the time in which a lecture, recitation or class discussion was taking place, praise the class at the end of approximately each 15-minute period in which no inappropriate talking had occurred. (c) When silent seatwork had been assigned, do not interrupt the period to praise, but praise the class at the end of the period if no inappropriate talking had occurred during the period. (d) At the end of each class make a summary statement concerning talking behavior, such as: "Thank you all for being so quiet today!" or "There has been entirely too much talking today, I'm disappointed in you!" or "You have done pretty well in keeping quiet today, let's see if you can do better tomorrow!"

The concentration of praising instances during the first 2-minutes of class was scheduled because the baseline data revealed inappropriate talking as particularly frequent at this time.

Although the teacher continued to record instances of turning behavior, she was instructed to ignore this behavior in the experimental class during Experimental Condition I. In effect, baseline recording of turning behavior continued during this Condition. No changes were made in the teacher's behavior in the control class.

Experimental Condition II

After Experimental Condition I had been in effect in the experimental class for 26 class days and had markedly reduced talking behavior (see "Results"), Experimental Condition II was put into effect on the 54th day of the study. In this condition, the contingent social consequences for talking behavior in the experimental class were continued and, in addition, the teacher initiated the same system of contingent social consequences for turning behavior, with the aim of reducing the amount of this behavior occurring. This subsequent provision of similar consequences, first for one behavior and then for another, constitutes the multiple baseline technique.

The procedures agreed upon for providing reprimands for inappropriate turning behavior were the same as those for talking behaviors, except that the teacher referred to "turning" instead of "talking" in her reproofs. She could now also mention both behaviors in her reproof if a student happened to be doing both. The procedures regarding the application of praise contingent on not turning around were also the same as before, except that the higher frequency of praising during the first 2 minutes of class was not used. Also, the teacher could now combine her positive remarks about not talking and not turning if such were appropriate to existing conditions. Finally, since inappropriate talking behavior had been reduced considerably by this time, the procedure of praising every 30 seconds during the first 2 minutes of class was dropped. As before, no changes were made in the teacher's behavior in the control class.

RESULTS

Because data were not collected on individual students, it is not possible to specify exactly how many students were involved in either inappropriate talking or turning behavior. The observers and teacher agreed that over one half of the students in both classes were involved in inappropriate talking behavior and that about one third of the students in both classes were involved in inappropriate turning behavior.

Talking Behavior

Figure 16-2 indicates the daily percentage of intervals of inappropriate talking behavior in the experimental and control classes throughout the study. During the Baseline Condition in the experimental class and the equivalent period in the control class (Days 1 through 27), the average daily percentage of inappropriate talking intervals was 25.33 percent in the experimental class and 22.81 percent in the control class. The two classes were thus approximately equivalent with respect to the amount of inappropriate talking behavior in each before the experimental interventions were made in the experimental class. As can be seen, the introduction of the contingencies in Experimental Condition I on Day 28 immediately reduced the percentage of intervals of inappropriate talking behavior in the experimental class. From this point on, the amount of inappropriate talking behavior in the experimental class continued to decrease and finally stabilized at a level below 5 percent. Meanwhile, the control class continued

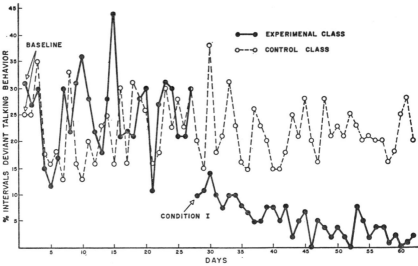

Figure 16-2. Daily percentages of intervals of inappropriate talking behavior in experimental and control classes during Baseline and Experimetal condition I periods.

to manifest its previous level of inappropriate talking behavior. In the period from Day 28 through Day 62, when the study was concluded, the average daily percentage of inappropriate talking intervals in the control class was 21.51 percent, compared with an average of 5.34 percent in the experimental class.

Turning Behavior

The results obtained with the second target behavior, inappropriate turning around, can be seen in Figure 16-3, which indicates the daily percentages of intervals of inappropriate turning behavior in both classes during the study. During the Baseline Condition in the experimental class and the equivalent period in the control class (Days 1 through 53), the level of inappropriate turning behavior was slowly increasing in both classes. The average daily percentage of inappropriate turning intervals during this time with 15.13 percent in the experimental class and 14.45 percent in the control class. As with talking behavior, the two classes were roughly equivalent in the amount of inappropriate turning behavior observed before experimental interventions were made.

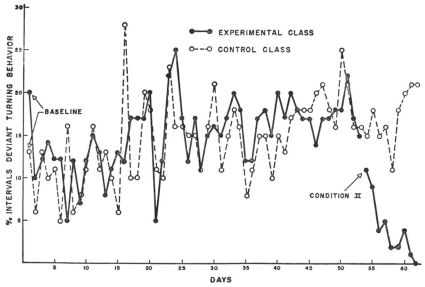

Figure 16-3. Daily percentages of intervals of inappropriate turning behavior in experimental and control classes during Baseline and Experimental condition II periods.

The introduction of Experimental Condition II contingencies on Day 54 again immediately reduced the percentage of inappropriate turning intervals in the experimental class. This behavior continued to decrease during the remaining days of the study. In the control class, the level of inappropriate turning behavior remained essentially the same. In the period from Day 54 through Day 62, the average daily percentage of inappropriate turning intervals in the control class was 17.22 percent and in the experimental class was 4.11 percent.

Teacher Behavior

During the Baseline period on talking behavior, the average number of instances of inappropriate talking per class period that received some type of verbal reprimand from the teacher was 25.76 percent in the experimental class and 22.23 percent in the control class. The majority of these verbal responses took the form of saying, "Shhh!" On occasion, observers noted that the teacher corrected students directly, using their names. On several occasions, she made general threats, stating that she would keep people after school if talking did not subside; however, she was never observed to carry out this kind of threat. During this period, there were no observations of the teacher's dispensing any praise for not talking. During Experimental Condition I, the teacher disapproved of an average of 93.33 percent of inappropriate talking instances per class period in the experimental class. In the control class during this time, she disapproved of an average of 21.38 percent of inappropriate talking instances per class period. She also praised on an average of 6.07 occasions per experimental class period, contingent on not talking, during this time. With two exceptions, she was not observed directly to praise not talking in the control class.

During the Baseline period on inappropriate turning behavior, the average percentage of inappropriate turning instances per class period that received verbal reprimands from the teacher was 12.84 percent in the experimental class and 13.09 percent in the control class. Most of these were simple instructions, like, "Turn around!" and she used the student's name in most cases. During Experimental Condition II, the average percentage of inappropriate turning instances per class period that occasioned disapproving responses from the teacher was 95.50 percent in the experimental class and 18.50 percent in the control class. In addition, she praised on an average of 5.75 occasions per experimental class period, contingent on not turning. In the control class, she was not observed to provide any such praise for not turning.

DISCUSSION

The results indicate quite clearly that the statements of praise and disapproval by the teacher had consistent effects on the two target behaviors observed in the experimental class. Both behaviors decreased. That the statements were, in fact, responsible for the observed modifications in behavior was demonstrated through the multiple baseline procedure in which the target behaviors changed maximally only when the statements were applied. The use of the control class data further substantiates this contention. The observations of teacher behavior in the study provide evidence that the program was being carried out as specified in the two classrooms.

The design of the study does not make it possible to isolate the separate effects of the teacher's statements of praise and disapproval on the students' behaviors. It is possible that one or the other of these was more potent in achieving the observed results. In addition to the possibility that statements of praise or disapproval, in themselves, might have differed in their effectiveness in modifying behavior, the different manner in which these two types of statements were delivered may have resulted in differing effects. The design, it will be remembered, called for disapproving statements to be delivered to individual students, while praise was delivered to the class as a whole. This resulted in a sudden onset of numerous disapproving statements delivered to individual students when Experimental Condition I was put into effect. The observers agreed that the students seemed "stunned" when this essentially radical shift in stimulus conditions took place. The immediate and marked decrease in inappropriate talking behavior at this point may have resulted because of this shift. The phenomenon can be compared to the sudden response rate reductions observed in animals when stimulus conditions are shifted suddenly. The decrease in inappropriate turning behavior observed when Experimental Condition II was put into effect, while immediate, was not of the same magnitude as that observed previously. Perhaps some measure of adaptation to this type of stimulus shift had taken place. Regardless of the possible reasons for the immediate effects observed when the experimental conditions were put into effect, it is also true that the direction of these effects was maintained thereafter in both experimental conditions. The combination of praise and disapproval undoubtedly was responsible for this.

Assuming that praise statements were functioning as positive reinforcers for a majority of the experimental class, they may have operated not only directly to reinforce behaviors incompatible with inappropriate talking and turning but also to generate peer-group pressure to reduce inappropriate behavior because such statements were contingent on the entire class' behavior. Further studies are needed to investigate the effects of peer-group contingencies on individual behavior.

Although it appears that the statements of praise and disapproval by the teacher functioned as positive reinforcers and punishers, respectively, an alternative possibility exists. These statements may have been operating primarily as instructions that the students complied with. It is conceivable that had praise statements, for example, been delivered as instructions independent of the occurrence of inappropriate behavior the same results might have been obtained. Also, it should be noted that results obtained in other studies (Lövaas *et al.*, 1964; Thomas *et al.*, 1968) indicate that disapproving adult behaviors do not have a unitary effect on children's behavior. What would appear to be punishing types of statements are sometimes found to function as positive reinforcers. Informal observations indicated that this seemed to be the case in this study, at least as far as one student was concerned.

Several comments may be made regarding the practical aspects of the present approach. The study further exemplifies the usefulness of the multiple baseline technique, which makes it unnecessary to reverse variables in order to demonstrate the specific effectiveness of the experimental variables. Many teachers and school administrators will undoubtedly find this approach more acceptable in their schools. The notion of reversing variables to reinstitute what is considered to be maladaptive or inappropriate behavior is extremely repugnant to many educators who are more interested in "getting results" than in experimental verification of the results obtained.

The study differs from most previous operant research in class-rooms in that the focus was on recording and modifying target behaviors without specific regard to the individual students in-volved. Most earlier studies have focused on observing the be-havior of one student at a time. With this approach, it takes con-siderable time to extend observations to an entire class and usu-ally this is not done. While observations of an entire class are not always necessary from a practical point of view (i.e. only a few students are involved in inappropriate behaviors), the present approach does seem feasible when the number of students involved in one or more classes of inappropriate behavior is large. From an experimental point of view, this study was deficient in not pro-viding more exact information as to the number of students actu-ally involved in the target behaviors. Once this facet is deter-mined, however, the essential approach seems quite feasible and practical.

It might be argued that a group-oriented approach will not function in the same way with all members of the group. This is potentially possible, if not probable. However, two practical as-pects should be considered. In the first place, such an approach could conceivably remediate the total situation enough to allow the teacher to concentrate on those students who either have not responded or who have become worse. Secondly, perhaps a gen-eral reduction in inappropriate behavior is all the teacher desires. In this study, for example, the results obtained were, according to the teacher, more than enough to satisfy her. She did not, in other words, set a criterion of eliminating the target behaviors.

A significant practical aspect of this study was the amount of difficulty encountered by the teacher in recording behavior and delivering contingent praise and disapproval. It might be asked how she found time to teach when she was involved in these activities. Perhaps the best judge of the amount of difficulty in-volved with these techniques is the teacher herself. She reported that, initially, recording behaviors was difficult. The task did take considerable time and did interrupt her on-going teaching. On the other hand, the large amount of talking and other inappropriate behaviors occurring at the beginning of the study also interrupted her teaching. She felt that as the study went on she became more accustomed to recording and it became easier for her to accomplish. She pointed out that the fact that she usually positioned herself at her desk or rostrum also made recording somewhat easier because the forms were readily available. This was her usual position in the classroom; she did not change to make recording easier. Considerable time was required to deliver contingent praise and disapproval at the beginning of the experimental conditions. This also tended to interrupt teaching tasks as far as the teacher was concerned. However, she felt that this state of affairs did not last long because the target behaviors declined so immediately and rapidly. The overall judgment of the teacher was that the procedures of recording and dispensing contingent consequences did, indeed, interfere with her teaching but that the results obtained more than compensated for this. When the levels of inappropriate behavior had been lowered, she felt she could carry out her teaching responsibilities much more efficiently and effectively than before. She felt strongly enough about the practicality and effectiveness of the techniques to present information and data on the study to her fellow teachers and to offer her services as a consultant to those who wanted to try similar approaches in their classrooms.

The senior author held frequent conferences with the teacher after class periods. The aim was to provide her with feedback regarding her performance in class. She was actively praised for appropriate modifications in her classroom behavior and for record-keeping behavior. Likewise, she was criticized for mistakes in her application of program contingencies.

Finally, the data of this experiment are considered significant by reason of the strong implication that teacher praise and disapproval can function to modify the behavior of high-school-level students. This potentially extends the implications earlier research accomplished on the preschool and elementary levels.

REFERENCES

Baer, D. M., Wolf, M. M. and Risley, T. R.: Some current dimensions of applied behavior analysis. *Journal of Applied Behavior Analysis 1*:91–97, 1968.

Becker, W. C., Madsen, C. H., Jr., Arnold, C. R. and Thomas, D. R.: The contingent use of teacher attention and praise in reducing classroom behavior problems. *Journal of Special Education, 1:* 287–307, 1967.

Bushell, D., Jr., Wrobel, P. A. and Michaelis, M. L.: Applying "group" contingencies to the classroom study behavior of preschool children. *Journal of Applied Behavior Analysis, 1:*55–61, 1968.

Cohen, H. L., Filipczak, J. and Bis, J. S.: *Case I: An Initial Study of Contingencies Applicable to Special Education.* Silver Spring, Md., Educational Facility Press—Institute for Behavioral Research, 1967.

Hall, R. V. and Broden, M.: Behavior changes in brain-injured children through social reinforcement. *Journal of Experimental Child Psychology, 5:*463–479, 1967.

Hall, R. V., Lund, D. and Jackson, D.: Effects of teacher attention on study behavior. *Journal of Applied Behavior Analysis, 1:*1–12, 1968.

Harris, F. R., Wolf, M. M. and Baer, D. M.: Effects of adult social reinforcement on child behavior. *Young Children, 20:*8–17, 1964.

Lövaas, O. I., Freitag, G., Kinder, M. I., Rubenstein, D. B., Schaeffer, B. and Simmons, J. B.: *Experimental Studies in Childhood Schizophrenia—Establishment of Social Reinforcers.* Paper read at Western Psychological Assn., Portland, April, 1964.

Madsen, C. H., Becker, W. C. and Thomas, D. R.: Rules, praise and ignoring: elements of elementary classroom control. *Journal of Applied Behavior Analysis, 1:*139–150, 1968.

Patterson, G. R.: An application of conditioning techniques to the control of a hyperactive child. In L. P. Ullmann and L. Krasner (Eds.): *Case Studies in Behavior Modification.* New York, Holt, Rinehart and Winston, 1966, pp. 370–375.

Rabb, E. and Hewett, F. M.: Developing appropriate classroom behaviors in a severely disturbed group of institutionalized kindergarten-primary children utilizing a behavior modification model. *American Journal of Orthopsychiatry, 37:*313–314, 1967.

Thomas, D. R., Becker, W. C. and Armstrong, M.: Production and elimination of disruptive classroom behavior by systematically varying teacher's behavior. *Journal of Applied Behavior Analysis, 1:* 35–45, 1968.

Zimmerman, E. H. and Zimmerman, J.: The alteration of behavior in a special classroom situation. *Journal of the Experimental Analysis of Behavior. 5:*59–60. 1962.

17

Behavioral Management
of School Phobia

T. Ayllon, D. Smith and M. Rogers

In an eight-year-old Negro child diagnosed as suffering from school phobia, the problem was redefined as zero or low probability of school attendance. The implementation of techniques for increasing the probability involved getting the child's mother to withdraw the rewards of staying at home. Then a home-based motivational system was used to reinforce school attendance and refusal to attend school resulted in punishment. School attendance was generated quickly and maintained even after the procedures were withdrawn a month later. No "symptom substitution" was noticed either by the parents or the school officials within the nine months of follow-up. An additional important finding was that when the child's school phobia was used to produce aversive consequences on the mother, it immediately led the mother to find a "natural" way to rectify her child's psychiatric condition.

THE MOST WIDELY accepted approach to neurosis is the psychoanalytical one. The phobic object is said to serve as a symbol of some danger that is extremely real to the patient and whose

NOTE: A portion of this paper was read at the Southeastern Psychological Association, New Orleans, 1969. We thank Dr. L. L'Abate for the use of material from psychodiagnostic evaluations. We also acknowledge our deep appreciation to Dr. Joseph Zimmerman and Dr. Zal Newmark for their critical reading of the manuscript.

From the *Journal of Behavior Therapy and Experimental Psychiatry,* *1*:125–138, 1970. Copyright 1970 by Pergamon Press. Reprinted with permission of authors and publisher.

origins are attributed to early childhood. Concern for the underlying dynamics of school phobia has resulted in provocative speculations. For example, sometimes the cause of the child's fear
of school is traced to "an unrealistic self-image" (Leventhal and
Sells, 1964). More often the mother is blamed for the child's
school phobia, as she is said to displace her own hostility onto
the school (Coolidge *et al.*, 1962). It has also been suggested
that the hostile impulses of sadomasochistic school personnel
toward school phobics leads them to reenact in the school setting
the sadomasochistic relationship alleged to exist between mothers
and their children (Jarvis, 1964). Unfortunately, such hypotheses
have not led to standardized techniques for its treatment.

An alternative approach to school phobia is that of Wolpe's
systematic desensitization technique. The pioneering work of
Wolpe constitutes the first effective translation of the conditioning
techniques of Pavlov and Hull to therapeutic procedures. Indeed,
Wolpe's systematic desensitization technique marks a departure
from methods used up to 1958 which was when his book *Psychotherapy by Reciprocal Inhibition* appeared in print.

The effectiveness of this approach, unlike the psychoanalytic
one, has received empirical validation (Garvey and Hegrenes,
1966; Lagarus *et al.*, 1965; Patterson *et al.*, 1964). The impact
of Wolpe's work has been such that even when modifications of
his work have been explored, such as Patterson's (1965) use of
M&M's to reinforce responses to the hierarchy of stimuli presented
to the phobic child or Lazarus and Abramovitz's (1962) use of so-
called 'emotive imagery', the conceptual rationale and procedural
details remain those advanced by Wolpe (1958).

A complementary approach to school phobia may now be available through the use of operant techniques. In dealing with "emotional" or behavioral problems this approach tries to determine
through observation and experimentation the particular environmental event likely to be responsible for the behavior. The rationale for an operant approach to school phobia, however, requires
that the condition or diagnosis of school phobia be behaviorally
redefined. Indeed, irrespective of the interpretation to be attached
to school phobia, the major feature of this condition is immediately
accessible to observation: the child's attendance at school. School

phobia, therefore, can be redefined behaviorally as an observable event of low frequency or probability of occurrence. Two major methodological advantages are obtained by such a redefinition. First, frequencies and rates of behavior constitute the data of a large body of experimental research. Techniques to increase or decrease rates of behavior initially developed in the laboratory (Skinner, 1938; Ferster and Skinner, 1957) have been successfully extended to the treatment of pathological behaviors in clinical settings (Ayllon and Michael, 1959; Isaacs *et al.*, 1960; Ayllon and Haughton, 1964; Wolf *et al.*, 1964; Ayllon and Azrin, 1965; Ayllon and Azrin, 1968b).

The second advantage of redefining school phobia as a low-probability behavior is that it immediately suggests what the relevant target for treatment is, namely reinstatement of school attendance. Our strategy then was to apply such behavioral procedures to the analysis and modification of school phobia.

It should be recognized that while a legitimate target of treatment may be self-understanding, growth and insight, these are important only insofar as they are presumed to facilitate the behavioral change from not going to school to normal school attendance. The observable datum, school attendance, then is a legitimate treatment objective if not the only relevant one, for school phobia. Another objective of the behavioral intervention reported here was to bypass treatment in a clinical situation or in a therapist's office, since success in such situations would still have to generalize into the school situation for the success to be relevant to the problem. Therefore, our attempt was to treat the phobia in the environment where it survived. In this manner, if our strategy succeeded, there would be no school phobia and the problem of generalization would simply not arise.

BACKGROUND
The Child

The subject of this study was Valerie, an eight-year-old Negro girl from a low-income area. In the second grade, she had exhibited episodes of gradually increasing absences from school until she stopped going to school in that grade; this continued on into the third grade.

The Family

She had three siblings, a sister who was nine and two brothers ages six and ten. None of her siblings had a history of school phobia. Her father was periodically employed as a construction worker and her mother worked as a cook in a restaurant. Both had high-school–level educations.

School Phobia

Valerie held an above-average school attendance record in kindergarten and the first grade. She started skipping school only gradually in the second grade and finished that year with 41 absences. According to school records, Valerie attended no more than the first 4 days of shool in the third grade. During her 4 days of attendance, her mother reported that Valerie refused to go to school. Whenever the mother attempted to take her to school, Valerie threw such violent temper-tantrums, screaming and crying, that it was nearly impossible to move her from the house.

Finally, the mother took Valerie to a number of specialists, including a school counselor, a medical specialist and a social worker. All these professionals offered extensive advice. The mother reported that the advice took several forms: "Ignore the behavior and it will go away"; "Give her plenty of praise and affection"; and "Punish her severely if she refuses to go." Unfortunately, none of this advice worked and Valerie continued to stay away from school.

Val, according to the mother's reports, had much trouble going to sleep and lay awake during much of the night. Val had no friends except for one cousin to whom she felt close. Children did not seek her nor did she seem interested in playing with children at school or in the neighborhood. According to the teacher's reports, when Val did attend school she was as quiet as a mouse in class and simply stood and watched at recess but would not join the games and activities. As the mother became convinced that Valerie had "something wrong with her nerves," she took her to the local hospital so that she could get some "pills for her nerves." Valerie was evaluated by the pediatric staff and her case diagnosed as school phobia.

Diagnostic Test Results

Several diagnostic psychological tests were administered to Valerie while her case was being presented at the local hospital. The test results were as follows:

> Valerie demonstrated a consistent variability in her overall functioning. Her problem-solving, visual-manual skills (WISC Performance IQ = 78) are considerably below her near-average verbal-expressive abilities (WISC Verbal IQ = 90). Within her verbal skills, she ranges from a defective level of functioning in comprehension of social situations and in her fund of information to an above-normal level of functioning in her ability to think abstractly. Within her performance skills, she also demonstrated variability (DAP IQ = 87; Peabody IQ = 76). Valerie's variable functioning is due to an extreme inability to concentrate, since on perceptual tasks not requiring concentration she performed at a normal level (Frostig Perceptual Quotient = 98). Emotionally, Valerie's inability to concentrate is related to her extreme fears—especially her fears about men. The only way she can cope with men is to see them as dead. The inconsistency in her functioning seems to be related to the amount of concentration required by various tasks—such as classroom activities. To handle such stressful situations she is likely to withdraw by not performing.

Social Intake Evaluation

A social intake evaluation was also done at the pediatric clinic. Excerpts of this evaluation indicate that "when the mother tried to accompany Valerie to school, even as far as getting on the bus with her, as they approached the school, Valerie would become very stiff and begin shaking, screaming and hollering. When Valerie was asked about this, she stated that she was afraid to go to school, that when she went to school she thought about the time she was molested." This was a reference to an incident which took place when the child was four years old. According to Valerie's mother, a boy had "played with Valerie's 'private parts.'" Neither the extent of this incident nor any physical evidence could be obtained at the time of its occurrence. After the child had been diagnosed as suffering from school phobia, the mother was advised that the nature of Valerie's difficulties required long-term psychiatric treatment. Since the cost of such treatment was beyond the family means, the mother was left with the understanding that she should resign herself to living with the problem. Quite by accident, one of the authors of this chapter was visiting the pediatric facility where Valerie's case was being discussed for the benefit of interns in pediatrics and child psychiatry. It was then that a suggestion was made by the senior author to attempt a behavioral treatment of Valerie's school phobia.

METHODOLOGY

Behavioral Strategy

The behavioral approach to school phobia requires to break it down into three major components.

First of all, there is the matter of response definition. The relevant dimension, insofar as the school, parent and child are concerned, is that of school attendance. Thus, we can define school phobia as a low or near-zero level of school attendance. This definition enables us to specify what the target behavior is for a treatment program. If the rate of going to school is low, our aim then is to increase it and maintain it, hopefully under the conditions that obtain in the "natural" setting of the school environment. The next component involves the matter of consequences or reinforecment for staying away from school. These consequences must be examined as they affect the child and the behavior of those living with her. Finally, there is the issue of redesigning the consequences provided by the environment so as to minimize the probability of skipping school while maximizing the probability of attending school.

To identify the relevant environmental consequences responsible for the child's refusal to attend school, the child's behavior was directly observed and recorded by trained assistant-observers. The initial step was to attempt to quantify the dimensions of the relevant behaviors in the three primary environments of the child: (a) home, (b) a neighbor's home (where she was cared for) and (c) school.

The systematic observational schedule that was conducted each day on a minute-by-minute basis started at 7:00 A.M. and ended at 9:00 A.M. The sampling of observations was conducted for 10 days at home and for 3 days at the neighbor's house. Behavioral observations and procedures designed to reinstate school attendance were implemented by two assistant observers. One observer conducted the prompting-shaping procedures and participated in the observations at the neighbor's apartment. The second observer was responsible for giving instructions to the mother and conducted the observations at Valerie's home. Once the child returned to school as a consequence of the procedures applied, the observations were extended to include the child's behavior at school and on the way to and from school.

Valerie's Behavior at Home

The observations in the home revealed that Valerie was sleeping an average of 1 hour later than her siblings in the morning, although according to the mother she retired at the same time as they, between 9:00 and 10.00, every night. Her mother had long abandoned any hope of Valerie's going to school and simply allowed her to sleep until she awoke or until it was time for the mother to leave for work at 9:00 a.m. The mother would usually leave for work approximately 1 hour following the departure of the siblings who left for school at 8:00 A.M.

Except for a few occasions when the mother made breakfast for the children, they frequently fixed their own food. Valerie was given no preferential treatment and was never asked what she would like for breakfast if she slept late. Upon arising, Valerie spoke on average of 14 sentences to the siblings, an average of 10 sentences to her mother and only 2 sentences to her father. The mother averaged one request each morning asking Valerie to go to school. Physical interaction such as touching, holding or other aggressive or affectionate behavior occurred seldom with her siblings and not at all with her father. On the other hand, Valerie typically followed her mother around the house, from room to room, spending approximately 80 percent of her time within 10 feet of her mother. During these times, there was little or no conversation. When the mother left for work, she would take Valerie to a neighbor's apartment. On every observational occasion, when the mother left the neighbor's apartment to go to work, Valerie would immediately leave and follow the mother. This behavior of quietly following her mother at a 10-foot distance occurred on each of the 10 days of baseline observations. Each time this occurred, the mother would look back and see Valerie, stop and warn her several times to go back, all of which had no effect on Valerie. When the mother began walking once more, Valerie continued to follow at a 10-foot distance, with no verbal response of any type. Also, it was noted that on three occasions that the mother resorted to punishing Valerie with a switching for following, Val would cry quietly but would make no effort to return home until the mother took her back to the neighbor's apartment. Once the mother left again for work, Valerie would continue to follow at about twice the distance, or 20 feet, behind the mother. This daily scene was usually concluded with the mother literally running to get out of sight of Valerie so that Valerie would not follow her into traffic.

Valerie's Behavior at the Neighbor's Apartment

Valerie was observed at the neighbor's apartment for 3 days, during which the observer had no interaction with Val but remained nearby recording whatever behavior occurred. During this time, Val watched the observer at times but made no effort to interact in any way.

At the neighbor's apartment, Val was free to do whatever she pleased for the remainder of the day. Val showed little interest in television or radio, preferring to be outdoors unless it was raining. If she had to stay inside, she pored over a mail order toy catalogue. Very rarely did the neighbor spend time interacting with Val. The few times she did, it was after Val's mother had left for work and Val was still crying.

Outdoors, Val found many ways to entertain herself. The observer watched while she played with a jump rope, exploded caps and found a dozen different ways to play with Play-Dough. If she ran out of things to play with, Val amused herself by hopping on one foot, jumping, running and turning in circles. In addition, Val had some money and at some time during the day made a trip to the corner store where she bought candy, gum or soft drinks.

Val was the only school-age child at the neighbor's house and children from toddlers to kindergarten age sought her attention. She was somewhat aloof but occasionally joined their play. In short, her day was one which would be considered ideal by many grade children—she could be outdoors and play as she chose all day long. No demands of any type were made on Val by anyone and she had the status of being the eldest among the children.

Valerie's Behavior in School

Two visits were made to the school to get acquainted with the principal and teachers and to gather information from them about Val's past school performance, work attitude and social adjustment. Copies were obtained of the official records of Val's attendance for kindergarten, first grade, second grade, and the current year (third grade). The records showed Val's attendance to have been above average during kindergarten and first grade but that absences had increased each quarter during the second grade: 1st quarter, 1; 2nd quarter, 7; 3rd quarter, 13; and fourth quarter, 20, for a total of 41 absences for the year. Excuses had been illness, oversleeping or missing the bus. Scholastic achievement had been normal or average until absences became numerous. Val, it was reported, had never cried or asked to go home. While described as shy, quiet and rather apathetic, Val had never given the impression that she was unhappy or afraid.

The Behavioral Assessment

The evaluation of Valerie's behavior at home, at the neighbor's apartment and finally at school suggested that Valerie's school phobia was currently maintained by the pleasant and undemanding characteristics of the neighbor's apartment where Val spent her day after everyone had left home in the morning.

Rather than speculating on the "real" causes or etiology of the phobia itself, our initial strategy was to determine the feasibility of having Val return to school by some prompting-shaping procedure (see Ayllon and Azrin, 1968a, for rationale and empirical basis for this procedure). Once this was done, it would then be possible to provide for some pleasant experience associated with being in school in order to maintain her school attendance. To design the prompting-shaping procedure, it was necessary first to assess Valerie's existing behaviors that had a component relation to the target behavior. Indeed, if attending school were to be meaningful, Valerie had to show sufficient interest to go to school voluntarily and consistently. In addition, she had to be prepared to work with school materials and perform academic work. To determine the presence or absence of these component behaviors, first one assistant took a coloring book, crayons, a set of arithmetic flash cards and other academically related items to the neighbor's apartment. While at the neighbor's apartment, she prompted Val to make the appropriate academically related responses to the stimuli. Val responded appropriately to the academic material and contrary to expectations, she did not panic, "freeze" or become at all upset when exposed to academically related material. The next objective was to assess the difficulties associated with leaving the neighbor's apartment. Therefore, the next probe was for the observer to invite Val for a car ride after both had worked on academically related activities. Val offered no resistance and went with the observer for a car ride and later had a hamburger on the way home.

This behavioral assessment assured us (a) that a prompting-shaping procedure could start by taking Val directly to school rather than in gradually increasing steps and (b) that she would do academic work once in the classroom. The next step was to develop the desired response chain eventuating in Valerie's attendance at school. It must be remembered that Val stayed alone with her mother after her siblings left for school at about 8:00 A.M. She remained with her mother until she left for work at 9:00 A.M. If staying with the mother alone was the reinforcing consequence that maintained her refusal to go to school, we reasoned, withdrawal of this consequence might lead Valerie back to school. Before we could try such a procedure, however,

TABLE 17-1

PROCEDURAL AND BEHAVIORAL PROGRESSION DURING
THE TREATMENT OF SCHOOL PHOBIA

Temporal Sequence	*Procedure*	*Valerie's Behavior*
Baseline observations Day 1–10	Observations taken at home and at the neighbor's apartment where Val spent her day.	Valerie stayed at home when siblings left for school. Mother took Val to neighbor's apartment as she left for work.
Behavioral assessment Day 11–13	Assistant showed school materials to Val and prompted academic work.	Val reacted well to books; she colored pictures and copied numbers and letters.
Behavioral assessment Day 13	Assistant invited Val for a car ride after completing academic work at neighbor's apartment.	Val readily accepted car ride and on way back to neighbor's apartment she also accepted hamburger offered her.
Procedure 1 Day 14–20	Taken by assistant to school. Assistant stayed with her in classroom. Attendance made progressively earlier while assistant's stay in classroom progressively lessens.	Val attended school with assistant. Performed school work. Left school with siblings at closing time.
Day 21	Assistant did not take Val to school.	Val and siblings attended school on their own.
Procedure 1 Day 22	Val taken by assistant to school.	Val attended school with assistant. Performed school work. Left with siblings at school closing time.
Return to baseline observations Day 23–27	Observations taken at home.	Val stayed at home when siblings left for school. Mother took Val to neighbor's apartment as she left for work.
Procedure 2 Day 28–29	Mother left for work when children left for school.	Val stayed at home when children left for school. Mother took her to neighbor's apartment as she left for work.
Procedure 3 Day 40–49	Taken by mother to school. Home-based motivational system.	Val stayed at home when siblings left for school. Followed Mother quietly when taken to school.
Procedure 4 Day 50–59	On Day 50, mother left for school *before* children left home. Home-based motivational system.	Siblings met mother at school door. Val stayed at home.

TABLE 17-1 (Continued)

Sequence Temporal	Procedure	Valerie's Behavior
	After 15 min of waiting ing in school, mother returned home and took Val to school.	Val meekly followed her mother.
	On Day 51, mother left for school *before* children left home.	Val and siblings met mother at school door.
	On Day 52, mother left for school before children left home.	Siblings met mother at school door. Val stayed at home.
	After 15 min of waiting ing in school, mother returned home and **physically hit and dragged Valerie to school.**	Valerie cried and pleaded with her mother not to hit her. Cried all the way to school.
	On Day 53–59, mother left for school before children left home.	Val and siblings met mother at school door.
Fading Procedure Day 60–69	Mother discontinued going to school before children. Mother maintained home-based motivational system.	Val and siblings attended school on their own.
Fading Procedure Day 70	Mother discontinued home-based motivational system.	Val and siblings attended school on their own.

it was necessary to determine the probability of Valerie remaining in the classroom once she returned to school. That was, in effect, the objective of the first procedure. Additional procedures were subsequently implemented to achieve the target behavior.

Specific Procedures and Results

Table 17 shows all procedural stages as well as their behavioral effects. The target behavior of voluntary and consistent (100%) school attendance was achieved in less than two months. Four distinct procedures were designed and implemented only after observing and recording their specific effects on Valerie's voluntary school attendance.

Procedure 1: Prompting-Shaping
of School Attendance

Our plan was to manage to have Valerie visit the school at a time when school was almost over for the day. By having the child go to school for a short time only, to be dismissed for the day along with the rest of the pupils, we attempted to use the natural contingencies of the school to maintain Valerie's presence in school. Permission was obtained from the teacher to bring Val to school for the last hour of the school day and for the assistant to remain in the classroom with her. The plan was to arrive at school progressively earlier until the child's presumed fears were extinguished, at which time she would then initiate voluntary school attendance. The first day of this procedure, the assistant told Val, about 1:30 P.M., that they would be going to school and that she would stay with Val. Val's eyes widened, but she offered no resistance. They drove to school, arriving 1½ hours before closing time; holding hands tightly they went to the third-grade classroom. Val was given a desk and the assistant sat nearby until the day was over. The teacher, in a very natural manner, greeted Val and gave her some classroom material. Val immediately starting doing some schoolwork. On the way out of school, the assistant found Val's siblings. To maximize the probability of Val's getting approval from her siblings, associated with the school, the assistant gave Val some candy to share with the siblings and left her to walk home with them.

The following day, the procedure was repeated, except that the assistant left Val in the classroom about 10 minutes before school was out. Again, the teacher worked with Val just as naturally as if she had been attending all day long. The assistant, before leaving the classroom, instructed Val to meet her siblings and reassured her that they would wait for her to walk home with them. The next day, the time of arrival was moved up so that Val spent 2 hours in school. By now Val had attended the third grade for a total of 4 hours. On the basis of her classroom performance, the teacher came to the conclusion that Val was too far behind to catch up with her third-grade classmates. Therefore, after careful consideration and discussion with the school principal, the teacher decided to place Val in a second-grade class to insure her learning the material she had missed during her prolonged absence from school. Again, the cooperation of the new second-grade teacher was obtained to allow Val to keep going to school at rather unusual hours, about 2 to 3 hours before the end of the school day.

The next day, Val was taken to the second-grade class for the first time. She gave no evidence of being upset with the shift from classrooms. On succeeding days, Val was taken earlier each day. By the time Val was arriving in school at 9:30 A.M. the assistant had gradually decreased her own time in the classroom from the initial 1½ hours to 5 minutes. Each day, the assistant left a sack containing some small prize like a children's magazine, a few pieces of candy, etc., with the teacher to be given to Val when school was over. On the eighth day of this procedure, Val left home with her siblings and went to school without the assistant for the first time. The teacher praised her, and the assistant went to school and told Val how happy she was that Val had come to school by herself.

On the next day Val stayed home until her mother left for work. As usual, she was then taken to the neighbor's apartment. The assistant picked her up and took her to school where she spent the remaining 4½ hours of the school day. The prompting-shaping procedure was discontinued at this time to allow for further behavioral evaluation. For the next 6 days she remained at home when her siblings went to school, and just as before, the mother took Val to the neighbor's apartment as she left for work.

Figure 17-1 shows the day-to-day behavior of Val under procedure 1. The prompting-shaping procedure demonstrated that Val could go to school and stay all day without running away, causing disturbance in the classroom or displaying any behavior that might suggest undue fear or panic. Just as significant, Val's behavior in school indicated that the natural reinforcing consequences provided at school were adequate to keep her there once she engaged in the first activity of a complex behavior chain including getting up on time, washing, dressing, leaving the house and going to school. True, this procedure reinstated Valerie's school

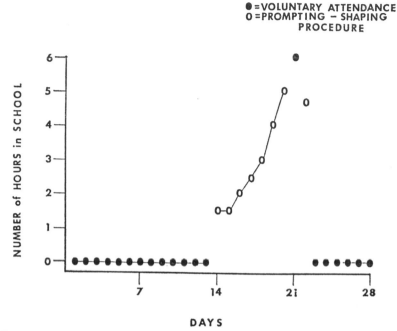

Figure 17-1. Valerie's school attendance both when she was escorted to school during the prompting-shaping procedure, and when she went on her own. Each dot represents the actual duration of her stay in the classroom per day. The start of Procedure 1 is indicated by the gap between day 13 and day 14.

attendance but failed to maintain it. This problem then was how to provide sufficient motivation to insure her leaving for school. At this point, it became necessary to examine and redesign the social consequences provided at home for Valerie's refusal to attend school.

Procedure 2: Withdrawal of Social Consequences Upon Failure to Attend School

As mentioned before, Val stayed with her mother for 1 hour daily right after her siblings had gone to school. The objective here was to eliminate such a social consequence for staying away from school. Therefore, procedure 2 involved instructing the mother that she was casually to inform all the children the night before that she was going to leave for work *at the same time they left for school.* When additional questions were asked, she was to reply that her working hours had been changed. Valerie gave no verbal or physical reaction to this announcement when it was given. Nothing else was changed. The children were treated the same as on previous occasions. One of the assistant-observers, who had had no interaction with Val, was in the house making standard observations the day the new procedure 2 was initiated and during subsequent intervention. The mother left for work along with the siblings, but Val refused to go. Therefore, she was taken to the neighbor's apartment. This procedure was continued for 10 days during which Val did not attend school and was taken to the neighbor's apartment. In addition, Val increased her "following behavior" when the mother left for work. Valerie followed at a distance of 3 to 6 feet behind the mother. When Valerie was punished by her mother, she invariably dropped back to about 8 to 10 feet and continued following her mother. As there were no other observable effects on Valerie's behavior at the end of 10 days, this procedure was terminated. In effect, we had spent over 20 days trying various procedures and we were now back to the original behavior pattern: Val did not go to school and was taken to the neighbor's apartment. As soon as the mother started to leave for work, Val followed her, despite her mother's efforts to discourage her.

Procedure 3: Prompting School Attendance Combined with a Home-Based Motivational System

Despite the fact that Val appeared to have remained as unchanged as ever through the various procedures, it was clear from results of procedure 1 that she could return to school through a prompting-shaping procedure. The problem was one of maintaining that attendance for any length of time. To find a solution, it was required that we find some source or sources of reinforcement to be used at home contingent on school attendance. Val's mother described some of the things Val liked most. Among these were having her cousin stay overnight with her, and having soda pop, chewing gum and ice cream. Therefore, the strategy for designing the new procedure included the prompting-shaping procedure that previously resulted in Val's return to school and a motivational system designed to reinforce Valerie for attending school. This time, the mother, rather than an assistant, was to use the prompting procedure. In addition and to facilitate implementation of the motivational system, a large chart with the name of each child in the family and the days of the week was given to the mother. She announced that a star would signify one day of going to school on a *voluntary* basis and was to be placed on the appropriate spot by each child at the end of each day. Five stars would equal perfect attendance and would result in a special treat or trip on the weekend. In addition to the above, each child who went to school on a voluntary basis would receive, each day, three pieces of a favorite candy. If anyone had to be taken to school (nonvoluntary attendance), the reward was only one piece of candy. It was felt to be important to attach some reward value to the school attendance, even if, in the beginning, attendance was not voluntary. The occasion of putting up stars, handing out rewards and verbal praise was to be made into a special event each evening when the mother returned home. When Valerie did not leave with the other children to go to school in the morning, the mother was to leave the house 15 minutes later, taking Valerie with her to school. No excuses were to be tolerated, with the exception of sickness. Since previously Valerie had used the excuse of being sick to avoid going to school, this time the mother was given a thermometer and taught to use it to decide whether or not Valerie was ill. If the thermometer reading was above 100, the mother would then be justified in allowing Val to stay home. This procedure resulted in Valerie's mother taking her to school daily for ten consecutive days. Once, Valerie stated she was sick, but since her temperature was within the normal range, her mother took her to school. Procedure 3, just as procedure, 1, resulted in Valerie attending school, but it failed to initiate Valerie's going to school on her own. In analyzing the procedure carefully, it seemed that what was happening was that the mother taking Valerie personally to school was perhaps adventitiously reinforcing and thus maintaining her refusal to go on her own. After the other children had left for school, the mother in a very matter-of-fact fashion, asked Valerie to get ready to go to school with her. On the way to school, Valerie and the mother appeared quite natural, and even after 10 days of this procedure there was no particular irritation or apparent inconvenience experienced by Valerie or by her mother. It should be pointed out here that prior to he present intervention, Valerie would kick and scream and simply refused to go to school even when her mother at-

tempted to take her by force. The results of procedure 3 suggested that the natural consequences for school attendance plus the motivational system employed here increased the probability of Val's going to school escorted, but it failed to prompt her going to school voluntarily. Procedure 4 was designed to introduce a mild aversive consequence for the mother if Val failed to go to school. In addition, the motivational system used in procedure 3 was maintained.

Procedure 4: The Effects of Aversive Consequences on the Mother

Procedure 4 involved having the mother get ready for work and leave the house 10 minutes *before* the children left for school. She was to inform all the children that she had to go to work much earlier but wanted to see that they got to school on time, so she would meet them at school each morning with a reward. This procedure was designed to have a twofold effect: one, to prompt the behavior on Valerie's part of voluntarily leaving for school with her siblings and to provide reinforcement through the mother upon arrival at school. If Valerie failed to arrive at school with her siblings, the mother had to return home and escort Valerie to school. Since the school was about a mile away from home, Val's failure to go to school required that her mother walk back home a mile and them walk another mile to school—this time with Valerie in tow, for a total of three miles walking. By having Valerie's behavior affect her mother's directly, it was hoped that this procedure would, in effect, have the mother become more actively interested in conveying to Val the importance of going to school. On the first day of this procedure 4, Val behaved just as she had throughout the previous ones: she remained at home after everyone, her mother and later the siblings, had left for school. The mother met the siblings at school, gave them a bit of candy and then waited for Val to come to school. Following the previous instructions, she remained at the school door for 15 minutes before going back home to find Val. Once there she very firmly proceeded to take Val by the hand and with hardly any words between them, they rushed back to school. Val did not protest and quite naturally followed her mother into school. After a few minutes, Val's mother left school for work. That evening, the mother rewarded each child with praise and candy for going to school. She gave stars to the siblings and placed them on the board made for that purpose. She also gave Val a piece of candy and noted that she could not get a star since Val had not attended school on her own. The children's reaction to the stars and praise seemed one of excitement. Val, however, appeared somewhat unsure of what was happening. The second day of procedure 4, Val got up along with her siblings, dressed, fixed herself some breakfast, and left for school with her siblings. When they arrived at school they met their mother who was waiting for them. The mother was obviously pleased with Val to whom she gave candy along with the siblings. At the end of the school day, the children again were praised at home and given stars by the mother on the special board that hung in the kitchen. Val appeared very interested, particularly when the mother explained to her that if she collected five stars she would be able to exchange them for the opportunity to have her cousin, of whom Val was very fond, spend a night with her. The next day, Val remained at home after the mother and the siblings had left for school. Again, the mother waited for 15 minutes in school. Then she returned home. As it was raining, it was a considerable inconvenience for Val's mother to have to go back home. Once she reached home, she scolded Val and pushed her out of the house and literally all the way to school. As Val tried to give some explanation, the mother hit her with a switch. By the time they arrived at school, both were soaking wet. That evening, Val received some candy but no stars as she had not gone to school on her own. This was the last time Val stayed away from school. The next day she went to school along with her siblings. The mother met the children at the school door and genuinely praised them for their promptness. That evening, Val received a star along with candy and was praised by the mother in front of the siblings. Within 5 days Val had accumulated enough stars to exchange them for the opportunity to have her cousin stay over-night with her. She appeared in very good spirits and seemed to enjoy her cousin's visit. The next school day, Val got up with her siblings, washed, dressed, fixed herself some breakfast cereal and left for school with them. When they arrived at school they were met by their mother, who again praised them, gave them some candy, and then the children went to their respective classrooms while the mother went off to work. Val and the children continued attending school without any difficulty, even after one aspect of the procedure was withdrawn: namely, the mother waiting for them at school. The home-based motivational system was maintained in force for one month and withdrawn at that time. Still, Val and the children continued attending school, unaffected by the withdrawal of these formal procedures.

To gain perspective on the dimensions of the school phobia presented here, it is necessary to look at Val's overall school attendance per quarter (45 days each quarter). Figure 17-2 shows that Val went from 95 percent school attendance to 10 percent within 5 quarters. This 10 percent represented the first 4 days of the fifth quarter, after which she quit going to school for the remainder of the quarter. The present behavioral inter-vention was conducted during the latter part of the sixth quarter. The net result was that Val's overall attendance in the sixth quarter increased from 10 to 30 percent. The next quarter, the seventh, her overall attendance increased from 30 to 100 percent. A follow-up for the next 3 quarters indicates that Val had maintained this perfect attendance.

Follow-up

Inquiries were made of Valerie's parents and teachers at 6 and 9 months subsequent to Valerie's return to school. Their

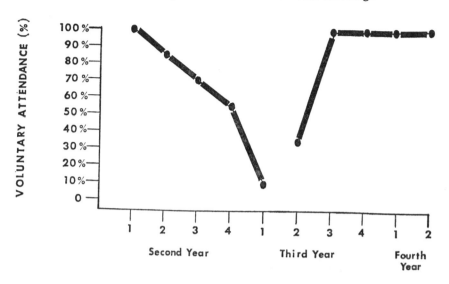

QUARTERS per SCHOOL YEAR

Figure 17-2. Valerie's voluntary school attendance. Each dot represents the percentage of voluntary attendance per school quarter (45 days). The behavioral intervention was initiated during the second quarter of the third year of school.

comments can be subsumed under school and home evaluation. Finally a psychodiagnostic evaluation was also obtained.

School Evaluation

Val's academic progress is shown by her current grades. While previously she was an average "C" student, she now has "A's" and "B's." Her teacher remarked that Val is well-behaved in class and helpful to the teacher. While she is pleased to volunteer for small errands and clean-up duties to assist the teacher, she has also shown sufficient social skills to be chosen as the school guide for a new girl admitted into her classroom. Val's specific duties as guide consisted of showing and explaining to the new girl the various school facilities such as the school cafeteria, the library, the gym and so on. The teacher was particularly impressed with Val's performance as a guide because the new girl came from Germany and asked more detailed questions than is usually the case for a standard transfer student. Her newly developed social skills appeared to have impressed the Brownie Scouts to extend a cordial invitation for Valerie to join their group. Valerie was thrilled with the prospect, and after requesting permission from her mother she joined the Brownies. Every Tuesday afternoon after class, she attends the group's meeting which is held in the school. After the meeting, she walks home with her girl friends.

A few months after Val resumed normal school attendance, an incident took place that suggests the strength of her newly acquired fondness for school. She was waiting for the school bus when another child snatched her money changer from her, took her bus money and ran away. Instead of crying and returning home, Val ran all the way to school, since she did not want to be late.

Home Evaluation

Val no longer complains of feeling sick or tired in the morning, nor does she suffer from insomnia. She goes to bed about 8:30 P.M. daily with her siblings and gets up at 7:00 A.M. Valerie now fusses and hurries her siblings to finish dressing in the morning in time to go to school. She brings her math and spelling work home to show her mother. The mother very naturally praises her child, as she does her other children. Whereas previously Valerie had been rather apathetic in school, she now takes pride in her work there and likes to discuss things she is learning.

Eight months after Val resumed school attendance, the mother initiated divorce proceedings against her husband. This situation introduced a definite strain into the home family relations. Still, Val appeared sufficiently motivated to continue attending school without any disruption in her academic or social progress.

Neither the mother nor the school teachers have noticed any other maladaptive behavior or possible "symptom substitution" since the child resumed normal school attendance. On the contrary, the mother, as well as Valerie's teachers, were very impressed with the astounding change in her behavior and the promise it now offers for her future both academically and socially.

Psychodiagnostic Evaluation

Because Valerie's school phobia was initially presented and diagnosed in the psychiatric unit of a pediatric department at a large urban hospital, the formal procedures for case referral included a psycho-diagnostic evaluation prior to and following treatment given to the child.

The conclusion now arrived at by the examiner is interesting!

> Her emotional development is characterized by deviations in the area of maturity and aggression. Her reality testing is marred by an extreme concern over sexuality and men, whom she sees as attacking, ever-fighting animal-like creatures. On the basis of the recent results, without considerations to results previous to behavioral management, it would seem that the school phobia may have been treated successfully, but it has not meant anything to this girl.

DISCUSSION

A child diagnosed as suffering from school phobia was cured within 45 days through the combined use of behavioral analysis techniques. The term *cured* is used here purposely since the functional characteristics of school phobia are straightforward: chronic absence from school. Therefore, reinstating the child's school attendance constitutes the only relevant criterion of successful cure.

The therapeutic intervention reported here is characterized by the following features.

1. Definition of the psychiatric problem is made in terms of behavioral dimensions. The observable and measurable dimension of school phobia is the child's frequency of school attendance. Hence this is the datum par excellence in the treatment of school phobia.

2. Evaluation of the treatment objective is made in terms that are amenable to direct observation and measurement. Since the treatment objective was defined as reinstatement of voluntary school attendance, it was easy to evaluate the effectiveness of the behavioral intervention. The psycho-diagnostic evaluation illustrates the dangers involved when evaluation of a treatment is on a nonbehavioral basis: speculation on personality factors

often are given importance at the cost of minimizing the observable behavioral changes.

3. The behavioral intervention is conducted in the very environment where the individual's behavior is to be displayed. Hence, rather than working in a clinic or hospital situation, the emphasis is on utilizing behavioral techniques right in the field environment to which any clinic-based therapeutic efforts must generalize for these efforts to be successful.

4. Description of the procedures used here is also consistent with the stress on directly observable and measureable dimensions. The above provides a self-corrective method for approaching psychiatric problems in general. Each of the several procedures used here gave empirical quantitative information that enabled us to revise each procedure in the light of its effects on the child's behavior. This ongoing, step-by-step self-corrective evaluation is particularly critical for developing effective and inexpensive methods of treatment.

One other finding here was that the use of differential consequences for attending school was more effective than the use of either positive reinforcement or negative reinforcement (punishment) alone. It must be pointed out that during the baseline observations, the mother was observed hitting the child, with no change in her refusal to attend school. Also, during procedure 2, she was observed hitting the child again without any effect on her refusal to attend school. Similarly, Valerie's refusal to attend school continued when positive reinforcement was made available for going to school escorted by her mother (procedure 3). However, when school attendance was reinforced by the mother immediately at the school door as well as at home with an incentive system that made use of the child's own motivation, while refusal to attend school was punished, it took but a few days to reinstate normal school attendance.

Why should punishment have worked this time? A parsimonious explanation of this finding lies in the fact that procedure 4 combined punishment for staying away from school with positive reinforcement for voluntary school attendance. Valerie's mother had used punishment previously but no positive reinforcement for going to school. These findings are consistent with those obtained by Holz *et al.* (1963) under more controlled conditions. In that study, they found that one of the most efficient methods for eliminating an undesirable response of mental patients was to schedule punishment for the undesirable response and concurrently, reinforcement for an alternative competing response.

An important procedural innovation introduced here was arranging the child's refusal to attend school to affect the mother's own behavior. When procedure 3 required that she take Valerie to school, she did so without ever appearing inconvenienced by it. It was only when Val's refusal to go to school resulted in her mother having to walk from the school back home and then again back to school that the aversive properties of the procedure led to the mother finding a "natural" way of putting an end to such inconvenience. Only twice did she have to be inconvenienced. The second time her reaction was such as to convince Valerie that it would be easier to go to school with her siblings. The aversive properties of the procedure set up an escape-avoidance type of behavior in the mother that led Val to prevent such occurrences in the future by attending school.

REFERENCES

Ayllon, T. and Azrin, N. H.: The measurement and reinforcement of behavior of psychotics. *Journal of the Experimental Analysis of Behavior, 8:*357–383, 1965.

Ayllon, T. and Azrin, N. H.. Reinforcer sampling: a technique for increasing the behavior of mental patients. *Journal of Applied Behavior Analysis, 1:*13–20, 1968a.

Ayllon, T. and Azrin, N. H.: *The Token Economy: A Motivational System for Therapy and Rehabilitation.* Appleton-Century-Crofts, New York, 1968b.

Ayllon, T. and Haughton, E.: Modification of the symptomatic verbal behavior of mental patients. *Behavioral Research and Therapy, 2:*87–97, 1964.

Ayllon, T. and Michael, J.: The psychiatric nurse as a behavioral engineer. *Journal of the Experimental Analysis of Behavior, 2:*323–334, 1959.

Coolidge, J., Tessman, E., Waldfogel, S. and Willer, M.: Patterns of aggression in school phobia. *Psychoanalytic Study of the Child, 17:*319–333, 1962.

Ferster, C. B. and Skinner, B. F.: *Schedules of Reinforcement.* Appleton-Century-Crofts, New York, 1957.

Garvey, W. P. and Hegrenes, J. R.: Desensitization techniques in the treatment of school phobia. *American Journal of Orthopsychiatry, 36*:147–152, 1966.

Holz, W., Azrin, N. H. and Ayllon, T.: Elimination of behavior of mental patients by response-produced extinction. *Journal of the Experimental Analysis of Behavior, 6*:407–412, 1963.

Isaacs, W., Thomas, J. and Goldiamond, I.: Application of operant conditioning to reinstate verbal behavior in psychotics. In Ullmann, L. P. and Krasner, L. (Eds.): *Case Studies in Behavior Modification.* New York, Holt, Rinehart and Winston, 1965, pp. 69–72.

Jarvis, V.: Countertransference in management of school phobia. *Psychoanalytic Quarterly, 33*:411–419, 1964.

Lazarus, A. and Abramovitz, A.: The use of 'emotive imagery' in the treatment of children's phobias. *Journal of Mental Science, 180*: 191–195, 1962.

Lazarus, A., Davidson, G. and Polefka, D.: Classical and operant factors in the treatment of a school phobia. *Journal of Abnormal Psychology, 70*:225–229, 1965.

Leventhal, T. and Sells, M.: Self-image in school phobia. *American Journal of Orthopsychiatry, 34*:685–695, 1964.

Patterson, G. R.: A learning theory approach to the treatment of the school phobic child. In Ullmann, L. P. and Krasner, L. (Eds.): *Case Studies in Behavior Modification.* New York, Holt, Rinehart and Winston, 1965, pp. 279–285.

Skinner, B. F.: *The Behavior of Organisms: An Experimental Analysis.* New York, Appleton-Century-Crofts, 1938.

Wolf, M., Risley, T. and Mees, H.: Application of operant procedures to the behavior problems of an autistic child. In Ullmann, L. P. and Krasner, L, (Eds.): *Case Studies in Behavior Modification.* New York, Holt, Rinehart and Winston, 1965, pp. 138–145.

Wolpe, J.: *Psychotherapy by Reciprocal Inhibition.* Stanford, Stanford University Press, 1958.

IV

SPECIAL EDUCATION

MANY TEACHERS and counselors have reported at some time or another that students fail to learn because of a "lack of motivation." This problem is often noted to be particularly acute among those students who have been categorized as socially and emotionally maladjusted. They have at times presented a wide range of behavioral problems which have prevented them from progressing satisfactorily in the typical school environment. Since many of these students have not responded to traditional classroom rewards such as praise and academic success, numerous psychologists and educators have recently advocated the use of tangible reinforcers. Such reinforcers might consist of things like candy, money, games or free time. At times, points or tokens are earned which can then be exchanged at a later time for the previously mentioned rewards. Such rewards are then referred to as "back-up" reinforcers. Paying students to learn has certainly been a topic of considerable debate. After all, are we not "bribing" the children? As soon as we stop paying them will they not stop learning? Will they learn only for material benefit? At the present time, it is not possible to given an unqualified answer to these questions. This is primarily because most studies to date have attempted to demonstrate that behavior changes can be effected in a very short time through behavior modification procedures. As such, these studies have emphasized the *acquisition* phase of learning, or that period in which the most dramatic gains are made. These gains may be stated in terms of an increased rate of positive behavior previously exhibited infrequently, or the substitution of adaptive responses for maladaptive responses. In both cases, few studies, if any, have been specifically designed to demonstrate how these behavior changes are *maintained*. That is, what natural reinforcers within the environment will maintain the behavior gains once such reinforcers as tokens, toys and candy are removed? The following example illustrates a probable sequence of events. If a child's classroom behavior is so disruptive that he never sits in his seat or attends to study materials, he may never become interested in reading. Therefore, a strategy is developed whereby the child is permitted to engage in his favorite activity only after he has completed a short reading activity. Once he begins to acquire new skills such as reading comics, sports or other items, reading activities may eventually become reinforcing in their own right. Still, some might argue, our ultimate goal is to produce students who will "learn for learning's sake." This, of course, does not mean that people work only because they enjoy their various tasks. When teachers are asked "If you were not paid for teaching, would you continue to teach?" very few respond in the affirmative. Hopefully this is not because they do not find teaching intrinsically rewarding. Rather, it is probably because material reinforcements are an integral part of life. We need them to survive. Therefore, both personal and tangible rewards are important sources of motivation. However, many children may never enjoy the privilege of reading for its own sake until reading has first been shown to be "worth something."

In the first paper of this chapter, Tyler and Brown provide an excellent example of how a token reinforcement system may be used to improve academic performance of delinquent boys. Importantly, they demonstrate that paying students to learn is effective *only* when rewards are contingent upon specific performance. In the second paper, Broden *et al.* also demonstrate that token reinformers are effective. In addition, they were found to be more powerful than systematic teacher attention and praise in increasing the study behavior of disruptive children. The fact that the students were involved in determining those behaviors which would earn or lose points emphasizes the importance of student involvement in the development of an effective token system.

Many problems may be encountered in attempting to establish a token system. Kuypers *et al.* point out problems that they experienced and make suggestions for avoiding them. Foremost among these problems was the lack of adequate teacher training which resulted in intermittent reinforcement of deviant behavior and a failure to recognize situations which required the use of shaping procedures. The authors also emphasize that systematic social reinforcement plays an important role in all classroom situations and should not be discarded when a token system is introduced.

Rarely have educational behavior modifiers described the classroom in which the entire environment has been restructured in order to allow each child to realize his potential. While the preceding studies allude to such classrooms, the next chapter, by Hewett, describes in detail a possible engineered environment for children with learning disabilities. Although the project was developed for use with children having emotional disturbances, many of the classroom operations and suggested physical arrangements can be generalized to regular public school classrooms. We urge teachers to apply the same systematic procedures of evaluation to changes in room design as they would in the case of manipulating social or academic behavior. To date, little is known about the functional relationship between classroom design and pupil performance. It is a necessary area of investigation if we are to achieve optimal learning conditions.

The previously mentioned investigations demonstrate that operant conditioning techniques are effective in changing the behavior of socially and emotionally maladjusted children. However, it is often implied that children who are retarded or brain damaged are inherently different from other children, and therefore the same principles of learning cannot be used to modify their behavior. The last two chapters take issue with that premise.

Zimmerman *et al.*, using token reinforcers, were able to teach retarded students to follow instructions. This study is of particular interest because the students were effectively taught and reinforced as a group rather than on an individual basis. Token rewards were found to be more effective in maintaining desirable behavior than social reinforcement (praise) alone.

Finally, Hall and Broden, using only social reinforcement, show how the maladaptive behavior of three brain-injured children was changed. Gains made in each of the specific behaviors reinforced permitted each child to improve his overall functioning and well-being.

SOCIALLY AND EMOTIONALLY
MALADJUSTED CHILDREN

18

Token Reinforcement of Academic Performance with Institutionalized Delinquent Boys

VERNON O. TYLER, JR. AND G. DUANE BROWN

Court-committed boys ages 13 to 15 in a training school observed a daily television newscast. The following morning in school their teachers administered a ten-item true-false test based on program content; S's were immediately shown their scores. After school, S's were paid tokens redeemable for candy, gum, etc. During Phase I (17 days), Group 1 (9 S's) received tokens contingent on test performance; Group 2 (6 S's) received tokens on noncontingent ("straight salary") basis. During Phase II (12 days), Group 1 received noncontingent reinforcement and Group 2 contingent reinforcement. The hypothesis that test scores would be higher under contingent than noncontingent reinforcement was supported in both be-

NOTE: This study was conducted at Fort Worden Treatment Center (Washington State Department of Institutions, Division of Juvenile Rehabilitation), Port Townsend, Washington. Grateful appreciation is due Superintendent Gus Lindquist and Assistant Superintendent Robert H. Koschnick and Principal John Kanarr for their support and encouragement of this study; teachers Sam Rust, Jr., and William Harrison for their original thinking, which made this study possible, and for preparing and administering the tests; Cottage supervisor Allen Hodge and his staff Edith Smith and Lew Streit for administering the "token economy"; John D. Burchard and Don R. Shupe for their invaluable consultative services; Don Blood and B. L. Kintz for their comments on statistical procedures; and Patricia Soapes, Sara Burchard, Doreen Beazley, and Mary Wagner for collecting and compiling data.

A version of this paper was read at the Western Psychological Association, San Francisco, California, May, 1967.

From the *Journal of Educational Psychology, 59*:164–168, 1968. Copyright 1968 by the American Psychological Association. Reprinted with permission of authors and publisher.

tween- (p < .05) and within-S (p < .005) comparisons. The conclusion was that contingent token reinforcement strengthens academic performance.

M ANY EDUCATORS prefer to motivate academic performance with "intrinsic" rather than "extrinsic" reinforcers; if used at all, they say, extrinsic reinforcers should be employed with caution (Marx, 1960). At the same time, it is recognized that delinquent youngsters often have academic difficulty in the usual school situation (e.g. Bloch and Flynn, 1956; Briggs *et al.*, 1962). Since the IQ's of delinquent youngsters may average well within the normal range (e.g. Tyler and Kelly, 1962), low motivation appears to be responsible for their poor school performance.

Various approaches have been suggested for motivating these "underachievers." As Birnbrauer *et al.* (1965) have indicated, these include (*a*) the use of "intrinsically reinforcing" materials which "are 'interesting,' 'meaningful,'" etc., (*b*) "using materials and procedures which combine interest value and high probabilities of success," and finally, (*c*) "presenting social and/or symbolic reinforcers, e.g. teacher approval, grades, and stars." But as Birnbrauer *et al.* point out, none of these methods may be adequate for the retarded, school dropouts and behavior problems. They suggest token reinforcement systems may be more effective. In such systems, the tokens which are exchangeable for tangible reinforcers become generalized reinforcers (Skinner, 1953). A few examples of token reinforcement systems which have strengthened academic performance include studies with youngsters having reading difficulties (Staats *et al.*, 1962), retardates (Birnbrauer *et al.*, 1965), nursery school youngsters (Heid, 1964) and elementary school children (Michael, 1965). However, work with delinquent youths appears to be quite rare. Cohen (Cohen *et al.*, 1965) has described a promising program for institutionalized delinquents. Of course, Slack (1960) and Schwitzgebel (e.g. Schwitzgebel and Kolb, 1964) have used operant techniques with delinquents but not directly in the area of academic performance so far as is known.

For the present study, it was assumed that many delinquent

youngsters lack reinforced practice in the skills that result in teacher ratings of satisfactory performance. Apparently, the typical school situation does not provide the type of reinforcements necessary to strengthen these skills. The purpose of this study was to develop procedures for improving the academic functioning of a group of delinquent boys. This essentially involved setting up a "token economy" based on academic performance. More specifically, it was hypothesized that academic performance with contingent reinforcement will be superior to performance with noncontingent reinforcement in both between- and within-group comparisons.

METHOD

The subjects (*S*'s) in this study were 15 court-committed boys, 13 to 15 years of age who resided in a one-cottage living unit of a state training school. They attended school in their own self-contained classroom, supervised by two team teachers. At 6 P.M. every evening, Monday through Friday, the television set in the cottage day room was turned on to the Huntley-Brinkley news broadcast. Youngsters were permitted, but not required, to watch the program; the only requirement was that all youngsters in the vicinity of the television set remain quiet so that those who wished to watch could do so. The following morning in school, *S*'s were administered a ten-item true-false test on the news program. The teachers wrote the questions the night before while watching the program. They wrote a new question every time there was a change of subject and two or three items to cover special subjects presented at the end of the program. The items were simple statements concerning the current events presented in the broadcast. Of course, this method meant the items were not standardized for difficulty. Immediately after administration, the tests were graded and the scores entered on a grade sheet which each student carried with him. Upon returning to the cottage, in the afternoon, those *S*'s on contingent reinforcement were paid in tokens according to the scores they had earned on the test; *S*'s on noncontingent reinforcement were paid a "straight salary." The tokens were redeemable for canteen items (candy, gum, etc.) and privileges in the cottage.

The *S*'s were paid the tokens according to a schedule designed by the experimenters (*E*'s). The *E*'s looked at each *S*'s scores on the true-false test for the 20 school days prior to the beginning of the experiment. Considering these data and *S*'s presumed level of motivation, a judgment was made as to what his schedule should be to maximize test performance; for example, if an *S* had been averaging six items correct, and had been earning approximately 20 cents a day in tokens, he would be given about 15 cents for six items correct, 20 cents for seven, 25 cents for eight, 27 cents for nine and 30 cents for ten correct. The goal was to let each *S* earn his previous average "income" with a slight improvement in performance and even more with greater improvements. The *E*'s' judgments were influenced by a subjective assessment of *S*'s level of aspiration, tolerance for frustration and limitations on the research budget for reinforcers.

Twenty *S*'s were randomly assigned to groups in the design

TABLE 18-1

DESIGN FOR ADMINISTRATION OF CURRENT EVENTS TEST REINFORCEMENT

Subjects	Phase I (Days 1–17)	Phase II (Days 18–29)
Group 1*	Contingent reinforcement	Noncontingent reinforcement
Group 2*	Noncontingent reinforcement	Contingent reinforcement

* For Group 1, *N* = 9; for Group 2, *N* = 6.

outlined in Table 18-1. However, because of the rapid turnover of population in a crowded institution, some *S*'s left the institution prior to completion of the study, resulting in unequal *N*'s in the two groups.

In Phase I, *S*'s in Group 1 were placed on contingent reinforcement and *S*'s in Group 2 on noncontingent reinforcement (paid 21 cents a day regardless of how well they did on the test). In Phase II, Group 1 was placed on noncontingent reinforcement and Group 2 on contingent reinforcement. A counterbalanced design was necessary to compensate for uncontrolled variability in the difficulty of the tests from day to day.

Although Group 1 (mean age 15.6) averaged a year older than Group 2 (mean age 14.6), both groups were functioning in the low-average IQ range (mean IQ's, 94 and 98, respectively).

In addition, problems in data collection should be mentioned. On some occasions, *S*'s were absent from school and could not take the tests. Because the tests were not equated for difficulty from day to day, the problem of missing data was a serious one. Only data for the days on which scores from at least 12 of the 15 boys were available were included for analysis. Missing scores for each *S* were replaced with the *S*'s mean score for the phase. From Phase I, data are reported from 17 of the 27 days on which tests were administered; from Phase II, data are reported from 12 out of 29 days. As is apparent, it was necessary to eliminate large quantities of data in order to make comparisons in which most of the *S*'s of both groups were represented.

RESULTS

Mean daily test scores for both groups for Phases I and II over the 29 days reported are presented in Figure 18-1. Means for each phase are also included. The data show a clear pattern:

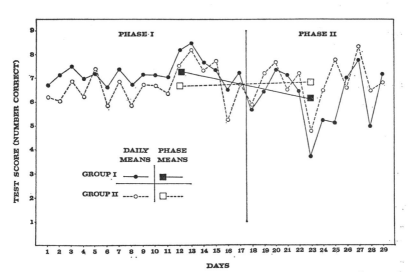

Figure 18-1. The effect of contingent and noncontingent token reinforcement on true-false test performance.

Phase I, Group 1 surpassed Group 2 on 15 out of 17 days; during Phase II, Group 2 surpassed Group 1 on 9 out of 12 days. Reversals, when they did occur, were quite small in contrast to the predicted differences between groups. The irregular, spiked form of the curves suggests that the tests varied a good deal in difficulty level from day to day, as was expected. The nearly parallel form of the two curves indicates the groups responded to these variations in difficulty in a highly consistent, reliable fashion.

The *S* means for each phase were treated with a Lindquist (1953) Type-I design analysis of variance. The summary of this

TABLE 18-2

ANALYSIS OF VARIANCE OF SUBJECT MEAN*
TEST SCORES UNDER CONTINGENT AND
NONCONTINGENT REINFORCEMENT

Source	*df*	*MS*	*F*
Between *S*'s			
B (Groups)	1	.02	
Error (b)	13	.43	
Within *S*'s			
A (Phases)	1	2.60	7.43**
AB	1	2.49	7.11***
Error (w)	13	.35	

* Analysis based on two values from each subject: the mean of his 17 daily scores from Phase I and the mean of his 12 scores from Phase II.
** $p < .025$; two-tailed.
*** $p < .0125$; one-tailed.

analysis in Table 18-2 indicates there was no difference between Groups 1 and 2 (B comparison) but that the difference between Phases I and II (A comparison) and the interaction between Groups multiplied by Phases (AB comparison) were both significant ($p < .025$ and $p < 0.125$, respectively). No difference was expected in the B comparison because of the counterbalancing of treatments. The difference between phases may be attributed to uncontrolled day-to-day variability in the difficulty level of the tests. The interaction effect indicates that under contingent reinforcement, performance was at a significantly higher level than under noncontingent reinforcement. Since the direction of the interaction effect was predicted, the probability value was halved (one-tailed test).

While the within-*S* variances against which the interaction effect was tested were not significantly heterogeneous, some question could be raised about the normality of distributions of within-S difference scores. To avoid the assumptions of homogeneity of variance and normality of distributions and to study individual S performance, the data were subjected to nonparametric treatment. Mean scores for each S for each phase (same data as for analysis of variance) were classified as to whether the trend in the data supports $(+)$ or does not support $(-)$ the prediction that each S will perform at a higher level when token reinforcement is contingent on his test score than when it is not. Twelve of the 15 S's did better under contingent reinforcement; only two S's did worse. The Wilcoxon matched-pairs signed-ranks test (Siegel, 1956) was applied to these data, yielding a highly significant T of 11 $(p < .005$; one-tailed test$)$.

The between-groups effects were also tested for each phase separately, using the Mann-Whitney U test for independent measures (Siegel, 1956). As predicted, using one-tailed tests, during Phase I Group 1 surpassed Group 2 $(U = 13$, approaches significance at the .05 level$)$; during Phase II, Group 2 surpassed Group 1 $(U = 12, p < .05)$.

DISCUSSION

Both between-groups and within-groups data clearly indicate that contingent reinforcement was associated with higher test performance than when reinforcement was noncontingent. This pattern emerged in spite of the use of quickly prepared unstandardized test items which varied considerably in difficulty from day to day and in spite of unstable conditions such as the shifting institutional population.

Moreover, this pattern appeared and was maintained with consistency over a 12-week interval. This would suggest more than a transitory effect, more than delinquents "playing games" with the program or a novelty that wore off.

While the effect of the contingent reinforcement is statistically significant, the practical educational significance appears limited at this point. The S's on contingent reinforcement averaged less than one test item better performance than when they were on noncontingent reinforcement. On the other hand, it should be noted that *S*'s were attending small classes (10 students per teacher) led by teachers who in *E*'s' judgment were about the most competent they had ever seen. These teachers had a knack with obstreperous youngsters; they knew how to discipline them and yet they were quite skilled and ingenious at devising methods of exciting the interests of even the most apathetic youngster. Thus the token reinforcement was tried against the severe competition of undoubtedly powerful social reinforcements supplied by these teachers.

That the reinforcement showed an effect in addition to what was generally regarded as an effective instructional program is further evidence of the importance of tangible reinforcers with delinquent and disadvantaged youngsters. It is doubtful that the tokens would have been this effective in a prosperous urban junior high school in which the youngsters were satiated with tangibles, enjoyed school and were achieving "success" in the middle-class culture.

Replication of this study with more precise controls would more clearly demonstrate the effectiveness of this procedure. These controls should include an unreinforced control group and test items constructed to be more nearly equal in difficulty. Previous efforts by the investigators to produce improved academic performance with token reinforcement showed no results, presumably because of inadequate controls, particularly with regard to the measurement of the criterion.

Ultimately, of course, efforts must be made to "wean" youngsters from token reinforcers and link academic performance to the more traditional reinforcers such as social approval and perhaps even the "intrinsic" reinforcement of work "for the joy of the working (Kipling, 1896)." However, the results of the present study are encouraging and suggest that many youngsters who are uninterested and antagonistic toward school work can learn that school work can "pay off."

REFERENCES

Classroom behavior of retarded pupils with token reinforcement. Birnbrauer, J. S., Wolf, M. M., Kidder, J. D. and Tague, C. E.: *Journal of Experimental Child Psychology*, 2:219–235, 1965.

Bloch, H. A. and Flynn, F. T.: *Delinquency, the Juvenile Offender in America Today.* New York, Random House, 1956.

Briggs, P. F., Johnson, R. and Wirt, R. D.: Achievement among delinquency-prone adolescents. *Journal of Clinical Psychology, 18:*305–309, 1962.

Cohen, H. L., Flipczak, J. A. and Bis, J. S.: *Case Project: Contingencies Applicable for Special Education, Brief Progress Report.* Silver Spring, Md., Institute of Behavioral Research, 1965.

Heid, W. H.: Nonverbal conceptual behavior of young children with programmed material. Unpublished doctoral dissertation, Seattle, University of Washington, 1964.

Kipling, R.: *The Seven Seas.* New York, Appleton, 1896.

Lindquist, E. F.: *Design and Analysis of Experiments in Psychology and Education.* Boston, Houghton-Mifflin, 1953.

Marx, M. H.: Motivation. In Liba, Marie R. (Ed.): *Encyclopedia of Educational Research.* New York, Macmillan, 1960, pp. 888–901.

Michael, J.: Personal communication, 1965.

Schwitzgebel, R. and Kolb, D. A.: Inducing behaviour change in adolescent delinquents. *Behaviour Research and Therapy, 1:*297–304, 1964.

Siegel, S.: *Nonparametric Statistics for the Behavioral Sciences.* New York, McGraw-Hill, 1956.

Skinner, B. F.: *Science and Human Behavior.* New York, Macmillan, 1953.

Slack, C. W.: Experimenter-subject psychotherapy: A new method of introducing intensive office treatment for unreachable cases. *Mental Hygiene, 44:*238–256, 1960.

Staats, A. W., Staats, C. K., Schultz, R. E. and Wolf, M. M.: The conditioning of textual responses using "extrinsic" reinforcers. *Journal of the Experimental Analysis of Behavior, 5:*33–40, 1962.

Tyler, V. O., Jr. and Kelly, R. F.: Cattell's HSPQ as a predictor of the behavior of institutionalized delinquents. *Psychology Research Report No. 2.* Port Townsend, Wash., Fort Worden Diagnostic & Treatment Center, 1962.

Wingo, G. M.: Methods of teaching. In Liba, Marie R. (Ed.): *Encyclopedia of Educational Research.* New York, Macmillan, 1960, pp. 848–861.

19

Effects of Teacher Attention and a Token Reinforcement System in a Junior High School Special Education Class

MARCIA BRODEN, R. VANCE HALL, ANN DUNLAP AND
ROBERT CLARK

Teacher attention and a token reinforcement system were
used to bring about control in a disruptive junior high school
special education classroom. Individual and group study levels
were recorded during a baseline period. Subsquent experimental
periods employing teacher attention and/or a token point system increased study levels and decreased disruptive behaviors
of class members. Reinforcement of appropriate behaviors was
withdrawn during short reversals producing lowered study rates.
Reinstatement of contingencies again resulted in increased
study levels.

A SERIES OF STUDIES carried out in nursery schools (Harris
et al., 1964), special education classes (Hall and Broden, 1967;
Zimmerman and Zimmerman, 1962) and regular public schools
(Hall *et al.*, 1968a; Hall *et al.*, 1968b; Thomas *et al.*, 1968) have
demonstrated that contingent teacher attention could be effective
in increasing appropriae classroom behavior.

NOTE: This research was partially supported by the National Institute
of Child Health and Human Development (HD 03144 01-02) and the Office
of Economic Opportunity (CG8180 to the Bureau of Child Research, University of Kansas).

From *Exceptional Children*, 36:341–349, 1970. Copyright 1970 by the
Council for Exceptional Children. Reprinted with permission of authors
and publisher.

Similarly, token reinforcement systems backed up by food, field trips, toys, money, and grades were demonstrated to be effective in increasing academic behaviors of pupils in special education programs including classrooms for the retarded (Birnbrauer *et al.*, 1965), remedial classrooms for poverty-area elementary-age children (Wolf *et al.*, 1968) and for elementary special education pupils (McKenzie *et al.*, 1968; O'Leary and Becker, 1967).

With the exception of the study by Hall *et al.*, 1968b), however, these studies were carried out by experienced teachers and dealt with preschool and elementary-age children. Those using token reinforcement systems used reinforcers primarily extrinsic to the classroom, and most often there was more than one teacher available to conduct the class and carry out the experimental procedures.

In contrast, the present study was carried out in a public junior high school special education classroom by a first-year teacher without prior teaching experience. When systematic teacher attention to appropriate behavior proved to be limited in its effect, a token reinforcement system backed by reinforcers available to most junior high school teachers was used to reduce extremely disruptive behavior and to increase appropriate study behavior.

SUBJECTS AND SETTING

The subjects were 13 seventh- and eighth-grade students, eight boys and five girls, in a special education class in Bonner Springs Junior High School, Bonner Springs, Kansas. All students were several years behind in at least one major academic area and had other problems, including severe reading deficits, almost incoherent speech, emotional instability and acts of delinquency. Some specific problem behaviors involved cursing the teacher; refusing to obey teacher requests or to do assignments; throwing pencils, pens, or paper; fighting; chasing each other about the room; and eating a variety of snacks.

The inappropriate behaviors described had persisted through the first four months of school, although the teacher had used generally accepted methods for maintaining classroom control, including some praise for appropriate behavior and reprimands or a trip to the counselor or principal's office for misconduct.

The class met for five periods of the eight-period day. The entire class was present for the first, fifth and eighth periods. Only the seven seventh graders were present for the second and sixth periods, and only the six eighth graders were present during the third and seventh periods.

Observations

The system used was essentially that developed by Broden (1968) for recording classroom study behavior. Daily observations were made by an observer equipped with a recording sheet and stopwatch. Data were recorded on the recording sheet at 5-second intervals. At the 5-second mark, the behavior of the first pupil was recorded, at the 10 second mark the behavior of a second pupil was recorded, at the 15 second mark that of the third student, and so on until every student had been observed once; then the sequence was begun again. Thus the behavior of a different pupil was recorded every 5 seconds on a consecutive rotation basis.

As is shown in Figure 19-1, the recording sheet was divided into triple rows of squares with a different pupil's name entered at the top of each column of three vertical squares. The middle row of squares was used to record whether or not the pupil was studying. An "S" (for study) was recorded if the pupil were attending to or oriented toward the appropriate book when he had been assigned reading to do, if he was attending to the teacher or another pupil who was speaking during class discussions, if

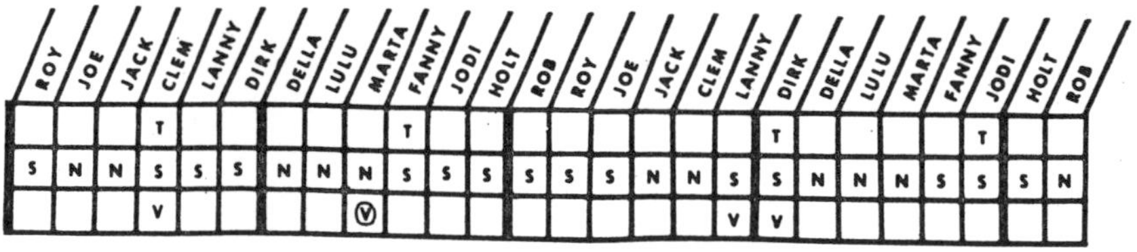

Row 1 T = Teacher verbalization directed to pupil
Row 2 S = Study behavior, N = Nonstudy behavior
Row 3 V = Appropriate pupil verbalization, v = Inappropriate verbalization

Figure 19-1. Observer recording sheet and symbol key.

he was writing spelling words during spelling period or if he was otherwise engaged in a teacher-assigned task. All other behaviors were designated as "N" except for the specific nonstudy behavior "out of seat" which was recorded as "O."

The top row of squares was used to record verbalizations by the teacher to a subject or to the class. A "T" designated teacher verbalization directed to an individual pupil during that 5-second interval.

The bottom row of squares was used to record pupil verbalizations. A "V" designated verbalizations recognized by the teacher.

Observations lasted from 30 to 40 minutes during any given period.

Computing the percentage of the total 5-second intervals in which "S" had been recorded revealed the class study rate. It was also possible to compute individual study rates by dividing the number of "S" intervals for the pupil by the total number of intervals that the individual pupil was observed and multiplying the result by 100. Thus both class and individual study rates could be obtained.

Reliability checks were made periodically throughout the study. A second observer made independent, simultaneous observations. This record was compared with that of the primary observer, interval by interval. The percentage of agreement was then computed. Observer agreement for this study ranged from 83 to 98 percent.

EXPERIMENT I

Initially, daily observations were begun during the fifth period when all 13 pupils were present. Assigned study tasks included reading, writing, and participation in class discussions.

During the first (baseline) 7 days of observation, the teacher was asked to conduct class in her usual manner and to ignore the observer. Care was taken not to mention possible experimental procedures. Pupils were told someone would be coming in at various times to assist the teacher. All contact between the observer and teacher or pupils was avoided during class sessions.

Figure 19-2 presents the data for the seven baseline sessions. The broken horizontal line indicates that the mean rate of study behavior was 29 percent. During baseline sessions, the teacher was observed giving attention to both study and nonstudy behaviors.

Prior to the eighth day of observation, a conference was held with the teacher. She was shown the baseline study data and was asked to begin giving attention to study behavior only and to ignore all nonstudying. During the next 11 days, the teacher went to pupils who were studying and commented on their good study behavior and work, called only on pupils who raised their hands and complimented the entire group when all were studying quietly.

As can be seen in the Social Reinforcement₁ phase of Figure 19-2, this procedure resulted in an increase in study behavior to a mean rate of 57 percent. Although this was an improvement over baseline rates, there were still frequent outbursts of inappropriate verbalizations, out-of-seat and other disruptive behaviors. Therefore, a new contingency for appropriate study was introduced.

During the next 18 sessions, a kitchen timer was placed on the teacher's desk and set to go off at random intervals averaging eight minutes. Pupils who were in their seats and quiet when the timer sounded were given a mark on a card taped to their desk tops. Each mark earned allowed them to leave one minute earlier for lunch. Teacher attention for study was continued during this phase.

As can be seen in the Timer₁ phase of Figure 19-2, an immediate increase in study behavior resulted. Beginning in the 25th session ("Quiet Entire Interval" in Fig. 19-2) pupils were required to be quiet during the entire interval between time rings in order to receive a mark. Beginning in the 31st session, marks (grades) were continued as before, but a grade of E (excellent) was also given if the pupil had been engaging in study behavior. These conditions seemed to have little additional effect on study level.

The mean study rate for the entire Timer₁ phase was 74 percent and, according to the subjective judgments of the teacher and observer, there was noticeably less disruptive behavior.

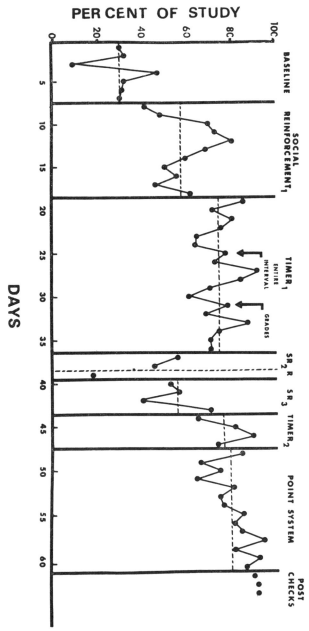

Figure 19-2. A record of fifth-period study behavior during baseline₁, social reinforcement₁, timer₁, social reinforcement₂ (SR₂), reversal (R), social reinforcement₂ (SR₂), timer₂, point system, and postcheck conditions.

In order to see if the reinforcement procedures were the primary factors in increasing study, a brief return to prior conditions was made. For 2 days, the timer—early-dismissal contingency was removed and only social reinforcement for study was given. This resulted in a drop in study behavior to 55 percent the first day and to 45 percent the second (Social Reinforcement$_2$). The following day (session 39), social reinforcement for study was also withdrawn. The teacher attended only to nonstudy behavior and ignored study behavior. This complete reversal of procedures resulted in a breakdown of study behavior and almost complete disruption of the class. As can be seen in Figure 19-2 (R-Reversal), the study level during this one day reversal was only 18 percent.

During the next phase (Social Reinforcement$_3$), the teacher again attended to study behavior and ignored nonstudy. The level rose to 55 percent. During the next 4 days, the timer and marks for early lunch dismissal plus grades for study were reinstituted. Under these conditions (Timer$_2$), the mean study level was 76 percent.

Beginning in session 48, the timer condition was discontinued and pupils were put on a token point system described in Experiment II. The data presented in the Point System phase of Figure 19-2 indicate that the higher study levels established with the timer were not only maintained but also slightly increased under the token point system. In fact, the mean study level rose to 90 percent.

Postchecks taken over the next month and a half after conclusion of daily monitoring indicated that the higher study levels were maintained through the remainder of the school year, despite the fact the teacher was not informed prior to observation time when these checks would occur.

EXPERIMENT II

After a few days of higher study levels achieved by the procedure described above, the teacher and principal concurred in their judgment that pupil behavior during fifth period was indeed under much better control. However, they reported that

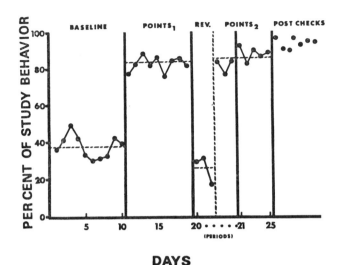

DAYS

Figure 19-3. A record of study behavior during the entire day, under baseline, points, reversal (Rev.), points₂, and postcheck conditions. Postchecks were taken periodically during the final six weeks of school after termination of regular observations.

the higher study rates had not transferred to the other five daily class periods. Therefore, an attempt to increase study during these periods also was made.

First, observations were made in order to determine the actual level of study during these five other periods. Nineteen 30-minute observations were made on ten different days. Although the mean number of observations was a little less than two per day, the number on any one day ranged from one to all five (the number monitored on days 7 and 8). As can be seen in Figure 19-3, the mean levels of study for the 10 days of observation ranged from 33 to 47 percent. The mean baseline level as indicated by the dotted horizontal line was 39 percent.

Following baseline, a token reinforcement system was instituted. A point system, using a combination of available privileges and punishments, was selected. (These periods were not followed by lunch, and therefore earlier dismissal for lunch could not be utilized as it had been for period five.)

TABLE 19-1

POINT SYSTEM

Earn Points:

5	in seat.
5	quiet.
5	doing assignment.
2	extra credit (after regular assignment is complete).
3	an "A" on an assigned task.
2	a "B" on an assigned task.
1	a "C" on an assigned task.
0	a "D" on an assigned task.

Minus Points:

15	out of seat without permission.
1	talking out of turn: hand is not raised, teacher hasn't called on you.
20	out of the room without permission.
5	incomplete assignment (per period).
3	namecalling, swearing.
20	throwing, hitting.
20	arguing with the teacher.
20	teacher must tell you more than once to stop.

Spend Points:

50	five minutes pass to the rest room.
50	permission to go five minutes early to lunch.
10	permission to get out of your seat for one minute.
50	permission to move your desk for one period.
100	permission to move your desk for one day.
300	permission to move your desk permanently.
20	pass to get a drink of water.
10	permission to talk to another person for five minutes.
50	Friday snack.
400	field trip.
20	nonacademic activities approved by the teacher such as knitting, puzzles, games, records.

To Earn Off Minus Points:

1	stay after school (per minute).
1	five earned positive points (earns off one minus point).
*	teacher assigned academic task.
*	the teacher determines the task and the point value.

Each pupil was given a copy of the point system values, similar to that shown in Table 19-1.

The "Earn Points" section was comprised of items suggested by the teacher, principal and observer as desirable pupil behaviors. Earn Points were assigned so that a pupil could accumulate about 20 points per class period by engaging in reasonably appropriate behavior such as remaining in his seat and being quiet. (Pupils were given the option of when and for what they would spend the points earned.)

The "Spend Points" section was comprised of activities and privileges which included those suggested by the pupils when they were asked, "What would you like to do if you had one free period?" Other Spend Point items were recommended by the teacher, principal and observer as probable reinforcers which could be administered within existing school policy. Spend Points were assigned so that behaviors thought to be highly desired were more costly than less desired ones.

The "Minus Points" section was comprised of undesirable pupil behaviors. Minus Points were assigned values so that the most disruptive behaviors cost the most. Pupils who accumulated 20 or more minus points were required to stay after school for 1½ hours on Thursday afternoon, which was the school-wide detention period. Minus points could also be bought off by Earn Points at a ratio of five earned points to one minus point.

The teacher kept account of points during the period on a form at her desk which listed all pupils and had columns for posting point totals earned, spent or lost. Point totals were posted on the chalkboard at the end of each period and pupils could see how many Earn Points and how many Minus Points each had acquired.

The results of instituting the point system were immediate and dramatic. As can be seen in the $Points_1$ phase of Figure 19-3, the mean class study rate rose to 83 percent on the first day. Study was maintained at high levels throughout the $Points_1$ phase of the experiment.

This increase in study level was recorded, even though three pupils argued that it was childish, stated that they would refuse to cooperate, would quit school and would complain to the principal and counselor. These remarks were largely ignored, and the second day, two of the three showed increased study rates. Over the next four days, the third objector, Rob, became extremely disruptive. He cursed the teacher, erased the board, tore up assignments, left the room, fought with other pupils and said he would not work and that no one could make him do it. When he was told to go to his seat or to the office, he refused. Under the point system he soon accumulated 512 minus points and 19 positive points. By the fourth day, other class members were spending increasing time watching Rob and laughing at his antics.

Wolf *et al.* (1964) had demonstrated that isolation procedures could be used effectively to reduce tantrum behaviors in a preschool child. Since much of Rob's behavior resembled tantrums, these procedures were explained to both the teacher and the principal and a modified version of isolation was decided upon. It was agreed that if Rob refused to obey the teacher's direction to be quiet or sit down he would be sent immediately to the office. Unlike other times he had been sent there, he was not to be allowed back into the classroom until he had stated that he would be quiet and stay in his seat.

During the first period of the fifth day, Rob refused to obey a teacher direction to be quiet and was sent directly to the principal's office. To reduce the chance that office procedures would reinforce him, the principal had an area screened off so that the student could not see who entered the office or what they were doing. He was not given work to do. He remained there until the end of the school day. The next day when he arrived at school he requested that he be returned to class and stated that he would stay in his seat and be quiet. When he returned to class, his talking and out of seat behaviors decreased and his study behaviors increased. From that point on, Rob presented no particular problem and obeyed the teacher. Though he refused to study for a time, he did begin to read a library book, then began to do individual work and finally began to participate in group discussions. He began accumulating earn points and working off the minus points. He freely spent points, seldom accumulating enough for a field trip. By the end of school, however, he was able to participate in a field trip and an auction which was held to use up surplus earn points.

After nine days of increased study under the point system, a reversal procedure was instituted. The experimenters agreed to allow reinstitution of the point system immediately if class behavior deteriorated to former levels and the teacher seemed to be losing control. It was thought that the effect of reversal might be observable over a 3- or 4-day period.

Reversal conditions were begun during the first period of day 20. The pupils were told that the point system was no longer in effect, and the teacher discontinued giving attention for appropriate study, although she provided verbal reprimands for nonstudy behaviors.

The data for day 20 are shown on a period basis in Figure 19-3 (Reversal). Study dropped to 29 percent in the first period. Second period it was 31 percent and third period it dropped to 16 percent. Because of the extremely chaotic situation and the prior agreement to discontinue reversal if control was lost, the point system was put back into effect during the fourth period. As can be seen in Figure 19-3, this resulted in a dramatic return to high study rates in the final three class periods of the day.

Period-by-period observations during the next 5 days showed that the mean study rate was above 80 percent.

Observations taken intermittently beginning 2 weeks later showed that over the next 1½ months of the remainder of the school year, high study rates were being maintained under the point system (see Postchecks, Figures 19-2 and 19-3).

The high Postcheck rate (90%) was maintained, even though the system was changed so that Minus Points were subtracted from earned points on a one-to-one basis in the interest of simplifying the record-keeping system.

The data indicated that in addition to study behavior, inappropriate talking and the number of times pupils were out of their seats were affected by the experimental procedures. During baseline, inappropriate verbalizations were recorded in 84 percent of the observed intervals. Under Points$_1$ conditions, inappropriate talking dropped to 10 percent. It rose to 44 percent during Reversal. It dropped to 5 percent when the point system was reinstated and was at 7 percent during the Postcheck period.

Pupils were out of their seats an average of 70 seconds per period during baseline. When the point system was instituted, the mean rate was 10 seconds per period. In the brief and chaotic three-period Reversal phase, the time out of seats rose to mean rate of 215 seconds per period. Out-of-seats time returned to 10 seconds per period during the Points$_2$ and Postcheck phases. These data indicated that control of these specific inappropriate behaviors as well as increases in study had been achieved.

INDIVIDUAL DATA

Since a record was kept of which student was being observed during each 5-second interval, it was possible to compute individual study rates for each experimental condition by dividing the number of study intervals by the total number of intervals that particular individual was observed and multiplying by 100.

An analysis of the data revealed that there was considerable individual variation in study rates and in the effects of the various experimental conditions on individuals. During the fifth period baseline phase, for example, study levels ranged from 11 to 62 percent. Although teacher attention was effective in increasing study for all pupils, it was much more effective for some than for others. For instance, one girl's study level increased from 14 to 64 percent while one boy's study increased only from 12 to 18 percent. Similarly, though the $Timer_1$ condition backed by early dismissal for lunch resulted in further increases in study for all other pupils, it resulted in an actual decrease in study level for one.

Reversal effects varied from pupil to pupil also. During the reversal phase, all showed decreased study levels, although study for six students remained at levels substantially higher than baseline rates, while almost no study was recorded for the three pupils who had the lowest baseline study rates.

An analysis of the data for the point system also showed variations in study levels. Marked increases in study levels over baseline were achieved for all pupils under the points system. All pupils showed a marked decrease in study during the brief reversal phase when the point system was withdrawn. In the $Points_2$ and Postcheck phases, data indicated that even though the three pupils who had the lowest baseline study levels were still studying less than their classmates, all three were above the 70 percent level, higher than the highest study rate recorded for any pupil during baseline.

DISCUSSION

This study showed that systematic reinforcement procedures using contingencies available in most junior high school classrooms could be used by a beginning teacher to gain control of an extremely disruptive junior high school special education class. Systematic teacher attention increased study levels but was limited in its effect. For most pupils, classroom privileges, including such activities as early dismissal to lunch, getting a drink, sharpening a pencil, and talking to another pupil for five minutes, were more powerful than teacher attention alone for motivating desired behavior. Reversal procedures demonstrated the functional relationship between the reinforcement contingencies and the increases in appropriate behaviors.

The data also revealed that the effectiveness of a given procedure varied from pupil to pupil. In the case of one pupil, it was necessary to institute a time-out procedure to gain participation in the point system. Once participation was gained, increases in study were dramatic.

In discussing the point system, it should be mentioned that there was no rationale for the number of points assigned for particular activities or for the selection of the activities, other than a seemingly suitable balance between the behaviors required to earn points and the reinforcing value of the activities and privileges for which they could be spent. Another teacher would doubtless have to adjust the system to fit his particular classroom group and the resources available to him.

Evaluating the point system in terms of value and convenience to the teacher is necessarily subjective but relevant to a discussion of the overall worth of the system. In her evaluation, the teacher stated that the system was helpful, for it gave both the student and the teacher "a black and white list of what is allowed in the classroom." She also stated that it was easier for her to be fair, since the clearly stated penalties and rewards stopped arguments over the teacher's handling of misconduct. She also reported that pupils did a great deal more classwork and made better grades. At times she had difficulty keeping up with the amount of extra-credit work, since pupils would choose extra work over any other activities if they were working for a highly prized privilege. She reported further that most pupils indicated they liked the order the system helped provide.

According to the teacher, the system could be improved by establishing a simpler system for computing point totals. She felt it was important to post the totals every hour so pupils would have more immediate feedback on their status, but daily instead of hourly computations would reduce the amount of teacher time needed to figure points. She also suggested that the pupils should be more involved in establishing the point system. Such involvement might reduce the initial resistance to the system. She reported that allowing the class to take part in modifying the system when problems arose had helped them accept it.

It is understood by the authors that the procedures used to bring about classroom control in this study are not new or startling. Good teachers have used teacher attention and access to privileges to motivate appropriate pupil behavior for many years. The results reported here are of interest, however, for they demonstrate a means by which a teacher who had not managed to do so was helped to organize the environmental consequences available to her and bring about desired classroom behavior. In essence, the point system acted as a convenient means for the teacher and the pupils to link desired study behavior with participation in desired activities.

It is conceded that a point system may not be necessary or appropriate in many junior high school classrooms. It may, however, be a valuable aid to teachers who have difficulty in maintaining classroom control over children with highly deviant and disruptive behaviors.

REFERENCES

Birnbrauer, J. S., Wolf, M. M., Kidder, J. D. and Tague, E.: Classroom behavior of retarded pupils with token reinforcement. *Journal of Experimental Child Psychology*, 2:219–235, 1965.

Broden, M.: Notes on recording. Observer's Manual for Juniper Gardens Children's Project, Unpublished manuscript, Bureau of Child Research, 1968.

Hall, R. V. and Broden, M.: Behavior changes in brain-injured children through social reinforcement. *Journal of Experimental Child Psychology*, 5:463–479, 1967.

Hall, R. V., Lund, D. and Jackson, D.: Effects of teacher attention on study behavior. *Journal of Applied Behavior Analysis, 1:*1–12, 1968a.

Hall, R. V., Panyan, M., Rabon, D. and Broden, M.: Instructing beginning teachers in reinforcement procedures which improve classroom control. *Journal of Applied Behavior Analysis, 1:*315–322, 1968b.

Harris, F. R., Wolf, M. M. and Baer, D. M.: Effects of adult social reinforcement on child behavior. *Young Children, 20:*8–17, 1964.

McKenzie, H., Clark, M., Wolf, M., Kothera, R. and Benson, C.: Behavior modification of children with learning disabilities using grades as token reinforcers. *Exceptional Children, 34:*745–752, 1968.

O'Leary, K. D. and Becker, W. C.: Behavior modification of an adjustment class: token reinforcement system. *Exceptional Children, 33:*637–642, 1967.

Thomas, D. R., Becker, W. C. and Armstrong, M.: Production and elimination of disruptive classroom behavior by systematically varying teacher's behavior. *Journal of Applied Behavior Analysis, 1:*35–45, 1968.

Wolf, M. M., Giles, D. K. and Hall, R. V.: Experiments with token reinforcement in a remedial classroom. *Behaviour Research and Therapy, 6:*51–64, 1968.

Wolf, M. M., Risley, T. R. and Mees, H. L.: Application of operant conditioning procedures to the behavior problems of an autistic child. *Behaviour Research and Therapy, 1:*305–312, 1964.

Zimmerman, E. H. and Zimmerman, J.: The alteration of behavior in a special classroom situation. *Journal of the Experimental Analysis of Behavior, 5:*59–60, 1962.

20

How to Make a Token System Fail

DAVID S. KUYPERS, WESLEY C. BECKER
and K. DANIEL O'LEARY

A token system was instituted in an adjustment class of six
third and fourth graders. The aim of the study was to examine
aspects of token systems critical in making them effective. The
results indicated a significant degree of improvement in behavior attributable to the token program, but when compared to
the highly effective program reported by O'Leary and Becker
(1967), it is apparent that an effective program requires more
than tokens and back-up reinforcers.

Token systems of reinforcement have usually been implemented
in classrooms when the available social reinforcers such as teacher
praise and approval have been ineffective in controlling the behavior of the children. Token systems involve the presentation
of a "token" (e.g. a checkmark) following the emission of specified responses. When the child has accumulated a sufficient number of tokens, he is then able to exchange them for "back-up"
reinforcers (e.g. candy, toys). The tokens initially function as
neutral stimuli, and they acquire reinforcing properties by being
exchangeable for the back-up reinforcers. Teacher praise and ap-

NOTE: This study was supported by the National Institutes of Health
Grant HD 00881-05.

From *Exceptional Children*, 35:101–109, 1968. Copyright 1968 by the
National Council for Exceptional Children. Reprinted with permission of
authors and publisher.

proval are often paired with the tokens, in order to increase the effectiveness of praise and approval as conditioned reinforcers. A general goal of token systems is to transfer control of responding from the token systems to other conditioned reinforcers such as teacher praise and grades.

Different investigators have reported upon the success of token systems in controlling the behavior of children in classrooms where the usual social reinforcers were ineffective (Birnbrauer *et al.*, 1965a; Birnbrauer and Lawler, 1964; Birnbrauer *et al.*, 1965b; O'Leary and Becker, 1967).

Teachers operating successful token programs in these studies have usually been explicitly trained in the systematic use of principles of operant behavior, and much of the success of the programs is most likely due to the general application of principles other than those governing the use of tokens per se. The central aspect of a token system is the pairing of teacher praise with tokens which are backed up by an effective reinforcer. In most effective studies, however, many other procedures have also been used. For example, praise for appropriate behavior and ignoring of disruptive behavior are used at times when tokens are not being dispensed. Time out (or isolation) is often used when intensely disruptive behaviors occur. Systematic contingencies in the form of privileges are often applied throughout the day. The children following the rules are the ones who get to help teacher, to be first in line, to choose an activity, etc. The principle of shaping is also systematically applied. Praise, privileges and tokens are not administered for achieving an absolute standard of performance but for improving behavior or for maintaining a high level of acceptable behavior.

The present study is one of several aimed at clarifying the important components of effective token systems. Our objective is primarily to make clear to those who might adopt such systems where things can go wrong if a token system is attempted without full consideration of the many variables important to success. The study uses a general procedure which was shown to be very effective when coupled with training in behavior theory, a time-out procedure, shaping and differential social reinforcement throughout the day (O'Leary and Becker, 1967). The present study, however, examines the effectiveness of the token system by itself in a classroom in which no other modifications were made in the teacher's handling of the class. The study approximates what might happen if a teacher read about a token system and tried to use it mechanically without a fuller understanding of those basic principles and supplementary procedures which are often used in successful studies but which are not emphasized or made explicit.

The study was planned to include additional phases to train the teacher in behavior principles; following this, a more effective program would have been established. However, at the request of the teacher, it was necessary to terminate the study prior to its completion. We will come back to this point in the discussion.

METHOD

The subjects who participated in this study were six third-grade and six fourth-grade children who were described as socially maladjusted. The children were typically assigned to an adjustment class when they showed such behaviors as temper tantrums, fighting, failure to pay attention in class, inability to work on their own and academic retardation. While the token system of reinforcement was in effect for the entire class, observations were conducted on only three of the children at each grade level—six children in all. Four of the children were selected because they engaged in a high rate of inappropriate and disruptive behavior, and two were selected because the teacher reported a low incidence of highly disruptive behavior in relation to the other class members. Two of the children had previously attended a classroom at another school in which a token system of reinforcement had been used (O'Leary and Becker, 1967).

Observations

The incidence of inappropriate classroom behaviors of the four highly disruptive children was recorded by two undergraduate students during the morning between 9:30 and 11:30. Between 1:00 and 2:00 in the afternoon, three undergraduate observers recorded the behavior of six children who included the four observed in the morning plus two children who were reported by the teacher not to show much disruptive behavior. Deviant behaviors were defined as behaviors likely to be incompatible with group learning conditions. Definitions used for six classes of deviant behaviors, and one class of relevant behavior, are as follows.

Coding Categories for Children

Deviant Behavior

Gross motor behaviors: Getting out of seat, standing up, walking around, running, hopping, skipping, jumping, rocking chair, moving chair, knees on chair. Include such gross physical movements as arm flailing, feet swinging and rocking.

Disruptive noise: Tapping feet, clapping, rattling papers, tearing papers, throwing book on desk, slamming desk top, tapping pencil or other objects on desk. Be conservative, rate what you hear, not what you see, and do not include accidental dropping of objects or noise made while performing gross motor behaviors.

Disturbing others: Grabbing objects or work, knocking neighbor's books off desk, destroying another's property, throwing objects at another without hitting, pushing with desk. Only rate if someone is there.

Contact: Hitting, pushing, shoving, pinching, slapping, striking with objects, throwing object which hits another person, poking with object. Do not attempt to make judgments of intent. Rate any physical contact.

Orienting responses: Turning head or head and body to look at another person, showing objects to another child, attending to another child. Must be of four-seconds duration to be rated and is not rated unless seated. Any turn of 90 degrees or more from desk while seated is rated.

Verbalizations: Carrying on conversations with other children when it is not permitted, calling out answers to questions or comments without being called on, calling teacher's name to get her attention, crying, screaming, singing, whistling, laughing, coughing, or blowing nose. Do not rate lip movements. Rate what you hear, not what you see.

Relevant Behavior

Time on task, e.g. answering questions, listening, raising hand for teacher attention, working at assigned task, reading.

Must include whole 10-second interval except for orienting responses of less than four seconds' duration.

The children were observed in a fixed order for 22 minutes each session, three times a week. Observations were made on a 20-second observe, 10-second record basis. Each observer had a clipboard with a stop watch and a recording sheet. Simple symbols were used to indicate the occurrence of a particular class of behavior. A given class of behavior could be rated only once in an observation interval.

Percentage of deviant behavior was defined as the percentage of intervals in which one or more deviant behaviors occurred. Reliability was checked on the average of once a week and was calculated by dividing the number of agreements on behavior code and time interval by the number of agreements plus disagreements.

Class Activities

For most of the day, the children were in a single classroom with one teacher. During the morning, the children's activities consisted of group reading lessons and individual seatwork. During the afternoon, the first 40-minute period consisted of a group arithmetic lesson and the second 40-minute period consisted of either art or music in another room for the fourth graders and art or spelling for the third graders.

Experimental Phases

Baseline

During the baseline phase, the teacher was asked to handle the children according to her usual techniques and procedures. Observers had recorded the children's behavior for approximately three weeks before the collection of baseline observations was begun. This initial period was instituted in order to allow the children to adapt to the observers' presence in the classroom.

Token Reinforcement Phase

The following written instructions were given to the teacher and discussed with her. These instructions were used as the basis for the token reinforcement stage.

1. Instructions for initial introduction of token program.

   a. Prior to the explanation of the token economy to the children, a list of rules should be written on the blackboard and left there while the program is in effect. (The rules worked out with the teacher were: *stay in seats, raise hand, quiet, desk clear, face front,* and *work hard.* For the art period for the third graders the rules were: *quiet, work hard* and *be polite.*)

   b. Explain to the children that they will be rated on how well they follow the rules from 1:00 to 2:30. Spiral notebooks will be attached to their desks, and every rating period the teacher will put a number from 1 to 10 in their notebooks. The better a child follows the rules, the higher the number he will receive.

   c. By earning points in this way, the children will be able to win prizes. They must have a certain number of points in order to win a prize. Show the children the prizes and explain that 10 points earns a prize from this box (show an example) and 25 points earns a prize from this box. Do not let the children handle the prizes.

   d. Emphasize that at all other times when the children are not being rated, their behavior will not affect their rating during the afternoon period.

   e. Explain to the fourth graders that their other teachers will rate them when they leave the classroom and that they will have to bring back a slip with their number on it signed by their teacher. If they do not bring back this slip, they will not receive any points that day. Also explain that the other children in the art and music class will not be told about their point system.

   f. Emphasize that they will not receive prizes every day, and that sometimes they will have to collect points over two or more days in order to obtain prizes. However, they will be told how long they have to work to earn a prize.

2. General instructions for operation of token program.

  a. Each day before the rating period, go over the rules with the children. Point out that they can earn prizes, tell them how many points they must have to win different types of prizes, and then show them some of the prizes they can win.

  b. When rating a child, point out the rules he followed in order to receive the points he did. "I'm giving you 8 points because. . . ," "I'm not giving you 10 points because. . . ." Also indicate what behaviors could be improved on to earn full points.

  c. At all times, except when prizes are being shown to the class or when the children are picking out the prizes they have earned, the prizes should be stored in a location where the children cannot reach them.

  d. If the children mention certain types of prizes they would like to be able to earn or if they do not appear interested in any of the prizes available, please notify the investigator as soon as possible.

  e. Record points on two pages. One will be picked up each day. Enter ratings from art and music teachers into the book also.

  f. Except for the first day of the token program, prizes should be given out at the end of the school day. On the first day, give out prizes after the third rating period.

  g. The children will be rated from 1 to 10 on how well they follow the classroom rules and behave in class. Rules can be modified or changed, but if this is done, notify the class and put the change on the blackboard.

  h. The value of the prize will be changed as the children are required to earn more points to win prizes. The number of points required will be indicated on the appropriate boxes.

  i. A child should be very well behaved to earn the highest-value prizes. Do not allow the children to try to talk you into giving them more points. Make a judgment and then explain that he earned only so many points, but he can earn more by behaving better.

Two values of prizes were used—one group in the 5- to 10-cent range, and one group in the 15- to 19-cent range. They included such things as candy, gliders, balls, pencils and clay.

For third graders, ratings were given after each 30-minute period. Since the fourth graders left for art or music during the second 30-minute period, the problem was initially handled by doubling the points earned in the first period and by having the art or music teacher give a rating for that period. After four days, the system was changed so that both third and fourth graders were rated after two 40-minute periods. During the first four days, prizes were distributed each day. After that, they were distributed every other day. The number of points required to earn prizes was gradually increased from 10 to 30 for lower-value prizes and 25 to 35 for higher-value prizes.

The teacher used her own judgment in making ratings within the guidelines given above. She was informed of how the observers rated the children the first few days of the program, but no attempt was made to determine her ratings. In all other aspects of her behavior, the teacher was expected to continue as she had before.

Baseline Two

The token system was withdrawn for two weeks and baseline conditions reestablished. It was during this period that the teacher decided not to continue with the study.

RESULTS

Reliability

During the afternoon observations, interobserver reliability for individual children for the 13-day baseline period ranged from 64 to 98 percent agreement with an average of 80 percent. During the token period, the interobserver reliability ranged from 69 to 100 percent with an average of 87 percent. For the second baseline, the range was 68 to 100 percent with an average of 82 percent. The reliabilities for morning observations ranged from 52 to 100 percent with an average of 85 percent.

Group Data

For all six children in the afternoon, the average percentage of deviant behavior during the baseline period was 54. During the token period, the average decreased to 27.8 percent and then increased to 41.5 percent when the tokens were removed. The daily averages for the different periods have been plotted graphically in Figure 20-1. If fewer than four children were observed on any day, then that day was eliminated from the analysis. The single day that a substitute teacher was in the classroom was also eliminated. An analysis of variance, using the average percentage of deviant behavior for each child during each period, indicated that the effects of periods were significant beyond the .01 level ($F = 11.27$, $df = 2$).

The average daily percentage of deviant behavior for the four children observed both in the morning and afternoon is plotted graphically by days for the different periods for both the morning and afternoon observations (see Figure 20-2). A child had to be observed in both the morning and afternoon for his percentage of deviant behavior to be included in the analyses, and if fewer

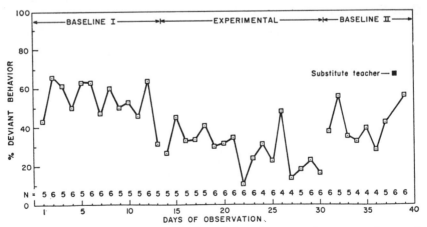

Figure 20-1. Percentage of deviant behavior as a function of experimental conditions for children observed during the afternoon.

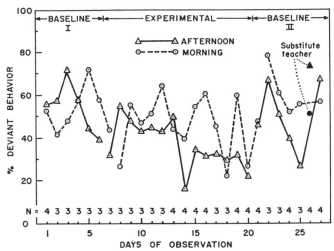

Figure 20-2. Percentage of deviant behavior as a function of experimental conditions for children observed during morning and afternoon.

than three children were observed on any day, then that day was eliminated from the analysis. The average percentage of deviant behavior for the first baseline period was 53.2 for morning and 54.3 for afternoon observations. For the token periods, the percentages were 45.0 (A.M.) and 35.5 (P.M.); and for the second baseline they were 58.5 (A.M.) and 50.4 (P.M.). These data show little, if any, generalization of improved behavior from the afternoon period when the token system was in effect to the morning period when the token system was not in effect. No statistical tests were carried out on the generalization data because of wide individual variations in effect. The important results of the study are made clear by examination of the individual graphs.

Individual Data

The individual graphs show that four children (1 through 4, Fig. 20-3) improved considerably under the token system, and two showed at best occasional good days. No consistent individual gains occurred during the morning period when individual data were examined (these graphs are not presented). Of interest is the fact that children 4 and 6 had participated in the earlier pro-

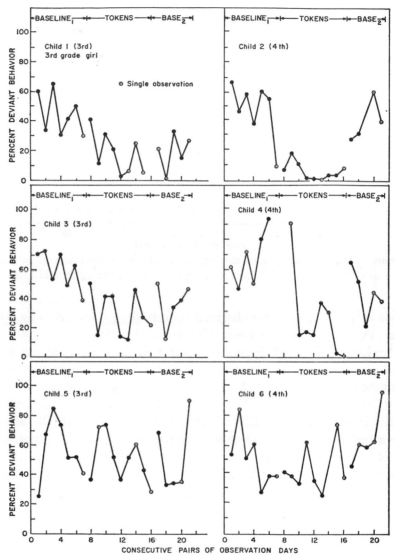

Figure 20-3. Percentage of deviant behavior for individual children based on afternoon observations.

gram by O'Leary and Becker (1967). Child 6 rarely responded to the new program, and often would not even keep his point book on his desk.

DISCUSSION

Although an average significant effect of the token program was demonstrated, it is quite clear from the individual graphs and the generalization measures that the program was only marginally effective. Many interpretations are always possible when there is a failure to establish experimental control over behavior; however, a number of the findings when compared with those from the earlier study by O'Leary and Becker (1967) suggest some reasonable conclusions. The reader should first keep in mind that the formal token system was very similar to that used by O'Leary and Becker, including the shift to a two-day delay in back-up reinforcers after the first four days. The programs were carried out at similar times during the day, on similar children in adjustment classes. In the first study (O'Leary and Becker, 1967), there were more Negro children and the general level of deviant behavior was higher during baseline. The token system in the first study produced a dramatic shift from approximately 80 percent deviant behavior to under 10 percent, and it was effective for all children. Furthermore, although generalization measures were not taken, repeated reports by diverse observers indicated a dramatic change in the behavior of the children throughout the day. Some of the keys to the differences in findings include the following.

1. Tokens or points were given for meeting an absolute standard in the present study, rather than for improvement. A shaping procedure was not used by the teacher. Under these conditions, the two children who were considered by the teacher to be less troublesome to begin with (children 1 and 2) responded very well to the program. While these two children had an average percentage of deviant behavior during baseline approximating that of the other children, it was qualitatively different behavior. Their behaviors involved talking and turning around in their seats rather than fighting, making loud noises and wandering around the room. It was easy for the teacher to give them high ratings and for them to respond to the reinforcement system. The children who could not as easily meet the standards set by the teacher could have been punished for improved behavior by receiving low point scores. The high degree of variability over days and between children is

precisely what would be expected when an absolute standard is applied.

2. No attempt was made to have the teacher systematically apply differential social reinforcement in between the times when points were awarded or at other times during the day. This aspect of the earlier program was probably responsible for much of its effectiveness. Points which are awarded 30 or 40 minutes later are not enough to help a child learn more appropriate behaviors. With effective and continuous use of praise for good behaviors and ignoring of deviant behaviors, immediate consequences can be brought to bear on such behavior, especially when praise has been made important to the children through its pairing with tokens. The lack of generalization effects are most likely due to this difference in procedures. (We had hoped to clearly show this by introducing systematic social reinforcement in the next stage of the experiment.) Observations of the teacher throughout the day indicated that she would intermittently pay attention to deviant behaviors and would often ignore the children when they were behaving well. If paying attention is reinforcing and if ignoring amounts to an extinction condition, these teacher behaviors would be affecting the children in a way opposite to that desired.

3. The teacher in this study was not trained through a workshop in the systematic application of behavioral principles. Such training may be important in knowing how to shape behavior and how to effectively use differential social reinforcement.

4. Some initial difficulties were encountered in getting the fourth graders to respond to the program (children 2, 4, and 6, Figure 20-3). They typically received high ratings (appropriately given) by their art and music teachers, which made it less necessary for them to behave in the classroom to earn points. The point system was eventually changed so that good behavior in both periods was essential (in the move to 30 points for a lower prize and 35 for a higher one).

5. Another potential problem was that during baseline, the teacher considered the level of deviant behavior to be close to an acceptable level. She had a great capacity for tolerating disrup-

tions in the class as long as they did not interfere with her work with an individual child. Also, in making judgments about following the rules, she was much more lenient than our judgment would deem appropriate. Her frame of reference would likely foster the reinforcement of deviant behaviors, as defined in the present study, and leave the level of improvement at a low level.

We titled this paper, "How to Make a Token System Fail." In actuality, the system functioned as expected—as far as it went. The minimal token system employed was statistically effective and could not have been much more effective if differential social reinforcement and shaping must be a central part of a workable system. The real failure in this experiment was the failure to give the teacher sufficient support and information to keep her working with the researchers so that subsequent phases of the study could demonstrate more definitively the importance of additional procedures. The behavior of the morning observers was a particular source of irritation for the teacher. Although instructed to fade into the background, two of them did not. Chewing and cracking gum, talking and obviously watching the children were among their behaviors found irritating by the teacher. Her warnings were not responded to soon enough, although eventually one of the observers was fired. By then it was too late to save the study. There were other failures in the administration of the study which produced unnecessary irritations for the teacher, such as intruding on her evening and week-end time to discuss problems.

We explicitly point out these problems so that others may profit from our mistakes. Great care should be exercised in selecting and training observers, in providing guidelines for the supervisory staff and in preparing the teacher for what is coming. While the teacher emphasized the role of the observer's behavior in her decision to stop the study, the study was not stopped until we had withdrawn the token system for about four days. Problem behavior as well as the concerns of the teacher had increased. Although the teacher agreed to let us finish the second baseline period, better preparation of the teacher on our part could have saved the study.

IMPLICATIONS

A token system is usually designed to make more usual social reinforcers effective for children and lead to an elimination of the token system. These objectives involve the use of a complex set of procedures. The findings of this study, when contrasted with those from O'Leary and Becker (1967), should suggest to the reader who is interested in applying a token system some of the important procedures which may be missed or not thought important in looking at the literature on token systems. If the token system involves delays in giving tokens or points (to simplify the procedure for the teacher), it is probably very important to use differential social reinforcement at all times. Explicitly, this involves giving praise and privileges for improvement in behavior and ignoring (rather than criticizing or distracting) children showing deviant behaviors—unless someone is being hurt. In the latter case, withdrawal of all social attention and loss of the opportunity to earn tokens by isolating the child (time out) is the procedure of choice. It is also important to use tokens and praise to shape improved behavior so that all children can be affected by positive reinforcement. Catch the child being good. Focus on that aspect of behavior which is an improvement (e.g. in seat rather than out, even if not yet working) and reinforce it. Look for sequential steps toward improvement which can be successively reinforced (in seat, not turning and talking to neighbors, desk cleared of excess materials, paying attention, working, working diligently).

A token system is not a magical procedure to be applied in a mechanical way. It is simply one tool within a larger set of tools available to the teacher concerned with improving the behavior of children. The full set of equipment is needed to do the job right.

REFERENCES

Birnbrauer, J. S., Bijou, S. W., Wolf, M. M. and Kidder, J. D.: Programmed instruction in the classroom. In Ullman, P. L. and Krasner, L. (Eds.): *Case Studies in Behavior Modification.* New York, Holt, Rinehart and Winston, 1965a, pp. 358–363.

Birnbrauer, J. S. and Lawler, J.: Token reinforcement for learning. *Mental Retardation,* 2:275–279, 1964.

Birnbrauer, J. S., Wolf, M. M., Kidder, J. D. and Tague, C. E.: Classroom behavior of retarded pupils with token reinforcement. *Journal of Experimental Child Psychology, 2:*219–235, 1965b.

O'Leary, K. D. and Becker, W. C.: Behavior modification of an adjustment class: A token reinforcement program. *Exceptional Children, 33:*637–642, 1967.

21

Educational Engineering with Emotionally Disturbed Children

Frank M. Hewett

An engineered classroom design based on the behavior modification model has been developed and used in institutional and public schools. It attempts to provide a setting for implementation of a hierarchy of educational tasks, meaningful rewards for learning and an appropriate degree of teacher structure. The classroom, students and techniques are described.

As EDUCATIONAL PROGRAMS for emotionally disturbed children receive increased federal, state and local public school support and become more widespread, several models for establishing these programs are available to teachers. There is the psychotherapeutic model with a psychodynamic, interpersonal emphasis; the pathological or medical model, which focuses on brain pathology and treatment of measured or inferred organic causal factors; and the pedagogical model, concerned with intellectual development, remedial techniques and academic goals. Each model has influenced school programs for emotionally disturbed children and, depending on the intuitive, diagnostic and curriculum skill of the teacher, has been useful to some degree. The need still exists, however, for a more generally applicable model to handle the ever-increasing number of inattentive, failure-prone and resistant children who are being separated from their more readily educable peers for special education. Such a model must be understandable to the teacher, translatable to the classroom and hold promise for more effectively educating the emotionally disturbed child.

NOTE: From *Exceptional Children*, 33:459–467, 1967. Copyright 1967 by the Council for Exceptional Children. Reprinted with permission of author and publisher.

Recently, a model called behavior modification has demonstrated usefulness with exceptional children. Rather than view the emotionally disturbed child as a victim of psychic conflicts, cerebral dysfunction or merely academic deficits, this approach concentrates on bringing the overt behavior of the child into line with standards required for learning. Such standards may include development of an adequate attention span; orderly response in the classroom; the ability to follow directions; tolerance for limits of time, space and activity; accurate exploration of the environment; and appreciation for social approval and avoidance of disapproval. Promoting successful development of these standards as well as self care and intellectual skills through assignment of carefully graded tasks in a learning environment which provides both rewards and structure for the child in accord with principles of empirical learning theory (Skinner, 1963) are the basic goals of the behavior modification model.

According to Ullman and Krasner (1965), the behavior modifier has three main concerns: (a) defining maladaptive behavior, (b) determining the environmental events which support this behavior and (c) manipulating the environment in order to alter maladaptive behavior. In the case of the emotionally disturbed child, his maladaptive behavior is readily distinguished in the classroom by poor concentration, hyperactivity, acting out, defiance, avoidance, withdrawal and other manifestations that make him a poor candidate for learning. Environmental events which maintain these behaviors might include positive reinforcement and recognition for misbehavior; association of school, teacher and learning with failure and negative reinforcement; and assignment of learning tasks inappropriate to the child. The third concern, what can be done to change school to remedy both the emotionally disturbed child's maladaptive behavior and its environmental supports, is the subject of this paper.

THE ENGINEERED CLASSROOM

In the engineered classroom, the teacher is assigned the role of behavioral engineer; she attempts to define appropriate task assignments for students, provide meaningful rewards for learning and maintain well-defined limits in order to reduce and hopefully eliminate the occurrence of maladaptive behavior. The teacher, then, engineers an environment in which the probability of student success is maximized and maladaptive behavior is replaced by adaptive behavior. The role of behavior engineer has been previously described by Ayllon and Michael (1959), with reference to application of behavior modification theory by nursing personnel working with psychotic patients. The engineered classroom concept has been explored by Haring and Phillips (1962), Whelan and Haring (1966) and Quay (1966) with emotionally disturbed children; and by Birnbrauer *et al.* (1965) at the Rainier School in Washington. I visited the latter research project, and aspects of the engineered design described here stem from these observations. Other authors, such as Staats *et al.* (1964), Zimmerman and Zimmerman (1962) and Valett (1966), have applied behavior modification principles to academic teaching.

One of the problems inherent in introducing theoretical concepts and research findings into the classroom is the inevitable involvement of a specialized and often alien vocabulary, as well as a frame of reference for implementation not usual to the educational background of the teacher. This dilemma arises in the psychotherapeutic and pathological models mentioned earlier, where libido, ego strength and psychosexual development; or dyslexia, perceptual motor dysfunction and strephosymbolia may be impressive but not always useful terms in the classroom. Successful application of behavior modification principles also requires understanding of such concepts as reinforcement, contingencies and scheduling; while simple and clear-cut in intent, they are not always easily grasped or accepted by teachers.

The engineered classroom design currently under investigation was introduced in the public school (Hewett, 1966), by a teacher who had no previous exposure to behavior modification theory. It attempts a translation of this theory—not rigidly, but pragmatically—to the school setting. Behavior modification principles are organized in terms of a learning triangle, the sides of which represent the three essential ingredients for all effective teaching: selection of a suitable educational task for the child, provision of a meaningful reward following accomplishment of that task and maintenance of a degree of structure under the control of the teacher. Figure 21-1 illustrates the relationship of certain behavior modification principles to these three factors.

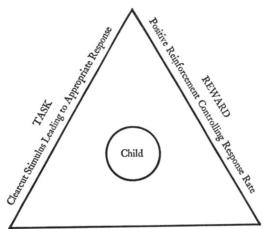

Withholding of Positive Reinforcement or Administration of
Negative Reinforcement Following Inappropriate Responses

Scheduling of Positive Reinforcement

Setting of Contingency for Receipt of Reinforcement

STRUCTURE

Figure 21-1. The learning triangle.

The engineered classroom design creates an environment for implementation of the learning triangle. Suitable educational tasks are selected from a hierarchy, presented in Figure 21-2, which describes seven task levels. The first five are readiness

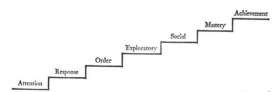

Figure 21-2. A hierarchy of educational tasks.

levels, largely mastered by normal children before they enter school. The final two are concerned with intellectual skill development which constitutes a primary educational goal with all children.

Emotionally disturbed children are usually not ready to be in school because they are unable to pay attention, follow directions, explore the environment or get along with others. For this reason, suitable educational tasks for these children must often be selected from the five readiness levels. The hierarchy encompasses many fundamental concepts of the psychotherapeutic, pathological and pedagogical models discussed earlier. However, it attempts to define these concepts in terms of educational operations rather than by psychoanalytic, neurological or narrow academic nomenclature. In this regard, the present hierarchy is a revision of one earlier described (Hewett, 1964). Table 21-1 summarizes the seven task levels of the hierarchy, children's problems relating to each, the type of learner rewards available and the degree of structure inherent at each level.

An assessment procedure enables the teacher to rate the child in terms of specific deficits on the hierarchy shortly after he enters the engineered classroom. This assessment becomes the basis for establishing an educational program for him and provides the teacher with an understanding of his basic learning deficits. This procedure is ongoing and is repeated three times each semester.

In helping an emotionally disturbed child get ready for intellectual training, the teacher can profitably use the behavior modification principle of shaping rather than holding out for the ultimate goal (e.g. student functioning appropriately on the mastery and achievement levels), successive approximations of that goal (e.g. functioning at attention, response, order, exploratory and social levels) are recognized achievements. The engineered classroom design attempts to provide an environment and program for shaping appropriate learning behavior.

CLASSROOM DESCRIPTION

The engineered classroom should be a large, well-lighted room (ideally 1200 to 1500 sq. ft.) with a double desk (2 x 4 ft.) for each of nine pupils. The class is under the supervision of a regular teacher and a teacher aide. The aide need not be certified or specially trained. High school graduates and PTA volunteers have been effective.

TABLE 21-1
DESCRIPTION OF THE HIERARCHY OF EDUCATIONAL TASKS

Hierarchy Level	Attention	Response	Order	Exploratory	Social	Mastery	Achievement
Child's problem	Inattention due to withdrawal or resistance.	Lack of involvement and unwillingness to respond in learning.	Inability to follow directions.	Incomplete or inaccurate knowledge of environment.	Failure to value social approval or disapproval.	Deficits in basic adaptive and school skills not in keeping with IQ.	Lack of self motivation for learning.
Educational task	Get child to pay attention to teacher and task.	Get child to respond to tasks he likes and which offer promise of success.	Get child to complete tasks with specific starting points and steps leading to a conclusion.	Increase child's efficiency as an explorer and get him involved in multisensory exploration of his environment.	Get child to work for teacher and peer group approval and to avoid their disapproval.	Remediation of basic skill deficiencies.	Development of interest in acquiring knowledge.
Learner reward	Provided by tangible rewards (e.g. food, money, tokens).	Provided by gaining social attention.	Provided through task completion.	Provided by sensory stimulation.	Provided by social approval.	Provided through task accuracy.	Provided through intellectual task success.
Teacher structure	Minimal.	Still limited.	Emphasized.	Emphasized.	Based on standards of social appropriateness.	Based on curriculum assignments.	Minimal.

The physical environment can be described as having three major centers paralleling levels on the hierarchy of educational tasks. The mastery-achievement center consists of the student desk area where academic assignments are undertaken. Adjacent to and part of this center are two study booths or offices where academic work may be done without visual distraction. These are carpeted and outfitted with desks and upholstered chairs. An exploratory-social center with three distinct areas is set up near the windows and sink facilities. Equipment for simple science experiments is available in one area, with arts and crafts activities in another. Social skills are fostered in the communication area of the exploratory center where group listening activities and games are provided. The attention-response-order center is in an opposite corner of the classroom and consists of two double desks and a storage cabinet where puzzles, exercises and materials for use in emphasizing paying attention, responding and routine are kept. Thus each level on the hierarchy has a designated area in the room where specific types of tasks may be undertaken by the child.

Mounted by the door is a work record card holder displaying individual work record cards for each student. The room has limited bulletin board displays and looks much like any elementary classroom. The hypothesis that all emotionally disturbed children need a drab, sterile, nonstimulating school environment is rejected in this design.

The class operates five main periods in the minimum 240-minute day required by California for programs for the educationally handicapped. Period I is a 10-minute order period (attention, response, and order levels); Period II consists of reading and written language (mastery level), and lasts 60 minutes; Period III is devoted to arithmetic (mastery level) and is 60 minutes in length; Period IV is a 20-minute physical education session; and Period V is for science, art and communication (exploratory and social levels) and lasts 60 minutes. In addition, a recess, nutrition break and evaluation period round out the class day.

A floorplan of the engineered classroom is illustrated in Figure 21-3.

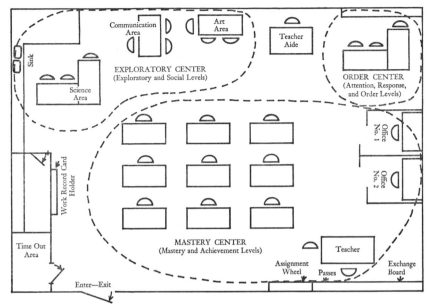

Figure 21-3. Floorplan of an engineered classroom.

STUDENTS

Two types of students have been enrolled in experimental engineered classrooms to date: public school children with essentially normal intelligence from Santa Monica and Tulare in California and the Palolo School district in Oahu, Hawaii, identified as educationally handicapped (underachieving due to emotional, neurological or learning disability factors) and emotionally disturbed children hospitalized on the Children's Service of the UCLA Neuropsychiatric Institute and enrolled in the Neuropsychiatric Institute School. The public school population consisted mostly of boys with conduct disturbances or neurotic traits including long-standing school phobias, psychosomatic and borderline psychotic problems, as well as minimal neurological impairment. The hospitalized group represented more serious emotional problems and included grossly psychotic and more markedly neurologically impaired individuals. All students were in the age group from 8 to 12.

ENGINEERED CLASSROOM OPERATIONS

As can be seen from Table 21-1, the range of rewards possible to offer the child in school includes tangible rewards, social attention, task completion, sensory stimulation, social approval and task accuracy and success. Normal children arrive in the classroom ready to learn in anticipation of such rewards as approval and accuracy, but emotionally disturbed children often are not motivated in the same manner. Levin and Simmons (1962) found that emotionally disturbed boys were more effectively motivated by tangible rewards of food than by social praise.

Since a meaningful reward for learning is essential in a successful teaching situation and emotionally disturbed children differ so greatly with respect to what is rewarding for them, the engineered classroom operates on the most basic reward level in an effort to insure gratification in school for even the most resistant learner.

As each student enters in the morning, he picks up his individual work record card which is ruled into 200 squares. As he moves through the day, the teacher and aide recognize his work accomplishments and efficiency to function as a student by checking off squares on the work record card. The student carries his card with him wherever he goes in the room. Checkmarks are given on a fixed-interval, fixed-ratio basis every 15 minutes. A time rather than a task contingency is used because it standardizes the total number of possible checkmarks in a single day, reduces competition and is useful in alerting the student to the work efficiency orientation of the classroom. Intermittent schedules for rewarding children may be more powerful, but in the author's experience, they have not proven as manageable and practical for the teacher.

Checkmarks are given in very specific ways. Normally, a maximum of 10 is given for any 15-minute period. Two checkmarks are given for starting the assignment (attention level), 3 for following through (response level), and a possible 5 bonus given for being a student (order, exploratory, social or mastery levels, depending on child's learning deficits). In addition, extra checkmarks might be given a particular child when necessary for motivation. In the main, however, the checkmarks are awarded conservatively by the teacher and attention is called to the specific reasons for the checkmarks being given or withheld. Since social reinforcement may actually be aversive for some emotionally disturbed children, the checkmark system functions as a neutral, nonconflictual meeting ground for teacher and student. The teacher attempts to convey the notion that checkmarks are objective measures of accomplishment and literally part of a reality system in the classroom over which she has little control. In this regard, the teacher functions as a shop foreman who pays workers what they actually earn according to standards set by the plant system. The teacher's message to the child is in essence: "That's just the way it is. I work here too." Students save completed work record cards and exchange them on a weekly basis for candy, small toys and trinkets. An exchange board in the room displays the tangible rewards available for 1, 2 or 3 cards filled with checkmarks.

While the checkmark system remains constant as the primary source of reward in the classroom, every effort is made to provide rewards at the higher levels of the hierarchy. The attention-response-order center offers activities such as tachistoscopic training, decoding exercises with symbol and flag code messages, puzzle making, simple construction kits, design copying with beads and blocks, and many other tasks useful in getting the child to pay attention, respond and follow directions.

The concept of order is also emphasized through the use of a system of passes to facilitate assignments to the offices and other centers in the room. When the child is assigned to a center, he picks up at the teacher's desk a pass which designates the area to which he will move. This pass is hung on the wall by the center during the period of time the child is away from his desk.

The exploratory-social center provides opportunities for multisensory exploration of the environment and communication. Materials for science experiments and demonstrations in electricity, magnetism, animal care and basic chemistry are available in one section. A listening post, Morse code activities, simple games for two or three children, and a tape recorder are in another section for communication and social tasks. Arts and crafts materials are available in another section. One of the main periods of the class day takes place at this center. Usually the teacher demonstrates several different science experiments each week. These experiments are pictorially illustrated on large cards with simple directions and filed at the center where they may be replicated by students assigned to the center at other times during the class day. Each day, students participate in art and communication tasks as part of the exploratory period.

The mastery and achievement center seeks to engage each child in a certain amount of academic work each day because in a majority of cases, emotionally disturbed children have failed to keep pace in acquiring reading, written language and arithmetic skills. A reading period is held three times weekly and consists of three different activities: individual oral reading with the teacher, independent activity reading for comprehension and development, and word study for review of reading and spelling words. Story writing takes the place of the reading period twice a week. Arithmetic assignments are individually prepared and based on diagnostic achievement test results. Assignment of mastery tasks coincides with the time contingency used as a basis for the checkmark system. Different tasks are assigned individual students every 15 minutes.

INTERVENTION

In accordance with principles of behavior modification, the teacher in the engineered classroom attempts to alter the environment to change maladaptive behavior patterns of students and to foster the development of more adaptive patterns through manipulation of assigned tasks and provision of success and rewards. The basic goal is to keep every child functioning as a student. So long as the child respects the working rights of others and displays a reasonable tolerance for limits of time, space and activity, he earns a full quota of checkmarks regardless what type of task he is assigned in the room. In order to help individual children earn as many checkmarks as possible, a series of interventions must often be used to alter the learning environment, including the nature of the assigned task, type of reward and degree of structure. These interventions are divided into two categories, student and nonstudent, and involve descending the hierachy of educational tasks until a level is found that enables the child to function successfully or provides for his exclusion from class.

If at any time during the class day the student begins to display signs of maladaptive learning behavior (e.g. inattention, day dreaming, boredom, disruption), his assignments are quickly changed. Table 21-2 summarizes the interventions which may

TABLE 21-2

HIERARCHY OF INTERVENTIONS TO MAINTAIN
STUDENT ROLE

Level	*Student Interventions*
1. Achievement	Assign student to study booth to pursue mastery work.
2. Mastery	Modify mastery assignment and have student continue at desk or in study booth.
3. Social	Verbally restructure expectation of student role (e.g. respect working rights of others, accept limits of time, space, activity).
4. Exploratory	Remove mastery assignment and reassign to exploratory center for specific science, art, or communication activity.
5. Order	Reassign to order center for specific direction following tasks (e.g. puzzle, exercise, game, work sheet).
6. Response	Remove child from classroom and assign him to a task he likes to do and can do successfully outside (e.g. running around playground, punching punching bag, turning specific number of somersaults on lawn).
7. Attention	Remove child from classroom, put on a one to one tutoring relationship with teacher aide, and increase number of check marks given to obtain cooperation, attention, and student behavior.
Nonstudent Interventions	
8. Time out	Take away work record card and explain to child he cannot earn check marks for a specific number of minutes which he must spend in isolation (never use more than three times in one day).
9. Exclusion	If child requires more than three time-outs in one day or fails to control himself during time out, or if he is verbally or physically abusive to teacher, immediately suspend him from class for rest of day, and if possible, send home.

be used in an attempt to foster adaptive student functioning. The teacher may select any intervention seen as appropriate or may try the student at each intervention level until his behavior improves. As long as the child is able to stabilize himself during any of the student interventions, he continues to earn checkmarks on a par with those students successfully pursuing mastery level assignments. He is in no way penalized for the shift in assignment. There appears to be little need to worry about other children reacting to what might be seen as inequality. They have seemed content to accept the teacher's explanation that "Johnny needs a different kind of assignment to help him learn right now."

When one-to-one tutoring on the attention level cannot be provided or is ineffective, the child loses his opportunity to earn checkmarks, is considered a nonstudent and is sent out of the room for a short period of isolation. Use of such isolation as an intervention has been described by Whelan and Haring (1966). If the child can successfully tolerate this period (usually 5, 10 or 15 minutes), his card is immediately returned and he may be reassigned at any level, depending on the teacher's assessment of his capacities for adaptive behavior at the moment. No lecturing or demand that he "promise to be a good boy" is given.

With respect to interventions, a question may arise regarding whether or not removing a child from a more demanding task and assigning him a less-demanding task in the classroom actually constitutes rewarding inappropriate behavior. Will not some children misbehave in order to be reassigned to a more inviting exploratory or order activity? In the author's experience with the engineered classroom this has occurred only rarely. When it does, the child is not permitted the choice of an alternate activity but is directly placed in an isolation intervention. In most cases, teachers anticipate such problems by limiting the amount of mastery work given the child, assigning him to an alternate center before his behavior becomes maladaptive.

With most children who become restless and resistant the teacher approaches the child and says, "You seem to be having trouble with this assignment. I want you to earn all of your checkmarks this period so go get a pass for the exploratory (or order) center and I'll give you a different assignment there." This is an expression of the basic philosophy of the engineered classroom which in essence tells the child: "We want you to succeed at all costs. If you will meet us half way and function reasonably well as a student we will give you tasks you can do, need to do and will enjoy doing, and we will reward you generously for your efforts."

DISCUSSION AND IMPLICATIONS

The engineered classroom design has been developed and observed in four public school systems and a hospital setting for the past two years. It has constantly been reassessed and changed and still is undergoing alteration in an effort to arrive at a practical and useful model for educating emotionally disturbed children. Preliminary observations suggest that changes in work efficiency and adaptive behavior occcur quickly. One of the aspects that most impresses observers is the purposeful, controlled and productive atmosphere in the classrooms. Despite the requirements for a teacher aide, a well-organized classroom and use of tangible rewards, it appears to be a feasible design for use in a public school.

Some educators are reluctant to use the behavior modification model because it has emerged from the experimental animal laboratory and some feel that tangible rewards for learning represent an unwholesome compromise with basic educational values. However, if one objectively and realistically views the emotionally disturbed child as a unique learner, not initially responsive to a conventional learning environment and often not rewarded by traditional social and intellectual rewards, then reducing one's goals so that he may be included in, not excluded from, school is just good common sense. To fail to teach a child because he lacks capacity to learn is one thing, but to fail because of a lack of flexibility and a realistic assessment of a child's needs is quite another.

The engineered class design is not viewed as an end in itself. Observations suggest that the value of checkmarks and tangible exchange items soon gives way to the satisfaction of succeeding in school and receiving recognition as a student from peers, teachers and parents. Transition programs have been worked out where children started in the engineered classroom have gradually been reintroduced into regular classes. While this stage is not wholly developed, it appears to be a natural evolutionary development in the program.

Some criticism of this approach has discounted improvements

seen in the adaptive functioning of the children as merely the result of the Hawthorne effect (Roethlisberger and Dixon, 1939); that is, anything novel or different in the environment produces an initial change in behavior. Even though some children have continued to improve for a full year in the engineered classroom, this possibility still exists. The answer to such a criticism is simply, "So what?" If one can create a unique learning environment that produces more adaptive learning behavior in emotionally disturbed children, perhaps we should capitalize on the Hawthorne phenomenon in special education and continuously introduce more stimulating and novel approaches with all exceptional children.

One major problem which has arisen from presenting the engineered classroom design to teachers in the field bears mention. Some of them are so desperate for ideas and directions to increase their effectiveness with emotionally disturbed children that they react to superficial aspects of the design and somewhat randomly apply them in the classroom. It is not uncommon to hear of a teacher rushing out, buying a large stock of M & M candies which are often used as exchange items, beginning to pass them out rather haphazardly in the classroom and then waiting for a miracle to occur. Needless to say, such a teacher will have a long wait. Checkmarks and candy are only a small part of the entire design. There is nothing new in the use of gold stars and extrinsic rewards in education, but there is a great deal that is unique in the systematic use of these to foster development of more adaptive learning behavior on the part of resistant and often inaccessible learners.

Behavior modification theory is a systematic theory, not a faddist theory based on gimmicks. To be useful, it must be understood and adhered to systematically, not sporadically. We are still trying to increase our understanding of its effectiveness in the engineered classroom, anticipating considerably more evaluation, exploration and experimentation before we can be certain of its applicability.

REFERENCES

Ayllon, T., and Michael, J.: The psychiatric nurse as a behavioral engineer. *Journal of Experimental Analysis of Behavior, 2:*323–334, 1959.

Birnbrauer, J., Bijou, S., Wolf, M. and Kidder, J.: Programmed instruction in the classroom. In Ullmann, L. and Krasner, L. (Eds.): *Case Studies in Behavior Modification.* New York, Holt, Rinehart and Winston, 1965.

Haring, N. and Phillips, E.: *Educating Emotionally Disturbed Children.* New York, McGraw-Hill, 1962.

Hewett, F.: A hierarchy of educational tasks for children with learning disorders. *Exceptional Children, 31:*207–214, 1964.

Hewett, F.: The Tulare experimental class for educationally handicapped children. *California Education, 3:*6–8, 1966.

Levin, G. and Simmons, J.: Response to food and praise by emotionally disturbed boys. *Psychological Reports, 11:*539–546, 1962.

Quay, H.: Remediation of the conduct problem in the special class setting. *Exceptional Children, 32:*509–515, 1966.

Roethlisberger, F. and Dixon, W.: *Management of the Worker.* Cambridge, Harvard University Press, 1939.

Skinner, B.: Operant behavior. *American Psychologist, 18:*503–515, 1963.

Staats, A., Minke, K., Finley, J., Wolf, M. and Brooks, L.: A reinforcer system and experimental procedures for the laboratory study of reading acquisition. *Child Development, 35:*209–231, 1964.

Ullmann, L. and Krasner, L.: *Case Studies in Behavior Modification.* New York, Holt, Rinehart and Winston, 1965.

Valett, R.: A social reinforcement technique for the classroom management of behavior disorders. *Exceptional Children, 33:*185–189, 1966.

Whelan, R. and Haring, N.: Modification and maintenance of behavior through systematic application of consequences. *Exceptional Children, 32:*281–289, 1966.

Zimmerman, E. and Zimmerman, J.: The alteration of behavior in a special classroom situation. *Journal of Experimental Analysis of Behavior, 5:*59–60, 1962.

BRAIN-INJURED AND RETARDED CHILDREN

22

Differential Effects of Token Reinforcement on Instruction-Following Behavior in Retarded Students Instructed as a Group

ELAINE H. ZIMMERMAN, J. ZIMMERMAN and C. D. RUSSELL

This study was addressed to the problem of applying behavior modification techniques on a group basis to a class of retarded students with "attentional deficits." Seven boys, age 8 to 15, characterized as showing severe "attentional" problems or disruptive behavior in their respective classrooms, participated daily for 30-minute sessions in a special class over a 1.5-month period. In each session, verbal instructions were given to the class as a whole. In control sessions, each appropriate instruction-following response by a child produced praise for that child. In experimental sessions, appropriate responses also produced tokens exchangeable for tangible reinforcers after the session. Token reinforcement differentially maintained instruction-following behavior in four children, while one responded appropriately to most instructions and a second improved continuously during the study. While the data suggest that the present approach can be successfully applied to the alteration of instruction-following behavior in retarded children, its major contribution may be that of providing objective quantitative information about such behavior.

NOTE: The authors wish to thank Mr. David Shearer, Principal, and the faculty of Noble School for their cooperation and interest. Special thanks go to Mrs. Marcia Yaver, the teacher next door, who volunteered her time and assistance whenever she was able.

Many behavior modification studies have been conducted in the classroom setting (*i.e.* Hall *et al.*, 1968; Harris *et al.*, 1964; Zimmerman and Zimmerman, 1962). Most such studies have focused upon the objective assessment of treatments applied to individual class members. In contrast, several classroom studies have involved (a) the concurrent, systematic treatment of each student participating in the class and (b) the application of a set of common treatments to all members of the class (*i.e.* Birnbrauer *et al.*, 1965; Burchard, 1965). These and similar studies have involved individually groomed classroom assignments but have placed greater emphasis upon treating the class as a whole in that every member of the class is exposed to similar sets of differential token-reinforcement contingencies.

A related set of classroom procedures was applied recently by Bushell *et al.*, (1968). Their procedures placed less emphasis upon the idiosyncratic treatment of individual class members and more emphasis upon the use of a set of common treatments. Classroom assignments were not explicitly groomed to specific individuals. Under conditions in which class members engaged in several different activities, all were exposed to one generally defined set of differential token-reinforcement contingencies.

To our knowledge, no published study has employed a procedure that exclusively involved the concurrent exposure of all class members to a single, specific set of differential-reinforcement contingencies. Although Burchard (1965, Exp. 1) applied such a set of contingencies to the sitting-at-desk behavior of each member of his class, this common treatment was employed in the context of the concurrent application of separate, individually groomed reinforcement contingencies.

The obvious need to develop techniques to facilitate the efficient instruction of an entire group of sudents under conditions in which behavior in each member can be monitored and examined as a function of common instructional procedures and common treatments gave impetus to the present study. The general purpose of this study was that of experimentally examining a classroom procedure designed for use with a group of retarded students characterized by their teachers as having "severe attentional deficits" and/or frequently displaying behaviors disruptive to ongoing classroom activities. The specific purpose was to examine behavior in each class member under conditions in which the class was addressed as a whole and as a function of the application of two sets of common response-contingent consequences.

Before implementing and conducting the study, the experimenters informally observed the tentatively selected subjects in their classroom settings and interacted with their teachers in informal conferences. The latter interactions suggested that the teachers tended to attribute disruptive behavior and other undesirable classroom performances to the students' "attentional deficits." The only generalization which could be made after informally observing the students' classroom performances was that each frequently failed to follow instructions. As a consequence, we designed a list of simple classroom instructions and used instruction-following behavior as the dependent variable. In line with the specific purposes of this investigation, instructions were presented to the group at large and as a whole, and appropriate behavior was examined as a function of response-contingent praise and response-contingent token reinforcement.

METHOD

Subjects and Setting

Seven retarded boys with "attentional problems," selected by teacher recommendation from three classes at the Noble School in Indianapolis, served as the members of the experimental class. A brief clinical description of each is provided in Table 22-1.

TABLE 22-1
AGE, IQ AND DIAGNOSIS OF EACH SUBJECT

Subject	Age (Years)	IQ	Diagnosis
S_1	8	46	Moderately retarded.
S_2	11	40	Moderately retarded, brain-damaged.
S_3	9	70	Mildly retarded, educable but deaf.
S_4	10	41	Brain-damaged, autistic, hyperactive.
S_5	11.5	48	Moderately retarded.
S_6	9.5	25 or below	Severely retarded, atoxic spinal deformity.
S_7	15	30	Cerebral dysgenesis.

The study was conducted in a 10 × 15 ft room that contained a teacher's desk and chair, a round table around which were placed seven student chairs, and the materials and props that were utilized in conjunction with the instruction list and token-reinforcement system. The seven students participated as a class in daily 30-minute sessions over a period of seven weeks. A dimly lighted, empty classroom immediately adjacent to the experimental room was used for time-out purposes, and occasionally served as an observation room for interested faculty. This observation was facilitated by a one-way vision mirror mounted in the door between the two rooms.

The Instruction List

Five initial sessions were devoted to observing the students in the experimental room and to constructing an instruction list that could be used to measure objectively the instruction-following behavior. The list was constructed on the basis of several considerations and criteria. First, items on the list were to call for many behaviors already within the repertoires of the subjects. Prior informal observations of the subjects in their classroom settings and interactions with their teachers permitted the listing of behaviors that were either observed to be or alleged to be in the subjects' repertoire. Second, and this was considered of paramount importance, items were to call for behaviors that could be easily and objectively monitored; observers would not be called upon to make judgments based on ambiguously defined behaviors. Finally, it was considered important to construct a list that would call for a broad spectrum of observable behaviors, since a functional repertoire generally accepted as being prerequisite for any student if he is to benefit from a classroom experience would include many different kinds of instruction-following responses. Classes of behavior called for by the instruction list included: motor performance, imitation, recognition, verbalization and other social behavior.

An initial list was constructed and tested. This was revised several times in order to improve the continuity and logical sequencing of the items and to replace ambiguous items with items that called for more readily and reliably monitored behaviors. In addition, to further emphasize the importance of "paying attention" on the part of the students, while at the same time maintaining the systematic and highly structured nature of the classroom procedures to be employed, the order of items on the final list was fixed, but equivalent choices of instructions were installed within more than half of the items. For example, item 21 always followed item 20, but the instruction: "Point to the picture of the *dog*," could be substituted for by "Point to the picture of the *rabbit* (*lion*)." In the subsequent formal application of the instruction list, choices within such items were varied randomly from session to session.

TABLE 22-2

THE FINAL INSTRUCTION LIST *

1. Sit down at the table and raise your hand. Reinforce and check only if seated for all "sitting" items.
2. Sit down at the table and do what I do. (clap hands   tap head   salute)
3. Get on the line. (point at the line on floor.)
4. Sit down at the table and point at your (nose   mouth   eyes   ears).
5. Stand behind desk. Come to me.
6. Take out some clean sheets of paper from desk and place on desk. Take one piece of paper. Paper is now always available.
7. Take out crayons. Take one crayon. Spare crayons now always available.
8. Sit down at the table and draw what I draw. Draw (A, B, C, D, E).
9. Sit down at the table and draw what I draw. Draw a (diamond, square, triangle).
10. Sit down at the table and give your paper to another child.
11. Sit down at the table and draw a (circle, face, round clock).
12. Stand behind desk. Come up and show your paper to me.
13. Take out and hold scissors. Take one scissors. Put them on desk.
14. Sit down at the table and cut out the (circle, face, round clock) that you drew. Must approximate circle.
15. Stand behind desk. Bring me what you cut out. Acceptable to bring anything he just cut out, providing it approximates circle.
16. There is a picture of a triangle on the wall. Point to the picture of the triangle.
17. Stand against one of the walls. Back to wall.
18. There are pieces of colored paper on the walls. Point to the (green   blue   pink) paper.
19. Sit down at the table and do what I do. (Tap table with one hand. Tap table with two hands. Place both hands in the middle of the table.)

20. Sit down at the table and touch another child's (hand, chest, arm).
21. There are animal pictures on the walls. Point to the picture of the (dog, lion, rabbit).
22. Sit down at the table and hold up (1, 2, 3, 4, 5) fingers.
23. There are pictures of numbers on the walls. Point to the number (1, 2, 3, 4).
24. Sit down at the table and do what I do. Hold up (1, 2, 3, 4, 5) fingers.
25. Sit behind desk. Pick up one scissors and bring it to me.

Individual Items

26. Sit down at the table. Individually to each child who is seated Get up and point to your name.
27. Sit down at the table. Individually to each child who is seated Say what I say (Good morning teacher. How are you? I am fine).
28. Sit down at the table. Individually to each child who is seated Tell me your name.
29. Sit down at the table. Individually to each child who is seated Count to (2, 3, 4, 5).
30. Sit down at the table. Individually to each child who is seated Say what I say (A, B, C, D; 1, 2, 3, 4; red, white and blue).

---

* Items are listed in the order that they were presented on the instruction list sheets. Underlined words were read to the class at large. Words not underlined served merely as information to the teacher. Alternatives within items appear in parentheses.

The final version of the 30-item instruction list is presented in Table 22-2. The first 25 items were group items presented to the class as a whole. The five final items were directed to specific individuals. Their inclusion permitted examination of behaviors that could not be reliably monitored in individuals under conditions in which two or more children responded concurrently.

Specific Experimental Procedures

The subjects, as a group, were exposed to a successive series of control and experimental conditions designed to assess the effects of token reinforcement delivered contingent upon the behavior of following instructions. In each of 11 control and 8 experimental (token-reinforcement) sessions, the following standard operating procedures were employed.

Each of three adults followed a copy of the 30-item instruction list. One adult served as instructor and the other two acted as independent observers. The instructor read items from the instruction list one at a time, and praised any subject who responded appropriately. The praise was simply the statement: "Very good, (name of subject who responded correctly)." Concurrently, and independently, each observer recorded correct responses. The roles of instructor and observers were alternated across sessions.

The first 25 items were exclusively directed to the group at large. Each was repeated once before the next item was read in order to provide two opportunities for appropriate responding. The final five items were each first directed to the group at large and then individually to each eligible (see below) child. As in the case of the other items, in order to provide two opportunities for appropriate responding, each individually directed item was repeated once to the same individual before the next individual was instructed.

The pacing of the instructions and repetitions was based upon the behavior of the subjects, rather than upon an arbitrarily prearranged set of temporal criteria. A subject's behavior-based pacing procedure was chosen because we wished to employ an instructional procedure that could not only be systematically employed and objectively defined but which would also be practical in the sense that it could be employed by a teacher working alone. While a time-based pacing procedure could probably be devised to meet all these criteria, the procedure employed (described immediately below) would probably be more readily negotiable by a teacher without props or outside aid.

In the case of each of the 25 group items, the instructor presented an instruction, monitored the group and praised any child immediately after he correctly followed an instruction, provided that the child was eligible for such praise. Eligibility was determined on the basis of a set of rules which involved, among other things, the differential pacing of given instructions. More specifically, in the case of 23 of the 25 items, praise was given to each child who responded to the instruction immediately after it was presented. If a child who did not immediately respond correctly did so while or immediately after another child was being praised, he too was praised. No child was praised twice for responding to the same item. As soon as the instructor failed to observe a single eligible child responding correctly, he immediately repeated the instruction. Praise was given to any remaining eligible child who immediately followed the repeated instruction. As soon as the instructor failed to observe any eligible child responding correctly, he proceeded to read the next instruction.

In contrast with most of the instructions, in the case of two of the alternative choices of item 11, and in the case of item 14, the instruction could not readily and/or immediately be negotiated by a subject with a single movement or set of movements. Thus, after items 11 or 14 were presented, the instructor paused as long as at least one child was in the process of correctly following the instruction. As soon as a correct instruction-following sequence was completed by a given subject, the latter was praised. This procedure obtained until no eligible child was observed to be in the process of correctly following the instruction. At that time, the item was repeated. The rule for going on to the next instruction was the same as the rule for repeating the item.

In the case of each of the five individually directed items, the instructor first presented the item to the group at large and then to a specific eligible individual. If the individual did not immediately respond correctly, the item was repeated to that same individual. If the individual did not immediately respond correctly to the repetition, the item was then presented to a different individual. If and when the item was correctly responded to by the individual to whom it was directed, the latter was immediately praised and the item was then immediately presented to the next individual. This procedure continued until all eligible children were given the opportunity to respond, and then the next numbered item was presented with the entire process repeated.

For each of the first 25 items, each observer independently monitored all members of the class, while for each of the final five items each observer focused upon the specific individual to whom an instruction was directed. Each observer placed a check in the appropriate space on the instruction list when he observed a subject responding appropriately to a given instruction. A subject was checked for a correct response even if the instructor failed to praise the child. Similarly, a subject was not checked for a correct response if it was not observed, even if the instructor praised the child. Finally, a child could be checked for a maximum of only one correct response per item, even if he responded correctly to it on each repetition.

Behaviors incompatible with following instructions (for example, running around the room or shouting) were generally ignored. Exceptions to ignoring inappropriate behavior took place when one subject aggressed physically against another or if a subject tampered with exchange items present in a compartmentalized box during token-training and token-reinforcement sessions. When the latter behaviors occurred, they produced a time-out for the offending subject. He was placed alone in a dimly lighted adjacent room by the instructor for a period of 10 to 20 seconds (the instructor counted silently to 15). No time-out termination delay contingency was applied because offenders neither kicked nor screamed when placed in the time-out room.

All other procedures employed were idiosyncratic to particular control and experimental conditions and will be specified under the description of those specific conditions.

Table 22-3 lists the order of presentation of the control and experimental conditions, together with the associated consequences of attending to instructions. The associated number of successive daily sessions is also given.

Precontrol (Pre-C₁) Condition

This was the first condition in which the standard operating procedures described above were employed. Subjects were exposed to each of two sessions in which a 30-item instruction list was used. A subject was praised by the instructor for each appropriate response, regardless of his physical place in the room.

Initial Control (C₁) Condition

In this condition, subjects were exposed to three sessions conducted exactly like the Pre-C₁ sessions with one exception. At this point and thereafter, the final version of the instruction list was used. In this list the words "Sit down at the table and . . ." were

TABLE 22-3

ORDER AND NATURE OF THE CONDITIONS TO WHICH
THE GROUP WAS EXPOSED

Condition	Consequence of Following an Instruction	Number of Sessions Exposed
Precontrol (Pre-C₁)	Verbal praise only. Instructor says, "Very good, *(name)*."	2
Initial control (C₁)	Same as Pre-C₁.	3
Token training	See text.	4
Second control (C₂)	Same as Pre-C₁.	3
Initial token (T₁)	Verbal praise as above plus token dropped into tumbler. Tokens exchanged for tangible reward at end of session.	3
Second token (T₂)	Same as T₁ except that the words "that's a token" are added to the verbal praise.	2
Final control (C₃)	Same as Pre-C₁.	3
Final token (T₃)	Same as T₂.	3

added to 17 of the items. Now praise was contingent upon both being seated at the table and responding appropriately to the given instruction.

Token Training

During the subsequent four sessions, standard operating procedures were not employed. In these sessions, the subjects were given a step-wise exposure to materials and procedures which would later form the basis of the token-reinforcement system. During the first session, poker chips (referred to as tokens) were dispensed to each subject on a response-independent basis. That is, each token was delivered to a subject regardless of what he was doing. Each time a token was handed to a subject, it was immediately accompanied by an edible, such as candy. The token was taken back upon receipt of the edible. During the first few such exchanges, subjects were assisted manually. Later, subjects had to independently return the token to receive the edible. These initial steps were scheduled first simply to pair tokens with tangible reinforcers and second to teach them to trade tokens for a reinforcer. During the initial part of the second session, similar exchanges were made, but each exchange involved a choice of three edibles. As this session progressed, the subjects were exposed to a series of exchanges in which gradually increasing delays between token delivery and token exchange were systematically scheduled.

Before the third session, additional materials were introduced into the room. These included a wooden block which contained seven colored transparent tumblers and a 16-compartment box (called "the store") which was filled with tangible rewards. The tumbler block was placed on the teacher's desk. Each subject was assigned a particular tumbler which could be distinguished from every other tumbler on the basis of several independent stimulus dimensions such as color, position in the wooden block and a geometric symbol painted directly under it on the block. To aid a fourth adult, who was to drop tokens into appropriate tumblers at appropriate times, each child's name appeared on the back of the block, beneath the appropriate tumbler. The "store" was placed on a chair in a corner of the room so that it was away from all other props. Articles "for sale" included small edibles, balloons, candy bars, whistles, toy cars, trucks and planes, and a variety of trinkets and other toys. They were arranged according to size and "price." The largest ("costliest") articles were placed in the two upper rows of four compartments each, while the smallest (" least expensive") articles were placed in the bottom row.

In the third and fourth token training sessions, the class was visually and functionally exposed to the tumblers and the store. Tokens were delivered into tumblers instead of directly to the children. In the first 10 minutes of the third session, tokens were delivered on a response-independent basis and subjects were called up one at a time to the teacher's desk after each delivery for the purpose of immediate exchange. Each removed his token from his tumbler, handed it to the teacher, and proceeded immediately to the store. Selection of a reward was permitted from the bottom row only at this point. Before one of these exchanges, and in an effort further to facilitate discrimination between the tumblers, each subject was asked to select and paste an animal sticker on his tumbler. During the remainder of this third session, tokens were delivered on a response-contingent basis. Instructions different from those on the instruction list were given to the group at large, and praise, together with token reinforcement, was given to each individual who responded appropriately. After several sets of immediate exchange transpired, exchange delays were increased by going through three and then more instructions before calling any subjects up to the desk. The final delay involved a period of no exchange for 7 to 10 minutes.

The last token-training session was conducted in a manner similar to that which would be employed during subsequent experimental sessions: *i.e.* throughout the session, appropriate responses produced praise and token reinforcement. As in the previous session, instructions were different from those on the instruction list, but in contrast, only a single token exchange was scheduled at the end of the session. Each given subject had to be seated at the table in order to be eligible for his exchange. A subject who had earned nine or fewer tokens could choose an item only from the bottom row of the store. A subject who had earned from 10 to 19 tokens could choose an item from the two bottom rows. Only 20 or more tokens allowed a child *carte blanche* at the store.

Second Control (C₂) Condition

To assess the effects of the token-training procedures, *per se,* on performance previously generated, the behavior of the subjects was again examined under control conditions. Data obtained after token training might reflect changes in behavior attributable to rapport and to the pleasant interactions implicit in the token-training procedure. Therefore, in an effort to avoid ambiguity of interpretation, the group was exposed to three additional control sessions immediately after token training terminated and before being exposed to the experimental conditions.

Initial Token (T₁) and Second Token (T₂) Conditions

The subjects were subsequently exposed to three sessions in which the behavioral effects of adding token reinforcement were examined. These sessions were conducted with the tumbler for tokens and the "store" present in the room. A fourth adult was available to drop tokens into appropriate tumblers when a subject was praised by the instructor. Tokens were exchanged for an article in the "store" at the end of the session.

During the initial two sessions under the T_1 condition, subjects were required to earn 20 tokens to gain free choice at the "store." Range of selection was restricted on the basis of the number of tokens less than 20 that were earned. In the third T_1 session and in all subsequent token-reinforcement sessions, choices and restrictions placed upon choices were determined on an individual basis. A subject was given free choice of anything in the "store" if he earned more tokens than in the previous session. Subjects whose earnings equalled those of the previous session were restricted to articles that appeared in the bottom two rows; those accumulating fewer tokens than in the previous session could select only from the bottom row.

Because of the possibility that some subjects may have failed to associate the verbal praise with the delivery of a token during the T_1 sessions, two additional token-reinforcement (T_2) sessions were conducted which differed from the T_1 sessions only in that the words, "that's a token" were added to the teacher's statement of praise.

Final Control (C_3) and Final Token (T_3) Conditions

To determine whether the differential effects of token reinforcement previously obtained could be reliably reproduced, the group was reexposed to three additional control sessions and then to three additional token sessions. The C_3 sessions were conducted in the same fashion as the C_2 sessions, and the T_3 sessions duplicated the T_2 sessions.

In each C and T session, two observers equipped with the instruction list placed a check mark in the appropriate space on that list whenever a given subject responded correctly. At the end of each session, the number of items responded to by each subject was independently totalled by each of the observers.

When there was disagreement between the two totals for a given subject, the average of the two was taken as the subject's score for that session.

RESULTS AND DISCUSSION
Overview

For four of the seven subjects (Student 1 through Student 4), token reinforcement generated and maintained higher frequencies of instruction-following behavior compared to that behavior maintained under control (praise only) conditions. The behavior of Student 5 and Student 6 did not appear to be differentially influenced by the token-reinforcement procedure, but the data did provide important quantitative information about their instruction-following behavior over the course of the sudy. Finally, one subject (Student 7) failed to follow any instruction throughout the study.

Specific Results

Figures 22-1 through 22-6 present the daily results obtained from Student 1 through Student 6, respectively. In each figure, the total number of items responded to appropriately, per session, is plotted as a function of the successive control and experimental conditions.

Figure 22-1 presents the data obtained with Student 1. This subject responded appropriately to approximately 25 of the items during the first two sessions in which the standard operating procedures were employed. During these two precontrol condition (Pre-C$_1$) sessions, he was out of his seat and moving about the room much of the time. The instruction list used at this time did not require that he be seated in order to be praised by the instructor. As a consequence of the observation of this subject's concurrent appropriate and disorderly behaviors (as well as similar observations with other subjects), the final revision of the instruction list was made. This revision was designed to maximize the incompatibility of obtaining reinforcement while at the same time engaging in disorderly conduct. In the first control (C$_1$) session, the number of correct responses for Student 1 did not change, but it was apparent that he spent more time sitting at the table.

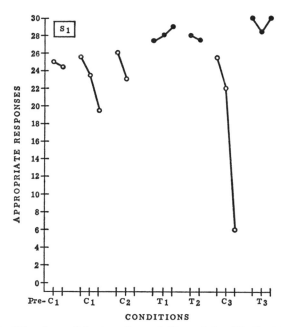

Figure 22-1. Number of instructions followed by Student 1. In every session, each such response produced praise ("Very nice, *name of student*"). In precontrol (Pre-C₁) sessions praise was never contingent upon being seated at the table. In initial control (C₁) sessions, and *all* sessions thereafter, praise was also contingent upon being seated at the table in the case of 17 instructions. In initial token (T₁) sessions appropriate responses also produced a token. In the remaining token (T₂ and T₃) sessions, the words, "that's a token" were added to the praise.

In each of the two subsequent C_1 sessions, his total number of appropriate responses decreased. During the token-training sessions he was orderly and seemed attentive. During the C_2 session that immediately followed token training, his appropriate response total was identical to that obtained in the first C_1 session. In his next C_2 session, this total decreased. This subject was not present for the final C_2 session.

In each of the first five (T_1 and T_2) token-reinforcement sessions, Student 1 responded correctly to between 27 and 29 items on the 30-item instruction list. Thus, each daily T_1 and T_2 total

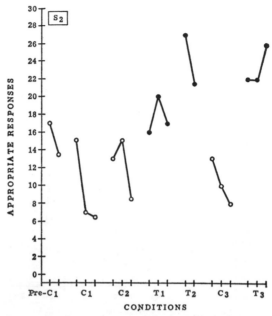

Figure 22-2. Number of instructions followed by Student 2.

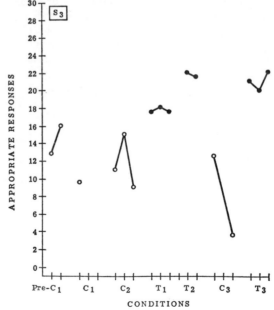

Figure 22-3. Number of instructions followed by Student 3.

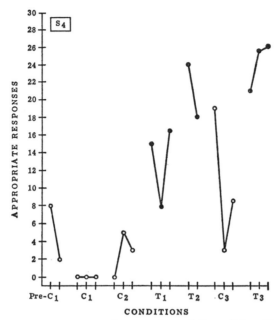

Figure 22-4. Number of instructions followed by Student 4.

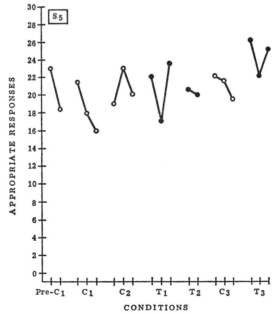

Figure 22-5. Number of instructions followed by Student 5.

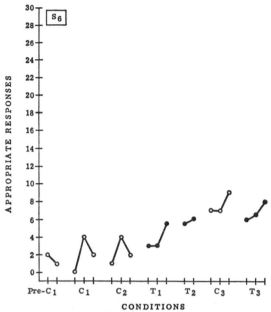

Figure 22-6. Number of instructions followed by Student 6.

exceeded any obtained previously. In the first C_3 session, his response total decreased to 25. In the two subsequent C_3 sessions, his totals decreased markedly, and his disruptive behavior appeared to increase and subjectively resembled his behavior in his regular classroom. The total of only six correct responses which he obtained in the third C_3 session clearly indicates the extent to which his instruction-following behavior deteriorated. Finally, with the reinstatement of the token-reinforcement procedures in the T_3 sessions, appropriate responding on the part of S_1 increased markedly. He actually followed each of 30 instructions in two of the three T_3 sessions. The beneficial effect of token reinforcement was, thus, clearly established for this subject.

The results obtained with Student 1 were representative of results obtained with Students 2, 3 and 4. These results are shown in Figures 22-2, 22-3 and 22-4, respectively. In the case of each of these subjects, the highest totals of correct responding were obtained in token reinforcement sessions. Each of these three subjects differed from Student 1 in one respect. Their response totals increased when the words "that's a token" were added to the verbal reinforcement in the T_2 sessions. This suggests that the use of this specific verbal bridge may have added to the effectiveness of the token-reinforcement system. This possibility must remain speculative, however, because this verbal factor was not systematically manipulated and because it is also quite possible that either (a) the changes in the token-exchange criteria introduced at the end of the third T_1 session and/or (b) continued exposure to token reinforcement, *per se*, could have accounted for the increases in appropriate response totals observed with these subjects after the third token-reinforcement session.

Two subjects did not appear to be differentially influenced by the application of token reinforcement over the study. Figure 22-5 presents the daily results for Student 5. Between the initial Pre-C_1 session and the final C_3 session, his totals of correct responding varied between 16 and 23. This range of values was obtained under both token-reinforcement and control conditions. That Student 5 may have been influenced by tokens is suggested only by the results obtained in the T_3 sessions. His highest totals in the study (26 and 25) were obtained in the first and third T_3 sessions. In general, however, it would be more appropriate to summarize his results by indicating that he responded appropriately to the majority of items throughout the investigation. We would point out that while Student 5's teacher reported that he "paid poor attention" in her class, the data obtained for him in the experimental class demonstrated that he was certainly capable of following simple instructions. In contrast, these data are not compatible with statements often made about this student which suggest that he has "severe attentional deficits." These data, when considered in combination with his reported classroom history and with the subjective interpretations of his regular classroom performance suggest that a systematic approach, *per se*, which is necessary to obtain objective behaviorial measurements, may be critically important to the future successful education of this subject.

Figure 22-6 presents the results for Student 6. An examination of his results suggests that he continuously improved with respect to following instructions during the study and independent of specific conditions. This subject was assigned the lowest IQ of all subjects in this study. While on the one hand it might be argued that his results are certainly compatible with this evaluation (he followed fewer total instructions over the study than all but one subject), they are not compatible with several subjective reports which indicated that he was "incapable of paying attention and learning much of anything." The data obtained for Student 6 demonstrate that under repeated systematic exposure to at least one general set of classroom conditions, this child's instruction-following behavior can be accelerated. It is quite probable that this acceleration, observed over the course of the study, would not have been detected had we either subjectively observed his performance or exposed him to fewer sessions. Thus, as in the case of Student 5, the data obtained with Student 6 suggest that a systemaic approach, *per se*, may also be critically important to his future education.

Student 7 failed to respond to any item on the instruction list throughout the study. He was thus a poor selection for the present approach. Informal efforts with this subject, in isolation, did indicate, however, that he might benefit from a reinforcement program applied on an individual basis.

Reliability of the Instruction List

In an experimental study such as the present one, the reliability of the data-gathering instrument depends upon the extent to which responses called for can be objectively monitored. On the basis of a comparison of the pairs of individual session totals obtained for each subject between the two independent observers across the study, the final list appeared to call for behaviors that were well defined and readily observable. In 55 percent of the daily individual subject totals compared, no disagreement was found between observers. Furthermore, a difference of only one response was obtained in the two totals in 33 percent of these comparisons. Finally, no difference greater than three responses was ever obtained in any comparison, and this occurred in no more than 5 percent of the comparisons.

Associated Results and Further Discussion

Three additional sets of observations remain to be described. They involve (a) some comments about the effectiveness of the time-out procedure, (b) some speculations about a possible relationship between the potency of the present token-reinforcement procedures and the nature of the subjects' "attentional" problems and (c) some impressions and speculations about the apparent development and differential maintenance of some social emergents.

Time-out

Time-out was primarily instituted to deal with occasions on which one subject aggressed physically against another. It was also used to discourage tampering with the store. Basically, this procedure involved the teacher's removal of an offending child from the experimental room. The offender was placed in the dimly lighted adjacent classroom. He was returned to the classroom after the teacher had completed a silent count of 15. Had an offender emitted tantrum-like behavior while in isolation, termination of such behavior would have been required before permitting him to return; no such delay contingency was necessary. The use of time-out appeared to discourage repeated offending within any given session. It never had to be used twice in a given session and was used twice in only two sessions. Generally, when a subject was placed in time-out, no further time-out–producing behavior on the part of any of the subjects was observed over the remainder of that session. No definitive conclusions can be drawn with respect to the effects of time-out over sessions. Time-out was used after Student 5 tampered with the store on two occasions. These were both delivered during the first token-reinforcement session. The fact that this procedure never required repetition for this subject, suggests (but does not prove) its effectiveness. Time-outs were employed 18 times following aggressive behavior over the course of the study. Student 4 produced 13 of these. The fact that he received 11 time-outs during the initial 12 sessions and only 2 over the final 11 sessions might suggest that this procedure was effective across sessions. It should be pointed out, however, that he tended differentially to produce time-outs during control sessions and that these comprised the majority of the initial sessions, while only three of the final 11 sessions were control sessions.

Potency of Treatment and "Attentional" Problems

In first proposing this study to the principal and faculty of Noble School, we emphasized an interest in working with children whose disruptive behavior in and out of the classroom often led to their being characterized, among other things, as being "hyperactive." Over the course of the investigation, it was the impression of all observers that behavior that might be "attributed" to "hyperactivity" occurred less frequently during token sessions than during control sessions. The data obtained with some subjects over the investigation are certainly in logical agreement with these subjective impressions. What appears to be most significant about this observation is the fact that those four subjects who were reported to be "extremely hyperactive" and/or extremely disruptive in their regular classrooms were the same four subjects who showed dramatic improvement in instruction-following behavior under the token-reinforcement situation. To the extent that our subjective impressions were valid, these findings support the notion that a major observable contributor to "attentional deficit" type inferences drawn by teachers about students may be the frequent failure of the latter to follow instructions.

The Apparent Emergence of "Helping" Behavior

Perhaps of greatest relevance to the potential benefits that might be derived from the present and similar approaches, above and beyond those of economy and objective information, is the description of what subjectively appeared to be the emergence of potentially significant and unexpected social behavior. During the Pre-C_1, C_1 and C_2 sessions, although the class was treated as a group with respect to instructions, there appeared to be little, if any, group cohesiveness. The only interaction between members of the group involved "playful" and "not so playful" fighting between pairs of subjects. There did not appear to be any instance of "cooperation" between subjects or "assistance of one by another." In contrast, after the initial token session and in all subsequent token sessions, we frequently observed behaviors on the part of each of five subjects (Student 1 through Student 5) which (subjectively) appeared to be socially directed toward another subject, and which we inferred to be designed to help the latter subject earn reinforcement. On one occasion, for example, Student 1 brought scissors to Student 6 when scissors were needed to fulfill the requirement of an item on the instruction list. Various subjects were seen to raise Student 7's hand for him when an instruction called for that behavior. Other dramatic examples of similar social behaviors included Student 2 leading Student 4 to the table, thereby making the latter eligible for reinforcement, and Student 4 pointing to the appropriate card with the name of a fellow subject on it, seeming to encourage imitation.

We can, at best, only speculate about these alleged cases of "helping" behavior, because no objective measurement procedures were utilized to monitor their occurrence and because no explicit contingencies were scheduled with respect to their occurrence. Tokens were not delivered to a subject as a consequence of "assisting another subject." The emergence of this behavior could have crucially depended upon one or more of the characteristics of the program. This behavior may have been controlled, in part, by the presence or absence of the props and cues associated with token reinforcement, since it was apparently not observed during control sessions. This behavior could have emerged as a consequence of addressing the group as a whole and/or of the fact that all children could equally obtain tangible goods (competition was not involved).

Since the instructor and observers focused their attention upon appropriate instruction-following behavior throughout this investigation, the observations reported above, while provocative, must be regarded as generally anecdotal in nature. Time limits set upon the present study did not permit a more systematic examination of these phenomena and excluded the possibility of further appropriate experimental manipulations.

A Final Comment

We have no special investment in token reinforcement, *per se*, as a method of generating and improving classroom behavior. A token-reinforcement system involves a complex set of procedures which demands much attention and includes vast numbers of stimulus elements and environmental variables. From an experimental point of view, those invested in the effects of token reinforcement would have to carefully isolate the numerous variables involved in order to determine objectively the factors necessary and sufficient for the generation of observed reliable behavioral changes. Instead, our bias is in the direction of a systematic arrangement of an environment and the systematic application of any given treatment in such way as to facilitate objective and reliable measurements. Quantitative data alone reveal whether a specific treatment (be it the use of token reinforcement, electric shock, M&M's, threats or instructions) is therapeutic, ineffective or noxious with respect to a chosen target behavior. In the case of the "treatment" applied and treatment effects assessed in the present study, the data suggest that the approach taken can be successfully applied to the problem of altering behavior of individuals treated as a group in a group setting. We would here reiterate that not every member of the group was differentially influenced by token reinforcement under the conditions which obtained. However, in the case of two of the three subjects who were not differentially influenced, the use of the present procedures provided objective information about their behavior which could be as valuable with respect to their further education as that provided for the subjects whose performances were differentially influenced by token reinforcement!

REFERENCES

Birnbrauer, J. S., Wolf, M. M., Kidder, J. D. and Tague, C. E.: Classroom behavior of retarded pupils with token reinforcement. *Journal of Experimental Child Psychology,* 2:219–235, 1965.

Buchard, J. D.: Systematic socialization: a programmed environment for the habilitation of antisocial retardates. *Psychological Record,* 17:461–476, 1967.

Bushell, D., Wrobel, P. A. and Michaelis, M. L.: Applying "group" contingencies to the classroom study behavior of preschool children. *Journal of Applied Behavior Analysis,* 1:55–61, 1968.

Hall, R. V., Lund, D. and Jackson, D.: Effects of teacher attention on study behavior. *Journal of Applied Behavior Analysis,* 1:1–12, 1968.

Harris, F. R., Wolf, M. M. and Baer, D. M.: Effects of adult social reinforcement on child behavior. *Young Children,* 20:8–17, 1964.
Zimmerman, E. H. and Zimmerman, J.: The alteration of behavior in a special classroom situation. *Journal of the Experimental Analysis of Behavior,* 5:59–60, 1962.

23

Behavior Changes in Brain-Injured Children Through Social Reinforcement

R. Vance Hall and Marcia Broden

Systematic adult social reinforcement brought about behavior changes in brain-injured children with developmental deficits not amenable to previous efforts at modification. Following baseline observations, systematic reinforcement procedures were successfully carried out by parents and teachers initially unskilled in operant conditioning techniques. The necessity of contingent reinforcement was demonstrated during a brief reversal of contingencies which resulted in a correspondingly brief decrease in the rates of the desired behaviors. A postcheck three months after termination of the experiment indicated the behavior changes were being maintained at rates higher than those observed prior to employment of experimental procedures.

SINCE SKINNER (1938) first outlined the principles of operant conditioning, the diversity of organisms to which the principles have been successfully applied has steadily increased. From infrahuman organisms, such as pigeons and rats, the application of an individual analysis of behavior and its systematic reinforcement has been broadened to include human retardates, psychotics, nor-

NOTE: This report is based on a dissertation by the senior author submitted to the University of Washington in partial fulfillment of the requirement for the Ph.D. degree.

From the *Journal of Experimental Child Psychology*, 5:463–479, 1967. Copyright 1967 by Academic Press Inc. Reprinted with permission of authors and publisher.

mal preschool and school-age children and culturally deprived children.

Among the operant studies involving retarded, psychotic and normal children are several which have modified behavior problems also found among children diagnosed as brain-injured. These behaviors include tantrums (Wolf *et al.*, 1964), crying (Hart *et al.*, 1966), isolate play (Allen *et al.*, 1964), hyperactivity (Patterson, 1965) and inactivity (Johnson *et al.*, 1966).

It has been open to question, however, whether such techniques could be successfully applied to these behaviors when they occur in brain-injured children. These behaviors of brain-injured children are often distinctively described as distractible, perseverative, disinhibited, catastrophically responsive and driven (Strauss and Lehtinen, 1947). It is widely thought that to bring about behavior changes in children diagnosed as brain-injured or neurologically impaired will often prove difficult, presumably because behavior resulting from brain damage is inherently different than that of normal organisms (Straus and Lehtinen, 1950; Lewis *et al.*, 1960).

The purpose of the present study was to examine the applicability of systematic reinforcement procedures to behaviors of brain-injured children and to determine whether adults initially unfamiliar with systematic reinforcement procedures could apply them successfully in a school setting. This is in contrast to studies by skilled researchers in laboratories where the choice of behaviors for study is not a matter of immediate urgency.

METHOD

S's

The subjects were three pupils in the Experimental Education Unit of the University of Washington.[1] They had been diagnosed

[1] The authors express appreciation to Dr. Donald M. Baer of the University of Kansas for advice and critical comment, and to Dr. Charles R. Strother and Dr. Alice H. Hayden of the University of Washington Mental Retardation and Child Development Center for providing facilities and encouragement during the course of the study, and to the staff of the University of Washington Pilot School (now the Experimental Education Unit of the MRCD Center).

as having a central nervous system dysfunction, evidenced by medical, neurological and/or psychological evaluations. The children exhibited behavior patterns considered by the school staff to be interfering with their developmental progress.

Method of Observation and Recording

Two to five informal predata observation sessions were employed in each experiment. Both the *E*'s recorded the types of activity engaged in by the *S* and the responses made by others following the *S*'s activity.

Subsequent to these observations, the observers and the *S*'s teachers established criteria for recording when the behaviors under study were or were not occurring. Once these criteria were established, experimental data were recorded by an observer utilizing a formal recording sheet and a stop watch.

The recording sheet consisted of a form marked with triple rows of squares, each square representing an interval of 10 seconds. One row was used to record the behavior engaged in by the *S*. The second row was used to record verbalizations by an adult directed toward the *S* which might function as reinforcement. The third row was used to record the occasions of an adult's proximity to the child which might function as reinforcement. A record of these data was made during each ten-second interval of each session. A second observer periodically made a simultaneous record of observations. Agreement of the two records was then checked interval by interval. The percentage of agreement of the record gave an indication of interobserver reliability. If the subject or others attempted to interact with the observers in any manner while they were recording, they ignored such attempts and refused to speak.

The observation and interobserver reliability check techniques were identical to those used at the University of Washington Developmental Psychology Laboratory (Allen *et al.*, 1964) and at the University of Kansas Laboratory Preschool (Baer and Wolf, 1966).

Each experiment consisted of a sequence of periods:

1. Baseline period.
2. Reinforcement period.

3. Reversal period.

4. Return to reinforcement period.

The baseline period was used to determine objectively the rates at which the behaviors under study were occurring prior to experimental use of social reinforcement. Following the recording of the baseline data, the rate of the behaviors under study was presented to those working with the children in graphic form. The basic principles of operant conditioning were discussed and procedures for changing the pattern of adult social consequences to the child's behavior were suggested by the *E*'s.

During the reinforcement period, these operant conditioning procedures were employed in an attempt to increase the rate of desired behaviors and decrease the rate of the undesired behaviors. When higher rates of the desired behaviors were achieved, the first reinforcement period was discontinued and reversal period conditions were instituted. Now adult social reinforcement was no longer contingent on emission of the desired behaviors; instead, it was given for other behaviors. When this resulted in a decrease in rates of the desired behaviors, a return to reinforcement of those behaviors was quickly reinstituted and maintained to the end of the experiment. A fifth period of observation was employed some three months after termination of experimental procedures to determine whether the modifications brought about were being maintained. The rates of the behaviors under study are presented graphically as percentages of total behavior for each session.

Experiments

S1

S1 was a six-year old girl who had been treated for hydrocephaly from infancy and had a history of multiple operations and over 50 hospital admissions. Her coordination and fine muscle control were poor, and she had difficulty in maintaining her balance. Thus she disliked writing, jig-saw puzzles and games which required good eye-hand coordination. She refused to participate in these activities in the public school special education class she had attended and from which she had subsequently been excluded.

At the time of the study, the girl's intellectual functioning appeared unimpaired and tested within normal limits. Her Metropolitan Achievement Test grade equivalent scores ranged from 1.8 to 3.9 in reading and arithmetic areas, although her teacher reported that she read at considerably above grade level with good comprehension when paper and pencil testing was not required. She participated in games and school activities which were highly verbal but shunned writing, coloring, drawing and other skilled motor activity.

S1's teacher asked S1's parents to engage the girl in manipulative eye-hand motor tasks at home. The mother had tried but said she was unable to get her daughter to cooperate to any great degree, even though a desk, crayons, pencils, paper and manipulative toys were made available.

The mother was consulted by the E's and expressed her willingness to cooperate in a study of S1's play behavior at home after school. Two informal observation sessions yielded a list of the girl's behaviors which were classified as nonmanipulative activities, including tricycle riding, standing, walking, climbing on a climbing frame, sitting and talking. S1's teacher provided a list of manipulative activities such as drawing, writing, coloring, pasting and working puzzles which she deemed desirable manipulative behaviors not observed in S1's repertoire.

The subsequent formal sessions ranged from 30 to 35 minutes in length. During these sessions, manipulative play was recorded. In addition, verbalization directed to S1 by her mother, and S1's proximity to her mother was recorded. (Proximity was recorded if S1 touched her mother or was within three feet of her during five seconds or more of any ten-second interval.)

Section A of Figure 23-1 presents baseline period data (sessions 1–7). During the baseline period, no activity which had been designated as manipulative play was observed except during session three (Point *a* in Fig. 23-1) when S1 spent less than a minute, or 2.3 percent of her observed time for that day, coloring in a coloring book.

The mean rate of S1's manipulative play for the baseline period was less than 1 percent (.33%). A functional analysis of the baseline period data indicated that S1 received a high rate

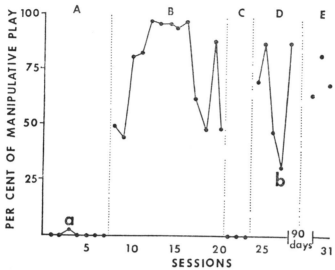

Figure 23-1. A record of *S*1's rates of manipulative play: A, baseline period, prior to experimental procedures; B, reinforcement period, social reinforcement of manipulative play by *S*1's mother; C, reversal period, reinforcement of nonmanipulative play; D, return to reinforcement period, reinforcement of manipulative play; E, postexperiment, three months after termination of the experiment.

of verbal attention and was in close proximity to her mother during much of her free play time at home. This high rate of attention and proximity was given to *S*1 as she played about the house and yard or talked to her mother as the latter performed her household tasks. Thus, the mother's attention and proximity were selected as the contingencies to be used during the reinforcement period.

Section B of Figure 23-1 presents the data of the first reinforcement period (sessions 8–20) in which *S*1's mother was instructed to give attention to and to approach her daughter only when she engaged in manipulative play. At these times, she was encouraged to talk to, give verbal approval of and place herself in proximity to *S*1. Otherwise she was encouraged to stay away and to refrain from speaking or giving attention to her in any way, although she was to allow *S*1 to engage in whatever play activities she chose.

A detailed description of the first reinforcement session gives an indication of the functional relationship of parent attention and proximity to *S*1's behavior. During the first session, *S*1's mother did not attend as usual to her daughter as she played about the home and yard. Rather, she silently stationed herself near the table where *S*1's paints, crayons and other materials were located. After the initial seven minutes of the session (in which *S*1 received neither attention nor proximity from her mother), she approached her mother and the materials, picked up a crayon and began to color. The mother commented appprovingly and talked to *S*1 as she colored. She received continuous attention and proximity as she continued coloring for three minutes and forty seconds. At that point, the telephone rang and the mother left to answer it. In the very same interval *S*1 moved away from the coloring and held on to her mother until the phone conversation was completed.

When her mother finished the call and moved back to the coloring activity area, in the same interval, *S*1 returned also and began once again to color. She maintained this behavior for the next eleven minutes as the mother remained by her and talked to her. At the end of that time, however, the mother left *S*1's side, stopped talking to her and began preparation of the evening meal. After twenty seconds, *S*1 also left the coloring activity, went outside briefly and then returned to watch her mother prepare pudding for supper. She did not engage in further manipulative play during the session.

As can be seen in section B of Figure 23-1, in the following sessions *S*1's manipulative behavior continued to show a similar responsiveness to her mother's attention and proximity. Manipulative play remained at a high level throughout the period, although it fluctuated during the last sessions. The lowest point was reached in the eighteenth session when an ice cream truck came by and *S*1 left to purchase and eat an ice cream bar. In the last session, the mother gave her attention for a considerable period as she played with a toy telephone, a nonmanipulative activity; even so, manipulative play remained above 50 percent. The mean rate of *S*1's manipulative play for the first reinforcement period was 76.4 percent. The manipulative activities observed included coloring, writing, cutting with scissors, pasting, drawing, playing with Play Dough and painting.

Section C of Figure 23-1 presents S1's manipulative play rates during a three-day reversal period (sessions 21–23). During these sessions, the rate of manipulative play observed was in fact 0.0 percent. The data appear perhaps unrealistically responsive to changed conditions, due to the fact that S1's mother began reversal procedures as soon as S1 came home from school some 15 to 30 minutes before the observer arrived.

Thus, even though upon arriving home, S1 had initially begun to engage in manipulative play, the mother had ignored her until she began engaging in other activities. By the time the observations began (some 15–30 minutes later), the mother had effectively reinforced her daughter for intensive behavior incompatible with manipulative play. Ostensibly the child had complete freedom to go back to manipulative tasks; however, she did not do so while her mother provided continuous attention and proximity for the other behaviors.

Once the effects of reversal had been demonstrated, S1's mother once again made social reinforcement contingent upon manipulative play. During the first session of the return-to-reinforcement period (sessions 23–27) the rate increased to 70 percent as shown in section D of Figure 23-1. In the following session it rose to 87 percent and then dropped sharply in the next two sessions. At Point *b* it was noted by the *E*'s that S1's mother was giving verbal attention for behavior other than manipulative play. This was pointed out to her. In the next and final session, the mother became more discriminating and S1's manipulative rate of play promptly rose to 88 percent. The mean rate for the entire period was 65 percent.

Observations made three months later indicated that manipulative play was being maintained at a mean rate of 71.2 percent (Section E of Figure 23-1). The mother reported she had continued systematically to reinforce manipulative play beyond the time of the experimental observations and soon found it possible to maintain a high rate with only occasional reinforcement. S1's parents and teacher agreed that the procedures had not only increased S1's rate of manipulative play but had improved her skills in writing, coloring and her general fine muscle coordination. Interobserver reliability checks made during the experiment showed a correspondence ranging from 97 to 100 percent.

S2

S2 was a five-year-old girl who had had encephalitis at the age of eight months. The illness resulted in seizures and a subsequent right hemispheric hemiplegia. Abnormal electroencephalographic readings were thought to be consistent with a left posterior frontal lesion. The seizures were controlled by medication which was later discontinued. S2's subsequent development was delayed; no walking or talking appeared until two years of age. There was a continued right spastic hemiplegia.

At the time of the study, the girl wore a brace on her right leg and had limited use of her right arm. S2 reportedly avoided use of the various pieces of climbing apparatus in the school play yard, and preferred to engage in activities such as swinging, talking to an adult or sandbox play. She exhibited a great amount of dependent behavior toward adults, often asking them to do things for her, clinging to them and asking them to watch her as she played.

Exercise of the right arm and leg had been recommended as a part of S2's educational rehabilitation program. Since regular physical therapy was not available, the staff recommended more use of the playground climbing apparatus.

The climbing apparatus was located in the preschool outdoor play area. It included a climbing tower with steps leading to a platform six feet high with a pole for sliding to the ground; a raised platform three feet × six feet, three feet high with inclined ramps up two sides and stair steps up a third side; an overhead ladder; a metal climbing frame five feet high consisting of three arched ladders leading to a central ring which served to join them; and planks and boxes placed on or between these devices. Since outdoor play was supervised by three graduate assistant teachers, the problem presented was to develop procedures which they could employ to bring about the desired increase in climbing.

Prior to recording data, informal observation of S2's activity was made by the E's. Behavior was then dichotomized into climbing and nonclimbing behavior. The method of observation used during subsequent formal sessions was essentially similar to that used with S1. Data were taken from the time the outdoor play period began until S2 left the play yard. The length of the sessions varied, depending on the daily schedule of activity and ranged from eighteen to forty-nine minutes in duration. Climbing behavior was recorded whenever S2 made physical contact with the climbing apparatus during five seconds or more of any ten-second observation interval. Verbal attention was recorded whenever someone talked to S2. Proximity was recorded whenever a teacher touched S2 or approached within three feet of her for half or more of each ten-second interval.

Section A of Figure 23-2 presents baseline period data (sessions 1–9). By coincidence, on the initial day of baseline observation, a new piece of climbing apparatus, the climbing tower, was installed. S2 spent three minutes of the first five minutes of ob-

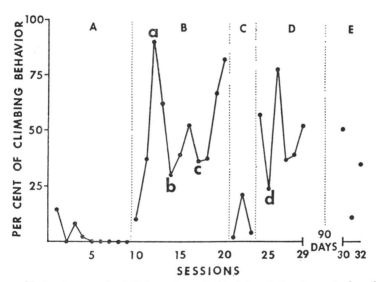

Figure 23-2. A record of S2's rates of climbing behavior: A, baseline period, prior to experimental procedures; B, reinforcement period, social reinforcement of climbing by S2's teachers; C, reversal period, reinforcement of nonclimbing behaviors; D, return to reinforcement period, social reinforcement of climbing behavior; E, postexperiment, three months after termination of the experiment.

servation on the tower. After this short burst of climbing behavior, she left the tower for other activity and was in contact with it for only two additional ten-second intervals during the remaining twenty-three minutes of the session. On subsequent sessions, she showed less and less activity on this or other climbing devices.

In the final four sessions of the baseline period her climbing behavior was observed to be zero. The mean of the rates of climbing behavior for *S*2 during the baseline period sessions was 2.3 percent. Typical behavior incompatible with climbing included sandbox play, swinging in a swing, riding in a wagon, standing, and clinging and talking to a teacher who had been assigned to give her special supervision.

Following the baseline period, the data of section A of Figure 23-2 were presented by the *E* to *S*2's teachers. The basic principles of operant conditioning were discussed and procedures for modifying the consequences of *S*2's behavior were agreed upon.

Section B of Figure 23-2 presents the data of the first reinforcement period (sessions 10–20). During the first reinforcement period, the teacher who had worked with *S*2 was assigned primary responsibility for carrying out the contingencies of approaching her, talking to her and giving her verbal approval when *S*2 approached or made use of the climbing apparatus. All teachers were to withhold these contingencies for other behavior.

As shown in Figure 23-2, the rate of climbing rose during these sessions. In session twelve (Point *a* in Fig. 23-2) *S*2's rate of climbing reached 90 percent and she was heard to state, "I want to do it by myself," as she climbed on the tower (previously she had required assistance in climbing). When told it was time to discontinue play, she said "I want to stay up here."

In session thirteen, *S*2 spent 20 of the first 23 minutes climbing. During her play, however, another girl began to climb on the same apparatus and to shove and hit *S*2. After a particularly strong exchange, *S*2 left the climbing apparatus and did not return until the other girl left the yard. Her rate of climbing for the session nevertheless was 60.8 percent.

At point *b* in Figure 23-2 the head teacher assigned a different teacher to *S*2. The original teacher was assigned to the girl who had struck S2, since there was concern about the "jealous" behavior shown by S2's classmate. The rate of climbing dropped to 30.1 percent. S2 seemed to spend a number of minutes watching her classmate and her "old" teacher interact.

Her rates of climbing increased, however, in the next two sessions. Then, at Point c in Figure 23-2, the head teacher again assigned a different teacher to S2. This teacher was new to the situation and, due to a misunderstanding, reinforced wagon riding as well as climbing behavior during this session. This resulted in an increase in wagon riding and a decrease in the total climbing rate. The misunderstanding was corrected, and in the final sessions of the period climbing behavior rose once again to high levels. The mean climbing rate for the entire experiment period was 49.6 percent.

There was general agreement by the staff that S2's behavior had changed markedly during outdoor play and that her play included a much higher rate of climbing, running and jumping, and less clinging to her teachers. Furthermore, it was noted she was indeed using both her right arm and leg to a greater degree, and the therapeutic aim of the program was being realized. Section C of Figure 23-2 shows S2's climbing rates during a three-day reversal period (session 21–23). The mean of the rates for the reversal period was 8.6 percent.

The effects of reversal having been demonstrated, the teachers once again began giving S2 verbal attention and placed themselves in proximity to her when she engaged in climbing behavior. As can be seen in this return-to-reinforcement period (Section D of Fig. 23-2), there was rapid increase in climbing rate.

The second session of this period (Point d of Fig. 23-2) was marked by an unexpected visit from a former teacher of the preschool group. Uninformed of the study being conducted, she interacted with S2 while the latter was engaged in nonclimbing activities, and a much lower climbing rate was recorded for the session.

In the following sessions of the period, climbing rates rose in spite of the fact the climbing apparatus was somewhat wet due to rain. S2 was observed to use all of the climbing apparatus available to her, and the mean of the climbing rates for all sessions of the return-to-reinforcement period was 48.7 percent.

Observations of S2 were made three months later (Section E of Fig. 23-2). Although the class was housed in new quarters, it was still headed by the same teacher. An assistant teacher present in the play yard during the follow-up observations was new to the group and had not participated in the experiment. During the course of these observations, S2 received teacher attention and teacher proximity for both climbing and nonclimbing behaviors. Even so, the mean of the rates of climbing for these observations was 34 percent and included climbing a ladder on the metal climbing frame, grasping the central ring at its apex with both hands and, after hanging suspended for a few moments, dropping to the ground. The head teacher reported S2 had continued making progress in the use of her affected limbs, as illustrated when she hung by both hands from the climbing frame unassisted. Interobserver reliability checks made periodically throughout the experiment show a range of from 93 to 98 percent agreement.

S3

S3 was a nine-year-old boy with a history of prematurity and depressed functioning in the neonatal period. He had been diagnosed as having a probable central nervous system dysfunction, and his record indicated marked perceptual problems, expressive language difficulties, impaired gross and fine motor coordination, and impaired tongue movements. The behavior problems noted included impulsivity, perseveration, temper tantrums, and demands for adult attention.

S3's teacher had requested the development of procedures for rapidly increasing the rate of S3's social (parallel and cooperative) play during school play periods. However, S3 had resisted previous attempts to increase his rate of social interaction with his peers. He engaged in game activity organized by the teacher, but during free play isolated himself or monopolized the teacher's time and attention.

Prior to recording data on the rate of social play, S3 was observed for five days during outdoor play periods. Notes were

made on the types of activity *S*3 engaged in and of the consequences which followed his behavior. *S*3's teacher was then
consulted and criteria for defining social play were agreed upon.
Social play included parallel and cooperative play during which
the *S*'s engaged in similar activities involving the same or similar
material in proximity to each other (within 6 feet). During the
experiment, data were taken from the time the daily play period
began until it ended and *S*3 left the playing area. The length
of the sessions varied, depending on the daily schedule, the mean
length being 51 minutes.

The graduate students acting as *S*3's teachers were informed
that a study would be conducted requiring daily observations of
pupil activity but were not given specific information regarding
the nature of the experiment. No prior explanation was given *S*3
or his classmates, since observers were frequently present during
play activity. *S*3 did approach an observer on one or two occasions. When the observer averted his gaze and said he was busy,
*S*3 permanently discontinued approaching and gave no further
indication of awareness of observers.

Section A of Figure 23-3 presents baseline period data (sessions
1–8). During the baseline period, *S*3 engaged in a preponderance
of isolate play or attempted to engage the teacher in a one-to-one
relationship in such activities as shooting baskets with a basket-
ball. Frequently when the other children were engaged in social
play, *S*3's teacher would encourage him to join them in the activity. *S*3 would usually resist these efforts. He spent considerable
time watching while the others played and in calling to a teacher
to come play with him. The mean of the rates of social play
during the baseline period was found to be 16.8 percent.

At the conclusion of the baseline period, the data depicting *S*3's
rates of social play were presented in graphic form by the *E*'s to
*S*3's teachers. The basic principles of operant conditioning which
involved positive reinforcement and extinction were discussed. It
was suggested that *S*3's nonsocial behavior might be being maintained by teacher attention. Systematic procedures for modifying
the consequences of *S*3's play behavior were agreed upon. It was
decided that approaching, talking to or giving verbal approval of

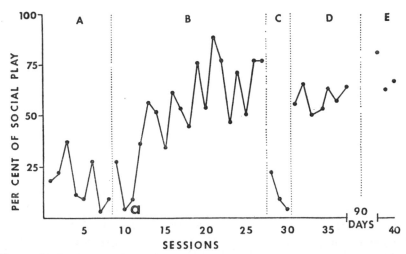

Figure 23-3. A record of S3's rates of social play: A, baseline period, prior to experimental procedures; B, reinforcement period, social reinforcement of social play by S3's teachers; C, reversal period, reinforcement of nonsocial play; D, return to reinforcement period, reinforcement of social play; E, postexperiment, three months after termination of the experiment.

S3 should be employed only when he engaged in social play with his peers.

Section B of Figure 23-3 presents the data of the first reinforcement period. During the first session of the reinforcement period, S3 engaged in almost no social play in the first half of the session. During the second half, he began engaging in social play (a series of bicycle races instituted by one of his classmates). S3 continued in this activity intermittently during the last 20 minutes of the session but was not attended to by the teachers. Toward the end of the session, he picked at his wrist until it bled, a mannerism which had previously resulted in a high rate of teacher attention. This behavior was ignored. The social play rate for the session was 27.5 percent.

The second session was marked by a good deal of isolate play, more wrist picking, calling to the teacher and squalling by S3. As agreed, these behaviors were not attended to by the teachers. On the other hand, only two of the eleven intervals in which social play did occur resulted in a teacher employing social attention. The rate of social play fell to 3.3 percent. In the third session, $S3$'s rate of social play was only 8.5 percent.

At the conclusion of this session (Point a in Fig. 23-3), the criteria for social play were restated and clarified, and the importance of attending to $S3$ during the first interval that social play occurred and during most subsequent intervals was stressed. It was also noted that $S3$ usually followed a pattern of isolate play at the beginning of the play period. Although he ignored his peers, he attempted to attract a teacher's attention—he called, squalled or picked at his wrist. If ignored further, he began looking toward his peers at play and if given teacher attention at this point, he would sometimes engage in social play. It was therefore decided to try a shaping procedure by reinforcing successive approximations of $S3$'s looking behavior to approaching and playing with his peers. More direct feedback on the results of each day's session was also arranged.

In the next session, social play rose to 36 percent and was maintained at this or higher levels in all subsequent sessions of the reinforcement period, except session fifteen when it dipped to about 28 percent. The mean of the rates of social play for the entire reinforcement period was 51.2 percent.

Section C of Figure 23-3 presents the data for the reversal period (sessions 28–30). In the first session of reversal, $S3$ repeatedly engaged in social play in short bursts. When he was given no adult social reinforcement, however, he turned to isolate activity. This was reinforced by teacher attention and resulted in several long periods of nonsocial play. During the second and third days of reversal, the amount and duration of social play decreased further. The mean of rates of social play for the reversal period was 11.9 percent.

Section D of Figure 23-3 presents the data of the return-to-reinforcement period (sessions 31–37). Once again, social play was reinforced whenever it occurred. In the first reinforcement session, the rate rose from 4.8 per cent to 55 percent. During the remaining sessions, social play was maintained at a level ranging from 48.9 to 64.9 percent, the mean of the rates being 57.4 percent.

At the conclusion of the experiment, the teachers were unanimous in their judgment that S3 had indeed increased his rate of social play, that his peers seemed to enjoy him more, that he laughed more and that he engaged in more physical contact with his classmates. They also reported that S3 was more cooperative in other activities during the day and that he had begun to derive reinforcement from the games engaged in and the responses of his peers. They reported that less adult social reinforcement was necessary to maintain social play.

Section E of Figure 23-3 presents data of follow-up observations made three months after termination of the experiment. At that time, S3 was enrolled in a special public school class for neurologically impaired pupils. Observations were conducted during regular recess periods for the special class. S3's teacher and the playground teacher were told only that an experiment involving S3's play activity had been made and the E wished to observe him during recess periods. During the recess observations, S3 engaged in a ball-bouncing game called "four square," took turns shooting baskets and played tag with his classmates. The mean of the rates of his social play was 65.7 percent. Interobserver reliability checks made periodically throughout the experiment showed an agreement of from 81 to 97 percent.

DISCUSSION

The results of this study indicate that techniques of operant conditioning were effective in modifying behaviors of children diagnosed as brain-injured. When systematic scoial reinforcement was employed, the reinforced changes were effected in a relatively short period. Thus there was no evidence indicating that the brain-injured child conforms to a basically different set of principles than that which has been shown to apply to other organisms.

Clearly enough, the behaviors of the brain-injured child often are related to the medical problems which may be a part of his history. Strauss and Lehtinen (1947), Lewis *et al.* (1960) and others note that the brain-injured child is more likely to have behavioral problems than a neurologically normal peer. However, the etiology of this deviant behavior may well be attributed to the fact that uncoordinated performance and poor perceptual organization have prevented reinforcement for activities relatively unavailable to the child. (*S*1 would seem to be an obvious example.) In such cases, a systematic program of differential reinforcement, including shaping procedures, may be necessary to initiate higher rates of desired behaviors. As more skillful performance is gained, he may well come in contact with the "natural" contingencies available, and further systematic programming may become unnecessary.

A second purpose of the study was to determine whether adults initially unfamiliar with systematic reinforcement procedures could apply them successfully in a school setting. It is probable that many more children will benefit from research in learning theory if it can be translated into procedures which can be carried out by teachers and parents in the school and the home (Staats, 1965). The results of the study indicated that the procedures used with parents and teachers were effective. Several problems had to be overcome in order to achieve this apparent success.

One major problem was obtaining an objective definition of the behavior under study so that it could be easily discriminated. This prompted the described attempts to establish objective criteria of identification prior to recording experimental data. Utilizing the baseline data during initial discussions of operant principles also seemed to help focus attention on the need for making this discrimination.

In spite of these attempts to identify the behaviors prior to application of reinforcement procedures, the participants experienced some difficulty in identifying the behaviors to be reinforced. Identifying what constituted social reinforcement and getting them to provide it as soon as the appropriate behavior occurred was a related problem.

To meet these problems, a pattern of almost daily conferences evolved. These conferences were used to clarify the criteria for subject behavior as well as criteria for reinforcement. The *E*'s also utilized these sessions to reinforce the adults socially when they carried out the procedures effectively.

Posting the results of each day's session in graphic form was used as a tool in this process of shaping the behavior of the participants. For example, when the daily graph posted on the rate of S3's social play showed an upswing, the E's would compliment the teacher responsible for having provided social reinforcement as soon as social play had occurred. Soon the teachers were able to look at the graph and the data sheets and to make self-evaluations of their effectiveness. Once this occurred, the data itself became reinforcing and helped to increase and maintain the teachers' rates of appropriate response as it gave them direct feedback on the results of their efforts.

Another problem which arose during the early stages of the experiments was that some teachers expressed reservations about applying operant procedures, since that entailed ignoring children without explanation when they were not engaged in desired behaviors. It was thought that this might cause confusion and feelings of rejection on the part of the child. In the first few sessions it was particularly distressing to the teachers when an S called out to them, pleaded and cried, or showed jealous behavior.

Cooperation was given during this early difficult period, however, partly because the behaviors chosen for modification were recognized as serious problems by all who participated. Since the problem behaviors were of long standing, there was a general receptiveness to trying a new approach. Objection and concern disappeared almost entirely as soon as the procedures began to bring about the desired modifications. The results shown by the data and the obvious improvement in S's behavior proved to be very reinforcing to those carrying out the procedures. Thus, credence in the procedures was established and resulted in greater proficiency of application once confidence, born of desirable results, had been gained.

The institution of the brief reversal period also presented a problem. In all cases, the adults expressed reservations about employing a reversal for they were convinced the procedures *had* been effective and were bringing about the desired changes. In the case of S3, reversal proved to be especially aversive, for it meant the return of behavior which was extremely repugnant.

In addition to the goal of demonstrating the causal relationship of the procedures, a benefit gained by reversal was that it illustrated with great clarity the effectiveness of systematic reinforcement. Thus it proved to be an effective teaching technique and seemed to result in more skillful and consistent reinforcement application after reversal than prior to it.

A final factor was the role of the natural contingencies once new rates of appropriate behaviors were established. The teachers usually noted during the course of the second reinforcement period that it was much easier to maintain a high rate of the desired behavior than it had been previously. They were able to shift to a variable ratio schedule of intermittent reinforcement which was much easier to maintain than the continuous reinforcement schedule used during the acquisition phase of the first reinforcement period. Reinforcement previously unavailable to the S's began playing a role. In some cases (as when a classmate said, "$S3$, we like you,") social reinforcement came from peers. It also was probably provided by intrinsic reinforcement (as when $S1$ manipulated objects with new-found skill or $S2$ stunted on the climbing apparatus).

In summary, the results indicate that systematic application of operant techniques can be effective in modifying problem behaviors of brain-injured children and that teachers and parents can be taught to employ the techniques after a brief period of training. Further use of operant procedures in training children diagnosed as brain-injured would seem to be warranted. Additional studies designed to develop and refine the techniques for training relatively naive adults to utilize operant procedures in school settings should also prove fruitful.

REFERENCES

Allen, K. E., Hart, B. M., Buell, J. S., Harris, F. R. and Wolf, M. M.: Effects of social reinforcement on isolate behavior of a nursery school child. *Child Development, 35*:511–518, 1964.

Baer, D. M., Wolf, M. M. and Harris, R. R.: Effects of adult social reinforcement on child behavior. *Young Children, 20*:8–17, 1964.

Baer, D. M. and Wolf, M. M.: In Hess, Robert D. and Bear, Roberta M. (Eds.): *Early Education: Current Theory, Research and Practice.* Chicago, Aldine, 1966.

Bijou, S. W.: Experimental studies of child behavior, normal and deviant. In Krasner, L. and Ullman, L. P. (Eds.): *Research in Behavior Modification*. New York, Holt, Rinehart, and Winston, 1965.

Ferster, C. B.: Personal communication, 1967.

Hart, M., Allen, K. E., Buell, J. S., Harris, F. R. and Wolf, M. M.: Effects of social reinforcement on operant crying. *Journal of Experimental Child Psychology*, 1:145–153, 1964.

Johnston, M. S., Kelley, C. S., Buell, J. S., Harris, F. R. and Wolf, M. M.: Effects of positive social reinforcement on isolate behavior of a nursery school child. Unpublished study, Seattle, University of Washington, 1963.

Lewies, R. S., Strauss, A. A. and Lehtinen, L. H.: *The Other Child.* New York, Grune and Stratton, 1960.

Patterson, R.: An application of conditioning techniques to the control of a hyperactive child. In Ullman, L. P. and Krasner, L. (Eds.): *Case Studies in Behavior Modification*. New York, Holt, Rinehart and Winston, 1965.

Skinner, B. F.: *The Behavior of Organism.* New York, Appleton-Century-Crofts, 1938.

Staats, W.: A case in and a strategy for the extension of learning problems of human behavior. In Krasner, R. and Ullman, L. P. (Eds.): *Research in Behavior Modification*. New York, Holt, Rinehart, and Winston, 1965.

Strauss, A. A. and Lehtinen, L. E.: *Psychopathology and Education of the Brain-Injured Child.* New York, Grune and Stratton, 1947.

Wolf, M., Risley, T. and Mees, H.: Application of operant conditioning procedures to the behavior problems of an autistic child. *Behavior Research and Therapy*, 1:305–312, 1964.

Section Two
Respondent Principles in Education

T HE VAST MAJORITY of behavior modification studies with school children are based on operant conditioning principles. As demonstrated in the previous chapters, these have generally been quite successful. There is, however, another area of behavior modification which has been primarily concerned with the learning and relearning of emotional responses. Many behavior modification specialists believe that these responses are acquired via classical conditioning (respondent learning) and that this theoretical framework is also most appropriate for deriving methods to modify negative emotional reactions (e.g. fear and anxiety). Therefore, the first paper of this section, by Roden and Hapkiewicz has been specially written to (a) explain the theory, (b) outline the methods recently derived from the theory (often referred to as "systematic desensitization") and (c) give an example of how the methods may be implemented. Throughout the paper, the authors emphasize that school subjects and feelings or attitudes toward those subjects are acquired simultaneously. One cannot teach algebra to his students in the first half of class and wait until the second half of class to teach them to like it.

To date, most of the investigations using respondent conditioning techniques have been primarily concerned with the modification of negative emotional reactions rather than the development of positive emotions. This emphasis is reflected in the selection of readings for this section. Following the introductory paper are two illustrative case studies which were conducted in classroom settings. Kravetz and Forness demonstrate how respondent principles were used to successfully eliminate a child's fear of speaking in class. Furthermore, they point out that initial attempts using only reinforcement principles derived from operant conditioning were unsuccessful. The next study, reported by McNamara, describes the procedures used to modify a young girl's fear of the bathroom. Importantly, both of these case studies used respondent principles in combination with operant principles. They demonstrate that in actual practice, the two are difficult to separate and that their combined use is probably the most effective approach.

After scrutinizing the case studies, many practitioners may be satisfied that respondent conditioning techniques are effective. However, behavioral scientists (as well as some practitioners) are not convinced by such evidence and demand experimental verification, using controlled investigations, to demonstrate the effectiveness of these methods. The fourth paper of this section, by Davison, provides such evidence. His subjects were female undergraduates who exhibited extreme fear of snakes. Only those students in the experimental group which received all treatment components of systematic desensitization succeeded in overcoming their fear. This study also rules out the possibility that results were due to the students' expectations of success or that they were caused by some social relationship that developed between the counselors and students. As noted in the first chapter of this section, all of these studies pair a positive unconditioned stimulus (US), such as candy or "relaxation" feelings, with attenuated aspects of the fear stimulus. Students participating in these studies typically listed the kinds that made them anxious or fearful (e.g. aspects of situations related to test anxiety), rank order this list of items from least to most disturbing and received individual counseling. However, in the fifth paper, Emery and Krumboltz, working with test-anxious college students, demonstrate that these lists may be standardized and successfully incorporated into treatment programs for numerous individuals.

The study reported by Emery and Krumboltz at least implies that respondent conditioning procedures may be implemented on a group basis. In the final paper of this section, Kondas demonstrates that group conditioning procedures are both possible and effective. Both school children and college students treated by systematic desensitization reported feeling less anxious about tests and oral reports than students who did not participate in the group sessions. These findings suggest such programs may be successfully implemented in schools by counselors or school psychologists.

24

Respondent Learning and Classroom Practice

AUBREY H. RODEN and WALTER G. HAPKIEWICZ

THROUGHOUT THE HISTORY of education, considerable attention has been focused on the social and emotional development of children. It is generally agreed that schools should provide conditions conducive for growth in such "affective domains" and that such growth may be just as important, or even more important, than academic achievement. Thus, virtually all sets of educational objectives, whether verbal or written, have featured important affective elements. Yet, progress toward achieving these objectives, as opposed to merely describing them, has been poor. Few systematic educational experiences have been designed to promote achievement of these objectives and adequate instruments for the measurement of affective outcomes of instruction are practically nonexistent. The lack of progress in this area reflects the overwhelming emphasis in recent years on cognitive, rather than affective, objectives. This is particularly evident upon observing the frequency of use of such phrases as cognitive or academic achievement, and the relative scarcity of the term "affective achievement." For example, upon examining the typical school report card, we notice that John's grades for each subject are listed. He may be achieving B's in word attack skills and A's in reading comprehension. Teachers may also comment about discipline problems. Nowhere, however, is there space to report John's attitude toward school. His feelings about school subjects are rarely, if ever, assessed and reported to parents.

The emphasis upon cognitive objectives and the students' subsequent academic achievement is also evident in the training of teachers. If one reviews the books written to teach teachers how to write objectives, it becomes immediately obvious that virtually all of them deal with the cognitive domain, while few are applied toward the affective domain (Mager, 1968, is the major exception). This is true in spite of the fact that there are taxonomies available in both of these areas (Bloom *et al.*, 1956; Krathwohl *et al.*, 1964).

The mere fact that these domains are different is not meant to imply that they operate independent of one another—quite the contrary. For example, we can maintain a sharp focus looking only at the acquisition of reading skills for any child over any reasonable time period. This gives us great precision and is very useful only so long as we remember that we have temporarily suspended the broader reality, ignoring many of the other things happening while this segment of learning occurred. We tend to define the teachers' responsibility to the child almost exclusively in terms of information, skills, subject matter and related cognitive material. Actually, many other events and processes have to be put into the picture before we see a real three-dimensional child in our class.

Is it possible for one to learn to read using cognitive processes without necessarily learning to like or dislike reading itself, reading materials, reading instruction and perhaps even oneself as a reader or reading student? Can a student learn competencies such as reading, arithmetic, science or writing as an isolated segment of knowledge or skill, without learning attitudes toward these areas and materials? Common sense and experience tell us No.

This chapter is based on the premise that a significant proportion of school learning is emotional or affective and that much of this learning is in the form of classical conditioning or respondent learning.

RESPONDENT LEARNING

Respondent learning takes place when an organism is exposed to two stimuli which occur very nearly or actually as simultaneous events. One stimulus is quite potent affectively and has been termed an unconditioned stimulus (US). The US is capable of automatically eliciting an unlearned response called an uncondi-tioned response (UR). A simple example is a loud noise (US) resulting in an immediate withdrawal response (UR). A second stimulus is affectively neutral or very weak and produces no inherent reflex-like reaction in the organism when it is initially presented. It is termed a conditioned stimulus (CS). Almost anything can be a conditioned stimulus; for instance, showing a book, paper clip, pencil or rabbit, or saying the words "math" or "reading" to a child who had never been exposed to them before might result in some curiosity behavior or puzzled expressions, but would not produce a UR. These objects or statements are initially neutral for most children in most settings and can be referred to as conditioned stimuli (CS). When a potent US such as a loud noise is frequently paired with a CS such as a rabbit, eventually a response resembling the UR occurs when just the rabbit is presented. This is a learned response called a conditioned response (CR). Schematically it might appear as follows:

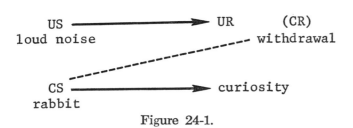

Figure 24-1.

This example is from Watson's (1920) classic study in which a little boy learned to fear a white rabbit. The boy (little Albert) (a) was initially indifferent to a white rabbit (CS); (b) he came to fear (CR) it after it had been (c) paired with a sudden loud noise (US) (d) which frightened (UR) him. These four basic elements, together with a learner, all put together with the proper timing and sequence, constitutes respondent learning. In brief, if you hit (US) a child over the head with a reading text (CS) for a period of time, he will tend to dislike (CR) both you (CS) and the book (CS). This is, admittedly, not a surprising consequence and hardly the kind of thing one needs a psychologist to point out. The examples outlined above represent a type of respondent conditioning called aversive conditioning. Naturally, the same procedures could be used to produce positive CR's simply by using positive, rather than aversive, US's. Yet, for all its obviousness, the previous examples reflect all too accurately the very backbone of educational practice.

An important consequence of the extremely simple and automatic quality of respondent learning is that it usually occurs without our being aware that it is happening. It goes largely unnoticed in classrooms. The learning is psychological rather than logical, it is nonrational; e.g. whatever little Albert happened to be attending to was what he learned to fear; it could have been almost anything. Volition is essentially irrelevant.

In many classrooms, an emotion such as fear of failure is activated and maintained during the learning period. If it shows signs of weakening, we frown, shout, demand public performance of some kind and in various ways insure its continuation. What this amounts to is a prolonged series of respondent learning sequences during the entire time the student is motivated to learn the cognitive material. It is as though we kept little Albert in the experimental situation for a full 50-minute period; he is shown the rabbit and frightened by the loud noise right at the beginning of the period. We then have an intensive course on the nature and nurture of rabbits. He is encouraged—required—to experience rabbits in as many ways as possible. He is closely observed and any time that his emotional state diminishes, i.e. he starts to relax, we maintain his motivation or interest with startling sounds. In effect, this is what Watson did with his experiments. The "class period" was relatively short, the subject matter was rabbits; the lesson plan was the experimental design; the measurable behavioral objective was the child's avoidant responses when faced with the sole exam item—a rabbit.

Make some simple substitutions in Watson's nursery school unit on rabbits. Bring it up to the first grade and change the curriculum from rabbits to reading. Fear and an urge to escape or avoid the situation will still be our unconditioned response; however, instead of a startling sound we will use *failure*. John wants to learn to read for many reasons. It is of fundamental importance to him. His parents and all of the other significant persons in his life expect him to learn to read, and they ask for progress reports on a regular basis. When classes start, some of the children can already read; others seem to be learning fast. He probably expects it of himself. The teacher gives various formal and informal tests designed to sort the children into at least three groups: readers, ready readers, not ready or "readiness group." After several weeks the stable class structure emerges and John can no longer avoid the horrifying facts. He is one of the goats, part of the chaff. This wise and powerful person, the teacher, has examined him and found him wanting. He is not quite sure which of his many inadequacies and shortcomings have been uncovered; he has plenty of them and has no doubt that she is right no matter how unjust it all seems. He lost without even knowing he was in a race. He tries to reassure himself with several thoughts: "Maybe tomorrow she will find that she has made a mistake and will put me in the other group, then I can read." "Tomorrow or very soon, she will teach me how to read. Then I will move up to that other group and everything will be alright." Meanwhile, back in the real world, teacher says, "Alright class, go to your reading groups." John sits down with the other unfortunates, takes his readiness materials in hand and proceeds to discriminate between drawings of ducks and ships by marking the appropriate picture while the privileged groups engage in ostentatious reading behaviors.

And so, the year moves on. George, who is experiencing success in reading, finds that the world is good and getting better in certain significant ways. He likes reading more and more. In fact, he likes school, his teacher, learning and himself. His parents are proud of him, and his mother is properly sympathetic with "poor John's" mother. He is beginning to read significant materials like some of the words in comics, advertisements and the words his parents spell out when the children are around. He finds that books and other written material have a certain attraction about them, and he is increasingly interested in handling them, finding words that he knows and guessing about some of the others. The more success he has, the more he wants to do and to be challenged. For John, things are going downhill. Some of the children in the readiness group find the activities quite satisfying. For them, it is not a failure situation. If John were fortunate, he would not see it as failure; or if he did, the aversive conditioning might be specifically attached to readiness materials themselves rather than reading. However, John is not so fortunate. He cannot read and does not appear to be making any progress. This is the bitter truth he has to report to himself and to others when he is asked to report on his status as a reader. With luck, his tenure in the readiness group will be short and his subsequent experience with reading will be so successful that it will wipe out the failure experience; we will follow this line of reasoning later. For now, John is undergoing aversive conditioning. Everything that has to do with reading is steadily increasing in potency as a negative stimulus. In addition to his inability to read, he now dreads the signs and symbols of reading. Truly, not all change is progress, nor all learning.

Show Albert a rabbit and he is frightened. Expose John to reading materials and/or experiences and he shows signs of anxiety. He may fidget, complain of stomach aches and ask to go home. He will probably rationalize e.g. "Reading isn't really important anyway. Not nearly as important as football or baseball. Wait till recess, I'll show them." However, in spite of the emotional Band-Aids, the process goes on. For Albert or George or John substitute any child anywhere anytime; for rabbits or reading substitute any school subject or activity. The message is the same. We cannot teach knowledge or skill without necessarily teaching affect at the same time in the same area. The issue is not whether or not we want to teach an emotional response; we will—it is explicit in the nature of the learner. The only real issue is whether we teach a positively eager approach or a dreadful avoidance.

Many educators and parents will, when presented with the reality of respondent learning, agree that it is important. This is immediately followed by several qualifications and disclaimers which can be summarized as: "Yes, the affective domain is important but let us keep our values straight. First things first. Teach the subject matter and whatever time is left over can be used for respondent learning."

When the average person is asked "What is the single most important objective for public education?" the most frequent response is "knowledge." Teachers, on the other hand know that knowledge is a means rather than an end. Most of us would tend to see choice as the heart of the educational enterprise.

But what does education have to do with choice in a general as well as a more specific way? If one were to compare the more educated individual with one who is significantly less educated, presumably the better-educated would, as compared with his less-educated colleague, be aware of a broader array of choices with more alternatives per choice; be able to bring a richer store of knowledge to bear on choices and alternatives; be more competent in choice-making processes; be more self-confident and willing to seek out choices and alternatives; be able to respond to some choices and select certain alternatives which the less well educated person would lack the competence of confidence to approach. We recognize that choice as a process has little meaning and no usefulness without knowledge.

However, competence and knowledge in our pupils is necessary but not sufficient. A positive affect for learning is also required. The ability to read is necessary by the time the child reaches the intermediate grades. However, if he is to acquire real competence as a reader, he must have the practice and growth which can only come from liking reading enough to seek it out on his own as an effective and desirable means for solving problems. By the time he leaves school, reading should be a kind of "cognitive hand"; something which you automatically use for work and pleasure, something taken for granted in either case. If the child learns to dislike reading early in his career, if he is convinced that he does not and cannot do it well, then he avoids it as he grows up and does not become as skillful with it as he could or should; it hurts a little, it is awkward and he takes too long to do a job that does not quite come up to his standards. At our best, we only provide a beginning in school. We teach only the fundamental skills and knowledge which will permit the subsequent development of mature competence. We make possible more choices and the competence to deal with them. Unfortunately we also teach children to fear and dislike some disciplines such as reading and mathematics to the point that they expect to fail. Such feelings may take on the quality of a self-fulfilling prophecy. An otherwise successful and bright third-grader who is convinced that he "is not good at" or "can not do" reading or mathematics can very quickly be proved right, at least in terms of performance criteria. The result in such a case can be the abolition of vast possibilities for choice, alternatives and methods. Unless successful remedial action is undertaken fairly rapidly, we may train yet another mathematical cripple. More arguments could be added at this point, but it hardly seems necessary. We all have experiences in which we fear and hate a subject and do not do well at it. In fact, we tend to fall progressively farther and farther behind, the longer we are exposed to it. If we can agree that we *learn* to fear or seek out, to like or dislike a subject, then we can approach the more promising questions such as: What can be done to control this kind of learning? and What can be done to overcome fear and dislike once it has been learned? It is this question to which we now turn.

MODIFICATION OF NEGATIVE ATTITUDES

It is clear from what has been said so far that for all practical purposes, cognitive and affective learning are related. The persistent pairing of *failure* with the learning setting tends to respondently condition the child *against* the salient features of the situation (e.g. self, subject matter, learning materials, teacher). Conversely, pairing a learning setting with persistent *success* experiences will tend to respondently condition the child to a *liking* for the salient features of the learning setting (e.g. self, subject matter, learning materials, teacher). While there are many seemingly logical arguments in favor of failure experiences as a desirable feature in education, if you review the immediately preceding two sentences, you know that the argument in support of planned failure experiences is not at all logical. Is it really good for a child to experience failure in order to get him ready for the "real world?" One can only speculate as to the reasons for the common acceptance of this notion. The fact that some children emerge from a failure-motivating system with reasonably intact self-confidence is more a testament to the individual child's ingenuity and competitive success than to the system itself. However, many teachers are faced with students who have already experienced destructive learning sequences. For example, what can he do with this seventh grader who is functioning, more or less, at the third-grade level in reading or arithmetic? He *can* read and has a fairly large sight vocabulary. He has fairly good word attack skills. By the standards of a century ago, he would be a good reader. However, he is convinced that he is a "non-reader;" he dislikes reading in all of its signs, symbols and activities. He is, in brief, negatively conditioned to reading. Failure and humiliation have been paired too many times with reading. He often gets the same gut response to reading that some people get when they see a snake. Even if the teacher had the time to work individually with each such student, which he does not, how can you provide reading materials appropriate to his reading level without losing the student? Third- and fourth-grade reading texts have been tried before, as have the materials with simple words but an older interest level. He knows those materials and they only serve to remind him of his deficiency when he knows that the other seventh graders are not reading "that kid stuff." From the upper elementary grades on, it is almost always safe to assume that the student has sufficient reading skills to be able to profit from practice, if they would only practice enough to increase their skill. The basic skills are there. What is needed is a reliable and practical US to pair with reading. Furthermore, he must read long enough for a positive US to begin making a difference.

Some years ago, Roden developed a procedure for working with seventh-grade students in an economically depressed urban area. The setting was three large sections, up to 45 students per class, Language Arts, each meeting for 1½ hours each day. The median reading level was approximately mid–third-grade. The lower 50 percent of each class was identified, and one-half of each of these groups were sent to remedial reading each day while the remaining half stayed in the room for the experimental treatment. The treatment itself was relatively simple: the last thirty minutes of each period was set aside for "reading time." The students were instructed "You must have a book open on the desk and you must keep quiet." The instructor had previously obtained several hundred books from various libraries which were stacked on the floor and around the windows. The books were largely picture books with relatively little written material—"baby books" suitable for early primary and preschool. The art work and in some cases the written material was excellent; they were carefully chosen and the instructor literally peddled the books to the classes. There was a 3x5 card file and whenever a student finished reading a book he came up, pulled his card and entered the name of the book on his card. Each Friday was oral report time with the instructor selecting the books to be reported on. No student was forced to read nor was any particular book forced on anyone. Initially it was supposed that the easy books would have to be urged on the better readers in some manner. This proved to be unnecessary, as the best readers selected the easier books first and read through them until only material at or above their reading level remained. At this point, they happily settled down to challenging reading. The poorest readers picked the most difficult books they could find. One can assume that all books were negative stimuli for them, with simple books having the greatest negative stimulus value. While more difficult books would still be negative, they had some offsetting status value. "If I'm going to be arrested for driving without a license in either case, then I would rather get it in a Rolls-Royce than in a student driving car or a rolling pile of junk." The actual situation developed quite different from what their past experiences had led them to expect. The teacher and all of the best readers were reading the easy books and seemed to enjoy them. The best readers were giving oral reports on the picture books and actually found something in them to report. However, this time the slow readers had more than enough reading skill to be able to compete with the best. All they had to do was pick up one of those books and read it in order to cease being different in a hurting way. It took almost eight weeks before the last of the slow readers finally got the message, put an ancient copy of *Tale of Two Cities* to one side of his desk and picked up a copy of *The Bear that Wasn't*. Some fifteen or twenty minutes later, the student who sounded like a bear made his noisy way through the file box by way of certifying to all that he had, By God, Read a Book. With only the expected occasional lapse the experimental group continued to read and function as fully certified readers. In brief, they were experiencing that powerful unconditioned stimulus, success, within the context of reading practice. The group of slow readers who had been going to remedial reading showed an increase in measured reading competence of about one month increment for each month in remedial reading. Had they been doing that well all along, there would have been no need for remedial reading. The slow readers who remained in the class for the experimental program showed somewhat more than two months of increment in reading achievement per month of program. Of more importance within the present context, these latter students began to really like reading and were the ones most likely to grumble if something interferred with the reading period. During parent conferences at the end of the year, these students were reported to be reading more than ever before and showing sharp increase in optimism about their academic futures.

To summarize the preceding study, the problem readers were assumed to have enough basic skills to be able to profit from practice, with their most fundamental problem consisting of a strong negative respondent conditioning to reading derived from years of experiencing failure and humiliation within the context of reading. The positive US selected for pairing with reading was success. The entire six months of experimental procedure was carried out simply to insure that reading (CS) and success (US) would be contiguous for sufficient pairings to cause positive conditioning toward reading (CR). The fact that the practice in reading was also a sufficient condition for increased skill in reading simply serves to further illustrate the necessary relationship between cognitive and affective processes. It would be a bitter day indeed if one had to choose one and reject the other.

The preceding example provides one possible application of the respondent learning model. A more recent experiment conducted by Early (1968) illustrates another application of this conceptually simple model. This study was a direct outgrowth of a series of studies designed to demonstrate that classical conditioning could establish and alter attitudes in classroom settings (Roden, 1962). Early was interested in increasing the number of social contacts of "isolate" children in fourth- and fifth-grade classes. These children rarely talked or played with their classmates. However, "talking with the children" or placing these children in charge of various class activities were certain to generate resistance from at least those students who react negatively toward any authority figure. One should keep in mind that Early's method is not presented as a general solution in any sense. Rather, it is an example of the kind of thing that can be tried with a good probability that the situation will at least be improved. The experimental procedure in this case was designed to increase the number of interpersonal contacts between isolates and other students using the following steps:

1. The children were given a list of words and were asked to indicate whether they liked, did not care about or disliked each word.
2. Ten of the words that they liked were chosen as positive US's and were printed on a card along with the name of one of the isolate children (CS)
3. The children were asked to memorize these pairs (as a part of a memory experiment)
4. Half of the class was shown the isolates' name paired with a neutral word (words that the children neither liked nor disliked)
5. The children were observed before and after the "memory experiment" to note any changes in the number of social contacts between isolates and other children.

These observations indicated that, indeed, the number of inter-actions involving the isolated children, whose names had been paired with positive words, increased. The frequency of social contacts for isolated children whose names had been paired with neutral words remained unchanged.

Thus it appears that the simple combination of pleasant words with the names of low-popularity children was sufficient to sig-nificantly effect a change in personal relationship between them and their classmates.

ELIMINATING FEAR AND ANXIETY

While the previous discussion was primarily concerned with methods used to modify negative attitudes toward learning, this final section deals with treatment techniques hat have been shown to be successful with children who exhibit more extreme maladap-tive emotional responses toward school learning.

Approximately fifty years has passed since the first American psychologists reported classical conditioning in children (Mateer, 1918; Watson and Rayner, 1920), and about 45 years ago, Mary Cover Jones (1924a, b) used classical conditioning as the theo-retical basis for a procedure oriented toward "the elimination of children's fear" (Jones, 1924a). At that time, it seemed to many psychologists that the long step had been taken in the affective domain. Rapid, sound progress could be expected now that there was an adequate general theory of affective learning and proto-type experiments had demonstrated the feasibility of external manipulation in children's affective learning and relearning. How-ever, up until the past few years, classical conditioning has re-ceived relatively little attention from American psychologists in general and educational psychologists in particular. There were few, if any, significant research efforts to expand or exploit the implications of these studies for emotional learning and develop-ment.

However, the advent of behavior modification within the past decade has accelerated the application of techniques first used by Jones (1924a). Today these techniques are generally referred to as "systematic desensitization" (after Wolpe, 1958) and are frequently used with children. For example, one of the most prevalent problems among students is test anxiety. As suggested by Emery and Krumboltz (1967), classical conditioning can be used to explain how this anxiety is learned. Children who do not meet the expectations of their parents are probably punished for receiving low grades on examinations. If punishment is repeatedly paired with examination performance, the child's anxiety level will probably increase when faced with test-like events in the future. Those events associated with test taking, such as studying or simply reading the word "test," may become conditioned stimuli (CS) and therefore capable of eliciting anxiety. Basically, the treatment involves pairing a positive stimulus (which elicits a positive emotional response) with the CS's for anxiety or fear. The procedure for desensitizing fear is as follows: (a) a hierarchy of fear situations is established, ranging from the least–to the most–fear-provoking situation; (b) the child is placed in each fearlike setting (least disturbing setting first) while (c) he simultaneously receives stimuli (e.g. candy or toys) which elicit positive emotional reactions. This is essentially the procedure used by Jones (1924a,b). However, it should be noted that others have discovered that this technique also works when the following modifications are made. Instead of the child actually being placed in attenuated fear-arousing situations (step b above), he may simply be asked to *imagine* that he is in that situation. Secondly, in place of stimuli such as candy and toys, the child is taught in one or two sessions how to achieve a state of *relaxation* which also serves to inhibit anxiety responses. As outlined above, step b involves the graded presentation of aversive conditioned stimuli (CS) which are paired with stronger unconditioned stimuli (step c). Since the stronger stimuli are selected for their capacity to evoke positive emotional reactions (e.g. the stimuli that are elicited when the child is completely relaxed), the child's anxiety responses are gradually replaced with positive or at least neutral responses. Another technique, usually referred to as "emotive imagery," is sometimes used instead of teaching a child how to relax. In using this technique, the child is simply asked to imagine his favorite hero (e.g. Superman) while items in his fear hierarchy are presented orally. Theoretically, such powerful, assertive heroes function as unconditioned stimuli and help the child overcome fear or anxiety.

While the use of relaxation and emotive imagery in desensitizing fear have been shown to be successful, these techniques appear to have limited application in schools, i.e. only school psychologists or counselors may be able to use them. However, a combination of the procedure originally outlined and those mentioned above would appear to be of widespread practical value to many teachers. That is, the technique of emotive imagery may be used while placing the child in the actual fear situations listed in the hierarchy (e.g. Kravetz and Forness, 1971). For example, one of the most common problems experienced by many young children, particularly boys, is oral reading. For those unfortunates, reading in front of the class is one of the most debilitating experiences they will ever face. Faced with such a child, what might the teacher do? In following procedures outlined above, the first thing that should be done is to identify the child's interests and strengths. Suppose that John feels particularly confident and comfortable in talking about rockets. He might be taken individually to a private sector of the room (screened off if possible) and asked to talk, all alone, into a tape recorder. Several means may be available to put him at ease in this situation. You may indicate that you are preparing stories for younger children and suggest that he imagine himself to be an astronaut and make up a short story. Or you may request his help in making up lessons to teach younger children about rockets. Having accomplished this, the length of stories or lessons he prepares may be increased and the following hierarchy introduced:

1. Speaks to teacher alone.
2. Speaks to best friend alone.
3. Speaks to teacher and friend together.
4. Speaks to small group while seated in a circle.
5. Speaks to small group while standing.
6. Speaks to entire class from his seat.
7. Addresses the class while standing at the front of the room.

Eventually, other topics or reading materials may be substituted for those initially used in aiding John to overcome his fear.

These problems are evident in some students of all ages, primary school through college. They become particularly acute when students avoid courses in which they must present topics to the class or perhaps in music class when they must sing (or play an instrument) solo to an audience. Hopefully, many of these fears can be recognized early and desensitization techniques implemented before these emotional states reach debilitating proportions.

SUMMARY

We have suggested that a significant proportion of school learning is affective and that much of this learning is in the form of classical conditioning. Furthermore, while emphasis in recent years has been on cognitive objectives and academic achievement, the cognitive and affective domains are interdepenent. We cannot teach school subjects without necessarily arousing emotional feelings and attitudes toward those same subjects. Although we inevitably teach students to like or dislike our various disciplines, only by teaching them to approach, rather than avoid, will we have successfully provided a wide array of choices from which they may select to develop mature competence. Finally we have suggested techniques from respondent learning theory which any teacher or counselor may use to change anxieties, fears or attitudes that children exhibit toward school content.

REFERENCES

Bloom, B. S. *et al.* (Eds.): *Taxonomy of Educational Objectives: Handbook I: Cognitive Domain.* New York, David McKay, 1956.

Early, C. J.: Attitude learning in children. *Journal of Educational Psychology, 59*:176–180, 1968.

Emery, J. R. and Krumboltz, J. D.: Standard versus individualized hierarchies in desensitization to reduce test anxiety. *Journal of Counseling Psychology, 14*:204–209, 1967.

Jones, M. C.: The elimination of children's fears. *Journal of Experimental Psychology, 7*:382–390, 1924a.

Jones, M. C.: A laboratory study of fear: The case of Peter. *Pedagogical Seminary, 31*:308–315, 1924b.

Krathwohl, D. R. *et al.* (Eds.): *Taxonomy of Educational Objectives: Handbook II: Affective Domain.* New York, David McKay, 1964.

Kravetz, R. J. and Forness, S. R.: The special classroom as a desensitization setting. *Exceptional Children, 37*:389–391, 1971.

Mager, R. F.: *Developing attitude toward learning.* Palo Alto, Fearon, 1968.

Mateer, F.: *Child Behavior, A Critical and Experimental Study of Young Children by the Method of Conditioned Reflexes.* Boston, Badger, 1918.

Roden, A. H.: A study of classical conditioning in some first grade classrooms. *American Psychologist, 17*:321, 1962.

Watson, J. B. and Rayner, R.: Conditioned emotional reactions. *Journal of Experimental Psychology, 3*:1–14, 1920.

Wolpe, J.: *Psychotherapy by reciprocal inhibition.* Stanford, Stanford University Press, 1958.

25

The Special Classroom as a
Desensitization Setting

RICHARD J. KRAVETZ and STEVEN R. FORNESS

IN THE TREATMENT of fear or anxiety responses in children, desensitization is a behavior modification technique used with considerable success (Lazarus and Abramovitz, 1962; Bandura, 1969; Patterson, 1965). The desensitization approach applies a hierarchy in which less threatening approximations of a feared situation are presented first. These are introduced in conjunction with a rewarding or relaxing stimulus. The child's response to this pleasant activity tends to overshadow his fear response. When the child demonstrates tolerance in that context, a slightly more threatening situation is introduced. The process is repeated at each level of the hierarchy until the child can eventually demonstrate assertive, nonfearful responses in the original fear producing situation.

Systematic application of desensitization has traditionally been restricted to the clinical setting. In this case, however, conditions merited its replication in a classroom context. The subject was a boy who had been hospitalized on the children's ward of a psychiatric hospital at the age of 6½. Referral at that time was prompted by his first grade teacher's report of his not talking in class. Medical and psychiatric evaluations at admission revealed no hearing problem, and the origin of the elective mutism was un-

NOTE: The research reported herein was performed in part pursuant to United States Office of Education Grant OEG-0-8-003019(031) and National Institute of Child Health and Development Grant HD 04612.

known. Achievement testing and academic performance showed him to be at or above grade level in most subjects. School prognosis, however, appeared poor, since even in the sheltered environment of the inpatient school classroom with its individualized instruction the child's only mode of communication was tugging the teacher's sleeve or, in rare instances, whispering in her ear. The boy also avoided interaction with classroom peers. Little progress was made during a year of treatment in conventional psychotherapy or in the inpatient school program, using token reinforcement.

The school plan during the year of hospitalization had focused on resolving the behavioral problem, i.e. the child's apparent deficiency in oral communication. Both primary and social reinforcement had been used for any oral response. Slow progress with conventional psychotherapy and in the token-reinforcement classroom appeared to warrant use of modified desensitization techniques.

PROCEDURE

The program took place within an engineered classroom (Hewett, 1968). In this type of classroom, the child works on individualized assignments and receives checkmarks for doing the work and following the behavioral rules of the classroom. Checkmarks are exchanged for candy or small toys at the end of each week. Three months prior to the program, the investigator had established initial contact with the boy in the same classroom with considerable rapport.

Before the desensitization process began, there were two sessions in which the investigator, functioning as a teaching aide in the classroom, assisted the child with a mathematics assignment requiring only minimal verbal exchange. Three sessions followed in which the boy was required to dictate a story to the investigator. The child received five checkmarks for each sentence dictated. He was allowed to whisper the story in the investigator's ear. However, in the last two sessions, the subject was required to read the finished story into a tape recorder with the instructions, "See how far up you can get the volume needle to go." After the last session, the investigator asked the boy to stand in front of the class and read the same story in order to establish some estimate of the boy's performance in front of a group. The child stood in front of the class but remained motionless and silent. After 30 seconds, he was told he did not have to continue. The investigator complimented the boy on his attempt and suggested that some day he might wish to try again.

Since an impasse had apparently been reached, it was obvious that some other approach was necessary. After discussion with hospital staff, it was decided that some form of systematic desensitization might well be the treatment choice.

Twelve sessions—two per week—were devoted to desensitization treatment. The first two sessions took place in a study room adjacent to the classroom. The investigator began by asking the child about his favorite heroes, eventually suggesting the names of folk heroes with which he might identify. The boy expressed reluctance to identify with assertive hero images, but the investigator verbally reinforced the child's expressed interest in Paul Bunyan, the legendary lumberjack, and suggested that he read the story of Paul Bunyan during the next session. The hero image was introduced and maintained as a supportive figure throughout the remainder of the treatment period. Use of a supportive or emotive image is described by Lazarus and Abramovitz (1962).

In the second session, discussion with the child of situations which involved oral communication enabled the investigator to arrive at a hierarchy of fearful situations. The hierarchy was comprised of seven steps, three of which were repeated to reinforce fully the assertive responses.

The hierarchy with repeated steps indicated is given below:

1. Reading alone to investigator.
2. Reading alone to roommate.
3. Reading to two classroom aides (repeated).
4. Reading to teacher and classroom aides (repeated).
5. Reading to teacher, classroom aides and small group of classroom peers (repeated).
6. Reading to entire class.
7. Asking question or making comment at weekly ward meeting when all patients, teachers and staff were present.

Over each of the remaining sessions, the boy was deconditioned to a situation on the hierarchy, then immediately placed in that situation and reinforced for adaptive responing. A typical session from step 4 of the hierarchy is described below.

Before the class period began, the investigator discussed with the boy's teacher the plan for the hour's treatment. The goal was to have the boy read a Paul Bunyan story and answer relevant questions in front of a group of five adults (teacher and classroom aides). Approximately one-half hour before the structured interaction was to begin, the boy and the investigator went into a small room adjacent to the classroom. The investigator began discussing how big, strong and assertive Paul Bunyan was and asked the boy to close his eyes and dream that he was sitting among a group consisting of the teacher and classroom aides (mentioned by name). Asked how he felt, the boy made no response, but he looked distressed. At this point, the investigator told the boy, "This time imagine that your big, strong friend Paul Bunyan is there standing next to you in the group and imagine that Paul had just told all the teachers that you were a good friend of his and that they had better pay close attention to what you were going to say." At this point, a smile appeared on the boy's face. The investigator asked him to open his eyes and proceeded to discuss the fact that Paul Bunyan would be extremely interested in hearing the boy read a story. The investigator then told the boy that if he read three pages in the above situation and answered all the questions that were asked, that he could play with the electric train during free time.

The adults formed a circle of chairs next to the wall where the boy's picture of Paul Bunyan hung. The boy sat next to the picture, and the investigator observed from a distance. The teacher reported afterwards that the boy had read three pages of the story, held up the book so that they could see the pictures, and answered questions loudly and clearly enough so most of what he said was understood. The investigator then praised the boy and allowed him to play with the electric train.

The procedure for each session consisted of specific steps, as illustrated above. First the boy was asked to imagine the fearful situation. The emotive image of Paul Bunyan was then introduced into the imaginary situation to overcome unassertive response tendencies. When preliminary deconditioning indicated relaxation, the investigator set agreeable reinforcement contingencies, and the boy then confronted the actual situation. Afterwards, he received reinforcement in the form of checkmarks or free time.

The last step on the hierarchy was achieved 6 weeks after the study began. At the weekly patient-staff meeting, the boy raised his hand and made easily audible comments on two separate occasions, the first time he had done so since his admission to the hospital. At the time of this writing, the boy has been discharged and is reportedly functioning well in a regular public school classroom.

DISCUSSION

Although it was apparent prior to systematic desensitization that the boy was able to speak in non–anxiety-provoking situations, this ability did not generalize to more threatening situations. The difference between speaking into a tape recorder and speaking in front of a group was too great to allow for generalization, since contextual cues were dissimilar. When systematic desensitization was initiated, people were gradually introduced. Assertive responses learned at one step of the hierarchy were more likely to transfer to the next, since the new setting contained only a few more people than that in which the boy had already demonstrated competence. The boy was confronted at each step with familiar cues associated with assertive responses and only a minimal number of new cues which might elicit anxiety responses.

Mention should be made of the combined use of desensitization and reinforcement techniques, an approach previously used by Patterson (1965). In the classroom, the boy had been receiving checkmarks or free time contingent on behavior or academic performance and continued to receive them during the desensitization. It is impossible to ferret our differential effects and maintain that desensitization was exclusively responsible for success. Reinforcement techniques alone, however, had done little to resolve the fear of speaking. Combined use of desensitization and reinforcement, as outlined by Bandura (1969), appeared to be necessary for maximum generalization to natural settings.

Another important aspect of the treatment centered around classroom routine. Studying the life of Paul Bunyan and drawing pictures of him were part of assigned academic tasks in the classroom and served as the focal point of a unit of academic instruction. Continued exposure tended to enhance the Bunyan image by focusing on such characteristics as "strong," "big" and "unafraid." This exposure gave the boy further opportunity to identify with a model incompatible with his own unassertive demeanor. Once assertive responses began to be demonstrated, reliance on the Paul Bunyan image was diminished and social reinforcement was sufficient to maintain assertiveness.

Desensitization, like other behavior modification teachniques, is a powerful tool and extreme care should be taken in its application. In the present case, it appeared warranted, since despite good academic performance, prognosis for success in school was decidedly poor until the behavioral deficit was removed. This technique would appear to apply in other areas of special education where generalization of learned responses to other settings is critical.

REFERENCES

Bandura, A.: *Principles of Behavior Modification.* New York, Holt, Rinehart & Winston, 1969.

Hewett, F.: *The Emotionally Disturbed Child in the Classroom.* Boston, Allyn & Bacon, 1968.

Lazarus, A. and Abramovitz, A.: The use of "emotive imagery" in the treatment of children's phobias. *Journal of Mental Science, 108:* 191–195, 1962.

Patterson, G.: A learning theory approach to the treatment of the school phobic child. In Ullmann, L. and Krasner, L. (Eds.): *Case Studies in Behavior Modification.* New York, Holt, Rinehart and Winston, 1965.

26

Behavior Therapy in the Classroom: A Case Report

J. Regis McNamara

This article describes the development, procedures and outcome of a behavior modification program on a preschool child enrolled in Head Start. The program used reciprocal inhibition techniques and shaping procedures to treat a five-year-old Negro girl with a bathroom phobia. Individual sessions in the classroom while the other children were on the playground utilized sequential presentation of fear associated cues in the presence of preferred toys and candy. During regular class routines, the teacher established body contact through hand holding in the bathroom to allay the fear. No fear combined with positive individual use of the bathroom was seen at the termination of the program. A three-month follow-up indicated short-term stability of the new positive bathroom behavior. Discussion centers upon the therapeutic effectiveness of such a program and its workability in a school setting.

IN A RECENT article, Woody (1966) discussed the application of behavioral stratagems in dealing with behavioral problems of children in school. The article dealt with the kinds of behavioral modification techniques that can be used by a psychologist functioning within a school setting. It should be noted, however, that these procedures are somewhat limited and do not adequately reflect the diversity of methods that could be potentially at the school psychologist's disposal. These techniques are multifaceted

NOTE: This is an amended version of a paper presented at a meeting of the Florida Psychological Association in May, 1968, Clearwater Beach, Florida.

From the *Journal of School Psychology*, 1:48–51, 1968–69. Copyright 1968, 1969 by the Journal of School Psychology Inc. Reprinted with permission of author and publisher.

and have been given a more extensive exposition elsewhere (Rachman, 1963; Ullman and Krasner, 1966). The work of Holmes (1966) represents an incipient attempt by the school psychologist to treat school behavior problems with the direct application of the major learning techniques. The present case report demonstrates the feasibility of behavioral techniques in treating a bathroom phobia of a preschool child in a school setting.

A behavior therapist views a phobia as a learned response, subject to the same principles of learning and unlearning as any other response (Wolpe, 1958) and, ontologically, equally related to the development of fear responses in children and adults alike (Rachman and Costello, 1961). One of the earliest illustrations of behavior therapy in practice was provided by Jones (1924). One of her techniques for eliminating a child's (Peter) fear of rabbits was the introduction of a powerful "pleasant stimulus," food, in the presence of the rabbit. The new response (eating) elicited by the food served to develop positive responses associated with the food, thus effectively inhibiting the fear response. Other methods (Jersild & Holmes, 1935) have been advocated for dealing with children's fears, but the reciprocal inhibition principle (Wolpe, 1958) seems to have gained the widest acceptance.

The present investigation primarily utilized the reciprocal inhibition method (i.e. positive reinforcement of a response antagonistic to fear in the presence of the stimulus that ordinarily generates the fear) in conjunction with the Skinnerian method (1953) of conditioning via approximations. In this case report, candy M&M's and affective responses toward preferred toys were used to elicit responses incompatible with fear. Candy was chosen for its easy manipulability; toys were chosen for their effectiveness in eliciting responses incompatible with fear in another case (Bentler, 1962).

CASE HISTORY

Brenda, a five-year, five-month-old Negro girl enrolled in Head Start, was first brought to the attention of the psychologist in a case conference at a Head Start center. She was described by her teacher as being very afraid of going to the bathroom alone, refusing to go unless accompanied by one or more adults. It was further related that Brenda would sometimes spontaneously verbalize that the "Boogie Man" would get her in there—meaning in the bathroom. The teacher commented that this had been a persistent problem since Brenda entered school and that the severity of the problem had not diminished, although the child had been in the program for three months. Repeated observations made by the psychologist suggested that the problem was not related to attention-getting factors or personal-social factors in the immediate situation. A conference with the mother provided no clear-cut information about the behavior in question at home. However, further investigation by the social worker on the case revealed that occasionally members of the family would tell her that the "Boogie Man" would get her if she were not good. It thus seemed, on the basis of the history and the ongoing behavior of the child, that this fear was a learned unadaptive response to a bathroom-like situation: the initial fear-provoking event had already occurred (probably as a result of her being frightened in a confined situation) and had generalized to the bathroom at school.

PROCEDURE

Brenda's classroom was a self-enclosed portable unit, consisting of an air-conditioned, practically windowless, semicarpeted, amply spaced preschool room and an adjoining bathroom. Arrangements were made with the teacher to take the children out to play on the playground while the psychologist saw the child in the room. Each session lasted 15 minutes and the sessions extended over a period of three weeks. The teacher and the aides in the room were also instructed to go into the bathroom with her, to hold her hand, to be warm and acceptant toward her while she was there and to leave the door fully open. This procedure with the teacher, extrapolated from the work of Harlow and Zimmerman (1959), complemented the individual sessions. It was thought that body contact established through hand holding with a warm, accepting mother figure would inhibit the phobic response, much as it had with infant monkeys in a strange environment when they clung to their terrycloth monkey mothers. The teacher and aide served in another valuable way: they noted each morning the toys that Brenda played with and set them aside for use in the individual sessions.

The modification program took place in several stages. First, systematic sequencing of fear-associated cues in the presence of the fear-inhibiting stimuli were presented. The component parts of the situation precipitating the fear response were hypothesized to be the closed space and the toilet. Therefore, a model bathroom situation was set up in the room in alignment with the bathroom but some 15 feet from it. A six-foot-square area was initially set off by four small rectangular dividers. The toys that the child had played with that morning were scattered in the area along with small plastic trays of candy. The child was initially introduced to the situation by the therapist who told her that they were going on a candy hunt. Once inside the model area, the therapist played with her while both ate the candy. This procedure continued over the first two sessions until no apprehension was noted. During the next two sessions, a cardboard toilet was introduced into the model area. When the child became accustomed to this new situation (sessions 3 and 4), it was decided to move toward the toilet itself. Three large outdoor play blocks were set in a line running from the model area into the bathroom. On and around each block was a differential distribution of candy and toys, with the greatest amount on the block in the bathroom itself. The child was introduced into the bare model area and told that the candy and toys must be somewhere else. Then the therapist and child went to the first block nearest the play area and lingered in that area to play with the toys and eat the candy. The therapist also told the child, "Maybe if you sit on the block you will get some more candy." This procedure was repeated for all three blocks until the child was sitting on the block in the bathroom (sessions 5 and 6).

It should be noted at this juncture that rewarding the sitting behavior on the blocks outside the bathroom would help shape the toilet-sitting behavior itself. For the next two sessions (7 and 8), two blocks were used: one in the bathroom itself and one on the edge of the bathroom and room. While sitting on the block in the bathroom, the child was told, "Maybe you will get candy for sitting on the paddy seat and wetting in the paddy." The child sat on the toilet and was rewarded with candy but did not immediately void. While sitting there, she received more candy and finally urinated. Immediately after she finished voiding, the therapist dispensed some final candy as a reward. This behavior was repeated a number of times throughout the final sessions.

At this point, it was thought that sufficient fear reduction had taken place to begin a gradual withdrawal of adults from the bathroom. The teacher and aides were instructed to take Brenda to the bathroom but not to hold her hand. Initially, they merely stood beside her. Later, they gradually started withdrawing physically from the situation and started closing the door. During sessions 9, 10 and 11, one block remained in the bathroom. The therapist started off in full visual sight of the child with the door fully open. He then gradually moved out of the child's visual field but maintained constant voice communication with her. During each of these sessions, the door was gradually closed and left open only wide enough for the therapist to give candy to the child. The modification program was concluded at the end of session 11. The girl was spontaneously going to the bathroom alone, both in the individual session and during regular class, and closing the door behind her. A follow-up study three months later indicated no remission of symptomatology.

DISCUSSION

Although behavioral change occurred with therapeutic intervention, it would be premature—in an experimental sense—to ascribe the change entirely to the modification program. In order to demonstrate the real effect that this procedure had on the behavior in question, it would have been advisable to reinitiate the bathroom fear, note the new responses and then reintroduce the aforementioned procedures. This, in effect, would have demonstrated a more substantial causal connection between the treatment techniques and the behavioral change. As it stands, the relationship can only be inferred. It should be noted, however, that this exposition of clinical intervention in a special setting is not a demonstration in experimental rigor. Perhaps the real value of this program, aside from the treatment aspects, was that it engendered cooperation among the people involved (principal, teacher, aides and psychologist) and that it demonstrated the feasibility of a modification program in a school setting.

REFERENCES

Bentler, P. M.: An infant's phobia treated with reciprocal inhibition therapy. *Journal of Child Psychology and Psychiatry, 3*:185–189, 1962.

Harlow, H. F. and Zimmerman, R. R.: Affectional responses in the infant monkey. *Science, 130*:421–432, 1959.

Holmes, D. S.: The application of learning theory to the treatment of a school behavior problem: A case study. *Psychology in the Schools, 3*:355–359, 1966.

Jersild, A. T. and Homes, F. B.: Methods of overcoming children's fears. *Journal of Psychology, 1*:75–104, 1935.

Jones, M. A.: A laboratory study of fear: The case of Peter. *Pedagogical Seminar, 31*:308–315, 1924.

Rachman, S.: Introduction to behavior therapy. *Behavioral Research and Therapy, 1*:3–15, 1963.

Rachman, S. and Costello, C. G.: The aetiology and treatment of children's phobia: A review. *American Journal of Psychiatry, 118*:97–105, 1961.

Skinner, B. F.: *Science and Human Behavior.* New York, Macmillan, 1953.

Ullman, L. P. and Krasner, L.: *Case Studies in Behavior Modification.* New York, Holt, Rinehart and Winston, 1966.

Wolpe, J.: *Psychotherapy by Reciprocal Inhibition.* Stanford, Stanford University Press, 1958.

Woody, R. H.: Behavior therapy and school psychology. *Journal of School Psychology, 4*:1–14, 1966.

27

Systematic Desensitization as a Counter-Conditioning Process

GERALD C. DAVISON

Systematic desensitization, demonstrated in both clinical and experimental studies to reduce avoidance behavior, entails the contiguous pairing of aversive imaginal stimuli with anxiety-competing relaxation. If, as is widely assumed, the efficacy of the procedure derives from a genuine counterconditioning process, a disruption of the pairing between graded aversive stimuli and relaxation should render the technique ineffective in modifying avoidance behavior. This hypothesis was strongly confirmed: significant reduction in avoidance behavior was observed only in desensitization S's, with none occurring either in yoked S's for whom relaxation was paired with irrelevant stimuli or in yoked S's who were gradually exposed to the imaginal aversive stimuli without relaxation. Other theoretical issues were raised, especially the problem of transfer from imaginal to actual stimulus situations.

R̲ECENT YEARS HAVE witnessed increasing application of the systematic desensitization procedure, as developed by Wolpe (1958), to the modification of a wide range of neurotic disorders. In this therapeutic method, the client is deeply relaxed and then instructed to imagine scenes from a hierarchy of anxiety-provoking

NOTE: This paper is based on the author's doctoral dissertation written at Stanford University under Albert Bandura, whose invaluable advice and direction at every stage of the research and composition he is pleased to acknowledge. For their aid and encouragement, sincere thanks are also rendered to Arnold A. Lazarus and Gordon L. Paul. The author is especially grateful to O. B. Neresen, who made available both the physical facilities and human resources at Foothill Junior College, Los Altos, California.

From the *Journal of Abnormal Psychology,* 73:91–99, 1968. Copyright 1968 by the American Psychological Association. Reprinted with permission of the author and publisher.

stimuli. Initially he is asked to imagine the weakest item in the list and, if relaxation is unimpaired, is gradually presented incremental degrees of aversive stimuli until eventually he is completely desensitized to the most upsetting scene in the anxiety hierarchy.

In numerous publications, both Wolpe (1952, 1958) and other clinical workers (Geer, 1964; Lang, 1965; Lazarus, 1963; Lazarus and Rachman, 1957; Rachman, 1959) have claimed a high degree of success in eliminating diverse forms of anxiety disorders by means of this therapeutic technique.

These clinical claims of efficacy find some support in recent laboratory investigations conducted under more controlled conditions and with more objective assessment of therapeutic outcomes (Lang and Lazovik, 1963; Lang et al., 1965; Lazarus, 1961; Paul, 1966; Paul and Shannon, 1966). Although results from these experiments have confirmed the effectiveness of systematic desensitization, they do not provide direct information on the relative contributions to the observed outcomes of the different variables in the treatment procedure (e.g. relaxation, graded exposure to aversive stimuli, temporal contiguity of stimulus events). Moreover, the learning process governing the behavioral changes has not been adequately elucidated. There is some suggestive evidence from Lang et al. (1965) that extensive contact with an E, along with relaxation training, does not effect behavior change. However, one can raise questions about the suitability of their control for relaxation, inasmuch as S's in this condition began imagining snake-aversive items but were then led away from this theme by means of subtle manipulation of content by E. It is possible that this imaginal snake avoidance may have counteracted the nonspecific effects built into the control.

Wolpe's (1958) theoretical formulation of the desensitization process as "reciprocal inhibition" is based on Hull's (1943) drive-reduction theory of classical conditioning, a fatigue theory of extinction ("conditioned inhibition") and Sherrington's (1906) concept of reciprocal inhibition, whereby the evocation of one reflex suppresses the evocation of other reflexes. The conditions which Wolpe (1958) specified for the occurrence of reciprocal inhibition were succinctly stated in his basic principle: "If a re-sponse antagonistic to anxiety can be made to occur in the pres-ence of anxiety-evoking stimuli so that it is accompanied by a complete or partial suppression of the anxiety responses, the bond between these stimuli and the anxiety responses will be weakened" (p. 71). This statement appears indistinguishable from Guthrie's (1952) view of counterconditioning, according to which notion the elimination of a response can be achieved by eliciting a strong incompatible response in the presence of cues that ordinarily elicit the undesirable behavior: "Here . . . the stimulus is present, but other responses are present shutting out the former response, and the stimulus becomes a conditioner of these and an inhibitor of its former response" (p. 62). Wolpe, in fact, used the terms "reciprocal inhibition" and "countercondi-tioning" interchangeably but clearly indicated a preference for the former in view of his inferences about the neurological process accounting for the observed changes in behavior. However, aside from the fact that he has as yet provided no independent evidence for the existence of reciprocal inhibition at the complex behavioral level that he is dealing with, one must be wary of basing a neuro-logical hypothesis, albeit an ingenious one, upon a behavioral sys-tem which itself has been shown to have serious shortcomings (Gleitman *et al.*, 1954; Kimble, 1961; Lawrence and Festinger, 1962; Mowrer, 1960; Solomon and Brush, 1956).

At the present time, it appears both unnecessary and pre-mature to "explain" behavioral phenomena in terms of an under-lying neural process whose existence is inferable solely from the very psychological data which it is invoked to explain. To me, it appears to be more fruitful to stay closer to the empirical data and to conceptualize the process of systematic desensitization in terms of counterconditioning, according to which the neutraliza-tion of aversive stimuli results from the evocation of incompatible responses which are strong enough to supersede anxiety reactions to these stimuli (cf. Bandura, 1969).

PROBLEM

In view of the fact that the behavioral outcomes associated with systematic desensitization are assumed to result from counterconditioning, evidence that such a process does in fact occur is particularly essential (cf. Breger and McGaugh, 1965). To the extent that desensitization involves counterconditioning, the contiguous association of graded anxiety-provoking stimuli and incompatible relaxation responses would constitute a necessary condition for fear reduction. It is possible, however, that the favorable outcomes produced by this method are primarily attributable to relaxation alone, to the gradual exposure to aversive stimuli or to nonspecific relationship factors. The present experiment was therefore designed to test directly the hypothesis that systematic desensitization involves a genuine counterconditioning process.

The *S*'s were individually matched in terms of strength of their snake-avoidance behavior and assigned to one of four conditions. For one group of *S*'s (desensitization), a graded series of aversive stimuli was contiguously paired in imagination with deep muscle relaxation, as in the standard clinical technique. The *S*'s in a second group participated in a "pseudodesensitization" treatment that was identical to the first procedure except that the content of the imaginal stimuli paired with relaxation was essentially neutral and completely irrelevant to snakes. This group provided a control for the effects of relationship factors, expectations of beneficial outcomes and relaxation per se. A third group (exposure) was presented the same series of graded aversive items but in the absence of deep relaxation. This condition served as a control for the effects of mere repeated exposure to the aversive stimuli. A fourth group (no treatment) participated only in the pre-treatment and posttreatment assessments of snake avoidance.

In order to ensure comparability of stimulus events, *S*'s in the pseudodesensitization and exposure groups were *yoked* to their matched partners in the desensitization group, whose progress determined the number of treatment sessions, the duration of each session, the number of stimulus exposures per session and the duration of each exposure.

Within three days following the completion of treatment, all *S*'s were tested for snake avoidance as well as for the amount of anxiety accompanying each approach response.

On the assumption that the temporal conjunction of relaxation and anxiety-provoking stimuli is essential for change, it was predicted that only S's in the desensitization condition would display significant decrements in avoidance behavior and would also be superior in this respect to S's in the three control groups.

METHOD

Subjects

The S's were 28 female volunteers drawn from introductory psychology courses at a junior college. Students who reported themselves very much afraid of nonpoisonous snakes were asked to assist in a study investigating procedures for eliminating common fears. In order to minimize suggestive effects, the project was presented as an experiment rather than as a clinical study, and no claims were made for the efficacy of the procedure to be employed. To reduce further the development of strong expectation of beneficial outcomes, which might in itself produce some positive change, E was introduced as a graduate student rather than as an experienced psychotherapist. To some extent, the results from all the experiments cited above might have been confounded by these variables.

Pretreatment and Posttreatment Assessments of Avoidance Behavior

These assessments were conducted by an E (E_1) who did not participate in the treatment phases of the study and had no knowledge of the conditions to which S's were assigned. The avoidance test was similar to that employed by Lang and Lazovik (1963) except for several important changes that were introduced in order to provide a more stringent and sensitive test of the efficacy of the various treatment procedures. First, whereas Lang and Lazovik used essentially a 3-item test, the present behavioral test consisted of 13 items requiring progressively more intimate interaction with the snake (e.g. placing a gloved hand against the glass near the snake, reaching into the cage and touching the snake once, culminating with holding the snake barehanded for 30 seconds). Second, rather than obtaining a single overall estimate of felt anxiety following the entire approach test, the examiner in the present study asked S to rate herself on a 10-point scale following the successful performance of each task. Third, the examiner stood at all times no closer than 2 feet from the cage, whereas the tester in Lang and Lazovik's study touched and held the snake before requesting an S to do so. Evidence that avoidance behavior can be reduced through observation of modeled approach responses (Bandura *et al.*, 1967) suggests that the behavioral changes obtained by Lang and Lazovik may reflect the effects of both vicarious extinction and counter-conditioning via systematic desensitization.

Any S who, on the pretreatment assessments, succeeded in touch the snake barehanded was excluded from the study. Eligible S's were matched individually on the basis of their approach behavior and then assigned randomly to the different treatment conditions so as to constitute "clusters" of equally avoidant S's across groups. Initially it had been planned to include an equal number of matched S's in the no-treatment control group. However, since preliminary findings, as well as data reported by Lang and Lazovik (1963), revealed virtually no changes in nontreated controls, it was decided to enlarge the size of the three treatment conditions. Therefore, eight S's were assigned to each of the three treatment groups, while the nontreated control group contained four cases. The experimental design is summarized in Table 27-1.

TABLE 27-1
SUMMARY OF EXPERIMENTAL DESIGN

Group	Pretreatment assessment (E_1)	Treatment procedure (E_2)	Posttreatment assessment (E_3)
Desensitization *	Avoidance test with anxiety self-reports	Relaxation paired with graded aversive stimuli	Avoidance test with anxiety self-reports
Pseudodesensitization*	Same	Relaxation paired with snake-irrelevant stimuli	Same
Exposure *	Same	Exposure to graded aversive stimuli without relaxation	Same
No treatment **	Same	No treatment	Same

* $N = 8$.
** $N = 4$.

Treatment Procedures

The treatment sessions were conducted in a room other than the one in which the avoidance behavior was measured. The *S*'s in conditions employing relaxation training reclined in a lounger, whereas for *S*'s in the exposure group the chair was set in an upright position to minimize the development of relaxed states.

Relaxation Paired with Graded Aversive Stimuli (Systematic Desensitization)

During the first session, these *S*'s received training in deep muscular relaxation by means of a 30-minute tape recording consisting of instructions to tense and to relax alternately the various muscle groups of the body, interspersed with suggestions of heaviness, calm and relaxation. This procedure which I used earlier (Davison, 1965b), is based on Lazarus' (1963) accelerated training in Jacobsonian relaxation and is very similar to the technique used by Paul (1966).

In the second session, *S*'s ranked 26 cards, each describing snake scenes, in order of increasing aversiveness; for example, "Picking up and handling a toy snake," "Standing in front of the cage, looking down at the snake through the wire cover, and it is moving around a little," "Barehanded, picking the snake up, and it is moving around." The desensitization procedure, modeled after Lazarus (1963), Paul (1966) and Wolpe (1961), was administered in a standardized fashion, with a criterion of 15 seconds without signaling anxiety on each item. (For specifics of the procedure, see Davison, 1965a.) A maximum of nine sessions, each lasting about 45 minutes, was allowed for completing the anxiety hierarchy.

Relaxation Paired with Snake-Irrelevant Stimuli (Pseudodesensitization)

The *S*'s assigned to this group received the same type and amount of relaxation training as *S*'s in the above-mentioned group. Similarly, in the second session they also ranked 26 stimulus items, except that the depicted scenes were entirely unrelated to snakes. Because of the widespread belief that exploration of childhood experiences may be important in alleviating objectively unrealistic fears, it was decided to employ descriptions of common childhood events, which S's were asked to rank chronologically. Some of the items were essentially neutral in content ("You are about age six, and your family is discussing where to go for a ride on Sunday afternoon, at the dinner table."), while the others had mild affective properties ("You are about five years old, and you are sitting on the floor looking sadly at a toy that you have just broken."). The use of generic content thus made it possible to use snake-irrelevant stimuli without reducing the credibility of the treatment procedure.

As in the desensitization condition, S's were deeply relaxed and asked to imagine vividly each scene presented by the E until told to discontinue the visualization. Each S in this condition, it will be recalled, was yoked to her matched partner in the desensitization group, whose progress defined the number of treatment sessions, the length of each session, as well as the number and duration of each imaginal exposure. Thus, S's undergoing pseudodesensitization received the same number and duration of pairings during each session as their desensitization mates, with the important exception that snake-irrelevant stimuli were contiguously associated with relaxation.

Exposure to Graded Aversive Stimuli Without Relaxation (Exposure)

The S's in this group were administered the same series of snake-aversive stimuli in the same order and for the same duration as determined by their respective partners in the desensitization group to whom they were yoked. However, exposure S's received no relaxation training (hence, had one session less with E), nor did they engage in anxiety-competing relaxation while visualizing the aversive situations. Because of the yoking requirements, on those occasions when S's signaled anxiety, they were instructed to maintain the images until E asked them to discontinue. Cooperation in this obviously unpleasant task was obtained through friendly but cogent reminders that such visualization was important for the experimental design.

No Treatment Group

The S's assigned to this group merely participated in the assessments of avoidance behavior at the same time as their matched partners in the desensitization condition.

TABLE 27-2

CHANGES IN SNAKE-APPROACH BEHAVIOR DISPLAYED BY SUBJECTS IN EACH OF THE TREATMENT CONDITIONS

| Matched Cluster | Condition | | | |
	Desensitization	Pseudo-desensitization	Exposure	No treatment
1	3	2	2	0
2	3	−1	0	....
3	6	0	−1	−1
4	5	1	−5	0
5	0	1	2	....
6	6	8	1	0
7	12	0	0	....
8	7	1	1	....
M	5.25	1.50	0.0	−0.25

RESULTS

Table 27-2 presents the change scores in approach behavior for each S in each of the eight matched clusters.

Between-Group Differences

Because of the unequal number of S's in the no-treatment group, these data were not included in the overall statistical analysis. Two-way analysis of variance of the change scores obtained by the three matched treatment groups yielded a highly significant treatment effect ($F = 6.84$; $p < .01$).

Further, one-tailed comparisons of pairs of treatment conditions by t tests for correlated means revealed that S's who had undergone systematic desensitization subsequently displayed significantly more snake-approach behavior than S's in either the pseudodesensitization group ($t = 2.57$; $p < .01$), the exposure group ($t = 3.60$; $p < .005$), or the no treatment control group ($t = 3.04$; $p < .01$). The pseudodesensitization and exposure groups did not differ significantly in approach behavior from the no treatment controls (t's = .92, .21, respectively), nor did they differ from each other.

Within-Group Differences

Within-group changes in avoidance behavior were evaluated by t tests for correlated means. Results of this analysis likewise disclosed that only S's in the desensitization condition achieved a significant reduction in avoidance behavior ($t = 4.20$; $p < .005$).

Performance of the Criterion Behavior in Posttreatment Assessment

If the desensitization treatment does, in fact, involve a genuine counterconditioning process, then one would expect to find relationships between factors that are known to affect the conditioning process (e.g. number of aversive stimuli that have been neutralized) and degree of behavioral change. In this connection, of the eight S's in the desensitization group, five completed their anxiety hierarchies within the allotted nine sessions. It is of interest to note that four of these five S's performed the terminal behavior at the posttreatment assessment, whereas not a single S whose desensitization had to be terminated before all anxiety items had been successfully neutralized was able to hold the snake barehanded. Moreover, no S in the exposure or no-treatment groups performed the terminal behavior, and only one out of the eight pseudodesensitization S's attained the criterion performance.

Anxiety-Inhibiting Function of Relaxation

The S's in both the desensitization and exposure conditions had been instructed to signal to E by raising their index finger whenever a particular imagined scene aroused anxiety. Since S's in these two groups were matched for the order, number and duration of stimulus exposures, any differences in the frequency of anxiety signaling provide suggestive evidence for the efficacy of relaxation in counteracting the development of emotional arousal during systematic desensitization (but see methodological problem raised in "Discussion" below).

The S's in the desensitization group signaled anxiety on 27 percent of the stimulus presentations, whereas the corresponding figure for the exposure group was 61 percent. This highly significant difference ($t = 3.30$; $p < .01$, two-tailed test) not only furnishes an independent check on the relaxation training but also attests to the anxiety-inhibiting capabilities of relaxation procedures.

Relationship Between Anxiety Decrements and Approach Behavior

All S's except those in the first cluster rated the degree of emotional disturbance that they experienced during the successful performance of each task in the pretreatment and posttreatment assessments. Since all but one S in the desensitization treatment surpassed their initial approach performance, it is possible to obtain a measure of anxiety decrement at the point at which S's were unable to proceed any further during the pretreatment assessment. Thus, for example, an S who, on the first test, went so far as to look down at the snake with the wire cover drawn back and reported an anxiety rating of 9 but subsequently performed this same task with an anxiety rating of 2 would receive a decrement score of 7 points. These self-report data were analyzed in order to determine whether desensitization, in addition to increasing approach behavior, also reduces the degree of emotional disturbance accompanying the overt responses.

Except for one S who exhibited no behavioral change and reported a 1-point increase in anxiety, the remaining six cases all showed decreases, the mean decrement being 3.28. The t value for the correlated differences is 3.31, significant beyond the .04 level, two-tailed test.

It will be recalled that some S's in the pseudodesensitization group showed small but nonsignificant increases in approach behavior (Table 27–2). These S's also displayed some decrease in anxiety ($M = 2.67$) but not of a statistically significant magnitude ($t = 1.76$).

A within-group correlational analysis for S's in the desensitization condition further revealed that the magnitude of anxiety decrement is highly predictive of the degree of increase exhibited by S's in approach behavior. The product-moment correlation obtained between these two measures is $r = .81$, significant beyond the .05 level. This strong relationship indicates that *S*'s who experienced the greatest amount of anxiety reduction also showed the most behavioral improvement.

Anxiety Accompanying Strong Approach Responses

Although *S*'s who had undergone systematic desensitization exhibited highly significant improvement in overt approach to the snake, it is evident from the data that the bold approach responses performed in the post-test were accompanied by considerable anxiety, ranging from 4 to 10 on the 10-point self-report scale, with a mean of 7.75. These findings, which are consistent with results obtained by Lang and Lazovik (1963) and Lang *et al.* (1965), will be discussed later.

DISCUSSION

The results of the present study provide strong support for the hypothesis that behavioral changes produced by systematic desensitization reflect a counterconditioning process. This is shown in the finding that only *S*'s for whom aversive stimuli were contiguously associated in imagination with the anxiety-competing response of relaxation (i.e. *S*'s in the desensitization group) displayed significant reduction in avoidance behavior; this reduction was also significantly greater than the nonsignificant changes observed in the pseudodesensitization, exposure and no-treatment control groups. The fact that *S*'s who were merely exposed to the aversive stimuli and those for whom relaxation was paired with snake-irrelevant stimuli showed no significant changes in snake avoidance indicates that neither graded exposure alone nor relaxation and expectations of beneficial effects were determinants of the outcomes yielded by the desensitization treatment. Moreover, the desensitization–no-treatment comparison replicates Lang and Lazovik (1963), while the desensitization-pseudodesensitization comparison provides some manner of confirmation of Lang *et al.* (1965).

In evaluating the treatment involving mere exposure to the graded aversive stimuli, it should be noted that in order to control for duration of visualization, *S*'s were often required to continue imagining a scene after they had signaled anxiety. It is possible that had *S*'s been allowed to control their own exposures to the aversive items, they might have produced some extinction of fear. In a pilot study by the author (Davison, 1965b), considerable extinction was observed when *S*'s controlled their own exposures to aversive stimuli. In comparison, it should be pointed out that Davison's experiment, as well as the earlier observations of Grossberg (1965), Herzberg (1941) and Jones (1924), used actual rather than symbolic stimuli. Nonetheless, it would be of considerable interest and importance to determine whether self-controlled exposure to aversive stimuli in imaginal form also effects significant reduction in avoidance.

In addition, this issue of forced versus self-controlled exposure necessitates caution in interpreting the finding that desensitization *S*'s signaled anxiety significantly less often than their matched and yoked exposure mates. This difference may be due not only to the anxiety-competing properties of deep muscular relaxation but also to the aversive nature of being unable to perform a response that will remove one from a fearful situation (cf. Mowrer and Viek, 1948).

Suggestive evidence was obtained indicating that the increased approach behavior of the desensitization group was due to a decrease in anxiety; that is, the actual avoidance gradient seems to have been lowered to allow for more approach. While performing on the posttreatment assessment the most difficult behavior encountered at the pretreatment assessment, desensitization *S*'s rated themselves as significantly less anxious; furthermore, a high positive and significant correlation was found in this group between decrements in self-reported anxiety and amount of overt behavioral improvement. These findings are consistent with the anxiety-avoidance paradigm of Mowrer (1940, 1947) and Miller (1948), as well as with theories of psychopathology based on animal learning experiments (Dollard and Miller, 1950; Mowrer, 1950) — all of which at least implicitly form the basis of Wolpian behavior therapy. According to this general view, avoidance responses are mediated by a secondary drive of fear; to the extent that a treatment method successfully reduces this fear, formerly inhibited approach responses will become manifest with the reduction of fear.

However, this anxiety-reduction analysis of the data is subject to several qualifications. First, questions can be raised as to the validity of self-report data on a numerical scale as a measure of anxiety (cf. Martin, 1961). Asking a naive *S* to rate herself on a scale from 1 to 10 may be making undue demands for rather fine discriminations among degrees of emotional arousal. A second problem is that *S*'s rated their anxiety *after* they performed a given behavior. In order to infer the role of fear in inhibiting a given hehavior, a logical requirement is that such measures be taken before or during the behavior. Although *S*'s had been asked to rate the anxiety they were experiencing while performing the behavior, it is impossible to estimate the effect of actually performing the behavior on their self-reported ratings. A third consideration is of a theoretical nature. The experiments of Solomon and Wynne (1954) and Wynne and Solomon (1955) raise doubts about a straightforward interpretation of avoidance behavior as mediated by covert fear responses. Indeed, the data reported in the present study are amenable to at least one alternative explanation, namely that anxiety and avoidance responses are *both* conditioned to the aversive stimuli, therefore being correlated classes of responses but not necessarily causally related. Systematic desensitization, then, may be reducing both components of avoidance behavior. Indeed, some suggestive evidence for the partial independence of anxiety and avoidance is the fact that *S*'s characteristically experienced high emotional arousal while successfully executing the terminal approach response, even after having completed their anxiety hierarchies. Unfortunately, these data, it will be seen below, may also be considered in support of the anxiety-avoidance hypothesis.

Limitations of Systematic Desensitization

Having confirmed that systematic desensitization significantly reduces avoidance behavior and having provided evidence that an actual process of counterconditioning underlies these effects, it would seem valuable at this point to examine both the practical and theoretical limitations of the technique.

The practical limitations concern levels of relaxation achieved, the clarity of aversive images and the signaling of anxiety. In the present study, as in clinical uses of the procedure, extensive reliance was placed on *S*'s self-reports. It is clear that the outcome of any desensitization study will greatly depend on how satisfactorily these problems are dealt with.

Perhaps more intriguing are the theoretical limitations. It will be recalled that desensitization *S*'s experienced considerable anxiety while performing the terminal behavior or approach responses high in the graduated series of tasks during the posttreatment assessment. Inasmuch as five of eight *S*'s in this group had been successfully desensitized in imagination, their anxiety reactions in the posttreatment assessment situation raise an interesting theoretical question regarding transfer effects.

One would expect, on the basis of the principle of stimulus generalization (Kimble, 1961) that the degree of transfer of counterconditioning effects from one stimulus situation to another is determined by the number of common elements. According to Guthrie's (1952) notion, for example, a complex stimulus (like a snake) consists of a finite number of stimulus elements, each of which can be attached to only one molecular fear response at any given time. The desensitization procedure, as the present author has heuristically viewed it, operates in two ways to render a given molar stimulus incapable of arousing the molar response of fear. First, by beginning with the weakest items of an anxiety hierarchy, one is presumably taking a very small sample of the "snake-object population of stimulus elements." Since this limited "amount of snake" elicits a limited "amount of fear," an incompatible response can be made dominant over the minimal fear response. This is why, second, deep muscular relaxation responses are induced prior to the introduction of the small dose of aversive stimuli. It is in this fashion that one "alienates" the small sample of fear stimuli from the limited number of molecular fear responses.

When a given anxiety item has been neutralized (defined as visualizing it for 15 seconds without signaling anxiety), another sample from the population of fear stimuli is presented, the incompatible relaxation response being set against that part of the total fear response which would ordinarily be elicited by the sample of fear stimuli. This process continues up the anxiety hierarchy until all items have been successfully desensitized.

When viewed in this fashion, the process of systematic desensitization would not be expected to effect complete transfer from the imaginal to the real-life situation. For even though an *S* succeeds in imagining the various anxiety items without becoming anxious, the facts remain that (a) the visualization is unlikely to involve all the stimulus elements for the respective level of the hierarchy and (b) the hierarchy itself cannot possibly provide an exhaustive sampling of the population of fear elements.

In the studies of Lang and Lazovik (1963), Lang *et al.* (1965) and Paul (1966), there was also a failure to find complete fearlessness on the part of successfully desensitized *S*'s. On the other hand, the clinical literature would lead one to expect perfect transfer, namely, "It has consistently been found that at every stage a stimulus that evokes no anxiety when imagined in a state of relaxation evokes no anxiety when encountered in reality" (Wolpe, 1961, p. 191). This discrepancy may in some measure be due to the unreliability of clinical reports. However, assuming that the clinical data are, in fact, valid, the greater generalization of counterconditioning effects in actual clinical practice may be a function of several factors which were intentionally excluded from the present experimental design. Among these would be *in vivo* desensitization based on differential relaxation (Davison, 1965b; Wolpe and Lazarus, 1966), the positive reinforcement of approach responses in interaction with presumed counterconditioning (Bower and Grusec, 1964; Davison, 1964; Lazarus *et al.*, 1965), the vicarious extinction of avoidance responses by means of modeling procedures (Bandura *et al.*, 1967; Jones, 1924), "placebo effect" (Frank, 1961; Paul, 1966) and the so-called "nonspecifics" of a therapeutic relationship (cf. Lazarus, 1963).

Etiology Versus Treatment

Having furnished evidence in favor of a conditioning interpretation of a particular technique of behavior modification, it would seem appropriate to comment briefly on the implications which these findings have for the development of neurotic anxiety. An error in logic is committed if one adduces data such as these as evidence in support of a conditioning model of the *acquisition* of inappropriate anxiety: from evidence regarding efficacy in changing behavior, one cannot claim to have demonstrated that the problem evolved in an analogous fashion (cf. Rimland, 1964). Whether in the present instance neurotic disorders, modifiable via counterconditioning techniques, originate in situations conceptualized in classical conditioning terms is a very important research and preventive therapy question; it is, however, separate from the corrective therapy issue. In fact, the author has sought vainly in the experimental literature for paradigms which illustrate the acquisition of *stable* fear responses in human beings under conditions bearing even a remote resemblance to what would likely hold in real life.[1]

---

[1] The author is indebted to Gordon L. Paul and Bernard Rimland for first pointing out these issues.

REFERENCES

Bandura, A.: *Principles of Behavior Modification.* New York, Holt, 1969.

Bandura, A., Grusec, J. E. and Menlove, F.: Vicarious extinction of avoidance responses. *Journal of Personality and Social Psychology, 5:*16–23, 1967.

Bower, G. H. and Grusec, T.: Effect of prior Pavlovian discrimination training upon learning an operant discrimination. *Journal of Experimental Analysis of Behavior, 7:*401–404, 1964.

Breger, L. and McGaugh, J. L.: A critique and reformulation of "learning theory" approaches to psychotherapy and neurosis. *Psychological Bulletin, 63:*338–358, 1965.

Davison, G. C.: A social learning therapy programme with an autistic child. *Behaviour Research and Therapy, 2:*149–159, 1964.

Davison, G. C.: The influence of systematic desensitization, relaxation, and graded exposure to imaginal aversive stimuli on the modification of phobic behavior. Unpublished doctoral dissertation, Stanford University, 1965a.

Davison, G. C.: Relative contributions of differential relaxation and graded exposure to the in vivo desensitization of a neurotic fear. In *Proceedings of the 73rd Annual Convention of the American Psychological Association, 1965.* Washington, D.C., American Psychological Association, 1965b.

Dollard, J. and Miller, N. E.: *Personality and Psychotherapy.* New York, McGraw-Hill, 1950.

Frank, J. D.: *Persuasion and Healing.* Baltimore, Johns Hopkins Press, 1961.

Geer, J.: Phobia treated by reciprocal inhibition. *Journal of Abnormal and Social Psychology, 69:*642–645, 1964.

Gleitman, H., Nachmias, J. and Neisser, U.: The S-R reinforcement theory of extinction. *Psychological Review, 61*:23–33, 1954.

Grossberg, J. M.: Successful behavior therapy in a case of speech phobia ("stage fright"). *Journal of Speech and Hearing Disorders, 30*:285–288, 1965.

Guthrie, E. R.: *The Psychology of Learning.* New York, Harper, 1952.

Herzberg, A.: Short treatment of neuroses by graduated tasks. *British Journal of Medical Psychology, 19*:36–51, 1941.

Hull, C. L.: *Principles of Behavior.* New York, Appleton, 1943.

Jones, M. C.: The elimination of children's fears. *Journal of Experimental Psychology, 7*:382–390, 1924.

Kimble, G. A.: *Hilgard and Marquis' Conditioning and Learning.* New York, Appleton-Century-Crofts, 1961.

Lang, P. J.: Behavior therapy with a case of nervous anorexia. In Ullmann, L. P. and Krasner, L. (Eds.): *Case Studies in Behavior Modification.* New York, Holt, 1965.

Lang, P. J. and Lazovik, A. D.: Experimental desensitization of a phobia. *Journal of Abnormal and Social Psychology, 66*:519–525, 1963.

Lang, P. J., Lazovik, A. D. and Reynolds, D. J.: Desensitization, suggestibility, and pseudotherapy. *Journal of Abnormal Psychology, 70*:395–402, 1965.

Lawrence, D. H. and Festinger, L.: *Deterrents and Reinforcement: The Psychology of Insufficient Reward.* Stanford, Stanford University Press, 1962.

Lazarus, A. A.: Group therapy of phobic disorders by systematic desensitization. *Journal of Abnormal and Social Psychology, 63*: 504–510, 1961.

Lazarus, A. A.: The results of behaviour therapy in 126 cases of severe neurosis. *Behaviour Research and Therapy, 1*:69–79, 1963.

Lazarus, A. A., Davison, G. C. and Polefka, D.: Classical and operant factors in the treatment of a school phobia. *Journal of Abnormal Psychology, 70*:225–229, 1965.

Lazarus, A. A. and Rachman, S.: The use of systematic desensitization in psychotherapy. *South African Medical Journal, 31*:934–937, 1957.

Martin, B.: The assessment of anxiety by physiological behavioral measures. *Psychological Bulletin, 58*:234–255, 1961.

Miller, N. E.: Studies of fear as an acquirable drive: I. Fear as motivation and fear-reduction as reinforcement in the learning of new responses. *Journal of Experimental Psychology, 38*:89–101, 1948.

Mowrer, O. H.: Anxiety-reduction and learning. *Journal of Experimental Psychology, 27*:497–516, 1940.

Mowrer, O. H.: On the dual nature of learning—a reinterpretation of "conditioning" and "problem solving." *Harvard Education Review*, *17*:102–148, 1947.

Mowrer, O. H.: *Learning Theory and Personality Dynamics*. New York, Ronald Press, 1950.

Mowrer, O. H.: *Learning Theory and Behavior*. New York, Wiley, 1960.

Mowrer, O. H. and Viek, P.: An experimental analogue of fear from a sense of helplessness. *Journal of Abnormal and Social Psychology*, *43*:193–200, 1948.

Paul, G. L.: *Insights Versus Desensitization in Psychotherapy: An Experiment in Anxiety-Reduction*. Stanford, Stanford University Press, 1966.

Paul, G. L. and Shannon, D. T.: Treatment of anxiety through systematic desensitization in therapy groups. *Journal of Abnormal Psychology*, *71*:124–135, 1966.

Rachman, S.: Treatment of anxiety and phobic reactions by systematic desensitization psychotherapy. *Journal of Abnormal and Social Psychology*, *58*:259–263, 1959.

Rimland, B.: *Infantile Autism*. New York, Appleton-Century-Crofts, 1964.

Sherrington, C. S.: *The Integrative Action of the Central Nervous System*. Cambridge, Cambridge University Press, 1906.

Solomon, R. L. and Brush, E. S.: Experimentally derived conceptions of anxiety and aversion. In Jones, M. R. (Ed.): *Nebraska Symposium on Motivation: 1956*. Lincoln, University of Nebraska Press, 1956.

Solomon, R. L. and Wynne, L. C.: Traumatic avoidance learning: The principles of anxiety conservation and partial irreversibility. *Psychological Review*, *61*:353–395, 1954.

Wolpe, J.: Objective psychotherapy of the neuroses. *South African Medical Journal*, *26*:825–829, 1952.

Wolpe, J.: *Psychotherapy by Reciprocal Inhibition*. Stanford, Stanford University Press, 1958.

Wolpe, J.: The systematic desensitization treatment of neurosis. *Journal of Nervous and Mental Disease*, *132*:189–203, 1961.

Wolpe, J. and Lazarus, A. A.: *Behavior Therapy Techniques*. New York, Pergamon, 1966.

Wynne, L. C. and Solomon, R. L.: Traumatic avoidance learning: Acquisition and extinction in dogs deprived of normal peripheral autonomic functioning. *Genetic Psychology Monographs*, *52*:241–284, 1955.

28

Standard versus Individualized Hierarchies in Desensitization to Reduce Test Anxiety

JOHN R. EMERY AND JOHN D. KRUMBOLTZ

Fifty-four test-anxious college freshmen were randomly assigned to either (a) desensitization with individualized anxiety hierarchies, (b) desensitization with a single standard hierarchy or (c) a no-treatment control group. Criteria consisted of self-ratings of anxiety before and during examinations, scores on a test-anxiety scale and final examination grades. Findings were (a) students who received desensitization rated themselves as significantly less anxious about examinations, both before and during their final examinations, as compared with a no-treatment control group, (b) final examination grades of the desensitization groups were slightly, but not significantly, higher than the control group, (c) there was no difference in the relative effectiveness of individualized versus standard hierarchies.

EACH YEAR college counselors work with freshmen who experience extreme anxiety before and during midterm and final examinations. Many of these students have the ability to do well on their examinations, but perform poorly because of their anxiety (Alpert and Haber, 1963; Paul and Eriksen, 1964). Some students

NOTE: This research was supported by a grant from the Proctor and Gamble gift to the Stanford University School of Education faculty research fund. The research is based in part on the doctoral dissertation of the first author. Appreciation is extended to Albert Bandura and Norman Giddan for their help on the research.

experience difficulty in organizing a logical and coherent answer to an essay question, while others report that their "mind goes blank" when they encounter a difficult mathematics problem. Still others find it difficult to eat or sleep normally the day before examinations start. Such problems are evidence of what can be labeled "test anxiety."

Little work has been done on finding an effective method to reduce students' test anxiety. Sarason (1958) found that reassurance did seem to have a facilitative effect on the verbal learning of high test anxious subjects. Hoehn and Saltz (1956) found that anxious students tended to be helped by interviews, although rigid students were more likely to fail if interviewed. The results were further affected by the type of interview. Interviews in which the student was encouraged to complain produced the interaction noted above, while interviews oriented toward the student's goal and sources of interest and satisfaction did not. Paul and Eriksen (1964) found that high test anxious students (as measured by Mandler and Sarason, 1952) did better on a comparable "experimental" examination given later on the same day of the real examination, while low test anxious students did poorly.

McKeachie *et al.* (1955) gave half their students answer sheets with spaces in which they were invited to "feel free to comment" on the test questions, while the other half of the students were given standard answer sheets. Students who had the opportunity to write comments made "reliably" higher scores than those who used the standard answer sheets. The authors believed that giving students an opportunity to comment on test questions reduced anxiety and its concomitant detrimental effects.

Only one case study (Paul, 1964) was found where the desensitization process was used as a means of reducing test anxiety. Wolpe (1952) was the first to publish an account of the desensitization procedure. Basically, desensitization consists of verbally presenting carefully graded situations which are increasingly anxiety producing (an "anxiety hierarchy") to a deeply relaxed client until he is able to visualize the most stressful scenes on the list without experiencing any anxiety. Wolpe's subsequent writings on the subject (1958, 1961, 1962, 1964) show further clinical evidence for the effectiveness of the procedure for eliminating objectively inappropriate fears in human beings.

Thus far, systematic desensitization has been shown to be an effective method of eliminating many types of phobic behavior, but no study has specifically evaluated desensitization in reducing test anxiety.

A classical conditioning paradigm can be used to explain how students become overly anxious about taking examinations. A child bringing home an examination with a grade lower than that expected by his parents is likely to be punished, directly or indirectly, by his parents. The repeated association of punishment with examinations will produce an increase in his anxiety whenever events associated with examinations occur in the future. The freshman year at college may heighten fear of examinations. An increased level of competition combined with more complex subject matter challenges many students for the first time. Thus, the test anxiety of most college students can be viewed as a fear of events associated with the testing situation.

Since desensitization has been shown to be an effective method of reducing other fears, this study was designed to test the efficacy of using desensitization as a procedure in reducing undue test anxiety in college freshmen.

Other studies have examined certain variables relevant to the desensitization process. Among these variables were training in muscular relaxation (Davison, 1965; Lang *et al.*, 1965), the importance of suggestibility within the therapeutic relationship (Lang *et al.*, 1965) and a comparison of group versus individual desensitization (Paul and Shannon, 1966).

One assumption in all these studies has been that the anxiety hierarchy must be adapted to each individual undergoing desensitization or must be capable of being modified to suit each individual within the group situation. Anxiety hierarchies are usually constructed by both counselor and client. The client lists relevant anxiety-producing situations which he then ranks from least to most anxiety producing. This individualized hierarchy, which may be modified at any time during the desensitization process, is thus specifically tailored to the individual client.

The individualized hierarchies from many subjects with the

same problem may be similar enough in content to permit their compilation into a single standard hierarchy. It is possible that a standard hierarchy could be used as effectively in reducing test anxiety as the individualized hierarchies and at the same time reduce the time necessary for completion of an effective desensitization treatment. However, both Lazarus (1961) and Wolpe (1958) emphasize the importance of placing the items in the anxiety hierarchies in an order which is specifically tailored to each individual. Items not in the "correct" order might cause repeated signaling by the client and negate any beneficial effects from the desensitization process.

METHOD
Sample

The sample was selected from the freshman class of Stanford University. Most freshmen ($N = 1,078$; males $= 830$, females $= 248$) took a test anxiety scale as part of a three-hour psychological assessment during orientation week. This scale is a refinement of a scale previously constructed by Emery and contains 18 items known to discriminate between a group of Stanford undergraduates who called themselves "test anxious" and another group containing a random sample of Stanford undergraduates. Those who called themselves test anxious scored significantly higher ($p \leqslant .05$) on all 18 items than the random sample group.

Item 19 asks each student to respond to the direct statement: "I feel that I am unduly anxious about taking examinations." Scores were computed by assigning the following values to each response on the 5-point scale: Rarely or Never, 1; Infrequently, 2; Occasionally, 3; Frequently, 4; Almost always or Always, 5. Total scores were the sum of the values obtained for each of the 19 questions. A total of 240 students (male $= 165$, females $= 75$) were identified as test anxious if they met the following criteria:

1. They answered the nineteenth question "Frequently" or "Almost always" or "Always." (This criterion was met by 145 students.)
2. Their total score on the scale exceeded one standard deviation above the mean score. (This criterion was met by 95 students; 117 students met both criteria.)

Shortly after students had received the results of their fall quarter midterm examinations, a letter was sent to each freshman identified as test anxious ($N = 240$) inviting participation in a project to reduce test anxiety. Students were informed that everyone desiring to participate could not be accommodated because of limited staff and facilities. The purpose, nature of treatment and time required were explained. Ninety-six freshmen (males = 72, females = 24) responded to this letter, indicating they desired to participate.

Since the male-female ratio in the freshmen class was approximately 2:1 (approximately 150 freshman females did not take the test-anxiety scale), the 2:1 ratio was also used in this study. Thus, of the 96 volunteers, 36 males and 18 females were randomly selected and randomly assigned to one of three groups: (a) desensitization using an individualized hierarchy, (b) desensitization using a standard hierarchy, (c) no-treatment control. Each group had 12 males and 6 females. Test anxiety scale means and standard deviations at each stage of the sample-selection process are shown in Table 28–1. After random assignment, no significant differences were found between groups on age, first quarter grade-point average, or College Entrance Examination Board (CEEB) scores.

Treatment

Nine counselors were selected from graduate students in clinical and counseling psychology and trained in the desensitization technique. Students in the two experimental groups met with counselors during the winter quarter, 2 times per week for up to 8 weeks, until the desensitization process was completed. Each counselor worked with four students—two from each experimental group.

The desensitization process was identical for each experimental group except for construction of the anxiety hierarchies. The standard test anxiety hierarchy was constructed by compiling the individualized hierarchies of 15 test anxious subjects collected in a pilot study by Emery. The standard hierarchy consisted of 16 situations ranked from least anxiety producing, "The teacher announces and discusses a course examination (to be held in three

TABLE 28-1
MEANS AND STANDARD DEVIATIONS FOR GROUPS
ON THE TEST ANXIETY SCALE

Group	Male			Female		
	N	M	SD	N	M	SD
Freshmen class taking anxiety scale, September 1965 *	830	43.26	11.11	248	44.76	12.38
Students receiving letters of invitation	165	57.18	10.13	75	58.23	11.31
Students indicating interest in special help	72	58.44	9.64	24	59.14	9.91
Students randomly assigned to final sample	36	58.98	8.41	18	59.40	8.78

* The corrected split-half reliability for the scale was .76 with $N = 1,078$.

weeks) with the class," to most anxiety producing, "Having thirty minutes left to complete an examination and an hour's worth of work to do."

The group receiving individualized hierarchies was given the same list of 16 situations, but in a random order. Each student in this group was then given the following directions:

Each statement on the following sheet describes a situation related to taking exams. If you found yourself in any one of these situations, you might be bothered quite a bit, somewhat or not at all. Look them over. If you can think of any other situations related to taking exams that bother you a lot, add them to the list. You may write on the back if you wish.

When the list is complete, look at the situations over again quickly. Then, pick the situation that would bother you the most and place a "1" in the column to the left of it. Next, look at the remaining situations. Of these, pick the one that would bother you the most and place a "2" in the column to the left of it. Continue this procedure until you have ranked all items.

Desensitization was accomplished using the same standard hierarchy for all students in one experimental group but using the individualized hierarchy developed for each student in the other experimental group. All of the students who received desensitization completed the treatment. The no-treatment control groups was informed that their cards had not been among those drawn by lot to participate but that they would be contacted later.

Criterion Measures

Three criteria were used to judge the efficacy of the treatment procedures.

1. Winter quarter final examination grades in freshman history adjusted for fall quarter final examination grades in freshman history. History was used because it was the only common examination taken by all freshmen. These grades were obtained by direct communication with all 26 freshmen history instructors and were then quantified so that A = 4.0, A— = 3.7, B+ = 3.3, etc. During fall and winter quarters, all freshmen took the same final examinations. The exams lasted four hours and consisted of four essay questions.

2. Posttest anxiety scale scores adjusted for pretest anxiety test scores. Posttest scores were obtained by mailing letters to all 54 students 1 week prior to the final examination week of the winter quarter, 1966. Almost identical letters were sent to the experimental groups and to the control group. Both letters contained the identical test anxiety scale these students had completed during September, 1965.

3. Self-ratings of anxiety during examinations and self-ratings before examinations. The mean difference of these two ratings as well as the absolute value of each was used. A lowering of anxiety during the examination would be expected to facilitate performance on the examination.

These self-ratings were obtained by a second letter sent to all 54 students 1 week later just as final examinations were beginning. Both experimental groups and the control group received identical letters. Each letter contained a rating sheet for each examination the student had. The students rated their level of anxiety both before and during each final examination on a 7-point scale from "1" ("Very calm") to "7" ("Very intense anxiety"). Intensive follow-up procedures were used so that all 54 students returned both the test anxiety scale and the self-ratings.

Analysis to Test Hypotheses

An analysis of covariance was used to examine for significant differences (.05 level) between groups on the first two criteria. A one-way analysis of variance was used to examine for significant differences (.05 level) between groups on the third criterion.

All three criterion measures were used in testing both hypotheses:

Hypothesis 1. Desensitization treatment (combined experimental groups) will be more effective than the control procedure.

Hypothesis 2. Desensitization using an individualized hierarchy will be more effective than desensitization using a standard hierarchy.

RESULTS

The means reported in Table 28–2 indicate that desensitization is an effective method of reducing test anxiety based on the test anxiety scale scores and the self-ratings. The final examination grades showed trends in the predicted direction which did not reach statistical significance.

The crucial dividing line on the self-rating scale is between a rating of 3 (mild anxiety—not bothersome) and a rating of 4 (mild anxiety—bothersome). The desensitization groups not only experienced a decrease in anxiety during the examination but also felt less anxiety before the examination.

On none of the criteria was one experimental group more efficacious than the other. Thus, the assumption that a specific hierarchy is necessary in the desensitization process was not verified under the conditions of this study. Complete descriptions of procedures and analyses are available in Emery (1966).

DISCUSSION

The following conclusions seem warranted:

1. Students who received desensitization rated themselves as significantly less anxious about examinations, both before and during their final examinations, than a no-treatment control group.
2. Final examination grades of the desensitization groups were slightly, but not significantly, higher than the control group.
3. No difference in the relative effectiveness of individualized versus standard hierarchies was found.

TABLE 28-2
MEANS, STANDARD DEVIATIONS, AND F VALUES
TO TEST EACH HYPOTHESIS

Criteria		Desensitization, Individualized Hierarchy (1)	Desensitization, Standard Hierarchy (2)	Control Group (3)	F for Hypothesis 1, (1) and (2) versus (3)	F for Hypothesis 2, (1) versus (2)
Final exam grades						
History, fall quarter	M	2.49	2.49	2.55		
	SD	0.88	0.93	1.00		
History, winter quarter	M	2.82	2.83	2.64	1.58	0.00
	SD	0.82	0.83	0.76		
Test anxiety scale scores						
September 1965	M	59.2	58.8	59.4		
	SD	9.0	8.6	8.6		
March 1966	M	54.4	58.9	64.0	6.83*	2.37
	SD	12.2	8.5	12.7		
Self-rating of anxiety scores						
Before final exams	M	3.07	3.23	4.42	13.52**	0.99
	SD	0.85	1.01	0.91		
During final exams	M	2.60	2.81	4.58	14.78**	1.23
	SD	0.78	1.61	1.33		
Difference	M	0.47	0.42	−0.16	6.25*	0.03
	SD	0.85	0.83	0.83		

* $p < .05$.
** $p < .01$.

However, several limitations of the study must be considered. The sample was not representative of ability in a normal college population. The mean score for combined mathematics and verbal sections of the CEEB examinations was 1,310 (90th percentile on national norms) for the 54 students participating. Considering Spielberger and Katzenmeyer's (1959) findings that academic anxiety evidenced by those students of high ability seems to have a facilitating rather than debilitating effect on academic performance, the use of Stanford students may restrict generalizability of the findings.

Selection of test anxiety criterion measures is another problem. Some of the students who returned their posttest anxiety scales the week before examinations indicated that they would not be sure of how they felt about taking examinations until after their examinations were over. Administering the posttests after examinations was not done for fear of measuring more of a "relief that examinations are over" rather than a reduction in test anxiety. More objective measures of students' test anxiety need to be developed. Physiological measures such as pulse rate and/or GSR may be more meaningful than the self-report scales used here.

Within the desensitization treatment itself, a number of assumptions were made which may not be warranted. For instance, it was assumed that (a) all students attained at least a minimal degree of muscular relaxation and (b) all students were clearly able to visualize items on their hierarchies. The number of times a student signaled that he or she felt anxious while relaxed was not controlled either. Some students never signaled that they felt anxious, others signaled quite frequently.

The 60 per cent overlap between the individualized and standard hierarchies may have ruled out any possibility of differential effectiveness. However, one can infer that the standard hierarchy was effective. Another alternative would have been to have the students who used an individualized hierarchy construct their own hierarchy "from scratch" rather than altering, adding to and deleting from the standard hierarchy. This would have reduced the overlap between hierarchies and enabled a clearer test of the differences between the two ways of constructing hierarchies.

REFERENCES

Alpert, R. and Haber, R. N.: Anxiety in academic achievement situations. *Journal of Abnormal and Social Psychology, 66*:207–216, 1963.

Davison, G. C.: The influence of systematic desensitization, relaxation, and graded exposure to imaginal aversive stimuli on the modification of phobic behavior. Unpublished doctoral dissertation. Stanford, Stanford University, 1965.

Emery, J. R.: An evaluation of standard versus individualized hierarchies in desensitization to reduce test anxiety. Unpublished doctoral dissertation. Stanford, Stanford University, 1966.

Hoehn, A. J. and Saltz, E.: Effect of teacher-student interviews on classroom achievement. *Journal of Educational Psychology,* 47: 424–435, 1956.

Lang, P. J., Lazovik, A. D. and Reynolds, D. J.: Desensitization, suggestibility, and pseudotherapy. *Journal of Abnormal Psychology,* 70:395–402, 1965.

Lazarus, A. A.: Group therapy of phobic disorders by systematic desensitization. *Journal of Abnormal and Social Psychology,* 63: 504–510, 1961.

Mandler, G. and Sarason, S. B.: A study of anxiety and learning. *Journal of Abnormal and Social Psychology,* 47:166–173, 1952.

McKeachie, W. J.: Anxiety in the college classroom. *Journal of Educational Research,* 45:153–160, 1951.

McKeachie, W. J., Pollie, D. and Speisman, J.: Relieving anxiety in classroom examinations. *Journal of Abnormal and Social Psychology,* 50:93–98, 1955.

Paul, G. L.: Modification of systematic desensitization based on case study. Paper read at Western Psychological Association, Portland, April, 1964.

Paul, G. L. and Eriksen, C. W.: Effects of test anxiety on "real-life" examinations. *Journal of Personality,* 32:480–494, 1964.

Paul, G. L. and Shannon, D. R.: Treatment of anxiety through systematic desensitization in therapy groups. *Journal of Abnormal Psychology,* 71:119–123, 1966.

Sarason, I. G.: Effects on verbal learning of anxiety, reassurance, and meaningfulness of material. *Journal of Experimental Psychology,* 56:472–477, 1958.

Spielberger, C. D. and Katzenmeyer, W. G.: Manifest anxiety, intelligence, and college grades. *Journal of Consulting Psychology,* 23: 278, 1959.

Wolpe, J.: Objective psychotherapy of the neuroses. *South African Medical Journal,* 26:825–829, 1952.

Wolpe, J.: *Psychotherapy by Reciprocal Inhibition.* Stanford, Stanford University Press, 1958.

Wolpe, J.: The systematic desensitization of neurosis. *Journal of Nervous and Mental Disease,* 112:189–203, 1961.

Wolpe, J.: Isolation of a conditioning procedure as the crucial psychotherapeutic factor: A case study. *Journal of Nervous and Mental Disease,* 134:316–329, 1962.

Wolpe, J.: Behavior therapy in complex neurotic states. *British Journal of Psychiatry,* 110:28–34, 1964.

29

Reduction of Examination Anxiety and "Stage-Fright" by Group Desensitization and Relaxation

O. KONDAS

The results of the experiment in group desensitization, relaxation and imagination of exam situations in groups of children ($n = 23$) and students ($n = 13$) show that systematic desensitization is an efficient method for reducing stage fright. Some transient positive effects were also achieved with a modification of the Schultz method of relaxation. Interviews, a Fear Survey Schedule and a test of palmar perspiration were used in the assessment of effects. The main conclusions are concordant with previous studies in desensitization (e.g. Lang and Lazovik, 1963; Rachman, 1965, 1966a,b; Lazarus, 1961; Paul and Shannon, 1966) and the present results provide interesting comparisons.

INTRODUCTION

FEAR OF FAILING in examinations and of giving reports in class are relatively common worries of pupils. They appear in 44 to 90 percent of sixth-grade pupils, and 20 percent of school children experience fear of school examinations (Eysenck and Rachman, 1965). In relation to school examinations, pedagogical psychology uses the term "preexamination" state to describe this condition,

NOTE: Thanks are due to colleague E. Borzová from Psychiatric Hospital V. Levare for her assistance with this research and to the school director V. Hudzovic for arranging good conditions for the research. Appreciation is further expressed to Dr. S. Rachman for his kind critical reading of the manuscript.

From *Behavior Research and Therapy*, 5:275–281, 1967. Copyright 1967 by Pergamon Press. Reprinted with permission of author and publisher.

which is characterized by excessive tension (Prihoda, 1924; Duric, 1965). This state of excitement generally has a positive influence on performance, and Prihoda found that only in 13.3 percent of pupils did their school performance deteriorate. This deterioration can be included in the term "stage-fright," which represents a state of higher emotive tension and fear in personally important situations such as examinations or facing an audience. The teachers found 18.1 percent of pupils suffering from stage-fright ($n =$ 414), and psychological examination showed that for 9.9 percent of them, stage-fright was a serious personal problem (Kondas, 1966b). Since stage-fright is characterized by learned fear and increased tension, one may assume that desensitization treatment and relaxation might reduce it.

In 1965 and 1966, Rachman published studies concerning the separate effects of relaxation and desensitization in treating spider phobias. The present paper investigates similar problems under group-treatment procedures, while the Schultz method of autogenic training was used to induce relaxation. It also allows us to compare group desensitization in children and in adults. Further it appears to give a support to Paul and Shannon's (1966) finding on the efficiency of group desensitization in treating social-evaluative anxiety. In comparison with Paul and Shannon's work with students, our research was centered mainly on sixth- to ninth-grade children.

METHOD
Subject Selection and Samples

In October, 1965, the teachers of a large school were requested to select all fifth- to ninth-grade pupils who appeared to experience stage-fright and then to describe their symptoms and degree on a standard schedule (Kondas, 1966b). Sixty-nine of the children concerned were examined by Raven's PM, Eysenck's MPI adapted for children, an adapted Fear Survey Schedule (Wolpe and Lang, 1964) and by interview. The examinations were conducted by two psychologists with randomized order of the methods used in 5 or 7-member groups.

The pupils of this sample with stage fright (according to their teachers' description, own data, and FSS score) were selected and divided into four 6-member groups. They comprised the first sample, consisting finally of 23 children (age range 11 to 15 years; average age, 13 years).

The second sample consisted of thirteen psychology students in the fifth to seventh semester of their studies (average age 21.9 years). These were divided into three groups. Each potential subject was interviewed and completed an examination questionnaire and the FSS. The final sample was selected from a larger group of thirty students.

Procedure

Group sessions were conducted as follows. In the first (school-children) sample one group ($n = 6$) was given only relaxation by autogenic training (AT), the second group ($n = 6$) was given systematic desensitization (SD), the third group ($n = 5$) presentation of hierarchy items without relaxation and the fourth group ($n = 6$) served as a control group. The control S's were examined and reexamined at the same time as experimental groups. The procedure in the second (student) sample was analogous to the first one; six subjects received SD, four received relaxation by AT, and three subjects formed a control group.

For relaxation, Schultz's autogenic training was used. The children sat in comfortable armchairs and the following exercises of relaxed breathing, relaxation of right hand, left hand, muscles of legs, and relaxation of abdomen and breast muscles were provided in single sessions. The AT exercises were led by two psychologists, and there were ten sessions given at weekly intervals. The children were also asked to practice the same AT exercises at home, once a day. After the seventh session, the AT group was requested to do 2 to 3 minutes of relaxation while in the classroom, at the beginning of a lesson and while the teacher was writing in the classbook.

The SD group began desensitization after the seventh AT session. Five desensitization sessions were conducted at 5- to 7-day intervals. Systematic desensitization was conducted by a psychologist with experience in individual desensitization treatment.

The third group was required to shut their eyes and to imagine two to three hierarchy items in each session with two presentations of each item. There were four sessions altogether.

Examination Fear Hierarchy

A. For sixth- to ninth-grade children.
   1. Going to school in the morning—you think that you may be asked to give reports.
   2. The lesson begins—the teacher begins to examine.
   3. Writing a written exam.
   4. Examination begins—you think that you will be asked to give a report.
   5. As above—the teacher pronounces your name.
   6. You stand up and answer questions while in your place.
   7. Answering questions at a map.
   8. Calculating an arithmetic example on the blackboard.
   9. Answering questions in front of the class.
   10. As above—while the school director is present.

B. For university students
   1. One week before an important examination.
   2. Two days before the examination.
   3. You are to sit an exam tomorrow.
   4. It is the morning of the exam-day—it is 1–2 hr before the time of exam.
   5. Sitting for the examination.
   6. Reading the questions and preparing answers.
   7. Selecting questions (i.e. from written questions in envelopes).
   8. Entering the exam room.
   9. Waiting for exam in front of an examination work-room.

Measures

In addition to the interview data, two parallel series of FSS were used as the main indicator of effects. The adapted FSS consists of 31 items, 11 of which referred to stage-fright situations, each being estimated in five degrees. In the first sample, a test of palmar perspiration with Boymond's mixture (Král, 1964; Barlogová, 1965) was conducted under school examination conditions before and after treatment. Perspiration turns the treated filter paper blue; the resultant colors have different intensities and extent. Its evaluation was done qualitatively by two judges. An advantage of this assessment is its technical easiness, and it can be used directly in the classroom; a disadvantage lies in its qualitative character.

The follow-up evaluation was done by FSS in the children's group five months after the termination of treatment. (The follow-up *n* is smaller, as some children had left the school.)

After the publication of Rachman's data (1965) where he gives an account of the absence of changes in the MPI after desensitization, this inventory was not repeated.

RESULTS

Both autogenic training and systematic desensitization can be provided in group conditions. In all six members of childrens' SD group, agreement was reached in the sequence of hierarchy items. This criterion could not be wholly fulfilled in the SD group of psychology students. The differences in hierarchy item sequences demanded a division of the 6-member group into two 3-member subgroups. As a consequence of differences in item sequences, there were more frequent disturbances of relaxation when presenting "dissequenced" items, and therefore the presentations times of each such item had to be abbreviated. In the children's SD group, however, two presentations of all items except items Numbers 5, 9 and 10 were sufficient. The possibilities and limitations of group desensitization have already been discussed (Kondas, 1966a).

The results of the experiment are given in Table 29-1.

The greatest decrease of FSS score appears in both groups with systematic desensitization. The decrease is 28 points in children and 14 points in university students. Statistical comparison with nontreated control groups shows, according to the Mann-Whitney test, that this difference is significant ($P = 0.001$).

The results in groups with relaxation by means of the Schultz method are interesting. The difference in FSS score in the student group is slight and insignificant, while in the children's group it reaches the 3 percent level of significance ($P = 0.03$). There was,

TABLE 29-1
MAIN RESULTS OF EXPERIMENT

Group	Full FSS score		The Sum of Cases with Decrease of 10 or More Points in FSS	De- crease of Palmar Perspi- ration $(n = 5)$
	Before	After		
	Treatment			
A. Children				
AT relaxation	87.6	81.6	2	1
Desensitization	81.7	53.0	3	3
Imagination of hierarchy items	78.8	73.0	2	0
Control group	84.2	88.5	0	0
B. University students				
AT relaxation $(n = 4)$	75.5	73.0	2	....
Desensitization $(n = 6)$	82.5	68.6	4	....
Controls $(n = 3)$	62.0	64.3	0	....

however, an important difference in doing AT relaxation. The children also carried out the relaxation before the beginning of a lesson (in the classroom), that it, right before the examination. This was not done by the students who had three AT sessions less than the children's AT group.

In the palmar perspiration test, there were distinct decreases in perspiration during the examination. In the AT group, only one *S* showed a decrease, while after systematic desensitization, all but two *S*'s showed a decrement of perspiration in the examination condition.

Regarding the interview data, it may be mentioned that all students reported a reduction or elimination of stage fright after desensitization. Two students described a feeling of calmness similar to indifference, and a further two ate breakfast prior to the last examination period in the eighth semester—something they had never done until undergoing desensitization. The children of SD group said that examination no longer disturbed their calmness (four cases), and two cases reported a reduction of examination fear. The mother of a pupil spontaneously reported that her daughter now speaks calmly about the course of school examinations where she had never done so before. Previously her sleep had been disturbed and she complained of diarrhea.

In the group receiving AT relaxation, one student reported

being more relaxed at interview, and three of the AT children said that they were calmer during examinations than they had been before the treatment.

The follow-up data in mean FSS score is presented in Table 29-2 (childrens' group).

TABLE 29-2
DIFFERENCES OF THREE TREATMENT PROCEDURES
AT FOLLOW-UP

	Mean FSS score		
Procedure	*Before* *Treatment*	*After*	*At follow-up*
AT relaxation ($n = 4$)	2.89	2.63	2.94
Desensitization ($n = 5$)	2.73	2.34	2.30
Imagination of hierarchy items ($n = 3$)	2.20	2.03	2.17

The follow-up evaluation shows the stable effect of systematic desensitization. The effect of AT was only transient, and after five months, the pretreatment level had been restored. The changes of main FSS scores after the simple imagination of hierarchy items were very slight.

DISCUSSION AND CONCLUSIONS

The results show that the method of systematic desensitization is efficient in reducing stage fright. The present outcome is similar to Lazarus's work (1961) on the method of group SD in adults; group desensitization, it appears, is also possible with children. Moreover, the comparison between our first sample (children) and the second sample (students) shows even better performance of group SD in children. This may be attributable to the difficulty in achieving uniformity in the hierarchy item sequence with the students. The more frequent disturbances of relaxation occurred precisely in those subjects where the group-presented situation did not correspond with their individual hierarchy. This observation is further evidence that it is essential in the SD method to order the sequence of hierarchy items correctly (Wolpe, 1963) and of the importance of a graduated approach to desensitization (Rachman, 1966a). This fact requires that the therapist has some experience in the construction of a hierarchy.

The limitation of group desensitization which arises from the difference between individually constructed but group-presented hierarchy items was minimized by Paul and Shannon (1966). They constructed hierarchy lists by group discussion. The hierarchy thus included common elements from all S's with some broadening of the items by elements from the most anxious group member. At the beginning of each desensitization session, they provided further discussion of social-evaluative anxiety situations which resulted in changes of the anxiety hierarchies or the construction of a new hierarchy. In this way, the combination of group desensitization with group discussion overcomes the problem of how to achieve uniformity of hierarchy items.

Paul and Shannon (1966) found combined group desensitization superior to both insight-oriented psychotherapy and an attention-placebo program in the treatment of social-evaluative anxiety (public speaking situations). Similarly to snake phobias (Lang and Lazovik, 1963) or spider phobias (Rachman, 1965, 1966a,b), social-evaluative anxiety, examination anxiety or stage fright are suitable problems for experiments in desensitization (also from the standpoint of the ethics of therapeutic research).

The reduction of stage fright by systematic desensitization may be accounted for by the fact that its main feature is that it is a learned fear in which punishment, feeling ashamed, criticism, decrease of prestige and similar effects work as negative reinforcing factors. Stage fright symptoms like tremor, excitement, muscle rigidity or a feeling of stomach spasm indicate the presence of tension in this state (Kondas, 1966b). Since the relaxation in itself does not seem to be efficient (Rachman, 1965; Franks, 1966), our better results in the childrens' group might be ascribed to the effect of another form of relaxation (Schultz's method which is supposed to reduce tension—Kleinsorge and Klumbies, 1961). A more probable explanation is, of course, that owing to the relaxation given in the classroom situation just before the examination, some fear reduction was obtained as a consequence of the connection of the real examination-fear situation with a reaction incompatible with fear (i.e. AT relaxation). This conclusion is supported by the absence of any effect in the student's AT group in which the connection of relaxation and examinations did not take place. The reciprocal inhibition effect is a probable explanation of some of the positive results (Kleinsorge and Klumbies, 1961) achieved by autogenic training. The effect of AT in our childrens' group was, however, only transient, while the effect achieved by group desensitization was stable for at least five months after treatment.

The imagination of examination-fear situations without inducing a state incompatibe with fear does not produce fear reduction. This supports the notion of reciprocal inhibition as the main basis of therapeutic effects in systematic desensitization (Wolpe, 1954). It may be mentioned that according to the data collected from students (Kondas, 1966b), as well as by common observation, stage-fright seems to be considerably resistant to extinction by natural events. Despite the fact that students, for example, have a large number of opportunities for public speaking as well as examinations, the stage-fright reaction had not been eliminated in many cases—even though some of them had tried to be calm before exams and had tried deep breathing or to think about pleasant things when stage fright had arisen. Contrary to the inefficient extinction occurring in natural circumstances, immediate reduction of fear occurs by SD, and "the desensitization of imaginal stimuli does indeed generalize to real-life situations" (Rachman, 1966b).

REFERENCES

Barlogová, D.: Stupen potivosti koze. CSc. Dissertation, Bratislava, 1965.

Duric, L.: Práceschopnost' ziakov vo vynucovacom procese. *Slov. pedag. naklad.* Bratislava, 1965.

Eysenck, H. J. and Rachman, S.: *The Causes and Cures of Neurosis.* London, Routledge & Kegan Paul, 1965.

Eysenck, H. J. (Ed.): *Behaviour Therapy and the Neuroses.* Oxford, Pergamon Press, 1960.

Eysenck, H. J. (Ed.): *Experiments in Behaviour Therapy.* Oxford, Pergamon Press, 1964.

Franks, C. M.: Clinical application of conditioning and other behavioral techniques. *Conditioned Reflex,* 1:36–50, 1966.

Kleinsorge, H. and Klumbies, G.: *Technik der Relaxation—Selbstentspannung.* VEB G. Fisher, Jena, 1961.

Kondas, O.: Experiences with Wolpe's method of systematic desensitization. Paper read at *Third Czechoslovakian Psyhiat, Conf.,* Brno, 1966a.

Kondas, O.: Tréma ako forma nauceného strachu. *Psychol. a Patopsycol. dieťaťa,* 1966b.

Král, J.: Fyziologie a biochemie potu. *Stát. zdrav. naklad.* Praha, 1964.

Lang, P. J. and Lazovik, A. D.: The experimental desensitization of phobia. *Journal of Abnormal Social Psychology, 66:*519–525, 1963. Cited in Eysenck (1964), pp. 40–50.

Lazarus, A. A.: Group therapy of phobic disorders by systematic desensitization. *Journal of Abnormal Social Psychology, 63:*504–510, 1961. Cited in Eysenck (1964), pp. 87–98.

Paul, G. L. and Shannon, D. T.: Treatment of anxiety through systematic desensitization in therapy groups. *Journal of Abnormal Social Psychology, 71:*124–135, 1966.

Prihoda, V.: *Psychologie a Hygiena Skousky.* Praha, 1924.

Rachman, S.: Studies in desensitization—I. The separate effect of relaxation and desensitization. *Behavioral Research and Therapy, 3:*245–251, 1965.

Rachman, S.: Studies in desensitization—II. Flooding. *Behavioral Research and Therapy, 4:*1–6, 1966a.

Rachman, S.: Studies in desensitization—III. Speed of generalization. *Behavioral Research and Therapy, 4:*7–15, 1966b.

Wolpe, J.: Reciprocal inhibition as the man basis of psychotherapeutic effects. *Archives of Neurology and Psychiatry, 72:*205–226, 1954. Cited in Eysenck (1960), pp. 88–113.

Wolpe, J.: Quantitative relationships in the systematic desensitization of phobias. *American Journal of Psychiatry, 119:*1062–1068, 1963.

Wolpe, J. and Lang, P. J.: A Fear Survey Schedule for use in behaviour therapy. *Behavioral Research and Therapy, 2:*27–30, 1964.

Section Three
Teacher Training

Until the last couple of years, classroom behavior modification investigations were conducted by a relatively small group of individuals whose primary concern was to demonstrate the effectiveness of these techniques upon a variety of behaviors and populations. Many of the teachers who participated were involved in more than one study and little attempt was made to implement training procedures for teachers on a large scale. Now that interest and approval of these techniques has become relatively widespread, there is a need to disseminate accurate information to teaching personnel and particularly to investigate the most effective methods of training such personnel.

The paper by Whitmore *et al.* describes the content, procedures and results of a series of workshops designed to teach classroom management procedures to administrators, teachers and aides. The workshop included training in the specification and development of behavioral objectives and the development of learning modules, and gives practice in the use of behavior modification techniques. The results indicated that the trainees improved in all three areas, with the greatest skill being shown in reinforcement procedures. Follow-up analyses of the teaching personnel by the administrators indicated continued maintenance of these skills.

The next paper, by MacDonald, examines the use of a training procedure with an important sample of teachers—those who are *not* interested in receiving advice on behavior management. Using two similar teams of teachers, MacDonald found that the team receiving support consultation (selective reinforcement of the teachers' own positive behaviors) was more effective in using contingency management techniques than the team that was simply provided with direct advice. Effectiveness was evaluated in terms of the amount of change each team exhibited from negative to positive types of student-teacher interaction as well as increases in the number of student work groups observed in the room. MacDonald emphasizes that consultants are often tempted to offer too much advice. He recommends shaping the teacher's behavior by reinforcing some of his already-existing practices as the most effective means of increasing the teacher's use of reinforcement procedures.

30

Report of In-Service Teacher Training Workshops in the Management of Classroom Behavior

PAUL G. WHITMORE, EDWARD W. FREDERICKSON and
WILLIAM H. MELCHING

THE IN-SERVICE teacher training workshops were initiated as a result of the growing dissatisfaction of school officials with the low achievement of children in the elementary grades of an industrial suburb. Corrective changes could be attempted either in the curricular materials used in the elementary grades or in the instructional practices used by the elementary teachers. Since there was no reason to believe that materials significantly superior to those already being used were available on the educational market, it was decided to attempt to make corrective changes in the classroom practices of the teachers.

The experience and background of the change agents contracted by the school district was the primary determiner of the specific changes to be sought in the teachers' classroom practices. The change agents have been primarily involved in the development and application of the technology of training to programs of instruction for adults. (Ammerman and Melching, 1966; Haggard, 1970; Smith, 1964, 1966; Whitmore, 1961a,b). This technology is basically a behavioristic approach to the design and implementation of curricula. Although new curricular materials were not to be introduced, significant improvement in the behavioral implementation of existing materials was judged to be

NOTE: Paper presented at the meeting of the American Educational Research Association, New York, 1971. Published by permission of the authors.

both possible and desirable. Obtaining such improvement requires that the teachers define the goals of their instruction in behavioral terms, that the teachers use effective techniques for modifying students' behavior toward those goals, and that the teachers require each and every student to exhibit the specified behaviors before progressing from one point of instruction to another. Thus, although the ultimate changes were to be in the behavior of children, the immediate changes were to be in the behavior of adult teachers—a target population well within the experience range of the change agents.

All too often, attempts at educational innovation have failed because members of the target population have simply been "exposed" to new concepts and techniques through readings and discussions. Although such activities may persuade members of the target population of the need for particular changes, they rarely lead to permanent changes in behavior. To counter failure on this basis, it is important that the initial change effort itself establish the desired behaviors in the teachers' classroom practices and that a long-term effort be undertaken to sustain such teacher behaviors once established (McClelland, 1968).

METHOD

A well-designed and well-executed instructional workshop can be an effective technique by which to bring about changes in the capabilities and attitudes of people. Through extended work-training sessions, workshop participants are able to acquire both the necessary skills and the confidence needed to initiate and pursue desired courses of action. It was proposed to conduct several such workshops for school system personnel. These workshops sought to enable school personnel to employ more effective procedures in the management of classrooms and in the control of student motivation, thereby serving to improve the academic performance of students.

A total of four workshops were planned and conducted. Three workshops were presented in whole to selected teachers and in part to the teachers' aides, and one workshop was presented to administrative personnel. The workshops for teachers and teacher aides focused on the following educational practices:

1. Development and use of behavioral objectives.
2. Implementation of concepts of learning modules and mastery tests.
3. Employment of contingency management techniques in the classroom.

Workshops on these topics were designed to provide participants with firsthand practice and experience. Insofar as possible, instruction in each workshop followed this general sequence of steps:

1. Rationales for the given educational practice were presented as a basis for persuading the participants of the merit of the practice.
2. Principles governing the application of techniques to specific situations were introduced as a basis for decision and action by the participants.
3. Descriptions of applications of techniques to specific situations were presented for analysis and discussion by the participants.
4. Techniques were applied by the participants in real situations under the observation and guidance of the change agents.

The first and second steps were designed to be accomplished quickly, so that a substantial portion of these workshops could be devoted to the third and fourth steps, both of which involve participants with applications. During the applications in real situations, participants were asked to use instructional materials, course content, specific behavior problems and so forth, from their own work environments and experiences.

The three teacher workshops were undertaken to establish the desired behaviors in the teachers' classroom practices. Several actions were undertaken to sustain such teacher behaviors once established. These were as follows:

1. A special workshop was conducted for administrative personnel in the school system. The participants in this workshop included the superintendent, the principals of the four elementary schools, the principal of the high school,

the curriculum coordinator, the director of federal projects and the school psychologist. This workshop was designed to prepare these administrators to do the following:

a. Explain and defend the teachers' innovative classroom practices to the public.

b. Formulate reasonably accurate expectations regarding the outcome of the teachers' innovative classroom practices.

c. Provide the teachers with appropriate reinforcement to sustain their innovative practices; i.e. contingency management of teachers, if you will.

2. Three of the elementary school principals and the director of federal projects received intensive training in contingency management techniques, so that they could provide assistance to participating teachers during the ensuing school year.

3. A follow-on program was developed as a supplement to the initial effort to help insure implementation by the participating teachers during the ensuing school year.

Rationales Underlying the Teacher Workshops

Instructional Objectives

The need for instruction in this area is based on the premise that although teachers have, in the past, customarily attempted to express the goals of their instruction, they have not stated these goals in explicit and unambiguous terms. A good indication of the skills acquired by teachers who attended the workshop on instructional objectives is contained in the set of goals established for the workshop. These goals, stated in terms of expected teacher behavior, were as follows:

1. Given a set of learning goals, identify those that are stated in behavioral terms and those that are stated in non-behavioral terms.

2. Given a set of learning goals, identify those in which conditions of performance are stated and those in which conditions of performance are omitted.

3. Given a set of learning goals, identify those in which stan-

dards of performance are stated and those in which no standards are stated.

4. Given a set of objectives in which the three structural components (action, conditions, and standards) are present, judge the precision (i.e., clarity, communicability, or explicitness) of each component. Judgments should be made as either "acceptable" or "unacceptable."

5. Given an instructional topic or body of content conventionally taught in grades 1, 2 or 3, write a set of behavioral objectives that will effectively communicate the instructor's intent with respect to student learning. As a minimum, each objective should contain

   (a) A statement of the desired student action
   (b) The important conditions under which the action must occur.
   (c) The minimum level of acceptable performance.

6. Given a set of behavioral objectives appropriate for grades 1, 2 or 3, prepare at least one criterion test item for each test item for each objective. To be acceptable, each test item must require behavior that is relevant to the behavior specified in the objective.

Learning Modules and Mastery Tests

Administrative requirements with regard to organizing and presenting instruction are frequently not compatible with the student's needs, expectations and capabilities. Because teachers are confronted with the need to cover a stated amount of material in a given period of time, there is often a tendency to present instruction faster or in greater chunks than some students can effectively assimilate it. While the student is still struggling to accomplish one segment of material, and before he has demonstrated mastery of it, new material may be introduced, and he may never have an opportunity to acquire the missing knowledge and skills. The result is that the student falls farther and farther behind and becomes increasingly frustrated with "the system."

An approach to this problem that has enjoyed some success is one in which the total amount of material to be learned in a semester or in a year is divided into more manageable segments

called units or "learning modules." Associated with each module
is an objective or set of objectives, and a corresponding criterion
or mastery test. The task for the student in learning the material,
then, is to undertake it module by module, advancing to a new
module only after he has satisfactorily accomplished the preceding
one. The goals for the teachers for this workshop were as follows:

1. Given a body of instructional content or material in an area
   in which the teacher has a demonstrated teaching competence, divide the content into modules or learning units.
   The basis for the division of material should be natural or
   logical, and the amount of material may vary from unit to
   unit. Ideally, each week of instruction should contain approximately two units of instructional material.
2. Given a body of instructional material that has been divided into modules or units, convert the content of each
   module into statements of behavioral objectives. Each objective should be worded so that the three structural components (action, condition and standard) are stated explicitly, and each objective should be designated as either
   terminal or enabling, if possible.
3. Given a list of objectives for a set of instructional modules,
   construct a set of test items (to be grouped into mastery
   tests) that will assess how effectively the student has
   achieved each objecive in each module. To be acceptable,
   each test item must require behavior that is relevant to the
   behavior specified in the associated objective. Also, so that
   students may be retested if their initial performance on a
   mastery test is not satisfactory, alternate test items must
   be constructed for each abjective.
4. Using the objectives and modules previously prepared for
   a body of content, outline the necessary learning materials
   and set of learning experiences that are intended to enable
   students to demonstrate mastery of the content, i.e. to perform successfully on the mastery test.

Contingency Management

Educational literature amply supports the contention that the teacher can modify and control the performance of her students, both academic and disciplinary, by controlling her own responses (Hall *et al.*, 1968; Madsen *et al.*, 1968; Schmidt and Ulrich, 1969; Thomas *et al.*, 1968).

A good indication of the range of skills acquired by the teachers in the contingency management workshop was provided by the goals stated below. The goals were stated in terms of the expected teacher behaviors.

1. When asked to describe a previously observed child, describe the child in terms of observable behaviors rather than in terms of motivation, moral or affective characteristics.
2. When asked to explain the causation of specific behaviors emitted by a previously observed child, cite stimuli in the child's classroom environment as causative factors rather than motivational, moral or affective characteristics.
3. Define children's behaviors in such a manner as to produce adequate reliability among several observers.
4. Specify techniques for observing and recording children's behaviors, that are appropriate to the nature of the behavioral modification which is to be made.
5. Cite specific instances of positive social reinforcers, high-probability behaviors, aversive social stimuli and social punishers common for children in the classroom.
6. Cite strengths and weaknesses of each of the following behavior modification techniques:
   (a) Positive reinforcement of desired behaviors.
   (b) Positive reinforcement of behavior incompatible to undesired behaviors.
   (c) Ignoring of undesired behaviors.
   (d) negative reinforcement of desired behaviors.
   (e) Token economies.
   (f) Performance contracting.
7. When presented with descriptions of specific undesirable classroom behaviors of either individual children or groups of children, prescribe an appropriate behavioral modification technique, identifying specific details in the situation appropriate to the application of the technique.

Conduct of Workshops

The workshops were conducted during the summer of 1970. Each workshop participant, including each teacher aide, received a copy of a special workbook prepared by the change agents. The workbook stated the objectives for each workshop, presented a schedule of activities, gave definitions of workshop terms and contained four sample "programs" in contingency management. The programs provided detailed instructions to the teacher. Using them as guides, the teacher could prepare her own procedures for modifying designated student behavior.

Table 30-1 shows the number and kinds of participants attending each workshop, and the total number of days and hours per day involved.

The contingency management workshop was scheduled to be accomplished in conjunction with the instruction of selected students from the district. Approximately 150 students from grades 1, 2 and 3 received instruction for two hours each morning for four weeks. The students were divided into 12 clasess of 10 to 15 students each, and all classes received instruction in reading and mathematics. Two teacher–teacher-aide teams were assigned to each class. Student presence during this workshop was necessary to enhance the special contingency management techniques

TABLE 30-1
WORKSHOP SCHEDULE

Workshop	Participants		Time
	No.	*Kind*	*Days and Hours per Day*
Supervisory	4	Project director and principals	3½ days, 6 hours/day
Administrative	11	District administrators	2 days, 6 hours/day
Contingency Management	24 24	Teachers Aides	19 days, 3 hours/day
Instructional objectives	24	Teachers *	9 days, 3 hours/day
Learning Modules	24	Teachers	10 days, 3 hours/day

* Twenty-four teacher aides also attended the workshop on instructional objectives but only for the first four training sessions.

and to provide a realistic setting for the practice of these techniques.

So that the workshop would not be unduly biased by the kinds of students attending summer school, participating schools were requested to send "representative" students. Thus, based on previous evaluations provided by the teacher, the students in attendance consisted of fast learners, average children and problem children. No pretesting or posttesting of students was undertaken during the workshops.

RESULTS AND DISCUSSION

The primary purpose of this series of workshops was to provide members of the school staff with sufficient practice and experience to implement the procedures in their classrooms in the ensuing school year. In the objectives and modules workshops, the teachers were formed into grade-level groups to produce a draft of sets of modules, with accompanying terminal and/or enabling objectives, for reading and for mathematics for grades 1, 2 and 3. In addition, statements of desired entry-level performances for grade 2 were also drafted. An indication of the efforts of the group to generate learning modules and behavioral objectives is shown in Table 30-2. Each teacher received a copy of all materials for her use during the coming school year. The materials provided a tie between the activities in the workshops and the teachers' subsequent classroom practices. They also provided a basis for establishing a common curriculum for each of these grades across all of the schools.

Many of the teachers have been using these objectives as a basis for preparing their daily lesson plans for the ensuing school year. Two have been using them as virtual checklists for individual students. Thirteen have used them as review guides of the previous year's work. A few are using them as goals to be met by each student. And a few have not used the objectives at all.

During the two-hour instructional periods when children were present in the classroom, the workshop staff visited the classrooms and observed teacher behavior to diagnose each teacher's use of CM procedures and techniques and to prescribe corrective treatments. It became evident that there was a need for the majority

TABLE 30-2
NUMBER OF TERMINAL OBJECTIVES DRAFTED
FOR EACH GRADE LEVEL

Grade Level and Subject Area	No. of Terminal Objectives
Kindergarten	
Reading and Mathematics combined	22
Grade 1	
Reading	
Word Study Skills	42
Comprehension	7
Mathematics	30
Grade 2	
Reading	
Desired entrance behaviors	11
Word Study Skills	18
Comprehension	7
Mathematics	
Desired entrance behaviors	14
End of course behaviors	14
Grade 3	
Reading	
Word Study Skills	23
Comprehension	7
Mathematics	15

of the teachers to increase their frequency of response opportunities provided to the children and to increase the number of approving behaviors provided. To do so, teachers were asked to use M&M candies as reinforcers and to dispense a minimum of 50 M&M's per hour. The teachers were further instructed to reinforce only academic behaviors at this time. They were not to use M&M's to control disciplinary problems. The level of 50 M&M's was selected because it represented a middle figure for approving behaviors as determined from the early observation recording sheets.

In going from room to room, the workshop staff observed that a variety of technical errors were being made by the teachers in dispensing the M&M's. For instance, some teachers were having their teacher aides hand out the M&M's, which tended to delay the reinforcement and kept the teacher from acquiring secondary reinforcement properties. Also, some teachers were not providing social or verbal reinforcement in conjunction with the M&M's, which was a problem for some teachers for a considerable period of time. During the initial observation, it was also noted that some teachers dispensed several M&M's at one time, hence reducing the reinforcing value of each M&M. At least one teacher had added an element of punishment in that she took M&M's away from the child if he misbehaved. Explanations regarding these technical errors were provided to the teachers so that they understood why they should not engage in such activities.

It was also pointed out that many teachers would have to change their teaching style slightly in order to dispense 50 M&M's per hour. Many would have to create more academic response opportunities, while others would have to gauge their questions to the level of the individual child, since they could not reinforce the child unless he answered correctly. It was also suggested that teachers might try drawing the children in close around them during the period of time in which they were providing response opportunities. In this way, they could dispense the M&M's immediately and unobtrusively. It was decided that the teachers should continue the M&M program for the rest of the workshop. The reinforcing of academic responses was chosen because it was noted that the instances of disruptive behavior were quite low. This situation was quite probably attributable to the presence of four adults in each classroom. Hence, it was not appropriate to establish a general contingency management program in any classroom to control disruptive behavior.

By the beginning of the third week, it was quite evident that many of the teachers had incorporated the CM procedures into their various teaching approaches. The term "various teaching approaches" was used because almost all teachers who were observed presented the academic materials in vastly different manners. The approaches varied from the extremely quiet classroom atmosphere of a few teachers to other classrooms where there was generally a high level of activity and noise. It was evident that teachers had different definitions of disruptive or inappropriate classroom behavior.

During the third week, it was also evident that some of the teachers still were not providing enough social reinforcement or verbal praise when they dispensed M&M's. In addition, other teachers still did not provide enough response opportunities for all the students in the classroom. Some teachers tended to call upon only those children who volunteered to answer questions, whereas other teachers seemed to respond only to those children who insisted upon being called upon.

Almost all teachers and teacher aids had some difficulty ignoring inappropriate behaviors. In many cases, basic concepts involved in the procedure had been misunderstood. During one discussion, it was pointed out that ignoring inappropriate behaviors could only be effective if the appropriate behaviors were reinforced. Teachers and aides both had been ignoring, or at least trying to ignore, inappropriate behavior or disruptive behavior without reinforcing appropriate behavior, and as a result, they were not having much success in eliminating the disruptive behavior.

During the third week, the teachers had progressed to the point that their behavior had begun to change sufficiently so that social reinforcement could be provided to them as a group and, in some cases, individually. By the end of the third week, the teachers began to ask more questions and bring up specific problems that they had noted in the classroom. The questions and problems were discussed with the entire group. In many cases, teachers suggested solutions to problems brought up by other teachers.

During the two-week period when teacher observations were recorded, data were obtained for three teacher behaviors: response opportunities (RO), approving behaviors (AB) and disapproving behaviors (DB). The means of the teacher behaviors are presented graphically in Figure 30–1.

Thirteen of the 22 teachers for whom data are reported increased their rate of providing response opportunities by at least 50 percent. The remaining nine teachers initially used a high rate of teacher-student interaction, which they maintained during the observation period. Thirteen teachers had an increasing rate of approving behaviors, but this was accompanied by a marked decrease in disapproving behaviors. The remaining teachers maintained a relatively high level of approving behaviors.

The changes in disapproving behaviors were quite noticeable in many teachers who routinely used punishment. A total of 15

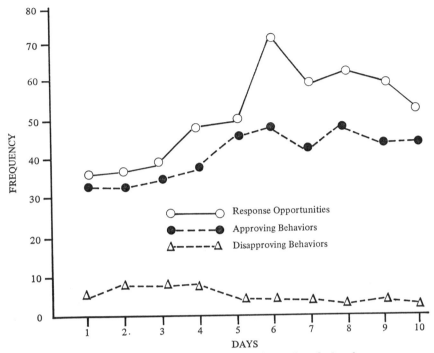

Figure 30-1. Mean frequency of teacher behaviors.

teachers showed a decrease in their rates of disapproving behaviors. Two teachers had increases in disapproving behaviors;
however, they also showed an increase in approving behavior.

In order to statistically evaluate the changes in teacher behaviors, analysis of variance (ANOVA) procedures were used.
Because of the problem of missing data decreasing the efficiency
of the procedures, a reduced amount of data was subjected to
statistical evaluation. For all three behaviors, there was a significant (.05) change in behavior (in the desired directions) from
the first to the last days of observation.

It can be concluded from the evaluation of the observation
data that the behavior of the teachers as a group changed significantly. They learned to present more response opportunities
to the students. They learned to use more positive reinforcing
statements and gestures, along with fewer aversive or punishing
behaviors.

As part of the follow-on program during the school year, the school district's director of federal projects visited each participating teacher's classroom once each week for the first six weeks and then once every two weeks. During these visits, he recorded the occurrence of the teacher's response opportunities, approving behaviors and disapproving behaviors. In general, the rate of response opportunities and approving behaviors has tended to hold at the level established during the latter part of the summer workshop. The rate of disapproving behaviors initially rose above the final workshop level but has declined steadily since then.

In order to help sustain the changes in the teachers' classroom practices, the director of federal projects has published several newsletters featuring activities of the participating teachers, which provides social reinforcement for those teachers whose activities are featured and designates them as models for others to emulate. In addition, the external change agents are providing the teachers with consultation according to a prearranged schedule, which also helps to direct and sustain changes in the teachers' classroom practices.

REFERENCES

Ammerman, H. L. and Melching, W. H.: The derivation, analysis, and classification of instructional objectives. HumRRO Technical Report 66-4, May, 1966.

Haggard, D. F.: An experimental program of instruction on the management of training. HumRRO Technical Report 70-9, June, 1970.

Hall, R. V., Panyon, M., Rabon, D. and Broden, M.: Instructing beginning teachers in reinforcement procedures which improve classroom control. *Journal of Applied Behavior Analysis, 1*:315–322, 1968.

Madsen, C. H., Becker, W. C. and Thomas, D. R.: Rules, praise, and ignoring: Elements of elementary classroom control. *Journal of Applied Behavior Analysis, 1*:139–150, 1968.

McClelland, W. A.: The process of effecting change. HumRRO Professional Paper 32-68, October, 1968.

Schmidt, G. W. and Ulrich, R. E.: Effects of group contingent events upon classroom noise. *Journal of Applied Behavior Analysis, 2*: 171–179, 1969.

Smith, R. G.: The development of training objectives. HumRRO Research Bulletin 11, June, 1964.

Smith, R. G.: The design of instructional systems. HumRRO Technical Report 66-18, November, 1966.

Thomas, D. R., Becker, W. C. and Armstrong, M.: Production and elimination of disruptive classroom behavior by systematically varying teacher's behavior. *Journal of Applied Behavior Analysis, 1*:35–45, 1968.

Whitmore, P. G.: Deriving and specifying instructional objectives. In P. Thayer: Automated teaching: Research problems. Symposium presented at the American Psychological Association, New York, September, 1961a.

Whitmore, P. G.: A rational analysis of the process of instruction. *IRE* (Institute of Radio Engineers) *Transactions on Education,* December, 1961b, Vol. E-4, No. 4, pp. 135–143.

31

The Kibitz Dimension in Teacher Consultation

Scott MacDonald

THE LAST DECADE has seen the rapid development of an effective technology in which essential management variables have been identified. Teachers, for example, may seek assistance in classroom discipline and with reasonable assurance, anticipate help in altering the behavior of one problem child, or at enhancing the study habits of an entire class. Whether called behavior modification, contingency contracting or classroom management, the application of learning principles to the behavior of students has become widely discussed in literature, (Benson, 1968; Hall et al., 1968; Meachum and Weisson, 1969; Staats, 1964; Tharp and Wetzel, 1970; MacDonald, 1971).

In response to the problem of conveying the information regarding the technology to teachers, an effective method has been described in which a college laboratory course format was used, with the teachers using their own classrooms as laboratories (MacDonald, 1970: MacDonald and Gallimore, in press). Thus, for those teachers who actively sought it, there was the technology and delivery system available through consultation which teachers could solicit to improve their management of classroom behavior problems.

Consultation in schools, however, does not always match the avid listener with the source of assistance. The school situation is one in which the teacher works in a structured hierarchy, often under several supervisors, some with vaguely identified authority over her. For numerous reasons, the consultant may

NOTE: Unpublished manuscript, 1970. Published by permission of author.

unexpectedly find himself in dialogue with a teacher who is at best, a polite listener. Whether the teacher has been forced, tricked, cajoled or simply become a passive partner to an active consultant, he responds differently than the one who actively sought advice. And the teacher who enters a consultative relationship with serious reservations about its potential value may regard a consultant as little more than a kibitzer.

Some teachers have formulated in their minds and perhaps articulated in public their lack of training in management skills. Others have not, though they are aware that children come to school for many reasons other than to obey the directives of the teacher. But for the teacher who is reluctant to discuss classroom management (even though she is aware that some training would increase her effectiveness), an effective consultative relationship requires more than an expert telling the teacher the essential facts and principles.

This paper deals with consultation involving teachers who, for various reasons, entered consultation reluctantly and/or under some degree of pressure to do so. This paper compares two styles of consultation with relatively reluctant clients. The focus is on consultant-teacher interaction when consultant and teacher find themselves working together even though the teacher may not have asked for help or had already met with consultants and, though problems had not been resolved, decided an optimum level of dialogue had been reached.

METHOD
Teaching Styles

In working with reluctant teachers, two rather different styles of consultation were selected. The first technique was an extension of the straightforward educative model in which the information is expressed directly to the teacher (Hall *et al.*, 1968; MacDonald and Gallimore, 1971). The information was handled as part of the relationship—delicately interspersed at the rate, in the judgment of the consultant, at which the teachers were prepared to use it. This will be called "traditional consultation," a style widely used by educational consultants, as well as mental health consultants who work with school personnel.

A second style was adopted from Sarason (Sarason *et al.*, 1966) who described support as an effective technique in assisting teachers. Since it was assumed that teachers in this situation (described below) behave in a variety of teaching acts, some more effective than others, it was decided to compare the traditional method with one which selectively supported the effective teaching acts in a manner described elsewhere (Verplanck, 1956) and referred to as "shaping." This will be called the "support consultation."

Setting

The study was done in an elementary school project intended to provide increased educational opportunities to economically disadvantaged children. The students were from families of heterogenous means, including those of middle as well as low income. The students were of varied ethnic origins, including Asian, Polynesian, Caucasian and mixes thereof.

The study concerned teaching teams working with classes comprised of pupils from two grade levels (to facilitate advantages of nongraded combinations of students). One level included students at kindergarten and first-grade level, and the other included students from second- and third-grade level. Two teaching teams operated at each joint-level, so that two kindergarten–first-grade classrooms as well as two second-grade–third-grade classrooms were targets for consideration. One team at each grade level was included in each of the two consultative styles.

The teaching teams were comprised of three teachers, a paraprofessional educational assistant and in most cases a parent who, though their time was volunteered, behaved similarly to the paraprofessionals and will henceforth be referred to as such.

In this federally funded project, there were "resource" people who included an active vice-principal, a school counselor, a public health nurse, two student social workers under the supervision of the University of Hawaii Department of Social Service, two part-time social workers, a mental health consultant, a psychiatrist and a consultant from the University College of Education!

Hiring one more consultant specifically for teachers of this project resulted not from the requests for help from the teachers but by the influence of the project manager, who felt that consultation might relieve the staff of some of the discipline problems the teachers were having. Thus the consultation was not delivered to an eager and requesting staff but to a group of teachers who had previous experience with consultants and *who were currently surrounded by them.*

Subjects

The subjects of this study were 20 teachers and classroom helpers who were the front-line personnel of this project. They were heterogeneous in experience, ranging from beginning teachers to veterans of over ten years in the classroom, with ethnic origin and characteristics similar to the student population, though not in the same proportions. The teaching teams were comparable in experience and ethnic background.

Procedure

There were four phases of the study. The first was to establish the consultative styles, the second to establish baseline data, the third to gather posttreatment data and the fourth to provide teachers with the information gained during the consultation. To give the reader a more complete feeling for the "field" nature of this study, a more complete description of the phases is included.

Phase I: Introduction. The consultant was contacted by the project manager and invited to speak to the faculty. The first meeting was cancelled because many teachers could not make the meeting. Another 90-minute meeting was scheduled and this time convened. The major topics of discussion were generalizations about dealing with students, and the experience of the consultant. Teachers were invited to bring up specific problems they had in class or to invite the consultant to their class for individualized assistance. No requests for help were forthcoming. A subsequent 90-minute faculty meeting was held, at which one teacher (who was employing a system of awarding M & M's to a student when he emitted favorable behavior, though the program was proceeding badly) asked if the consultant was another of "those behavior modifiers." The consultant answered questions directly (he admitted some people might, indeed, call him such names as "behavior modifier") and agreed with several teachers who expressed the opinion that faculty meetings were a waste of time. The classroom was the place where it happened. The consultant suggested he visit some rooms and get a better picture of what the project was about.

Phase II: Observation. The consultant was first invited to visit one team. He obtained a seating chart, a list of the troublesome children and a description of behaviors he should be especially alert to observe. The consultant then came to class equipped with a stopwatch, graph paper and a handful of pencils and began to record the behaviors of the children, using a behavioral code especially adapted to this task (Table 31-1). While recording the behaviors of the students served as discussion topics

TABLE 31-1
OBSERVATIONAL CODE

Student Behavior Categories

W: Student is working out of a textbook, or assigned work.
A: Actively attentive to teacher: A— attending to teacher, but slumped back or non-responsive when response is indicated: A+ actively attentive and responsive, squirming to give answer, fidgeting with excitement with what is happening, etc.
SW: Student is talking with other student, or oriented posturely with one, while doing assigned work.
DD: Day dreaming, staring out window, picking nose, sitting with eyes closed, sleeping.
D: Student is disruptive—actively trying to gain attention of another pupil to distract from work, or hitting, striking or throwing objects at another student such that will obviously distract him.
Pg: Occupied with some personal activity: combing hair, looking in purse, eating, scratching, playing game.
R: Responds verbally at appropriate time.
M: Moving about room—out of seat.
Z: Close to adult and not in verbal interaction with adult.

Teacher Behavior Categories

S: Supports student with verbal compliment or encouragement, gesture of approval, pat on back, etc.
D: Desist: tells student to desist an action, or makes gesture indicating the same.
Cont: Actually handles child in attempt to direct or redirect student's actions.
Dir: Giving specific instructions to perform an act without implying dissatisfaction with previous performance.
IG: Ignoring a student—scored when student makes bid for attention, especially scored when teacher has decided to use ignoring rather than D with a student either by own choice, or suggestion by consultant.
Q: Asks question (attempting to solicit student response).
I: Giving information to class—lecturing, reading instructions, etc.

in dealing with teachers, it was the recordings of teacher behavior which were important to this study. From a research standpoint, this period of observation—some four weeks long for the first team—served as a baseline during which usual frequencies of target behaviors could be obtained. Contact of consultant with teachers of the first team aroused the curiosity of the others who heard via the grapevine that the consultant did nothing but code behavior all day. When it became known that the consultant could describe in detail what target children (and teachers) did and for how long they did it, the consultant was invited to observe the other classes. During Phase 2, the consultant observed and did not answer questions about handling of problems, with the excuse that he first had to determine accurately what the problems were.

Phase III: Consultation. After establishing expected frequencies of pupil and teacher behavior in each of the classrooms, the consultant began informal consultations with teachers who sought advice by having coffee with them in the teachers' lounge or chatting with them after class and in some instances after school. With one kindergarten team and one third-grade team, he consulted in the *traditional consultation* style; with the other teams he used the *support consultation* style. During the consultation phase, the consultant continued to spend at least half of his time recording teacher and student behavior (necessary to evaluate the consultative effort).

Phase IV: Critique. At the close of the semester, the faculty was again assembled on two afternoons for exchange of information, summary of techniques and critique of the consultation's efforts.

Consultation Styles

The two styles of consultation may be identified as traditional or support.

Traditional Consultation. Consultant first made observations on identified "problems" (recorded student behavior) and shared the results with teachers. He then discussed alternative actions (teacher actions described below) that might lead to resolution of the problem. Suggestions of the teacher were solicited and made at least a part of the set of recommended teacher acts. Each discussion ended with a review of the steps involved; where there were several alternatives, the consultant suggested which should be tried first. Usually, the teachers and consultant discussed implementation, though some teachers did not request such specific information.

Support Consultation. When the teachers of the support consultation style met with the consultant, they received specific results of observations and were told where they had done well. The consultant selected out acts of teaching which achieved especially good results with the teachers. When teachers asked for specific techniques or advice, the consultant replied with, "What do you think about that?" or "I've noticed you're really pretty good with that. How do you think you could handle it?" When the teachers discussed several alternatives, the consultant reacted positively to those that were identified as "desirable." In this way, teachers left the consultation with support for advice supplied by themselves.

Recording

Student and teacher acts (Table 1) and programs utilizing student participation were recorded during Phases 2 and 3. Three types of observation described more fully elsewhere (MacDonald with Gallimore, 1971) were used.

Sweep. Each student in class was scored in a prearranged plan (e.g. those from left to right, or from seat #1 to #25). Normally, a class of 25 students were rated in from 60 to 90 seconds.

Contingency-Observation. Surveillance was maintained of the whole classroom until teacher directed a response to a student. The student was rated for the behavior shown before the teacher's attention, then the teacher's behavior was rated, and when the teacher's attention shifted away, the subsequent student behavior was again rated. This estimated the effect of the teacher's action on the student's activity.

Interaction. When the teacher worked directly with pupils, her behavior was rated into the prescribed categories, or if none applied to her actions, a description was made. Length of time spent in each action was recorded, as well as the student's behavior toward which her actions were directed.

The sweep provided frequency counts of student and teacher behavior. The contingency-observation provided frequency counts of student behavior and provided teachers with an evaluation of their effectiveness as well as describing the ratio of behaviors afforded to the identified students. The Interaction enumerated teacher behaviors, as well as identifying and enumerating student-participation programs.

A procedure unique to field situations was obtained in this study. Rather than establishing a pattern of observations in advance, the consultant observed by teacher request. When teachers wanted to know the effectiveness of a new technique, regardless of other considerations, he was obliged to use sweep. Thus, the pattern of data was dictated by teacher demand, though the amount of time spent observing each teacher was carefully balanced.

Target Behaviors

From previous work (MacDonald with Gallimore, 1971), the consultant identified two classes of teacher behavior: those related with high probability of success with students (referred to as support behaviors and programs eliciting high student involvement) and those related to low probability of success (referred to as desist behavior and programs eliciting little student involvement).

Support behaviors included verbal encouragement, pats on back, watching students, approaching them. Desist behavior included verbal and gestural acts of desist, physical restraint, giving commands, etc.

High-participation programs were those in which students responded with a verbalization (question and answer), a physical act, etc. Low-participation programs were typified by the lecture, seat drill, individualized audio-visual equipment, etc.

It was the explicit intent of the consultant to increase teacher support behavior with "problem" children and increase participation programs while decreasing desist behaviors and nonparticipa-

tive programs. Each strategy, i.e. encouragement of support behaviors and encouragement of high participation programs, was
associated with a specific type of problem.

Type #1: A Student Exhibiting Undesirable Behavior. The
first kind of problem brought to the consultant by members of
each team were those of individual students exhibiting undesirable
behavior. In these "opening" or "introductory" cases, the problem
could clearly be established as within the student. Teachers stated
that they did not wish to have their own feelings examined but
wanted help with the problem students. Thus, they were quick
to agree that regardless of where the locus of the problem lay,
it was the teachers who had to initiate action in order to bring
about a change in the behavior of the student. In some cases,
manipulation in the child's environment would be indicated
(change his seat; etc.); in some cases it was necessary to alter
his physical status (provide hungry student with snack), but
usually it came to the teacher-pupil interaction, and regardless of
who was "at fault," it was the teacher who needed to initiate
change. In fact, in many cases, the consultative effort could be
reduced to a simple formula: get the teacher to behave positively
to preferred behaviors of the student, and ignore misbehavior
(reduce desists).

The consultant's effectiveness could not, in this situation, be
accurately evaluated in terms of the altered behaviors of the target
student. For with so many persons involved in an identified
problem, it would be presumptuous to attribute either success or
failure with a pupil to the consultant's efforts with the teacher.
And since the target of the consultant's efforts were in terms of
teacher behavioral change, her behavior became the focus of
evaluative data.

Type #2: Enhancing Group Study. After several individual
cases were examined and mutually discussed, some teachers expressed concern over the fact that they had problems with several
students at a time or with the entire class. This was a shift in
emphasis from the behavior of a problem student to a concern
for their general effectiveness in teaching entire groups of students.
In effect, they were asking for suggestions directly relating to
their own pattern of behaviors. They described their desire to

command the attention of students or their desire to "hold the class" for entire segments of class work. In these requests, students were not considered as "problems" but, rather, simply respondents to whatever techniques the teachers utilized.

While some of the desired results could be obtained by considering the acts of the teachers as in problem Type #1, there were other, more complex, sets of teacher behaviors which were the target of consultation efforts. These behaviors were involving students in the lesson: again, past experience indicated that student involvement was a desired technique, and the increased use of programs involving student participation was the intent of consultation efforts.

RESULTS AND DISCUSSION

Type #1 problems were those in which the consultant simply tried to increase the number of support behaviors and decrease the desist behaviors. An example of Type #1 behavior, using traditional consultation style is as follows:

> A girl was identified by one teacher as being rather "dull" and not capable of work—she rarely attended to her lessons. The girl spent time during math lessons wandering about the room and chatting with others. She was pleasant to the teacher when teacher talked to her. Observations revealed that the teacher rarely spoke to the child and only when the girl *was out of seat*. In the *traditional consultation* style, she was told to attend to the child early in the hour, while the child was still in her seat. The teacher was told to announce periodically, "now let's see who is studying," and to comment favorably when the girl was in seat and reading. The teacher's behavior showed a considerable increase in supportive comments toward the girl and no discernible decrease in critical remarks.

Table 31–2 presents the number of support and desist behaviors detected per 25-minute observation period (some of the instruction was one in 25-minute modules, and hence all rates of student and teacher behavior will be reported in behaviors per 25-minute period). The activity of a teacher during any 25-minute period is somewhat determined by the subject matter and the specific objectives. In view of this, figures shown are from periods of comparable subject matter.

TABLE 31.2

DESIST AND SUPPORT BEHAVIORS BEFORE AND AFTER CONSULTATION BY THE FOUR TEAMS IN DEALING WITH INDIVIDUAL STUDENTS

Traditional Consultation

		D			S		
		Before	After	Change	Before	After	Change
Team 1	T	7	11	−4	5	14	+9
	P	13	9	+4	10	11	+1
Team 3	T	21	15	+6	10	5	−5
	P	23	19	+4	4	4	...

Support Consultation

		D			S		
		Before	After	Change	Before	After	Change
Team 2	T	7	2	+5	4	11	+7
	P	4	0	+4	4	13	+9
Team 4	T	6	1	+5	17	49	+32
	P	11	4	+7	4	17	+32

T = Teachers
P = Paraprofessionals

Number of 25-minute periods upon which above averages are based:

	Team			
	1	2	3	4
Before	5	3	4	2
After	6	7	9	8

Chi square values for comparisons of teacher and paraprofessional behaviors by consultation style:

	x^2	df	P
Teachers:			
Desist behaviors	6.1	1	.02
Support behaviors	3.5	1	.10
Paraprofessionals:			
Desist behaviors	3.9	1	.05
Support behaviors	6.45	1	.02

Table 31–2 shows that, contrary to expectations, the paraprofessionals were at least as active (numbers of *D*'s and *S*'s) in the classrooms as the professionals, at least in the management of the children. It is crucial to this analysis to understand that facial and gestural behaviors were a large part of the "vocabulary" used in scoring and that the nonverbal communications were a large part of the behaviors exhibited by the paraprofessionals. The active participation of the paraprofessionals is an index of success of the entire project, which deliberately attempted to achieve such active participation. The response of the paraprofessional over the time period studied shows that responsiveness of this source of manpower and suggests that perhaps more paraprofessionals could be involved in these programs, especially as classroom managers. Second, the table shows that the paraprofessionals tended to used more D behaviors. This was probably due to the essential "maintain order" orientation they had— a role which is consistent with their role prescription. Paraprofessionals are often counted on by teachers to maintain order while teacher presented academic content. It was a pleasant surprise that the paraprofessionals *did* respond as quickly as they did to consultation. Table 31–2 shows further that there is great variability in the numbers of D and S behaviors exhibited by members of the various teams. While the table does not show it, there tended to be variations within each team, with some members being highly active while others were less so.

To make the Table 31–2 easier to read, a change score is reported. The change score reflects an increase or decrease over time in the average behaviors exhibited by the particular team. The + denotes a fevorable shift in behavior (increase in S behavior, decrease in D behavior); − denotes the reverse).

Also included in the Table are chi-square comparisons computed directly from the table entries (McNemar, 1955). While all of the comparisons are not statistically significant, the reader will note that in each of the comparisons, the support consultation style yielded an advantage in the preferred direction. Thus, since the cumulative comparisons were all in a single direction, the pattern tends to reflect the enhancement of preferred teacher behavior by support style to a degree underestimated by the statistics.

This unexpected result might have resulted because the teachers in teams #2 and #4 developed a stronger rapport with the consultant and encouraged other team members to accept the "positive" approach that was supported. But the "positive rapport" was an advantage of support consultation, so part of the rapport effect is actually built into the comparison. Team members of #1 and #3 did not generate a "team spirit"; the traditional consultation style developed a rapport between consultant and teacher, and one composed of many elements, not all positive. While in some instances the team members of teams 1 and 3 banded together against administration and perceived criticism of the consultant, they also competed against each other in a tacit

TABLE 31-3
AVERAGE NUMBER OF PHYSICAL CONTROL BEHAVIORS

Traditional Consultation		Support Consultation	
Before	After	Before	After
7	15	3	1/2

contest to see who could gain most approval from the consultant for initiating the best program. It is impossible to tell from this study whether this was a part of the consultative style or whether it was a natural inclination of the teachers involved.

There is some evidence that the traditional consultative teachers adopted consultative advice in behavior but not attitude, at least among paraprofessionals. In some instances, they tended to grab misbehaving children firmly and force them to a conforming behavior (desist behaviors). Table 31-3 shows the average numbers of physical control behaviors per 25-minute period before and after consultation by consultation style. The data suggest that the support calculation was successful in reducing this behavior while traditional was not. Actually, it appeared to the consultant that two paraprofessionals, who accounted for most of the physical control behaviors, had reduced the number of verbal D behaviors they exhibited and adopted the more subtle strategy of physical control (which is difficult to discriminate from patting children or hugging them which are scored as S's and highly desirable forms of it).

The teachers in the support consultation, in one form or another, expressed their delight with the results of the S strategy over the D. In spite of the fact they had some reservations of "bribing" students, the increase in S behavior of this group supports their verbal claims: that they generally tried to encourage positive results.

It must be concluded that in direct consultation, the traditional form, even the very carefully and often indirectly applied use of specific advice sometimes results in the opposite of what the consultant intends in regard to the behavior of teachers. While the results of the traditional consultation may be considered as positive, the surprising superiority of support style consultation is clear in individual problems.

Type #2 problems were those in which the consultant attempted to foster the number of programs or teaching efforts in which student participation was used. An example of type #2 consultation is as follows:

> A teacher in the support consultation group wanted to increase student interest in spelling lessons, hoping that it would reduce the number of careless errors they made. When asked what she thought she might do, she stated that the students needed to take more part in the lesson. She got each a blackboard, formed teams, and when she tested, she stated the word and selected student whose hand was first raised. This technique was all she needed, as the public participation alone stimulated considerable interest.

While the objectives of the consultant in type #2 problems involved a decrease in the amount of attention teachers gave to students who were involved in nonstudy or nonattentive behavior, the major objective was to influence teachers to develop programs in which they intentionally elicited student response of some sort. The specific behaviors of the teacher were not the target of observation but rather the numbers of groups of students involved in participation learning. The consultant noted the use of such programs during observations, tallying credit for favorable response with each instance of such a program. Thus one teacher received three notations at once when it was observed that she was working concurrently with three groups of students, demanding from each of the groups that students within them respond to her or each other. Thus the notations may be inflated by the tendency for those teachers that used any participative programs to use *more than one*. The numbers of notations are compared in Table 31–4.

TABLE 31-4
NUMBER OF STUDENT INVOLVEMENT PROGRAMS PER
25-MINUTE PERIOD BEFORE AND AFTER
CONSULTATION

Traditional Consultation					*Support Consultation*			
	Before	*After*	*Change*			*Before*	*After*	*Change*
Team 1	5	10	+5		Team 2	1	3	+ 2
Team 3	7	7	....		Team 4	8	22	+14

Number of 25-minute periods upon which above averages are based:

		Team			
		1	*2*	*3*	*4*
	Before	2	2	2	2
	After	5	4	4	6

While Table 31–4 suggests that both consultation styles had a net positive effect, the support style not only increased the number of participative programs used by teachers already employing such techniques, but stimulated a team which was generally oriented to more lecture-style class presentation. Interestingly, the teachers in the support consultation attributed to the consultant several ideas that they employed in their programs of student participation. That is, while the consultant at no time made any substantive suggestions about program, the teachers frequently attributed to him effective suggestions that worked. At first it was difficult to understand. Reflection of the events suggests that the consultant supported certain alternatives that were made in his presence, and when these alternatives were employed and worked, he was given credit, not for supporting them, but rather for originating them!

The unexpected superiority of the support consultation over the traditional style and the use of subtle control techniques by the teams exposed to traditional consultation suggests that teachers in this urban setting do not suffer from a lack of information or alternatives from which to choose. Indeed, the major problem seems to involve a combination of their being exposed to many pieces of advice regarding their individual actions and at the same time feeling as if they are under constant surveillance, the major purpose of which is to detect "problem children." Teachers felt great pressure when being subjected to diverse and frequent advice. The pressure stimulated by the consultation does not result in acceptance of the advice but in attempts to eliminate problem behaviors. Teachers sometimes point out that the advice of one consultant is often opposed to that from another. And the teacher, exposed to multiple and conflicting consultations, responds by attempting to tighten her operation by increased compliance. The situation of frequent traditional consultations to teachers is analogous to the card player who, when subjected to constant and insistent kibitzing, inadvertently performs well below his usual level.

Support consultation, by utilizing the principle of selective reinforcement, enhances teacher effectiveness by increasing the frequency of effective teacher acts. Further, when the consultant rewards the teacher through the process of identifying effective teacher behavior, he is encouraging the teacher to seek, from her already adequate supply of alternatives, those which lead to the preferred student behavior. At the same time, supportive interaction lessens the emphasis on the teacher's perceived need for compliant behavior, and the teacher seeks other forms of student behavior, such as participation in the lesson, with the inevitable result of enhanced student academic performance. Based on evidence from this study, the teacher benefits from support— not in turning up new alternatives but from selecting from those already ringing in her ears.

A third type of problem may appear similar to either of the other two but is a problem of a different sort and one common only to team teaching. While the variations of this problem are limitless, the basic elements are easily identified: one teacher initiates action in regard to a pupil who is identified as a delinquent but is opposed by another teacher who reports that the problem is one of mismanagement. These problems are often accompanied by various staff members pulling the pupil in different directions.

The consultant's objective in this case may seem at first to be that of identifying those teacher acts which lead to positive student actions and those which lead to disruptive behavior. In the traditional consulted teams, for example, the consultant suggested which teacher behaviors elicited the observed behaviors on the parts of the students, and it was clear from the data who was effective and who was not. However, the teachers in the traditional consultation teams heightened the number and intensity of competitive remarks they made to the consultant about co-teachers, and the adverse effects on the target children were obvious. Thus the traditional consultation contributed to the increased competitive behavior among the teachers.

The support consultation teams were encouraged to develop solutions as a team and carry out their program as a unit. In one case, a student was switched from one teacher to another (normally an act which would shame a teacher) and in another, a team decided to discuss one example of this type of problem each week, in a systematic effort to present a "united front" to these students.

SUMMARY

The consultant in an urban area must be alert to the needs of the teacher early in the consultative effort. The problem of the teacher may be that of being advised and, at the same time, criticized for the number of "problems" she refers. The teacher may be trying too many things rather than not enough, or she may be trying to eliminate problems rather than teach new skills. She may be overstimulated to improve and develop ideas rather than the reverse. Where there are many resources available to the teacher, as is encountered in large population centers, the teacher may not only have many resources upon which she can call but she may have resources brought to her when she did not, in fact, ask for them. In such cases, the problem for the consultant is to avoid the role of just another kibitzer. When the teacher has too many sources of advice, the consultant may achieve his best results by cutting through all the advice and asking her what she thinks and what seems to be working, and in supporting her actions. An analogy might be appropriate in the situation of the urban teacher: in a sea of advice, she looks for a raft of confidence.

REFERENCES

Benson, Arthur M. (Ed.): *Modifying Deviant Social Behaviors in Various Classroom Settings.* Eugene, Oregon, Department of Special Education, College of Education, University of Oregon, 1969.

Hall, R. V., Panyan, M., Rabon, D. and Broden, M.: Instructing beginning teachers in reinforcement procedures which improve classroom control. *Journal of Applied Behavior Analysis, 1:*315–322, 1968.

MacDonald, W. Scott: Presenting behavior management principles to teachers, Paper read at Western Psychological Association Meeting, April, 1970, Los Angeles. Available from Psychology Department, University of Hawaii, Honolulu.

MacDonald, W. Scott (with Gallimore, Ronald): *Battle in the Classroom.* Scranton, International Textbook, 1971.

MacDonald, W. Scott and Gallimore, R.: A classroom method of teaching management skills to teachers. *Journal of Educational Research,* in press, 1972.

Meacham, M. L. and Wiessen, A. E.: *Changing Classroom Behavior: a Manual for Precision Teaching.* Scranton, International Textbook, 1969.

McNemar, Q.: *Psychological Studies.* New York, Wiley, 1955.

Sarason, S. B., Levine, M., Goldenberg, I. I., Cherlin, D. D. and Bennett, E. M.: *Psychology in Community Settings: Clinical, Educational, Vocational, Social Aspects.* New York, Wiley, 1966.

Verplanck, W. S.: The operant conditioning of human motor behavior. *Psychological Bulletin, 53:*70–83, 1956.

Section Four
Issues and Problems

Mᴏsᴛ ᴘᴜʙʟɪsʜᴇᴅ ʀᴇᴘᴏʀᴛs of classroom behavior modification investigations are concerned with detailing a specific set of procedures, analyzing the results and providing some discussion about the findings. There have been few papers which have attempted to outline in a general fashion either suggestions for teachers to follow in applying modification techniques or problems which may arise in the course of such applications. The first paper in this section, by O'Leary, provides a brief summary of practices, difficulties and suggestions concerning one specific area of classroom modification techniques, that of token systems. O'Leary is careful to point out certain crucial aspects of token systems such as the rules for exchanging tokens for back-up rewards, the need for consultation in designing and evaluating the token program and the importance of combining a social reinforcement with tangible rewards. He also discusses the necessity for providing a solid academic program and the difficulties encountered in withdrawing a token system. His suggestion that reinforcement procedures be applied at all levels within the educational hierarchy, from children in the classroom right up to the superintendent of schools, may possibly lead to even more effective ways of using behavior modification techniques.

The articles included in this book of readings have presented classroom behavior modification in a very favorable light. There have, however, been numerous criticisms of the area, and in the last article, MacMillan and Forness discuss some of these concerns. Although they specifically criticize behavior modification as applied to exceptional children, their comments are equally applicable to all behavior modification programs. These authors point out that while these techniques can enable teachers to alter the behavior of their students, there are no guidelines as to what the changes should be. They state that education goals are not determined by learning theory and that while the educator may acquire considerable skill in applying behavior modification techniques for the purpose of either accelerating desirable behavior or decelerating undesirable behavior, the nature of what behavior is desirable or undesirable is left to the individual teacher. Thus, having acquired the skills, it is possible for teachers to misuse them by attempting to eliminate behavior that they find annoying but which may not interfere with the child's learning. The authors suggest that the work of other theorists such as Piaget may prove useful in helping teachers to specify certain desired terminal behaviors in students.

The authors also criticize what they believe is behavior modification's preoccupation with extrinsic motivation and lack of interest in the intrinsic and cognitive aspects of reinforcement. We would argue that behavior modifiers are very much concerned with intrinsic motivation. One of the problems, however, is that so much effort has gone into developing powerful systems which change behavior rapidly that adequate procedures designed to fade out extrinsic reinforcers (and promote intrinsic motivation) have not yet been specified. The arguments presented by MacMillan and Forness concerning the necessity of utilizing empirical data from different theoretical positions in an effort to produce the best educational practices are well founded and will hopefully help to prevent the belief that behavior modification procedures will cure all of our educational ills.

32

Establishing Token Programs in Schools: Issues and Problems

K. Daniel O'Leary

ANY ATTEMPT to establish a token reinforcement program in a public school will prompt a barrage of questions from principals and teachers. Some of these questions are little more than reflections of resistance to change, but others are well-intentioned and often probe at the critical issues inherent in a token program. It is to the latter type of question that my presentation will be directed. Since a large proportion of you may be deciding whether or not to establish a token program in your schools, I will try to answer questions frequently posed by administrators and teachers themselves when proposals for token programs are presented to them.

The questions posed by principals frequently concern cost, necessary consulting time, teacher training and probability of success. Let us discuss the cost of reinforcers first. Consider a class of 15 disruptive children in an elementary school. If they all received back-up reinforcers worth 25 cents every day for one month (20 school days), then received 40-cent prizes every other day for one month, received 60-cent prizes every third day for one month, and finally received 1-dollar prizes every fifth day for one month, the cost of back up reinforcers would be less than 300 dollars for a four-month program.[1] If the aim of the project director is to transfer control from back-up reinforcers

---

NOTE: Paper presented at the meeting of the American Psychological Association, Washington, D.C., August, 1969. Published by permission of the author.

[1] One might use less expensive back-up reinforcers and quickly increase the behavioral criterion required for various reinforcers in order to maximize the possibility of maintaining prosocial behavior after the tangible back-up reinforcers are withdrawn.

such as candy and toys to praise and other social reinforcers, one should make a transition to social reinforcers as soon as possible. From my own experience with children from first to fourth grade, such a transition could certainly be made within three to four months without loss of appropriate behavior. In a junior or senior high school, the transition to social reinforcers would probably take longer and the cost of back-up reinforcers would undoubtedly be greater. However, McKenzie *et al.* (1968) have significantly changed the academic behaviors of 10- to 13-year-old children in a learning disabilities class by using grades as tokens and allowances as back-up reinforcers. The parents managed the exchange of tokens for back-up reinforcers under supervision of the experimenters, and since the parents were accustomed to giving their children allowances, neither parents nor the school assumed added costs.

Although some school systems or organizations like the PTA, the Rotary and Kiwanis have provided for the cost of back-up reinforcers for children, most published studies of token reinforcement programs have had government or university research funds cover such costs. The use of token programs has grown dramatically, but because of the dearth of outcome and follow-up research with token programs in classrooms, it seems best to continue to have the cost of back-up reinforcers covered by research funds where possible. In fact, it is my contention that any token program would be best conducted on a research or "pilot study" basis, even if it is not the intention of the psychologist to publish his results. Having an observer or teacher keep some records of the child's progress provides all people concerned with constant feedback and evaluation about the effectiveness of the program— one of the most beneficial effects of the whole behavior modification thrust.

Administrators and teachers will also wish to know about the necessary consultation time. It is of prime importance that a token program get off to a good start, and I suggest that any program receive at least one hour of consultation time per day during the first week of the program from someone knowledgeable in the application of learning principles to classroom management. The consultation time could then gradually taper off to two hours per week. Compared to the number of therapist hours spent in more traditional therapeutic centers where children are seen individually outside the classroom setting, such consulting time is probably an extremely effective use of professional services.

It has been demonstrated that teachers can use a token program and effect some change in children's behavior without participating in a course in learning principles or without having extensive consultation (Kuypers *et al.*, 1968). However, care must be taken not to rely solely on the "heavy duty" back-up reinforcers, since only partial change will result. Token and back-up reinforcement is but *one* method of producing change in the children's behavior, and it is critical that attention be paid to the types of cues, threats, and frequency and consistency of social reinforcement the teacher uses on a minute-to-minute basis. Particularly important is the effective shaping of the children's behavior in the time between the distribution of ratings or token reinforcers. In addition, adherence to the rules concerning exchange of back-up reinforcers is critical. Several years ago I dealt with a teacher who became so frustrated with the children that she occasionally allowed them to take any back-up reinforcers—regardless of the amount of token reinforcement. As you might guess, the program had little effect on the children's behavior.

The amount of time a teacher has to spend in giving out the token and back-up reinforcers may be a teacher's greatest concern. Even where we used ratings which were placed in children's booklets every 20 or 30 minutes, the amount of time it took the teacher to place a rating in each of 20 children's booklets and give just a few words of feedback to each child was only 3 to 4 minutes. Furthermore, we have found that after a token program has been in effect, the teacher can use less aversive control and spend less time in simple classroom management. Thus, the initial time spent in giving ratings and exchanging back-up reinforcers may be well worth the effort. It also should be emphasized that simply having the teacher send home a statement about the child's good behavior or giving the child a plastic token which the parent knows is indicative of good behavior can be used to effectively change a child's classroom behavior with a minimum amount of effort and time.

Questions about the probability of success of such a program are much more difficult to answer. From a review of token programs now being completed by Drabman and me, I would estimate roughly that 70 to 80 percent of the children in a token program in a preschool or elementary school class for emotionally disturbed, retarded or educationally disadvantaged children would show significant gains in appropriate social behavior and that these gains would be appreciably greater than those shown by control children in a regular special education class (O'Leary and Becker, 1967; O'Leary *et al.*, 1969). With regard to academic improvement, and particularly to changes on standardized tests, conclusions are more difficult to make, but studies by Birnbrauer *et al.*, 1965; Hewett *et al.*, 1969; Miller and Schneider, 1969; Walker *et al.*, 1968 and Wolf *et al.*, 1968 suggest that academic behaviors per se can indeed be significantly enhanced by a token program. However, it should be emphasized that a token program is no panacea for increasing the academic repertoire of children. A token reinforcement program is a means of effectively reinforcing behavior, but any token program is intrinsically bound to the adequacy of the presentation of academic materials. In a sense, a token program is an emergency device for prompting and maintaining academic and social behavior, but it tends to remain a prosthetic device if the presentation of academic material is boring and poorly programmed.

It has been quipped that behaviorally oriented psychologists are wart removers while analytically oriented psychologists are the heart surgeons of psychological problems. This remark may be particularly relevant to men who apply token programs but worry little about academic programs and the factors that will control the child's behavior after he has graduated from the token program. With regard to this issue of generalization, the question posed by an administrator or teacher is simply: What will happen when the token program is withdrawn? The answer to that question is straightforward. If special procedures are not devised specifically to maintain the children's appropriate behavior when the program is withdrawn, the children's appropriate behavior will decline. On the other hand, it appears that if some procedures are followed, the appropriate behavior of the children can be maintained after the formal token program is withdrawn. Because the problem of maintaining gains in a token program is presently such a key issue, a number of suggestions for enhancing long term effects of token programs follows:

1. Provide a good academic program, since in many cases you may simply be dealing with deficient academic repertoires, not "behavior disorders."

2. Give the child the expectation that he is capable and that his good behavior is the result of his own efforts. This suggestion has been amply followed in the Englemann-Becker Follow-Through Program where immediately following a child's correct answer, the teacher very enthusiastically says "Yes, that's a smart answer; you're a smart boy!" In this regard, it should also be emphasized that the teacher should convey an attitude that she feels or expects the token system to work and succeed.

3. Have the children aid in the selection of the behaviors to be reinforced, and as the token program progresses, have the children involved in the specification of contingencies—a procedure effectively used by Lovitt and Curtiss, (1969). For example, the child rather than the teacher could specify the amount of recess he should earn for a certain number of correct responses.

4. Teach the children to evaluate their own behavior.

5. Try in every way possible to teach the children that academic achievement will pay off. For example, pick something you know a child likes, e.g. clothes, and tell him how he will be able to buy many nice clothes if he studies hard and gets a good job.

6. Involve the parents. Most published studies on token programs in classrooms have not involved parents, probably for reasons of experimental control. However, I have not yet been involved in a token program where it was not thought that its long-term effectiveness could have been enhanced by parent involvement. The effective use of parents in school-related token programs has been well illustrated by McKenzie *et al.* (1968) and by Walker *et al.* (1968).

7. Withdraw the token and the back-up reinforcers gradually, and utilize other reinforcers existing within the classroom setting such as privileges, recess and peer competition, e.g. boys vs. girls and group contingencies.

8. Reinforce the children in a variety of situations and reduce the discrimination between reinforced and nonreinforced situations. Most of the evidence at this point strongly suggests that behavior is very situation specific and when it is clear to the children that their behavior pays off in one situation but not in another, they behave accordingly.

9. Prepare teachers in the regular class to praise and shape children's behavior as they are phased back into the regular classes and bolster the children's academic behavior—if needed—with tutoring by the undergraduates or parent volunteers.

10. Last, in order to maintain positive gains from a token program, it may help to look at the school system as a token system at large with a whole chain or sequence of responses and reinforcers from the children to the teacher, to the principal, to the school superintendent and finally to the school board. When viewed in such a manner, the consultant or research investigator should attempt to facilitate the process of reinforcement not only for the children but for the teachers, the principal and the school board. Praise to a teacher from a principal, frequent feedback and follow-up results given to the principal from the investigator, and some publicity about the program in local papers sent especially to school board members are but a few examples of the types of interactions which may serve to maintain interest in both the long- and short-term effects of token programs.[2]

In conclusion, a word of encouragement and a word of caution is in order. First, there definitely are a number of studies which demonstrate that a token program can be successful in changing the behavior of children in a classroom. However, a token program is only one of a variety of techniques which can be used to help a teacher. Because of the problems of withdrawal of token and back-up reinforcers, other procedures should be tried first, such as making rules clear, using praise and shaping, ignoring some

---

[2] Consulting fees paid to the teachers for their extra time commitment, university course credit, daily feedback concerning the behavior of the teacher and the children, frequent discussion with the teacher by the principal investigator and modeling and rehearsal of appropriate teacher behavior have been especially effective for us in gaining control of teacher's behavior.

disruptive behavior, diminishing the use of threats and verbal reprimands and focusing on a good academic program. Where such procedures fail and where there is a great deal of peer reinforcement for disruptive behavior (not just one or two disruptive children in a class), a token program may well be a very useful procedure for you.

REFERENCES

Birnbrauer, J. S., Bijou, S. W., Wolf, M. M. and Kidder, J. D. Programmed instruction in the classroom. In Ullmann, L. and Krasner, L. (Eds.): *Case Studies in Behavior Modification.* New York, Holt, Rinehart, and Winston, 1965, pp. 358–363.

Hewett, F. M., Taylor, F. D. and Artuso, A. A.: Santa Montica Project: Evaluation of an engineered classroom design with emotionally disturbed children. *Exceptional Children, 35:*523–529, 1969.

Kuypers, D. S., Becker, W. C. and O'Leary, K. D.: How to make a token system fail. *Exceptional Children, 35:*101–109.

Lovitt, T. C. and Curtiss, Karen A.: Academic response rate as a function of teacher and self-imposed contingencies. *Journal of Applied Behavior Analysis, 3:*49–54, 1969.

McKensie, H. S., Clark, Marilyn, Wolf, M. M., Kothera, R. and Benson, C.: Behavior modification of children with learning disabilities using grades as tokens and allowances as back-up reinforcers. *Exceptional Children, 34:*745–752, 1968.

Miller, L. K. and Schneider, R.: The use of a token system in Project Head Start. Unpublished manuscript, University of Kansas, 1969.

O'Leary, K. D. and Becker, W. C.: Behavior modification of an adjustment class: a token reinforcement program. *Exceptional Children, 33:*637–642, 1967.

O'Leary, K. D., Becker, W. C., Evans, M. B. and Saudargas, R. A.: A token reinforcement program in a public school: a replication and systematic analysis. *Journal of Applied Behavior Analysis, 2:*3–13, 1969.

Walker, H. M., Mattson, R. H. and Buckley, N. K.: Special class as a treatment alternative for deviant behavior in children. Monograph, Department of Special Education, University of Oregon, 1969.

Wolf, M. M., Giles, D. K. and Hall, V. R.: Experiments with token reinforcement in a remedial classroom. *Behaviour Research and Therapy, 6:*51–69, 1968.

33

Behavior Modification:
Limitations and Liabilities

DONALD L. MacMILLAN AND STEVEN R. FORNESS

The discussion concerns limitations inherent in the behavior modification paradigm and common misuses of the strategy by naive practitioners. The behavioristic explanation of learning often oversimplifies the human situation. Some pure behaviorists view motivation as extrinsic to learning and commonly separate the reward from the behavior. The separation may be justifiable in early stages of a shaping program, but desired behavior must come under the control of natural reinforcers as soon as possible. Various programs have been adapted to incorporate some of the evidence presented herein. Others have been less flexible, in which cases one can only speculate about the benefits derived by those whose behavior was modified.

WITHIN RECENT YEARS, the application of behavior modification techniques in classrooms of exceptional children has increased greatly. Evidence abounds regarding the efficacy of behavior modification with retarded children (Bijou and Orlando, 1961), learning disabled children (Hewett, 1965; Lovitt, 1968), autistic children (Ferster and DeMeyer, 1961; Hewett, 1964; Lovaas, Freitag, Gold and Kassorla, 1965), emotionally disturbed children (Levin and Simmons, 1962a; Levin and Simmons, 1962b), brain-damaged children (Patterson, 1965) and assorted behavior problems in the

NOTE: The research reported herein was performed in part pursuant to the University of California Intramural Grant No. 9109, USOE Grant No. 0-9-141269-3366 (031), and NICHD Grant No. HD04612, Mental Retardation Center, UCLA.

classroom (Hively, 1959; Hewett, 1966; Valett, 1966; Whelan and Haring, 1966). Hence, the contention that behavior modification is an effective technique with atypical children appears to be well documented.

Hewett (1968) contends that behavior modification assigns the teacher the role of a learning specialist, the role she is best prepared to assume. Alternate strategies (i.e. psychoanalytic, sensory neurological) place the teacher in the role of psychotherapist or diagnostician, roles which teachers are generally ill-prepared to assume. In light of successes in teaching atypical children with behavior modification techniques, Bijou (1966) contends that one can no longer categorically explain the failure to learn in terms of a child's deficiencies but rather must consider the tutorial inadequacies of the teacher. The combination of the factors above—teachers in roles of competence and the emphasis on what the child can do with properly sequenced and correctly reinforced material—provides a more positive approach to the education of exceptional children than did previous approaches which attributed the failure to learn to the child's defect.

By focusing on the consequences of altering and maintaining behavior, certain long-standing assumptions of educators have been questioned. One such assumption is that certain rewards, such as letter grades and teacher approval, have universal applicability. For certain children, the above rewards are ineffective. In attempts to identify rewards for children who do not respond to the traditional ones, investigators have utilized rewards considered unconventional by some (candy, checkmarks, tokens) with considerable success.

Research has further sensitized teachers to the power of their attention and how their attending to misbehavior may have the effect of increasing its occurrence (Zimmerman and Zimmerman, 1962). Premack (1959) describes the use of activities the child prefers (high-probability behavior) as an accelerating consequence for less-preferred behavior (low-probability behavior). Hence, if the child enjoys building model planes, the teacher can use this behavior as a reward for his performing tasks he enjoys less. Such evidence has had an impact on the ongoing practices in the special education classroom.

Enthusiasm over the reported successes of behavior modification with atypical children coupled with teacher's desperation for something that works may blind us to what behavior modification does not, or cannot, do. Mann and Phillips (1967) point out that a number of practices presently operative in special education are designed to fractionate global or molar areas of behavior. While their discussion did not include mention of behavior modification, their contention may also be valid with regard to this strategy. It is important that behavior modification be put in perspective with respect to the overall picture of education. Three limitations in the application of behavior modification to exceptional children will be discussed. Some of the limitations are inherent in the theoretical paradigm itself; others lie in the application, or misapplication, of that theory by practitioners. Specifically, the three limitations to be discussed are as follows:

1. Learning theory does not guide the teacher in determining educational goals.
2. A view of motivation as exclusively extrinsic in nature is limiting in scope.
3. The operational definition of reinforcement ignores certain cognitive aspects of reinforcement.

EDUCATIONAL GOALS
Behavioral Goals

Ullmann and Krasner (1965) state that the first question asked by the behavior analyst is, "What behavior is maladaptive, that is, what subject behaviors should be increased or decreased?" (p. 1). To the experimental psychologist, this is a question answered only through objective analysis of behavior. Too often, however, the real question that gets answered is "What behavior manifested by the child most annoys me as his teacher," regardless of whether or not that behavior is interfering with the child's learning or development.

The behavior modification strategy does not determine educational goals for the child. This is not to suggest that the behavior modification strategy claims to determine goals, but in its inability to do so may lie the reason for its lack of acceptance in public school programs. Hewett, Taylor and Artuso (1969) discuss the lack of balanced emphasis on goals and methods. They write:

> In general, selection of these goals is based on a desire to aid the child in changing maladaptive behavior to adaptive behavior. At best, these concepts of "maladaptive" and "adaptive" provide only the broadest of guidelines for selection of specific behavioral goals. In this sense the powerful methodology of the behavior modification approach is not matched by concern with goals in learning. Teachers are provided with an efficient means of taking emotionally disturbed children someplace but are not substantially aided in the selection of where to go.
>
> It is this lack of balanced emphasis on goals and methods that may preclude the acceptance of behavior modification in the field of education, particularly in the public school, and thereby may greatly limit its usefulness (p. 523).

Once the teacher has determined what the child is to be taught, the behavior modification techniques can be employed to achieve that end. Alternate developmental theories (e.g., Erikson, Piaget) may be more helpful for determining goals, in that they suggest to the teacher the developmental tasks that the child must master, and what skills he must acquire in order to achieve subsequent levels. Lacking a developmental framework, the teacher rather arbitrarily decides what the child must learn.

Wood (1968) expressed concern over the possibility that teachers are provided with a powerful tool in behavior modification techniques without simultaneously developing an understanding of its implications and potential misuse. In light of evidence suggesting that teachers, in general, are more concerned with maintaining power over students than in transmitting knowledge and skill, his concern seems well founded (Eddy, 1967; Henry, 1957; Landes, 1965; Moore, 1967). Implicit in the application of behavior modification techniques with children is the right of the behavior modifier to define what represents adaptive or appropriate behaviors. Wood (1968) described the teacher's role in such a relationship as follows. Having defined the child's present behavior as inappropriate, *he* plans to shape it toward behavior *he* has defined as appropriate. In describing the teacher most likely to misuse this tool without considering the child's rights to participate in defining the goal behavior, Wood states:

These teachers may often be those against whose already abusive application of their authority pupils have the greatest need to be protected. Like many "tools," behavior modification techniques are themselves morally blind. Like a stout sword, they work equally well in the hands of hero or tyrant. Any person of moderate intelligence can, with assistance if not independently, apply them with great effectiveness for good or ill (p.14).

In the case of many exceptional children, a number of their rights were abridged at the time of classification or labeling, thus making them more susceptible to abuse than had they not been so labeled.

Academic Goals

When the educational goal is related to the teaching of subject matter and the teacher employs a strict behaviorist strategy to achieve this goal, certain limitations inherent in the paradigm should be realized. The usual learning situation is much more complex than is suggested by the behavioristic paradigm. Enthusiastic proponents of behaviorism tend to be blinded by the framework and deny other possible explanations for human learning. The analysis of human learning in terms of discrete operational steps may ignore or violate the inherent logic in the material to be learned. Flavell (1963) explains Piaget's theory that schemata (organized information) develop as a consequence of assimilation and accommodation, and learning is facilitated by presenting materials in a manner amenable to reorganization of previously existing cognitive structures (schemata). In addition, Gagné (1962), operating within a different theoretical framework than Piaget, states that the nature and structure of the task to be learned is of greater importance that the behavioristic principles of learning, for example, reinforcement and practice.

It may be that behavior modification strategy fails to adequately consider the goals to which the shaped behavior is related. Determination of goals is left to the teacher who may or may not be a good judge of appropriate behavior. When the principles of behavior modification are applied to the teaching of subject matter, the reductionistic conception of the learning process is a definite limitation. Autoinstructional techniques suffer from many of the same limitations, which are elaborated upon by Stafford and Combs (1967).

MOTIVATION
Extrinsic

From the behavioristic point of view, motivation is seen as extrinsic to learning. Bijou and Baer (1961) stress the importance of behavioral scientists concerning themselves only with events which can be observed and quantified. In the application of reinforcement theory to behavioral management, an attempt has been made to observe the suggestions of Bijou and Baer. In attempts to get children to read, sit in their seats, attend to materials and develop other school appropriate behavior, the emphasis has been placed on the use of tokens, checkmarks and candy in association with the desired behavior. In programs developed to shape behavior through extrinsic rewards or consequences which are observable and able to be quantified, it is postulated that the child will ultimately want to engage in these appropriate behaviors because he will pair the social rewards of teacher or peer approval with the extrinsic rewards used during the shaping program. Inherent in such an approach is the belief that desire or motivation can be manipulated by simply applying consequences when the organism behaves in a desired fashion. The theoretical approach described above is extremely limited, ignores much of the available evidence presented in summary below and discounts alternative explanations of motivation.

Intrinsic

Piaget describes the equilibration process, wherein cognitive adaptation and growth result from the dynamic functioning of the processes of assimilation and accommodation. Exploratory behavior is inherently interesting and rewards the child if it relates to the child's existing mental structures (schemata). Not only is it important to present material in a fashion commensurate with the child's previous level of cognitive development, but material thus presented can become a source of intrinsic motivation to the child (Hunt, 1961). There is no observable or quantifiable "payoff" for such behavior; however, when a match between schemata and task exists the child finds the task inherently interesting.

Stimulation-seeking behavior appears to be another source of intrinsic motivation in higher order organisms. Festinger's (1957) "theory of cognitive dissonance" concludes that when incoming stimulation differs from existing perceptions or conceptions, one is motivated to resolve the discrepancy. Festinger (1957) postulated that cognitive incongruities are a primary source of motivation in human beings, a source which is intrinsic in nature and one which cannot be observed or quantified.

Although working outside of the two preceding theoretical frameworks, Harlow (1949, 1953) suggests that there may be an innate drive of curiosity, which is more likely to operate when the learners' primary needs have been satisfied (Maslow, 1943). Harlow (1953) explained that children and monkeys can enjoy exploration for its own sake. He cites the monkey who continues to solve problems despite the fact that his cheeks are full of food with which he was rewarded for correct or incorrect responses. Despite such unsystematic schedules of reinforcement, the monkeys increased their ability to learn how to learn (Harlow, 1949).

White (1965) offers another framework within which one can consider motivation. He contends that it is in studying the satiated child that one is truly able to understand human nature. In his paper critical of the traditional Freudian position which views motivation in terms of need reduction, White suggests that such a framework is unable to explain satisfactorily the apparent play behavior of the infant, or the one-year-old who tries to spoon feed himself despite the fact that he could gain greater oral satisfaction by allowing his mother to feed him. It may be added that neither can the reinforcement theory explain this behavior in terms of the observable events. Rather, White contends, the child is concerned with achieving mastery over his environment. Regarding play behavior, he writes, "It is directed, selective, and persistent, and it is continued not because it serves primary drives, which indeed it cannot serve until it is almost perfected, but because it satisfies an intrinsic need to deal with environment" (White, 1965, p. 15). The goal of behavior which White sees as an attempt to achieve competence may be to effect familiarity with the environment, or in more global terms, autonomy. In other words, the "payoff" is a feeling or sense of competence.

The point to be made with regard to motivation is that the behavioristic viewpoint is not the only framework within which one can consider motivation. In fact, the behavioristic paradigm is unable to explain adequately the behaviors described by Piaget, Festinger, Harlow and White. One is unable to observe the consequences for behaviors that result from exploration, cognitive dissonance, curiosity and competence as motives. Yet these sources of motivation must not be ignored or discounted as one attempts to reach the atypical child, or any child for that matter. Certain programs, such as Hewett's (1968), which are essentially behavior modification oriented, have altered their initial approaches and now attempt to utilize intrinsic sources of motivation. To the extent that this is practiced, however, such programs violate the pure approach suggested by Bijou and Baer (1961).

REINFORCEMENT

Within the behavior modification framework, reinforcement is commonly defined as "a stimulus which increases the probability of a response." The reinforcement does not have to be directly related to the behavior, and often the separation is intentional. An example of this separation is the use of candy to reinforce problem solving or seat sitting. Theoretically, such a definition does not adequately explain the verbal confirming response discussed by Jensen (1968). In addition, certain practical ramifications should be considered by the practitioner prior to the application of reinforcers which are unrelated to the behavior they are reinforcing.

Verbal Confirming Response

Jensen (1968) describes the "verbal confirming response" (V_c) or feedback, which is a type of self or symbolic reinforcement used by humans. It is extremely limited in lower forms of animals and young children. V_c is more than merely a secondary reinforcement. A secondary reinforcer is a previously neutral stimulus which has gained reinforcing power through being paired with a primary or biological relevant reinforcer. Secondary reinforcers are known to extinguish very rapidly in animal studies. Such is not the case with V_c, which has the effect of strengthening behavior even through the verbal confirming response itself has no reinforcing properties in the biological sense. "The V_c response is most often covert, especially in adults, and may even be unconscious. It consists, in effect, of saying to oneself *Good* or *That's right* or *wrong*" (Jensen, 1968, p. 124). The function of language in the above manner has been demonstrated by several Russian psychologists (Razran, 1959). An interesting feature of the V_c is that it must be self initiated. To the extent that it is necessary in efficient problem solving, the use of extrinsic reinforcers that are unrelated to the specific behavior they are reinforcing preclude the necessity for developing the V_c. In depriving the child of the opportunity of this V_c, are we hindering his development as a problem solver?

Arbitrary vs. Natural Reinforcers

Turning to more practical considerations, Ferster (1966) distinguished between arbitrary and natural reinforcers in a paper on aversive stimuli. He pointed out that arbitrary reinforcers differ from natural reinforcers in two ways: (a) when arbitrary reinforcers are used, the performance that is reinforced is narrowly specified rather than broadly defined, and (b) in the case of arbitrary reinforcers, the individual's existing repertoire of responses does not influence his behavior nearly as much as is the case with natural reinforcers. Therefore, natural reinforcers lead to more integrated general learning.

In the first case, a positive consequence is promised for a specific behavior, seat sitting, and a child can obtain that consequence only by conforming to specific demands. He sits in his seat to obtain the reward, but learning does not necessarily generalize to global behaviors, that is, adequate classroom behavior. In the second case, arbitrary reinforcers benefit the controller, not the controlled. The teacher who says, "If you sit in your seat, I'll give you five checkmarks" is arbitrarily reinforcing seat sitting, which is reinforcing to the teacher for employing the strategy. But the child is not being reinforced by a consequence that naturally exists in his environment. His natural environment has never reinforced his sitting in his seat with a checkmark, nor is it likely to in the future. In fact nonsitting has probably been rewarded through satisfying the curiosity drive.

While checkmarks, tokens, M & M's, and the like may be justifiable as initial means of bringing behavior under control, they must not represent an end in themselves. In several instances, teachers employing the behavior modification strategy, as they interpret it, have had their children on checkmarks for an entire year. When asked the reason the children were still functioning at this low reward level, the teacher indicated, "I'm not about to change something that is working." This teacher has failed in her responsibility to bring the child's behavior under the control of reinforcers that will exist in the child's natural environment, (e.g. social praise). Whelan and Haring (1966) distinguished between the acquisition of behavior and its maintenance. The arbitrary reinforcers are useful in the acquisition stage, but in the maintenance stage they suggest:

> When the behavior needs to be maintained, then it is no longer necessary to provide accelerating consequences to each behavioral response. Maintaining behavior requires that the teacher reduce considerably the number of accelerating consequences provided; indeed, it is a necessity if a child is to develop independent learning skills and self control. It is during this maintenance process that appropriate behavior is accelerated by consequences which are intrinsic to completion of tasks, social approval, feelings of self worth, and the satisfaction of assuming self responsibility. Therefore, dependence on numerous teacher applied consequences gradually loses significance to a child (Whelan and Haring, 1966, p. 284).

It is interesting to note that the above authors, two of the most commonly cited behavior modification advocates, refer to intrinsic consequences, feelings of self worth and satisfaction of assuming self responsibility. It may be that the problem lies with the practitioner who has learned the *how* of behavior modification and rigidly adheres to its doctrines. In training teachers to utilize the strategy, it seems essential that the instruction should include a heavy dosage of the possible misuse of this potentially useful strategy.

CONCLUSIONS

In conclusion, the behavior modification strategy has tremendous potential for work with atypical children. Its use with these children is promising; however, its misuse could be terrifying. It is not a panacea. It gives no direction in determining educational goals; it reduces constructs of learning, motivation and reinforcement to simplistic terms on occasion. To the unsophisticated practitioner, it may be blinding to broader frames of reference regarding the constructs listed above. Furthermore, it may preclude children from learning how to learn and thus becoming independent of teachers as such—a major goal of education. It is time we admitted the short-comings and limitations of the approach as well as extolling its virtues. In an address to a group of autoinstructional technique enthusiasts, Howard Kendler at the 1964 American Psychological Association Convention said the following: "You have a system called Socrates, but you don't have one called God." This statement applies to the present discussion, and should be heeded by the rigid behaviorist.

REFERENCES

Bijou, S. W. and Baer, D.: *Child Development.* New York, Appleton-Century-Crofts, 1961, Vol. I.

Bijou, S. W. and Orlando, R.: Rapid development of multiple-schedule performances with retarded children. *Journal of Experimental Analysis of Behavior, 4:*7–16, 1961.

Bijou, S. W.: A functional analysis of retarded development. In Ellis, N. R. (Ed.): *International Review of Research in Mental Retardation.* New York, Academic Press, 1966, Vol. I.

Eddy, E. M.: *Walk the White Line: A Profile of Urban Education.* New York, Doubleday Anchor, 1967.

Ferster, C. and DeMeyer, M.: The development of performances in autistic children in automatically controlled environments. *Journal of Chronic Diseases, 25:*8–12, 1961.

Ferster, C. B.: Arbitrary and natural reinforcement. Paper delivered at the meeting of the American Association for the Advancement of Science, Washington, D.C., 1966.

Festinger, L.: *A Theory of Cognitive Dissonance.* Evanston, Illinois, Row, Peterson, 1957.

Flavell, J. H.: *The Developmental Psychology of Jean Piaget.* Princeton, N.J., Van Nostrand, 1963.

Gagné, R. M.: Military training and principles of learning. *American Psychologist* 17:83–91, 1962.

Harlow, H.: The formation of learning sets. *Psychological Review,* 56:51–65, 1949.

Harlow, H.: Mice, monkeys, men, and motives. *Psychological Review,* 60:23–32, 1953.

Henry, J.: Attitude organization in elementary school classrooms. *American Journal of Orthopsychiatry,* 27:117–133, 1957.

Hewett, F.: A hierarchy of education tasks for children with learning disorders. *Exceptional Children,* 31:207–214, 1965.

Hewett, F.: Teaching reading to an autistic boy through operant conditioning. *Reading Teacher,* 17:613–618, 1964.

Hewett, F.: The Tulare experimental class for educationally handicapped children. *California Education,* 3:608, 1966.

Hewett, F. M.: *The Emotionally Disturbed Child in the Classroom.* Boston, Allyn and Bacon, 1968.

Hewett, F. M., Taylor, F. D. and Artuso, A. A.: The Santa Monica project: Evaluation of an engineered classroom design with emotionally disturbed children. *Exceptional Children,* 35:523–529, 1969.

Hively, W.: Implications for the classroom of B. F. Skinner's analysis of behavior. *Harvard Educational Review,* 29:37–42, 1959.

Hunt, J. McV.: *Intelligence and Experience.* New York, Ronald Press, 1961.

Jensen, A. R.: Social class and verbal learning. In Deutsch, M., Katz, I. and Jensen, A. R. (Eds.): *Social Class, Race, and Psychological Development.* New York, Holt, Rinehart and Winston, 1968.

Landes, R.: *Culture in American Education.* New York, Wiley, 1965.

Levin, G. and Simmons, J.: Response to food and praise by emotionally disturbed boys. *Psychological Reports,* 11:539–546, 1962a.

Levin, G. and Simmons, J.: Response to praise by emotionally disturbed boys. *Psychological Reports,* 11:10, 1962b.

Lovaas, O. I., Freitag, G., Gold, V. J. and Kassorla, I. C.: Experimental studies in childhood schizophrenia: Analysis of self-destructive behavior. *Journal of Experimental Child Psychology,* 2:67–84, 1965.

Lovitt, T. C.: Operant conditioning techniques for children with learning disabilities. *The Journal of Special Education,* 2:283–289, 1968.

Mann, L. and Phillips, W. A.: Fractional practices in special education: A critique. *Exceptional Children,* 33:311–317, 1967.

Maslow, A. H.: A theory of human motivation. *Psychological Review,* 50:370–396, 1943.

Moore, G. A.: *Realities of the Urban Classroom: Observations in Elementary Schools.* New York, Doubleday Anchor, 1967.

Patterson, G. R.: An application of conditioning techniques to the control of a hyperactive child. *Behavior Research and Therapy, 2:* 217–226, 1965.

Premack, D.: Toward empirical behavior laws: I. Positive reinforcement. *Psychological Review, 66:*219–233, 1959.

Razran, G.: Soviet psychology and psychophysiology. *Behavioral Science, 4:*35–48, 1959.

Stafford, R. R. and Combs, C. F.: Radical reductionism: A possible source of inadequacy in autoinstructional techniques. *American Psychologist, 22:*667–669, 1967.

Ullmann, L. and Krasner, L.: *Case Studies in Behavior Modification.* New York, Holt, Rinehart and Winston, 1965.

Vallett, R.: A social reinforcement technique for the classroom management of behavior disorders. *Exceptional Children, 33:*185–189, 1966.

Whelan, R. J. and Haring, N. G.: Modification and maintenance of behavior through application of consequences. *Exceptional Children, 32:*281–289, 1966.

White, R. W.: Motivation reconsidered: The concept of competence. In Gordon, I. J. (Ed.): *Human Development: Readings in Research.* Glenview, Ill., Scott, Foresman, 1965.

Wood, F. H.: Behavior modification techniques in context. *Newsletter of the Council for Childern with Behavioral Disorders, 5*(4): 12–15, 1968.

Zimmerman, E. H. and Zimmerman, J.: The alteration of behavior in a special classroom situation. *Journal of the Experimental Analysis of Behavior, 5:*59–60, 1962.